Film
Review
2010-2011

Film Review
2010-2011

Michael Darvell and **Mansel Stimpson**

EXECUTIVE EDITOR:
JAMES CAMERON-WILSON

SIGNUM BOOKS

For Peter Ritchie (1942-2010) and Robert Darvell (1925-2010) – MD

To Vernon Dobtcheff, distinguished actor and celebrated first-nighter, in appreciation of his earlier role when, in his late teens, he took so much trouble to act as mentor to a youngster – myself – making his first attempts at film criticism – MS

Acknowledgements

The editors of *Film Review 2010-2011* would like to thank the following, without whose invaluable help this book might not have appeared: Charles Bacon, Alex Buchan, Jeremy Clarke, Peri Godbold, Marcus Hearn, Marshall Julius, Jonathan Rigby, George Savvides and Derek Winnert.

In Memoriam pictures supplied by The Tony Hillman Collection.

Frontispiece: Jennifer Lawrence and Isaiah Stone in *Winter's Bone*.

First published in Great Britain in 2011 by Signum Books, an imprint of Flashpoint Media Ltd
22 Signet Court
Cambridge
CB5 8LA

© Michael Darvell and Mansel Stimpson 2011

Michael Darvell and Mansel Stimpson have asserted their right to be identified as the authors of this work, in accordance with the Copyright, Designs and Patents Act, 1988.

A CIP catalogue record for this book is available from the British Library.

ISBN 9780956653437

Designer: Peri Godbold.
Managing editor: Marcus Hearn.

Printed and bound in China by 1010 Printing International Ltd.

Contents

Introduction

by **Michael Darvell**

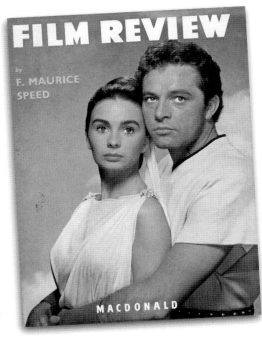

Jean Simmons and Richard Burton in *The Robe*, on the jacket of *Film Review 1953-54*.

Here we are again, a little later than usual as there was no *Film Review* annual last year. The hiatus was caused by the recession, when our then publisher ceased trading. However, we now look forward to a brighter future for the annual under its new imprint, Signum Books.

Volume 66 is a catch-up issue covering the 18 months we were off the bookshelves. Here you will find reviews and credits for all the films released between July 2009 and December 2010. In future we hope to cover the precise calendar year, which should be a better guide anyway to the annual output from the film industry. In Volume 65 of *Film Review* we covered some 400 films out of the 440 released between July 2008 and June 2009. This time we have over 700 releases, of which we have managed to cover around 650.

There are always some titles that escape our attention for one reason or another, such as specialised movies for club screenings; films that sometimes had a limited run; other titles that were belatedly released; and some of the Bollywood product which often creeps into cinemas without press shows. Still, between us *Film Review*'s critics see most of the major films on release.

Earlier in the year I attended the Grand Film Memorabilia Fair and Bazaar at the Cinema Museum in south London, the first in a series of money-raising events with the aim of securing

the lease of this important building, the Master's House in Renfrew Road, Kennington, SE11 (see www.cinemamuseum.org.uk or telephone 020 7840 2200). While there I happened to find a copy of the first volume of F Maurice Speed's *Film Review* for 1944. He had then been in the film reviewing game for about ten years, seeing five or six films a week, and had come to the conclusion that "what the ordinary moviegoer lacks is a more or less complete annual record, in picture and in story of his year's filmgoing." Apart from the various Christmas fan annuals at the time, he thought that nothing of this sort had been attempted. In order to fulfil his purpose he decided to close the gap himself. And here we are some 66 years later, still doing what Maurice Speed had in mind all those decades ago.

The entries for the film releases are much the same as Maurice intended: a short synopsis of the film with a critical summary followed by a list of players, director and producer. Nowadays we tend to list only the major actors but include more of the technical credits for screenplay, cinematography, editing, art direction, music and costumes. Basically, however, *Film Review* remains a digest of all the films released in any one year, plus features on aspects of the year's movies, awards and festivals, and obituaries of film people who have died during the period under review. Sadly, in this volume all the extra

Moneyspinner of the year: James Cameron, director of *Avatar*.

film reviews to be accommodated has made it impossible to include all our regular features, but we hope that normal service will be resumed in Volume 67. Meanwhile, do enjoy our survey of 18 months' worth of world cinema.

What kind of a year and a half has it been? Does a week go by in the cinema world when we don't have the statutory US rom-com or three opening? Then there are the many 3D releases, although some 3D effects today are not that brilliant. James Cameron's *Avatar* is a case in point. With all its other special CGI effects it didn't really need 3D as well, and the extra dimension didn't add very much to the enjoyment of the film. Although *Avatar* cost some $237 million to make, it has made more money than any other film in the history of the cinema. However, if you allow for an adjustment in the rise of ticket prices, then it comes in at number 14 in the top box-office takings of all time. It certainly beat commercially any other film made in 2009, the year it was released, but dollar for dollar or pound for pound, *Gone with the Wind* is still the top-grossing moneyspinner, with *Titanic*, James Cameron's other blockbuster hit, coming second, although *Avatar* is bound to knock that film off its bankable perch when *Avatar 2* and *Avatar 3* are released.

At the other end of the scale, *Motherhood*, the Uma Thurman film, opened in London at one cinema in March 2010 and took precisely £9 on its first day. That's just one concessionary ticket. The first weekend's takings amounted to all of £88. It's not the biggest flop in British film exhibition history, however, as that distinction goes to *My Nikifor* in 2007, which took just £7 at its opening. But then that was a small, independent Polish film; not, like *Motherhood*, a multi-million-dollar Hollywood production.

Apart from blockbuster action movies, rom-com date movies and 3D ventures, the US cinema still seems to be relying on old formulae to get its patrons' bums on seats. Every so often there's yet another instalment of *Pirates of the Caribbean*, an idea that must surely have been well and truly hammered into the ground by

now, but when each film in the series garners millions in revenue, the Disney organisation will carry on producing sequels to what only started out as a Disney theme-park ride. This has become quite a common practice now, with films increasingly being sourced from games or graphic novels rather than the world of literature.

Now that the *Harry Potter* film franchise is about to come to an end, something else is needed to replace it, so we can look forward to more bouts of that incurable movie industry disease, namely sequelitis. The sequels industry knows no bounds, which is why we have the continuing story of *Meet the Parents*, *Space Chimps*, *St Trinian's*, *Cats and Dogs*, *Toy Story*, *Saw*, *Piranha*, *Sex and the City*, *Iron Man*, *Nanny McPhee*, *TRON*, *Wall Street*, *Jackass*, *Twilight* etc, all of which have lately gone into sequels mode. Surely they daren't make any more sequels to *Ocean's 11*, would they, could they, should they?

Still, if it's not a sequel in the US, then it's invariably a remake and remakeitis is just as pernicious as sequelitis. Can a remake ever improve on an original? No, not if it's *Disney's A Christmas Carol*, *Fame*, *Sherlock Holmes*, *The Taking of Pelham 123*, *Clash of the Titans*, *Alice in*

Below left: Uma Thurman demonstrating the none too popular art of *Motherhood*.

Below: Penélope Cruz and Johnny Depp at Disneyland, California, for the latest *Pirates of the Caribbean* premiere.

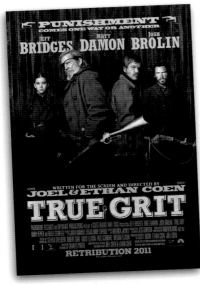

The Coen Brothers remade *True Grit* – but did they really need to?

Wonderland, *The Karate Kid* or *True Grit*, all of which have been subjected to recent remakes. There are more on the horizon too: *Evil Dead*, *The Dirty Dozen*, *1984*, *Footloose*, *Westworld*, *Hellraiser*, *Gambit*, *Logan's Run*, *Death Wish*, *Beverly Hills Cop*, *Die Hard*, *Jurassic Park*, *Terminator*, *Conan the Barbarian*, *Trainspotting* – the list goes ever on, and yet some of the originals were not great films the first time around. But *Fahrenheit 451*? Could you improve on Truffaut? Or Sam Peckinpah's *Straw Dogs*? And Jim Henson's *The Witches* is already a minor classic, so leave it alone.

What is even worse, however, is the remaking of foreign films into English-speaking versions as Hollywood tramples on fine pieces of writing and direction and churns out dud substitutes. Some films are perfect left as they are, so how does one explain the delightful French comedy, *Le diner de cons*, ending up in the US as the appalling *Dinner for Schmucks*? And I dread what America might do to that brilliant German film, *The Lives of Others*.

So many film books are released these days it's sometimes difficult to keep up with them all, but we'll single out one of them – an absorbing new book called *Dorset in Film* – because it's written by erstwhile *Film Review* contributor Anwar Brett. Anwar lives in Dorset and his research on the films that were made in that county from the silent days to the present time has obviously been a labour of love. Apart from detailing all the films that were made in Dorset (starting with several by Britain's pioneer film-maker Cecil Hepworth), Anwar interviews the actors and technicians who worked on Bill Douglas' *Comrades*, John Schlesinger's *Far from the Madding Crowd*, Karel

François Truffaut on location for *Fahrenheit 451* – but will a remake be any better?

Reisz's *The French Lieutenant's Woman*, Douglas McGrath's *Emma* with Gwyneth Paltrow, and Tony Richardson's *Tom Jones* with Albert Finney and Susannah York, giving a fascinating insight into the perils of filming on location. *Dorset on Film* is a large format, well-illustrated volume published by Dorset Books (ISBN: 978 1 871164 71 8).

Researching the entries for the *Film Review* releases section throws up all sorts of odd names and companies. There would appear to be a competition at the moment to see who can invent the wackiest name for a film production company. For instance, Closed on Mondays is responsible for *Scott Pilgrim vs the World*, Fresh and Smoked did *Bustin' Down the Door*, Roister Doister Films have *Mad, Bad and Sad*, Giant Seafood served up *Mega Sharks* (what else?), Babe Ruthless said *Whip It*, Six Point Harness must mean something to *Black Dynamite*, Oops Doughnuts Productions presented *You Again*, while New Boots and Panties (named after the Ian Dury album of the same name) worked on *Sex & Drugs & Rock & Roll*.

Favourites here are those with either a literate or a punning quality to them such as Cinequanon for *Still Walking*, Quentin Tarantino's company A Band Apart (a nod to Jean-Luc Godard) for *Inglourious Basterds*, and, perhaps best of all, They Are Going to Kill Us Productions, which gave us Joaquin Phoenix in *I'm Still Here*. One of the great individual names for personnel, since *King Kong* in 2005 and for his musical contribution this year to *Nanny McPhee and the Big Bang*, is composer and orchestrator Chris P Bacon.

Diversification would appear to be the thing in all aspects of cinema right now. Apart from the usual multiplexes and chains such as the Odeon, Vue, Cineworld, Empire and Showcase cinemas, there are many other movie houses literally popping up all over the shop – and in some cases, such as the HMV Curzon in Wimbledon, the cinema is actually in a music and DVD store, while Selfridge's in Oxford Street has also been showing films.

In London alone new cinemas have been opening up on a regular basis, such as the Rich Mix in Bethnal Green, a locale which also boasts a cinema at the Bethnal Green Working Men's Club, the Borough Roxy Bar & Screen in Southwark, the Shortwave in Bermondsey, the Kensal Rise Lexi, the Shoreditch Aubin, the Balham Exhibit and Bar, the Haringey Independent Cinema, while further out are the Windsor Fire Station and the Maidenhead Norden Farm, all showing films.

The Electric Cinema in Portobello Road, Notting Hill may well be the most luxurious cinema in the UK, with its low-slung armchairs with foot-rests and a 'back row' of double-beds for couples who can either watch the film sitting up or take it, as it were, lying down. The Phoenix in East Finchley, the oldest extant cinema in Britain, built in 1910,

is now a community cinema run by a charitable trust for the community, an independent house that still has just one single screen.

The same goes for the Rex Berkhamsted, which dates from 1938 but closed 50 years later and remained derelict until local businessman James Hannaway and friends refurbished it in its original Art Deco style and re-opened it in 2004. Since then its evening performances are invariably sold out, demonstrating that there is a demand for a local cinema that the big chains couldn't be bothered to satisfy. The Rex is now a Grade II-listed building and Mr Hannaway and his team are working on re-opening the Odeon in St Albans as the new Alpha cinema.

Cinema exhibitors have also been diversifying their programming by scheduling live relays of plays from the National Theatre and operas from the Royal Opera House and the Metropolitan in New York. This diversification is only to be applauded because it allows more people the chance to see quality productions that they may otherwise miss if they are not play- or operagoers and at just a fraction of the ticket price. What is also encouraging about these relays is that the productions come over better in a cinema, with the use of close-ups, so that, as in a film, the audience can feel part of the action, whereas in a large live theatre many of the nuances of a play or opera are lost if you're seated way back from the stage.

If cinemas are diversifying, then so are those film directors who have lately branched out into opera production, albeit not always successfully. The late John Schlesinger was successful as both film and opera director but this year has seen Mike Figgis directing *Lucretia Borgia* for English National Opera at the London Coliseum, with his own filmed inserts (of course). Terry Gilliam has done *The Damnation of Faust* at the same address,

while his former Monty Python colleague, Terry Jones, has been staging children's opera at the Royal Opera House, Covent Garden.

Other crossovers from film to theatre have been in the adaptations of famous films going live on stage. The longest running of these is *The 39 Steps*, based on Hitchcock's movie, which is still running in London and all around the world. Kneehigh Theatre had an enormous success staging *Brief Encounter*, a very clever combination of film and theatre, but their latest effort, a stage version of Jacques Demy's unique film *The Umbrellas of Cherbourg*, came and went like a brief summer shower. However, that hasn't put anybody off because we are now promised the premieres of theatre adaptations of *Ghost* (a musical), which we hope is better than the musical version of *Love Story*, and *The Ladykillers*, which can only be better than the Coen Brothers' filmed attempt at updating the famous Ealing comedy, or at least it surely couldn't be worse.

If film directors can be opera directors, then actors can be rock stars – at least that's what they hope. Woody Allen has for years played clarinet at Michael's Pub in New York every Monday, or perhaps not so regularly lately, as he is always making films in Europe. Many of Hollywood's glitterati have had a background in music at one time or another. Recently Steve Martin has been playing around, as it were, and Hugh Laurie has been gigging and recording an album. Jeff Bridges sang his way to an Oscar in *Crazy Heart* and has signed a record deal, while Gwyneth Paltrow has several singles and albums to her name. The likes of Bruce Willis, Don Johnson, Russell Crowe, Keanu Reeves, Dennis Quaid, Jack Black, Jeff Daniels and Johnny Depp are just a few Hollywood alumni who have sung for their suppers in the past.

So, if the film parts dry up... Well, they can always go back on the road and join the other boys in the band and earn an honest crust.

Jeff Bridges sang his way to an Academy Award in *Crazy Heart*, with Maggie Gyllenhaal.

Top 20 UK *Box-Office Hits*

by **James Cameron-Wilson**

1 January – 31 December 2009

1. *Avatar*
2. *Harry Potter and the Half-Blood Prince*
3. *Ice Age: Dawn of the Dinosaurs*
4. *Up*
5. *Slumdog Millionaire*
6. *Transformers: Revenge of the Fallen*
7. *The Twilight Saga: New Moon*
8. *Sherlock Holmes*
9. *The Hangover*
10. *Alvin and the Chipmunks: The Squeakquel*
11. *Star Trek*
12. *Monsters Vs. Aliens*
13. *Night at the Museum: Battle of the Smithsonian*
14. *Disney's A Christmas Carol*
15. *2012*
16. *Angels & Demons*
17. *X-Men Origins: Wolverine*
18. *Bolt*
19. *Brüno*
20. *Terminator Salvation: The Future Begins*

1

1 January – 31 December 2010

1. Toy Story 3
2. Harry Potter and the Deathly
    Hallows Part 1
3. Alice in Wonderland
4. Inception
5. Shrek Forever After
6. The Twilight Saga: Eclipse
7. Sex and the City 2
8. Despicable Me
9. Little Fockers
10. Iron Man 2
11. Clash of the Titans
12. How to Train Your Dragon
13. Gulliver's Travels
14. Nanny McPhee and The Big Bang
15. Robin Hood
16. The Chronicles of Narnia:
    The Voyage of the Dawn Treader
17. The Karate Kid
18. Paranormal Activity 2
19. StreetDance 3D
20. The Social Network

2

3

4

5

Faces of the Year

by **James Cameron-Wilson**

RUSSELL BRAND

Born: 4 June 1975 in Grays, Essex, England.

Russell Brand appeared out of nowhere like a comet. Akin to a rock star with his own arcane vocabulary, he was part Mick Jagger (the hips), part Freddie Mercury (the showman), part Ben Elton (the exuberant comic) and part John Wilmot, second Earl of Rochester (the womanising bard). In no time at all he had conquered TV, the chat show circuit, the tabloids, Hollywood, the publishing industry and the heart of pop diva Katy Perry.

A true original, Brand's brand of self-confident peacock strut is both bizarre and endearing. An Essex lad, he struggled through a terrible childhood, in which he was sexually abused by a teacher (aged seven), watched his mother battle cancer (aged eight) and suffered from bulimia (aged 14). His father, who left Mrs Brand when the boy was just six months old, took him to brothels in the Far East. "Of course, that's not a particularly healthy endeavour for a father and son to pursue together," Brand notes with typical candour. All is revealed in his best-selling autobiography, *My Booky Wook*, which was hotly pursued by a follow-up, *Booky Wook 2: This Time It's Personal*.

Then, after a bout of experimenting with illegal substances (cannabis, ecstasy, LSD), he enrolled at London's Drama Centre but was expelled for stabbing himself in a fit of pique. Turning to stand-up comedy, Brand worked his way up through the trenches until landing a TV spot, hosting *Big Brother's Big Mouth*. His early life is worth chronicling because, well, it's just so damned colourful (and we haven't even touched on the sex addiction).

On film, Brand appeared in *St Trinian's* (in a weird re-imagining of George Cole's original spiv) and then played an outrageous English rock star in the American *Forgetting Sarah Marshall*. This was successful enough to produce a spin-off, *Get Him to the Greek* [qv], and then he found himself in the incredible position of featuring in both the No 1 and No 2 spots of the American box-office chart in the same week (in April 2011). These box-office vehicles were, respectively, *Hop* and *Arthur*, the latter showcasing Brand as a dipsomaniac playboy, batting bon mots off Helen Mirren. Mirren and Brand also co-featured in *The Tempest* (in which he played the jester Trinculo), and he then joined Tom Cruise and Catherine Zeta-Jones in the jukebox musical *Rock of Ages*.

BRADLEY COOPER

Born: 5 January 1975 in Philadelphia, Pennsylvania, USA.

With those icy-blue eyes, that strong chin, the blinding and immaculate teeth, the swept-back golden hair, the mystery is that Bradley Cooper didn't become a movie star sooner. It wasn't until he was a mature 34 and teamed up with some relatively unknown comic goons that Cooper's boat sailed in a big way. The movie, the *event*, was called *The Hangover* and has become the highest-grossing R-rated film of all time. Let's count the figures: that's 467,483,912 worldwide dollars.

With his movie star looks, it comes as no surprise that Cooper has been romantically linked with some of the hottest actresses around. There were Cameron Diaz and Jennifer Aniston and he was briefly married to the Italian-American actress Jennifer Esposito. Most recently he was joined at the hip to Renée Zellweger. "I can't say enough about her," he gushed. "I just love her. I love acting with her." It's a pity that the movie they made together, *Case 39*, was such a dog.

The first time Cooper made an impact on screen was as Rachel McAdams' preppy, sociopathic boyfriend in *The Wedding Crashers*. The movie grossed over $285 million and Cooper segued into a series of so-so vehicles. He was Matthew McConaughey's best buddy in *Failure to Launch*, had a bit in the sports spoof *The Comebacks*, appeared with Rainn Wilson in *The Rocker* and was Jim Carrey's best mate in *Yes Man*. He had a good role in *He's Just Not That Into You*, in which he strayed from wife Jennifer Connelly to yoga instructor Scarlett Johansson, and then came *The Hangover* – with Ed Helms, Zach Galifinakis, et al.

Since that comic juggernaut Cooper has coasted somewhat. He played the romantic lead opposite Sandra Bullock in the execrable *All About Steve* [qv], partnered Ms Zellweger in the abominable *Case 39* [qv] and then spent some quality time with Julia Roberts in the *Love Actually*-lite *Valentine's Day* [qv]. The last-named was successful enough to spawn a companion piece, *New Year's Day* (with Cooper this time teamed with Jessica Biel). He also played Templeton Peck in *The A-Team* [qv] and then proved that he was a leading man in his own right, getting top-billing over Robert De Niro in Neil Burger's *Limitless*. In the last-named, he starred as a washed-up novelist whose life jumps into first gear when he's prescribed an illegal designer drug. It was a gripping, stylish and imaginative thriller – and a box-office hit. At last, Bradley Cooper had arrived.

ANDREW GARFIELD

Born: 20 August 1983 in Los Angeles, USA.

Three years out of London drama school Central, Andrew Garfield won the best actor BAFTA for *Boy A* (2007). The same year he starred opposite Robert Redford in *Lions for Lambs*, in which the two of them played psychological chess for the entire movie – in one room. It was an awesome start.

After that Garfield took supporting roles in *The Other Boleyn Girl* and *The Imaginarium of Doctor Parnassus* [qv] before joining Carey Mulligan and Keira Knightly in *Never Let Me Go*. The latter, combined with the critical success of *The Social Network* [qv] – in which he played Facebook founder Eduardo Saverin – earned Garfield a slew of nominations for best supporting actor, including a BAFTA and Golden Globe.

The rest could be history but turned into Marvel Comic mythology when Garfield was cast in the title role of the $220m *The Amazing Spider-Man*. And after that he was signed up to star in *Back Roads*, the first film in ten years to be directed by Adrian Lyne.

TOM HARDY

Born: 15 September 1977 in Hammersmith, London, England.

At once imposingly physical and charismatic, brutish and classically trained, Tom Hardy brings a true danger to the parts he plays. It is this intimidating, unpredictable nature that made him ideal for the role of the career criminal *Bronson*, Heathcliff in *Wuthering Heights* (the 2009 TV version) and as the successor to Mel Gibson in the *Mad Max* franchise.

Hardy is just one hell of an actor and has been building a head of steam – and recognition – since joining the grunts in TV's *Band of Brothers* and Ridley Scott's *Black Hawk Down*. He was a memorable villain in *Star Trek: Nemesis* (as the Jean-Luc Picard clone Praetor Shinzon), the mentally unstable Stuart Shorter in *Stuart: A Life Backwards* (for which he was nominated for a BAFTA) and as Bill Sikes in the 2007 TV version of *Oliver Twist*.

There have been a number of supporting bits (in *Marie Antoinette*, *Scenes of a Sexual Nature*, *RocknRolla*), but suddenly the future looks very bright indeed. Besides being virtually the only actor in *Inception* [qv] that one could decipher, Hardy has lined up Gavin O'Connor's *Warrior* (co-starring Nick Nolte), *Tinker, Tailor, Soldier, Spy*, McG's *This Means War* (co-starring Reese Witherspoon), John Hillcoat's Prohibition-set *The Wettest County in the World* and Christopher Nolan's *The Dark Knight Rises*, in which he plays the seemingly indestructible Bane. And, of course, there's *Mad Max 4*.

AARON JOHNSON

Born: 13 June 1990 in High Wycombe, Buckinghamshire, England.

In quick succession Aaron Johnson played a would-be rock legend and a would-be superhero in two high-profile movies. In *Nowhere Boy* [qv], he gave a convincing, cocky show as a Liverpudlian rebel and trouble-maker (John Lennon) in search of his mother, and in Matthew Vaughn's *Kick-Ass* [qv] he was a credible, vulnerable all-American teenager determined to best the criminal fraternity.

Johnson started acting young, playing the son of Macduff to Rufus Sewell's *Macbeth* on the London stage (aged eight) and, opposite Owen Wilson, a 12-year-old Charlie Chaplin in *Shanghai Knights*. He was also the male attraction in *Angus, Thongs and Perfect Snogging* and bedded Carey Mulligan in *The Greatest*.

In real life, Johnson became involved with his *Nowhere Boy* director Sam Taylor-Wood and fathered her daughter, proposing to the photographer-filmmaker in October 2009. (She said "yes".) Being 23 years her junior, the engagement generated considerable column inches in the press.

Since *Kick-Ass*, Johnson has starred in Hideo Nakata's internet thriller *Chatroom* [qv] and will next be seen with Glenn Close and Mia Wasikowska in the period drama *Albert Nobbs*. After that he stars as a marijuana farmer ("a genius botanist") in Oliver Stone's *Savages*, with John Travolta and Uma Thurman in support. Boyishly handsome and adept at an American accent, Johnson has found an instant niche on both sides of the Atlantic.

JENNIFER LAWRENCE

Born: 15 August 1990 in Louisville, Kentucky, USA.

When, in Los Angeles, Jennifer Lawrence auditioned for the lead role in *Winter's Bone* [qv] she was turned down flat. She was told she was too pretty. She auditioned again, and was turned down again. When auditions started up in New York, she took the 'red eye' to the Big Apple and, red-eyed, she auditioned yet again. Somewhere along the line her stubbornness chimed with the pig-headedness of Ree Dolly, the character she was up to play. By the third audition she had learned not to shower or to brush her hair. "We talked for hours and did some improv and I basically convinced them I was ugly enough to do it," she says now.

Ree Dolly is not ugly but she is hewn from the stark, hardscrabble backwoods of the Missouri Ozarks. And Lawrence, aged 18, conveyed as much by what she didn't say as by what she did. The performance earned her a shelf-full of awards as well as an Oscar nomination.

Since then she played the love interest of Anton Yelchin in Jodie Foster's *The Beaver*, turned blue as Mystique in *X-Men: First Class* and teamed up with Yelchin again in *Like Crazy*, winner of the Grand Jury Prize at Sundance. Next, she landed the lead in the horror film *House at the End of the Street* and played survivalist Katniss Everdeen in the $75m sci-fi actioner *The Hunger Games*.

Romantically, she has been linked with the English actor Nicholas Hoult, with whom she co-starred in *X-Men*.

AMANDA SEYFRIED

Born: 3 December 1985 in Allentown, Pennsylvania, USA.

Career-wise, *Mean Girls* did not have the same effect on Amanda Seyfried as it did on her co-stars Lindsay Lohan and Rachel McAdams. It would be four years until she found herself at the top of the Hollywood food chain, starring as the ingenue in the highest-grossing film in British box-office history. This, of course, was *Mamma Mia!* and Seyfried belted out such chart-toppers as 'Thank You For The Music', 'Honey, Honey' and 'I Have a Dream', dated her leading man Dominic Cooper and became an overnight star. She has hardly looked back, although the quality of her choices has puzzled some.

Jennifer's Body [qv] was an underwhelming horror film and *Boogie Woogie* [qv] went virtually unseen, as did the melodramatic *Chloe* [qv], in spite of co-stars Julianne Moore and Liam Neeson. Her next box-office hit was *Dear John* [qv], powered partly by the physical appeal of Channing Tatum and a poke in the eye to the critics, who hated it. Worse still was *Letters to Juliet* [qv], a Mills & Boon affair packed with unintentional laughs; yet, this too, managed to attract an audience.

Meanwhile, Ms Seyfried courted the tabloids with high-profile liaisons with Emile Hirsch, Alexander Skarsgård and Ryan Phillippe, before going on to star in the horror-lite take on *Red Riding Hood*. Next, she teamed up with Justin Timberlake for Andrew Niccol's *In Time*, a sci-fi thriller in which the currency of the future is time itself. As Niccol previously directed the thought-provoking *Gattaca*, *S1m0ne* and *Lord of War*, Seyfried could find herself with some decent reviews for once. After that she stars in the serial killer thriller *Gone*.

HAILEE STEINFELD

Born: 11 December 1996 in Tarzana, Los Angeles, California, USA.

It happens once in a blue moon. Goldie Hawn pulled it off in 1969, Tatum O'Neal in 1973, Anna Paquin in 1993 and Keisha Castle-Hughes in 2002. An actress comes along with little or no experience of the cinema and, in her very first film, blows away the public, the critics and the American Academy.

In the Coen brothers' *True Grit* Hailee Steinfeld was playing a girl a year older than herself. She also had to

ride horseback, handle a gun and stand up to Jeff Bridges while delivering some pretty difficult dialogue. She was 13 at the time and beat out 15,000 other girls for the part in a talent search that took 18 months.

Besides a few commercials and a couple of TV appearances, Steinfeld is very much a newcomer – but one with a commanding presence. Had all things been equal she should have secured her Oscar nomination for best actress – she does have the biggest part in *True Grit* – but thanks to studio politics she was relegated to the supporting category (and lost out to Melissa Leo).

To prove she is no flash in the pan, Steinfeld has decided that for her second film role she will try a bit of Shakespeare. One cannot accuse her of a lack of ambition. She is playing the Capulet girl in Julian Fellowes' adaptation of *Romeo and Juliet* with, at the time of going to press, Holly Hunter cast as the Nurse. Oh, and, censorship permitting, Steinfeld has agreed to a nude scene.

MIA WASIKOWSKA
Born: 14 October 1989 in Canberra, Australia.

At the time of going to press, Mia Wasikowska's *Jane Eyre* was generating the best buzz of any British movie in the US. She also happened to have the title role (Alice) in the second highest-grossing movie of 2010 (in the US) and appeared alongside Annette Bening and Julianne Moore in the critically acclaimed *The Kids Are All Right* [qv]. Not bad for a 21-year-old.

Mia Wasikowska was raised in Canberra. Having trained as a ballerina from the age of nine, she hung up her tutu at 14 and turned to acting. A year later she landed her first film, *Suburban Mayhem*, and was nominated for a Young Actor Award by the Australian Film Institute. After the Australian croc thriller *Rogue* (2007), she was Jamie Bell's love interest in *Defiance*, played the aviatrix Elinor Smith in *Amelia* [qv] and was then chosen by Tim Burton to be his grown-up *Alice in Wonderland* [qv].

When *Jane Eyre* opened in the States, the critics generally agreed that Wasikowska gave the best

interpretation of the role to date, with Peter Travers of *Rolling Stone* praising her "innocence and carnal curiosity". She then starred in Gus Van Sant's *Restless* (which was chosen to open the Un Certain Regard at Cannes), joined Glenn Close and Aaron Johnson in *Albert Nobbs* and was teamed with Shia LaBeouf and Tom Hardy in *The Wettest County in the World*, directed by fellow Australian John Hillcoat. Next, she signed up to play a girl in mourning in Chan-wook Park's *Stoker*, with Nicole Kidman in support.

It is a testament to Wasikowska's mettle that she opted to use her Polish mother's maiden name to act under, rather than stick to her father's more pronounceable 'Reid'. 'Mia Reid' may have appealed more to the Hollywood movers and shakers, but Ms Wasikowska is doing just fine as she is.

KRISTEN WIIG
Born: 22 August 1973 in Canandaigua, New York, USA.

Kristen Wiig has been the secret weapon of many a film comedy. She will sneak in, steal a laugh – or several – and slip out again. However, it was on television where she found her wings, and she excelled on *Saturday Night Live*, the revue that has launched a host of comedy stars – John Belushi, Steve Martin, Eddie Murphy, Mike Myers…

But she was also poached by Hollywood, the critics singling out her performances as the courteous but cutting TV producer in *Knocked Up*, the permanently pregnant wife of John C Reilly in *Walk Hard: The Dewey Cox Story*, the distracted surgeon in *Ghost Town*, the cringingly strait-laced theme park manageress in *Adventureland* [qv] and the big-haired Vicki St Elmo in *MacGruber* [qv], expanded from a *SNL* sketch.

As her fan base grew on *SNL*, so the parts in the movies got bigger. She was hysterical as the suppressed, God-fearing Ruth Buggs in *Paul*, prompting co-star Simon Pegg to call her "the funniest woman on the planet". But it took Wiig to turn producer and writer in order to secure her first big-screen starring role, in which she plays the bride of honour to Maya Rudolph (another *SNL* alumnus) in *Bridesmaids*.

The film was declared by many as the funniest of 2011 and, to prove it, grossed $100 million in a little over three weeks. It is satisfying to witness such a genuinely funny performer achieve her triumph, both critically and commercially. And with the actress-friendly *Friends With Kids* already in the can, Ms Wiig seems primed to take the world by storm.

Releases of the Year

This section contains details of all the films released in the UK between 1 July 2009 and 31 December 2010, the period covered by all the reference features in this volume.

Each film review is followed by the main credits for the film, beginning with names of the leading actors, then the Director, Producer(s), Screenplay Writer, Cinematographer, Production Designer or Art Director, Editor, Soundtrack Composer and Costume Designer.

For technical credits the normal abbreviations operate and are as follows:

Dir – for Director; Pro – for Producer; Ph – for Cinematographer; Pro Des – for Production Designer; Art Dir – for Art Director; M – for Composer; and Cos – for Costume Designer.

The production companies involved are listed, with the final name in the list being the distributor. The credits end with the film's running time, the country or countries of origin, the year of production, the UK release date and the British Board of Film Classification certificate.

Reviewers: Charles Bacon (CB), James Cameron-Wilson (JC-W), Jeremy Clarke (JC), Michael Darvell (MHD), Marshall Julius (MJ), Jonathan Rigby (JR), George Savvides (GS), Mansel Stimpson (MS) and Derek Winnert (DW).

Star ratings

★★★★★ **Exceptional**
★★★★ **Very Good**
★★★ **Good**
★★ **Mediocre**
★ **Poor**

Adam ★★½

This is a rom-com about a man suffering from Asperger's syndrome – yes, that's what I said, a rom-com about a man suffering from a form of autism. Predictably, the drama of his situation totally fails to fit in with the escapist exaggerated comedy of the rom-com genre. Hugh Dancy and Rose Byrne are truly valiant in their efforts to make it work but there was never a chance of success. MS

▶ Hugh Dancy, Rose Byrne, Frankie Faison, Mark Linn-Baker, Amy Irving, Peter Gallagher.
▶ *Dir* and *Screenplay* Max Mayer, *Pro* Leslie Urdang, Miranda de Pencier and Dean Vanech, *Ph* Seamus Tierney, *Pro Des* Tamar Gadish, *Ed* Grant Myers, *M* Christopher Lennertz, *Cos* Alisia Raycraft.
Fox Searchlight Pictures/Olympus Pictures etc-20th Century Fox.
99 mins. USA. 2009. Rel: 7 Aug 2009. Cert. 12A.

Adoration ★★★½

Long before the internet became so prominent, Atom Egoyan was fascinated by the role that technology and recorded images play in our lives. In this drama it's the internet that promotes a

Opposite:
Noomi Rapace in *The Girl With the Dragon Tattoo*.

With strings attached: Devon Bostick and Scott Speedman in Atom Egoyan's *Adoration*.

schoolboy's story linking his dead parents to terrorism and spreads the notion that his tale is true. Mixed in with this are other ideas – too many perhaps – and, although intriguing, the whole thing never quite comes together as *The Sweet Hereafter* did. Consequently it is not Egoyan at his best, but it will interest his admirers all the same. MS

▶ Devon Bostick, Arsinée Khanjian, Scott Speedman, Rachel Blanchard, Noam Jenkins.
▶ *Dir* and *Screenplay* Atom Egoyan, *Pro* Egoyan, Simone Urdl and Jennifer Weiss, *Ph* Paul Sarossy, *Pro Des* Phillip Barker, *Ed* Susan Shipton, *M* Mychael Danna, *Cos* Debra Hanson.
Serendipity Point Films/ARP Sélection/Ego Film Arts/ The Film Farm etc-New Wave Films
101 mins. Canada/France. 2008. Rel: 29 Jan 2010. Cert. 15.

Adrift ★★★½

A new view of Brazil is provided in this coming of age story which draws on the personal memories of writer/director Heitor Dhalia and features the beaches of the Buzios. The tale charts, too, the collapse of a marriage and Vincent Cassel reveals his ability to act in Portuguese. It's watchable enough, but as a study of children and of those bringing them up it fades beside the vivid impact of *The Kids Are All Right* [qv]. (Original title: *À deriva*) MS

▶ Vincent Cassel, Debora Bloch, Camilla Belle, Laura Nelva.
▶ Dir and Screenplay Heitor Dhalia, Pro Fernando Meirelles, Andréa Barata Ribeiro and Bel Berlinck, Ph Ricardo Della Rosa, Art Dir Guta Carvalho, Ed Gustavo Giani, M Antônio Pinto, Cos Alexandre Herchovitch.
O2 Filmes/Lei do Audiovisual/ANCINE/Lei de Incentivo à Cultura, Brasil etc-Revolver Entertainment.
102mins. Brazil. 2008. Rel: 17 Nov 2010. Cert. 12A.

Fair ground: Kristen Stewart and Jesse Eisenberg in Greg Mottola's warm and funny *Adventureland*.

Adventureland ★★★★

Unlucky on its release, when it was overshadowed by *(500) Days of Summer* [qv], this is in fact the superior study of adolescence. It has a pitch perfect performance from Jesse Eisenberg, who is admirably supported by *Twilight*'s Kristen Stewart. It's a romantic comedy written and directed by Greg Mottola, whose film is set in the small-town America of the 1980s as a direct reflection of the autobiographical elements in the tale. The ending may be a bit of a cliché but there's a subtlety and truth here often missing in this genre. MS

▶ Jesse Eisenberg, Kristen Stewart, Martin Starr, Kristen Wiig, Ryan Reynolds.
▶ *Dir* and *Screenplay* Greg Mottola, *Pro* Sidney Kimmel, Anne Carey and Ted Hope, *Ph* Terry Stacey, *Pro Des* Stephen Beatrice, *Ed* Anne McCabe, *M* Yo La Tengo, *Cos* Melissa Toth.
Miramax Films/Sidney Kimmel Entertainment/This Is That-Buena Vista International (UK).
107 mins. USA. 2008. Rel: 11 Sep 2009. Cert. 15.

Africa United ★★★★

This is the story of two young Rwandan boys whose passion for football takes them across Africa. They want to audition for the opening ceremony of the 2010 World Cup in South Africa but they take the wrong bus and end up in the Congo. They are penniless and time is running out... The young actors' immense enthusiasm makes up for their lack of experience in this charming and thought-provoking adventure which is fresh, original and makes great use of its stunning locations. GS

▶ Eriya Ndayambaje, Roger Nsengiyumva, Sanyu, Joanita Kintu, Yves Dusenge, Sherrie Silver.
▶ *Dir* Debs Gardner-Paterson, *Pro* Mark Blaney, Eric Kabera and Jackie Sheppard, *Screenplay* Rhidian Brook, *Ph* Sean Bobbit, *Pro Des* Mike Gunn, *Ed* Victoria Boydell, *M* Bernie Gardner, *Cos* Pierre Vienings.
Pathé Productions/Footprint Films/Link Media Production/BBC Films etc-Pathé Distribution.
88 mins. UK. 2010. Rel: 22 Oct 2010. Cert. 12A.

Afterschool ★★★½

The first proper feature from Antonio Campos of *Buy It Now*, this is a study of youngsters influenced by the internet and is set in an American East Coast school where two pupils collapse and die. Campos claims to ask questions about modern life, not to supply answers, and his sometimes stylised approach to his subject matter will not appeal to all. But there's no denying that in its best scenes it is both powerful and provocative. MS

HIV FC: Eriya Ndayambaje with his improvised football in Debs Gardner-Paterson's *Africa United.*

❭ Ezra Miller, Jeremy Allen White, Michael Stuhlbarg, Addison Timlin, Gary Wilmes.
❭ *Dir* and *Screenplay* Antonio Campos, *Pro* Josh Mond and Sean Durkin, *Ph* Jody Lee Lipes, *Pro Des* Kris Moran, *Ed* Campos and Zac Stuart-Pontier, *Cos* Catherine Akana.

BorderLine Films/Hidden St. Productions etc-Network Releasing.
107 mins. USA/France. 2008. Rel: 21 Aug 2009. Cert. 18.

Aftershock ★★★

Immensely popular on its home ground in China, this drama centres on a family driven apart by the earthquake of 1976 which devastated the town of Tangshan. Despite the real-life basis the tale told here is akin to soap opera. A mother forced to choose which of her two children to save is central and the child not chosen, a girl, survives with the conviction that her mother did not love her. Tears are in plentiful supply – and if this kind of popular drama appeals to you it's just possible that they will include yours. (Original title: *Tangshan Dadizhen*) MS

❭ Xu Fan, Zhang Jingchu, Li Chen, Zhang Zifeng, Chen Jin, Lu Yi.
❭ *Dir* Feng Xiaogang, *Pro* Guo Yanhong. Han Sanping and Wang Zhongjun etc, *Screenplay* Su Xiaowei, from Zhang Ling's novel, *Art Dir* Huo Tingxiao, *Ed* Xiao Yang, *M* Wang Liguang.

Tangshan Broadcast and Television Media/China Film Group Corporation/Huayi Brothers Media Corporation etc-Metrodome Distribution.
135 mins. People's Republic of China/Hong Kong. 2010. Rel: 12 Nov 2010. Cert. 15.

The Agent ★★½

Filming his own stage play about a writer's relationship with his agent, Martin Wagner displays a wholly misplaced confidence. There are interesting things to be said about the book trade today which someone like David Mamet could have brought to life. Wagner, however, has no gift for characterisation and this unconvincing piece lacks any dramatic force. As a stage work it was called 'riveting' by the *Sunday Times*, but I'll go with the contrary verdict of *The Independent* ('witless'), despite the efforts of the cast here. MS

❭ William Beck, Stephen Kennedy, Maureen Lipman.
❭ *Dir* and *Ed* Lesley Manning, *Pro* Martin Wagner and Manning, *Screenplay* Wagner, *Ph* Jonathan Harvey, *Pro Des* Humphrey Jaeger, *M* Simon Lambros.

Pinter & Martin-Pinter & Martin Ltd.
81 mins. UK. 2009. Rel: 18 Sep 2009. No Cert.

Agora ★★★

For an epic that attempts to bring the fourth century AD alive, *Agora* sticks pretty close to its narrative. In fact, there's way too much narrative for one film, precluding the opportunity for deeper characterisation. Alejandro Amenábar certainly brings the city of Alexandria to life with impressive CGI wizardry, but his characters remain ciphers stuck with recycled dialogue. Yet, while these people don't have time to eat, they do seem to cogitate on the shape of the universe. It all looks wonderful, though, and Rachel Weisz is ace as the Egyptian philosopher Hypatia. JC-W

Culture clash: tempers fray in the hyperactive neighbourhood of Jaffa, in Scandar Copti and Yaron Shani's *Ajami*.

▶ Rachel Weisz, Max Minghella, Oscar Isaac, Michael Lonsdale, Rupert Evans.
▶ *Dir* Alejandro Amenábar, *Pro* Alvao Augustin and Fernando Bovaira, *Screenplay* Amenábar and Mateo Gil, *Ph* Xavi Giménez, *Pro Des* Guy Dyas, *Ed* Nacho Ruiz Capillas, *M* Dario Marianelli, *Cos* Gabrielle Pescucci.

Mod Producciones/Himenóptero/Telecinco Cinema/ Canal +/Cinebiss-Paramount Pictures.
127 mins. Spain. 2009. Rel: 23 Apr 2010. Cert. 12A.

Ajami ★★★½

The setting is Jaffa but there are echoes of *Gomorrah* in this drama which, divided into chapters, tells a series of interlinked tales. It shows conflicts in this area involving Jews, Muslims and Christians but invites a non-partisan human response. The shifting focus is not always beneficial in maintaining the initial tension, but the non-professional actors are fine and you would never guess that much of the dialogue was improvised. MS

▶ Shahir Kabaha, Ibrahim Frege, Fouad Habash, Youssef Sahwani.
▶ *Dir, Screenplay* and *Ed* Scandar Copti and Yaron Shani, *Pro* Mosh Danon and Thanassis Karathanos, *Ph* Boaz Yehonatan Yacov, *Art Dir* Yoav Sinai, *M* Rabian Buchari, *Cos* Rona Doron.

Inosan Productions/Twenty Twenty Vision Filmproduktion-Vertigo Films
125 mins. Israel/Germany/UK 2009. Rel: 18 June 2010. Cert. 15.

Alamar ★★★½

This very personal film by Pedro González-Rubio was conceived as a hybrid between documentary and fiction. It charts with absolute conviction a five-year-old boy's discovery of the world and, in showing how his father, a Mexican fisherman, lives, it is as atmospheric and poetic as Flaherty's classic *Louisiana Story*. However, as a drama about a child torn between two lifestyles (his mother is returning to Rome and wants the boy to go with her), it is underdeveloped. MS

▶ Jorge Machado, Natan Machado Palombino, Roberta Palombini, Nestor Marin 'Matraca'.
▶ *Dir, Screenplay, Ph* and *Ed* Pedro González-Rubio, *Pro* Jaime Romandía and González-Rubio.

Xcalakarma Mantarraya Producciones etc-New Wave Films.
73 mins. Mexico. 2009. Rel: 10 Sep 2010. Cert. U.

Alice in Wonderland ★★★★

Not all admirers of the Alice books will agree but in my eyes Lewis Carroll and Tim Burton make for a fine partnership. Mia Wasikowska brings both strength and vulnerability to Alice and if the idiosyncratic tone of the original yields to a Narnia-like second half that's all right by me. The 3D version is not necessarily to be preferred, for these adventures chime with Burton's visual imagination in either case. Good work, too, from Bonham Carter and Depp. MS

▶ Johnny Depp, Anne Hathaway, Helena Bonham Carter, Crispin Glover, Matt Lucas, Mia Wasikowska, Frances de la Tour, Lindsay Duncan, Geraldine James and with the voices of Alan Rickman, Stephen Fry, Michael Sheen, Timothy Spall, Barbara Windsor, Christopher Lee, Michael Gough, Imelda Staunton.
▶ *Dir* Tim Burton, *Pro* Richard D Zanuck, Suzanne Todd, Jennifer Todd and Joe Roth, *Screenplay* Linda Woolverton, based on Lewis Carroll's *Alice's Adventures in Wonderland* and *Through the Looking Glass*, *Ph* Dariusz Wolski, *Pro Des* Robert Stromberg, *Ed* Chris Lebenzon, *M* Danny Elfman, *Cos* Colleen Atwood *Visual Effects/Animation* Sony Pictures Imageworks Inc. etc

Walt Disney Pictures/Roth Films/Team Todd/Zanuck Company-Buena Vista.
108 mins. USA. 2010. Rel: 5 Mar 2010. Cert. PG.

Aliens in the Attic ★★

The Pearson family are in for a surprise when they arrive at their holiday home in the middle of nowhere. They have visitors from outer space but only the children are aware of their existence and have to join forces in order to send them back where they came from. In this average family film, which is probably suited to younger undemanding children, Robert Hoffman nearly steals the show as the smug boyfriend who gets his comeuppance from the aliens. GS

▶ Carter Jenkins, Austin Butler, Ashley Tisdale, Ashley Boetticher, Doris Roberts, Robert Hoffman.
▶ *Dir* John Schultz, *Pro* Barry Josephson, *Screenplay* Mark Burton and Adam F Goldberg, *Ph* Don Burgess, *Pro Des* Barry Chusid, *Ed* John Pace, *M* John Debney, *Cos* Mona May.

Twentieth Century Fox/Regency Enterprises/Josephson Entertainment/New Upstairs Productions etc-20th Century Fox
86 mins. USA/Canada. 2009. Rel: 12 Aug 2009. Cert. PG.

All About Steve ★½

Mary Horowitz (Sandra Bullock) is a cruciverbalist – crossword compiler to you – and a complete nut. When she falls for handsome CNN cameraman Steve Mueller (Bradley Cooper), she composes a crossword all about Steve… A satire on mental illness – and, tiresomely, the media – this belongs more to the oeuvre of Lars von Trier. Here, we're given a strong dose of the zany, and 'funny' music to drive the jokes home, without so much as a hint of black humour to add colour. JC-W

▶ Sandra Bullock, Thomas Haden Church, Bradley Cooper, Ken Jeong, D J Quails, Keith David.
▶ *Dir* Phil Traill, *Pro* Bullock and Mary McLaglen, *Screenplay* Kim Barker, *Ph* Tim Suhrstedt, *Pro Des* Maher Ahmad, *Ed* Rod Dean and Virginia Katz, *M* Christophe Beck, *Cos* Gary Jones.

Fortis Films/Fox 2000 Pictures/Radar Pictures-20th Century Fox.
99 mins. USA. 2009. Rel: 15 Jan 2010. Cert. 12A.

Alpha and Omega ★★½

This pleasant 3D animation follows the story of two wolves – Kate (Hayden Panettiere) and Humphrey (Justin Long) – as they begin a long journey back home after they are taken away by a group of park rangers and shipped halfway across the country. Kate is a bossy Alpha wolf while Humphrey is fun-loving Omega. It is inoffensive and suitable for little children but not very exciting. GS

▶ Voices of Justin Long, Hayden Panettiere, Dennis Hopper, Danny Glover, Christina Ricci, Larry Miller.
▶ *Dir* Anthony Bell and Ben Gluck, *Pro* Ken Katsumoto, Steve Moore and Richard Rich, *Screenplay* Chris Denk and Steve Moore, *Ed* Scott Anderson, *M* Chris P Bacon.

Crest Animation Productions/Lions Gate Family Entertainment-Lionsgate.
88 mins. USA/India. 2010. Rel: 22 Oct 2010. Cert. U.

Alvin and the Chipmunks 2: The Squeakquel ★★

The singing chipmunk global pop stars Alvin (voice of Justin Long), Simon (Matthew Gray Gubler) and Theodore (Jesse McCartney) go back to school, where they come up against a new female trio called The Chipettes when they compete in a fundraising music competition to save their school. This movie musical comedy sequel is definitely for younger children only, with little entertainment and only a few laughs for adults, but it was a monster hit, taking $180million in the US alone. Paying the rent, *My Name Is Earl*'s Jason Lee is back as Dave. DW

▶ Zachary Levi, David Cross, Jason Lee and the voices of Justin Long, Matthew Gray Gubler and Jesse McCartney.
▶ *Dir* Betty Thomas, *Pro* Janice Karman, *Screenplay* Jon Vitti, Jonathan Aibel and Glenn Berger based on the

Gated community: Mia Wasikowska enters her old stamping ground in Tim Burton's extraordinarily successful *Alice in Wonderland*.

characters created by Ross Bagdasarian Jr, *Ph* Anthony B Richmond, *Pro Des* Marcia Hinds, *Ed* Matthew Friedman, *M* Alexander Welker, *Cos* David Newman.

Bagdasarian Productions/Fox 2000 Pictures/Regency Enterprises-20th Century Fox.
88 mins. USA. 2009. Rel: 21 Dec 2009. Cert. U.

Am I Black Enough For You?
★★★★

This is a fascinating documentary about legendary Philadelphia soul artist Billy Paul, who hit the big time in the 1970s with 'Me and Mrs Jones' but whose career nearly came to an end after his controversial follow-up single, 'Am I Black Enough For You?', flopped. Paul speaks eloquently about his life, his long marriage to his supportive wife Blanche and the civil rights movement that gave rise to the birth of soul music. GS

▶ Billy Paul, Malik Abdul-Basit, Clive Davis, Kenny Gamble, Schooly-D.
▶ *Dir, Screenplay* and *Ph* Göran Hugo Olsson, *Pro* Jenny Ornborn, *Pro Des* Stefania Malmsten, *Ed* Anders Refn.

Story AB-Verve Pictures.
87 mins. Sweden. 2009. Rel: 3 July 2009. Cert. 12A.

Amelia ★★★★

Undervalued by many critics, this is a good traditional biopic. In this case the subject is the famous flyer Amelia Earhart (1897-1937). The men in her life – the publisher George Putnam (Richard Gere), whom she married, and Gore Vidal (Ewan McGregor) with whom she had an affair – are portrayed as subsidiary figures, with the spotlight firmly on Amelia herself. With Hilary Swank ideally cast in this role, that's absolutely fine. MS

▶ Hilary Swank, Richard Gere, Ewan McGregor, Christopher Eccleston, Cherry Jones, Mia Wasikowska
▶ *Dir* Mira Nair, *Pro* Ted Waitt, Kevin Hyman and Lydia Dean Pilcher, *Screenplay* Ron Bass and Anna Hamilton Phelan, based on the books *East to the Dawn* by Susan Butler and *The Sound of Wings* by Mary S Lovell, *Ph* Stuart Dryburgh, *Pro Des* Stephanie Carroll, *Ed* Allyson C Johnson and Lee Percy, *M* Gabriel Yared, *Cos* Kasia Walicka Maimone.

Fox Searchlight Pictures/Avalon Pictures etc-20th Century Fox.
111 mins. USA/Canada. 2009. Rel: 13 Nov 2009. Cert. PG.

The American ★★★★

George Clooney is on fine form as the American of the title, a hit man in Europe who wants to start a new life but finds himself endangered. It's not too fresh a subject but director Anton Corbijn, he of *Control*, handles it brilliantly and the location shooting in Italy is a model of how such things should be done. Writer Rowan Joffe

The life of another: Nina Hoss in Max Färberböck's sincere and harrowing *Anonyma: A Woman in Berlin*.

shows more affinity with Graham Greene here than in his new version of *Brighton Rock*. MS

▶ George Clooney, Violante Placido, Thekla Reuten, Paolo Bonacelli, Lars Hjelm.
▶ *Dir* Anton Corbijn, *Pro* Anne Carey, Jill Green, Grant Heslov, George Clooney etc *Screenplay* Rowan Joffe, from Martin Booth's novel *A Very Private Gentleman*, *Ph* Martin Ruhe, *Pro Des* Mark Digby, *Ed* Andrew Hulme, *M* Herbert Grönemeyer, *Cos* Suttirat Anne Larlarb.

Focus Features/This Is That/Greenlit/Smokehouse etc-Universal.
105 mins. USA/UK. 2010. Rel: 26 Nov 2010. Cert. 15.

American: The Bill Hicks Story
★★★★

The American comic Bill Hicks died at the age of 32 in 1994 but is still coming into his own through albums and DVDs. This documentary has the footage to illustrate his work and relates it to his life story as told by family and friends. The stage act developed into a serious attack on those aspects of American life that he detested and this film, enlivened by animation techniques, has a freshness that helps to do justice to its subject. MS

▶ With Bill Hicks, Dwight Slade, Mary Hicks, Steve Hicks, Lynn Hicks, Kevin Booth.
▶ *Dir, Pro* and *Animation* Matt Harlock and Paul Thomas, *M* Bill Hicks, Kevin Booth, Marblehead Johnson etc

Halflife Films/Jackamo Television-Verve Pictures.
107 mins. UK. 2010. Rel: 14 May 2010. Cert. 15.

Animals United ★★½

Animals from all over the world join forces in order to teach the nasty humans a lesson or two about the global warming that threatens their survival. The pairing of Vanessa Redgrave and Jim Broadbent as the wise turtles works a treat while the double-act of Dawn French's elephant and Joanna Lumley's giraffe fails miserably. The 3D in

this likeable but uneven German animation feature is unremarkable, while the colourful animation and lovable animals will keep most children satisfied. (Original title: *Konferenz der Tiere*). GS

▶ Voices of Billy Beach, Jim Broadbent, Omar Djalili, Jason Donovan, Billie Piper, James Corden, Dawn French, Joanna Lumley, Vanessa Redgrave, Stephen Fry.
▶ *Dir* and *Pro* Reinhard Klooss and Holger Tappe, *Screenplay* Klooss and Erich Kästner, *Pro Des* Henning Ahlers and Jens Benecke, *Ed* Alexander Dittner, *M* David Newman.

Constantin Film Produktion/Ambient Entertainment GmbH/White Horse Pictures-Entertainment Film Distributors.
93 mins. Germany. 2010. 17 Dec 2010. Cert U.

Anonyma: A Woman In Berlin ★★★

This is another recent film from Germany which looks back to the Nazi era with eyes wide open. Here Max Färberböck chronicles the horrors of life in Berlin after the Russians entered the city in 1945. Sincere, unsensational but harrowing (it's based on the real-life diaries published by a woman as 'Anonyma'), the film features a fine performance from Nina Hoss. Unfortunately, it's also excessively long and the often nameless characters caught up in this horror make less impact than they should. (Original title: *Anonyma – Eine Frau in Berlin*) MS

▶ Nina Hoss, Evgeny Sidikhin, Irm Hermann, Rüdiger Vogler, August Diehl.
▶ *Dir* and *Screenplay* (from the diary *Eine Frau in Berlin* by Anonyma) Max Färberböck, *Pro* Günter Rohrbach, *Ph* Benedict Neuenfels, *Art Dir* Uli Hanisch, *Ed* Ewa J Lind, *M* Zbigniew Preisner, *Cos* Lucia Faust.

Günter Rohrbach/Constantin Films/ZDF – Zweites Deutsches Fernsehen/Tempus etc-Metrodome Distribution. 126 mins. Germany/Poland. 2008. Rel: 12 Feb 2010. No Cert.

Another Year ★★★½

Highly praised by many, this is a must-see for admirers of Mike Leigh and much of it is excellent. This time he is looking at characters becoming aware of their age and in so doing he contrasts a contented couple (Jim Broadbent and Ruth Sheen) and a friend of theirs, Mary (Lesley Manville), who, with two failed marriages behind her and no children, drinks too much. I found that the film's length reduced sympathy for Mary (she's pathetic but increasingly tiresome) and thought *Vera Drake* far better structured, but some will certainly disagree. MS

▶ Jim Broadbent, Lesley Manville, Ruth Sheen, Peter Wight, Oliver Maltman, David Bradley, Karina Fernandez, Martin Savage, Phil Davis, Imelda Staunton.
▶ *Dir* and *Screenplay* Mike Leigh, *Pro* Georgina Lowe, *Ph* Dick Pope, *Pro Des* Simon Beresford, *Ed* Jon Gregory, *M* Gary Yershon.

Focus Features International/UK Film Council/Thin Man Films etc-Momentum Pictures.
130 mins. UK. 2010. Rel: 5 Nov 2010. Cert. 12A.

Antichrist ★★★½

This Lars von Trier film, which created a furore at Cannes in 2009, is not a horror film. Brilliantly acted by Charlotte Gainsbourg and Willem

Another year, another Mike Leigh movie: Jim Broadbent and Ruth Sheen ooze content in *Another Year*, Oscar-nominated for best original screenplay.

Dafoe, it is instead a study of the grief felt in very different ways by a mother and father whose young son dies through a fall while the couple are making love. In the last section, however, psychological investigation yields to Grand Guignol and to an attempt to suggest that nature itself is inherently evil. Here the film goes right off the rails. Even so, for those who can take it (this is the film that shows genital mutilation), the movie is one to see and discuss. MS

‣ Willem Dafoe, Charlotte Gainsbourg, Storm Acheche Sahlstrøm.
‣ *Dir* and *Screenplay* Lars von Trier, *Pro* Meta Louise Foldager, *Ph* Anthony Dod Mantle, *Pro Des* Karl 'Kalli' Juliusson, *Ed* Anders Refn, *Cos* Frauke Firl.
Zentropa Entertainments/Memfis Film/Lucky Red/ZDF Arte etc-Artificial Eye.
109 mins. Denmark/Germany/France/Sweden/Italy/Poland/Belgium. 2009. Rel: 24 July 2009. Cert. 18.

The Ape ★★★

The rating for this Swedish drama is not high because, as a portrait of a killer's descent into hell told from his own viewpoint, the story lacks the explanatory detail that would make it meaningful. Furthermore, one finds improbabilities here. Nevertheless, writer/director Jesper Ganslandt is revealed as a film-maker capable of making minimalism riveting and his lead actor, Olle Sarri, is fine. (Original title: *Apan*) MS

‣ Olle Sarri, Françoise Joyce, Niclas Gillis, Sean Pietrulewicz, Eva Rexed.

Country living: Charlotte Gainsbourg regrets leaving the city in Lars von Trier's highly controversial *Antichrist*.

‣ *Dir*, *Screenplay* and *Ed* Jesper Ganslandt, *Pro* Jesper Kurlandsky, *Ph* Fredrik Wenzel, *Pro Des* Catharina Nyqvist Ehmrooth, *M* Erik Enocksson, *Cos* Kajsa Severin.
Fasad/Film i Vast and Sveriges Television, SVT etc-ICA Films.
79 mins. Sweden. 2009. Rel: 22 Jan 2010. No Cert.

The Arbor ★★★★★

Clio Barnard's brilliantly original film concerns the playwright Andrea Dunbar, who died in 1990 and was best known for *Rita, Sue and Bob Too*. She uses actors who lip-synch to the recorded comments of Dunbar's children and friends, while outdoors in the Brafferton Arbor of Dunbar's native Bradford players perform extracts from her work. The odd mix, extending to historical footage, works triumphantly. None of Dunbar's failings as a human being are hidden but the film celebrates her nevertheless. That's because the comments of those heard here make one realise more than ever the stunning authenticity of the dialogue in her plays. MS

‣ Manjinder Virk, Christine Bottomley. Neil Dudgeon, Monica Dolan, Danny Webb, Kathryn Pogson, Natalie Gavin, George Costigan.
‣ *Dir* and *Screenplay* Clio Barnard, *Pro* Tracy O'Riordan, *Ph* Ole Birkeland, *Pro Des* Matthew Button, *Ed* Nick Fenton and Daniel Goddard, *Cos* Matthew Price.
Artangel Trust/UK Film Council etc-Verve Pictures.
94 mins. UK. 2010. Rel: 22 Oct 2010. Cert. 15.

Armored ★★★★

This may be yet another American crime thriller about a robbery but Nimród Antal's direction displays a great feel for cinema and the film, although modest, has been underrated. As the innocent Ty (Columbus Short) gets sucked into a security team's plan to rob one of the company's own vans, the suspense is all the greater because we don't know if Ty is a character destined to survive or one as disposable as Janet Leigh in *Psycho*. MS

‣ Matt Dillon, Laurence Fishburne, Fred Ward, Jean Réno, Columbus Short, Skeet Ulrich.
‣ *Dir* Nimród Antal, *Pro* Joshua Donen and Dan Farah, *Screenplay* James V Simpson, *Ph* Andrzej Sekula, *Pro Des* Jon Gary Steele, *Ed* Armen Minasian, *M* John Murphy, *Cos* Maya Lieberman.

Screen Gems/Stars Road Entertainment/Farah Films-Sony Pictures Releasing.
88 mins. USA. 2009. Rel: 22 Jan 2010. Cert. 12A.

The Army of Crime ★★★★

Robert Guédiguian forsakes his usual Marseilles location for Paris and a story about the role played by the Resistance there during the Second World War. There's an emphasis here on the Jews who were involved and, if the narrative is occasionally somewhat over-complex, the sincerity and commitment behind the piece are well in evidence. Some elements are already familiar but the film's portrayal of those in the French police who gave support to the German military is uncommonly powerful and new. (Original title: *L'Armée du crime*) MS

‣ Virginie Ledoyen, Simon Abkarian, Robinson Stévenin, Lola Naymark, Jean-Pierre Darroussin, Grégoire Leprince-Ringuet. Arianne Ascaride.
‣ *Dir* Robert Guédiguian, *Pro* Dominique Barneaud, Marc Bordure and Guédiguian, *Screenplay* Guédiguian, Gilles Taurand and Serge Le Péron, from the latter's original idea, *Ph* Pierre Milon, *Art Dir* Michel Vandestien, *Ed* Bernard Sasia, *M* Alexandre Desplat, *Cos* Juliette Chanaud.

Agat Films & Cie/StudioCanal/France 3 Cinéma etc-Optimum Releasing.
139 mins. France. 2009. Rel: 2 Oct 2009. Cert. 15.

Arthur and the Great Adventure ★½

Since his early achievement as a director (*Nikita*, *Leon*, etc), the endlessly prolific Luc Besson has proved to be an even more accomplished producer. And writer. Then, following the commercial success of *Arthur and the Invisibles* – which was based on two of his own children's novels – Besson has revisited his literary oeuvre with this wildly uneven follow-up. This time Arthur (Freddie

Highmore) returns to the micro-universe of the Minimoys, where he is double-crossed by the megalomaniac Maltazard (voiced by Lou Reed). Frankly, it's a shambles. (Original title: *Arthur et la vengeance de Maltazard*) CB

‣ Freddie Highmore, Mia Farrow and the voices of Selena Gomez, Iggy Pop, Stacy Ferguson, Snoop Dogg, Will.i.Am, Lou Reed.
‣ *Dir* Luc Besson, *Pro* Besson and Emmanuel Prévost, *Screenplay* Besson and Céline Garcia, *Ph* Thierry Arbogast, *Pro Des* Hugues Tissandier, *Ed* Julien Rey, *M* Eric Serra, *Cos* Olivier Bériot.

EuropaCorp/TF1 Films Production/Apipoulaï Production/Avalanche Productions/Canal + etc.- EuropaCorp Distribution.
93 mins. France. 2009. Rel: 24 Dec 2010. Cert. PG.

Heist society: Matt Dillon in Nimród Antal's cinematic *Armored*.

Astro Boy ★★★

David Bowers' futuristic animation based on Tezuka Osamu's manga is a cross between *Artificial Intelligence* and *Metropolis*. In Metro City, Astro Boy (Freddie Highmore) is a young robot with superpowers created by his scientist father Dr Tenma (Nicolas Cage). But when Astro flies away to a different planet he is determined to be accepted as one of the gang when he meets a group of children led by Cora (Kristen Bell). It is enjoyable but the comedy scenes could have been sharper. GS

‣ Voices of Nicolas Cage, Samuel L Jackson, Kristen Bell, Charlize Theron, Matt Lucas, Bill Nighy, Freddie Highmore, Donald Sutherland, Nathan Lane.
‣ *Dir* David Bowers, *Pro* Mary Ann Garger, *Screenplay* Timothy Harris, from a story by Bowers,

The top-grossing film of all time: Stephen Lang and Sam Worthington discuss the box-office figures in James Cameron's *Avatar*.

based on the comic series by Tezuka Osamu, *Ph* Pepe Valencia, *Pro Des* Jake Rowell, *Ed* Robert Anich Cole, *M* John Ottman, *Cos* Jane Poole.

Imagi Animation Studios/Imagi Crystal/Tezuka Production Company Limited-E1 Entertainment. 94 mins. Hong Kong/USA/Japan. 2009. Rel: 5 Feb 2010. Cert. PG.

The A-Team ★

A contemporary restyling of a beloved 1980s adventure show that, let's be honest, was never very good, *The A-Team* lives up to its source material by being equally crummy, though in a far more modern way. Telling the mindlessly action-packed tale of how four eccentric military men transform into a crack mercenary squad of innovative do-gooders, the movie strives to retain the camaraderie of the original, but tries too hard and comes off as desperate. Sharlto Copley's Murdock enjoys the occasional inspired improv, but Liam Neeson's Hannibal is so far off-base it's AWOL. It's all just a bore. MJ

▶ Liam Neeson, Jessica Biel, Bradley Cooper, Patrick Wilson, Sharlto Copley
▶ *Dir* Joe Carnahan, *Pro* Stephen J Cannell, Tony Scott, Jules Daly, Spike Seldin etc, *Screenplay* Carnahan, Brian Bloom and Skip Woods, based on the television series, *Ph* Mauro Fiore, *Pro Des* Charles Wood, *Ed* Roger Barton and Jim May, *M* Alan Silvestri, *Cos* Betsy Heimann.

Twentieth Century Fox/Stephen J Cannell Productions/

Dune Entertainment/Top Cow Productions/Scott Free Productions etc-20th Century Fox. 117 mins. USA. 2010. Rel: 30 July 2010. Cert. 12A.

Avatar ★★★

James Cameron's *Titanic* was a world-beating moneymaker. Now *Avatar* is the same only more so, with Cameron's imagination running riot. Earthlings invade a remote planet peopled by Na'vi, a race of ten-foot-tall blue aliens, and other creatures who live in an atmosphere poisonous to humans. Genetically controlled beings (avatars) are sent to the planet under the guidance of paraplegic ex-Marine Jake Sully (Sam Worthington) and chief scientist (Sigourney Weaver) in order to mine for a rare mineral called unobtainium (the film's only joke). But love will out and Sam falls for a Na'vi princess (Zoe Saldana). Despite all the special CGI effects and 3-D, unless you can swallow the basic premise, the film is lost on you. However, enough cinemagoers loved it to make it the world's most profitable movie ever. Two sequels are already on the way. Phew! MHD

▶ Sam Worthington, Zoe Saldana, Sigourney Weaver, Stephen Lang, David Moore, Giovanni Ribisi.
▶ *Dir* and *Screenplay* James Cameron, *Pro* Cameron and Jon Landau, *Ph* Mauro Fiore, *Pro Des* Rick Carter and Robert Stromberg, *Ed* Cameron, John Refoua and Steven Rivkin, *M* James Horner, *Cos* Lilia Mishel

Acevedo, John Harding, Mayes C Rubeo, Deborah Lynn Scott.

Twentieth Century Fox Film Corporation/Dune Entertainment/Grant Studios/Ingenious Film Partners/Lightstorm Entertainment-20th Century Fox. 162 mins. USA/UK. 2009. Rel: 17 Dec 2009. Cert. 12A.

Away We Go ★★

This road movie directed by our own Sam Mendes is a very American work. A couple, unmarried but firmly established and expecting their first child, travel to find a suitable home in which to settle. Engagingly, Maya Rudolph and John Krasinski lack the obvious looks that Hollywood usually insists on for leading players. However, the characters they encounter irritate more than they amuse and the film ends up being tiresomely simplistic and sentimental – in contrast to Mike Leigh's warmly engaging *High Hopes* (1988), of which I was reminded. MS

➤ John Krasinski, Maya Rudolph, Jeff Daniels, Maggie Gyllenhaal, Allison Janey.
➤ *Dir* Sam Mendes, *Pro* Edward Saxon, Marc Turtletaub and Peter Saraf, *Screenplay* Dave Eggers and Vendela Vida, *Ph* Ellen Kuras, *Pro Des* Jess Gonchor, *Ed* Sarah Flack, *M* Alexi Murdoch, *Cos* John Dunn.

Focus Features/Big Beach/Neal Street Productions etc-E1 Films. 98 mins. USA/UK. 2009. Rel: 18 Sep 2009. Cert. 15.

Baarìa ★★★½

Giuseppe Tornatore, he of *Cinema Paradiso*, now offers this epic movie about three generations of a Sicilian family. It's a panoramic piece which adroitly sustains its length of two and a half hours. However, despite the political elements in a tale moving from the 1930s to the recent past, the film's tone is more popular than art-house. Italian audiences will more readily pick up social references, but for the most part it delivers on its chosen ground and technically it is of high quality. MS

➤ Francesco Scianna, Margareth Madè, Lina Sastri, Ángela Molina, Gaetano Aronica.
➤ *Dir* and *Screenplay* Giuseppe Tornatore, *Pro* Giampaolo Letta and Mario Spedaletti, *Ph* Enrico Lucidi, *Pro Des* Maurizio Sabatini, *Ed* Massimo Quaglia, *M* Ennio Morricone, *Cos* Luigi Bonanno with Antonella Balsamo.

Medusa Film/Exon Film/Quinta Communications etc-E1 Films. 151 mins. Italy/France. 2009. Rel: 23 July 2010. Cert. 15.

The Back-Up Plan ★★

Despite a few laughs and its easy-going nature, this is an irritating, vacuous rom-com memorable only for Jennifer Lopez's bland performance as Zoe, a businesswoman who's so unlucky in love she decides to conceive via artificial insemination. Then she meets hunky, persistent Stan (Alex O'Loughlin), drop-dead gorgeous like a calendar boy with his shirt off. Zoe resists but Stan keeps pursuing her. The good news is it's twins for Zoe, but the bad news is she thinks Stan might not be perfect after all! Lopez needs a more original script and, if Alex O'Loughlin can survive this, he'll survive anything. DW

➤ Jennifer Lopez, Alex O'Loughlin, Michaela Watkins, Eric Christian Olsen, Tom Bosley, Robert Klein.
➤ *Dir* Alan Poul, *Pro* Jason Blumenthal and Steve Tisch, *Screenplay* Kate Angelo, *Ph* Xavier Pérez Grobet, *Pro Des* Alec Hammond, *Ed* Priscilla Nedd-Friendly, *M* Stephen Trask, *Cos* Karen Patch.

CBS Films/Escape Artists-Sony Pictures Releasing. 106 mins. USA. 2010. Rel: 7 May 2010. Cert. 12A.

Bad Lieutenant ★★★½

The full title, *The Bad Lieutenant: Port of Call: New Orleans*, underlines the claim that, despite featuring a cop compromised by his own drug habit, this is not intended as an actual remake of Abel Ferrara's *Bad Lieutenant* of 1992. It features Nicolas Cage on strong form, but the film segues from an able but conventional account of criminal detection into a quirkily humorous tale that will appeal to some more than others. Werner Herzog presides and is personally responsible for footage of iguanas and alligators! MS

➤ Nicolas Cage, Eva Mendes, Val Kilmer, Alvin Xzibit Joiner, Fairuza Balk, Brad Dourif.
➤ *Dir* Werner Herzog, *Pro* Edward R Pressman, John Thompson. Randall Emmett and others, *Screenplay*

Swimming with the fishes: Nicolas Cage (left) as the ultimate corrupt cop in Werner Herzog's delightfully idiosyncratic *Bad Lieutenant*.

Bloody history: Anna Friel takes on the mantle of the notorious Countess in Juraj Jakubisko's visually audacious *Bathory*.

William Finkelstein, *Ph* Peter Zeitlinger, *Pro Des* Toby Corbett, *Ed* Joe Bini, *M* Mark Isham, *Cos* Jill Newell.

Millennium Films/Saturn Films/Polsky Films etc-Lionsgate UK.
122 mins. USA. 2009. Rel: 21 May 2010. Cert. 18.

The Ballroom ★★★★

Made in 2008, this is a relaxed and engaging movie set in a traditional dance hall in São Paulo; it was indeed filmed in one. The regular patrons, some aged, are the main characters, each with their own problems in life. Easily overlooked, this utterly unpretentious piece has been underestimated. It is remarkably successful in capturing life in its own quiet way and never resorts to anything approaching melodrama. (Original title: *Chega de saudade*) MS

➤ Leonardo Villar, Tônia Carrero, Cássia Kiss, Stepan Nercessian, Elza Soares, Marku Ribas, Clarisse Abujamra, Raul Bordale, Luiz Serra.
➤ *Dir* Laís Bodanzky, *Pro* Caio Gullane, Fabiano Gullane, Bodanzky etc, *Screenplay* Luiz Bolognesi, from a story by him and Bodanzky, *Ph* Walter Carvalho, *Art Dir* Marcos Pedroso, *Ed* Paulo Sacramento, *Cos* André Simonetti.

CCR/Bradesco/Gullane Films/Buriti Filmes etc-Matchbox Films.
95 mins. Brazil/France. 2009. Rel: 2 July 2010. No Cert.

Bananas! ★★★★

Fredrik Gertten's compelling documentary examines the controversial legal case of a dozen Nicaraguan banana plantation workers against Dole Food Corporation. The workers claim that Dole's usage of a deadly banned pesticide has been causing them many diseases, such as cancer and sterility, for generations. Everything is at stake but luckily the workers get the legendary Los Angeles-based attorney Juan Dominguez to represent them, so the David and Goliath battle begins... GS

➤ Byron Rosales Romero, Juan J Dominguez, Duane Miller, Rick McKnight, David Delorenzo.
➤ *Dir* Fredrik Gertten, *Pro* Margarete Jangård, *Ph* Joseph Aguirre and Frank Pineda, *Pro Des* Rebecca Medez, *Ed* Jasper Osmund, *M* Nathan Larson.

WG Film/Magic Hour Films ApS-Dogwoof Pictures.
80 mins. Sweden/Denmark. 2009. Rel: 16 Apr 2010. No Cert.

Bandslam ★★★

Shy teenager Will Burton (Gaelan Connell) is reluctant to move to New Jersey with his single mother Karen (Lisa Kudrow), but at his new school he can't believe his luck when the attractive and talented musician Charlotte (Alyson Michalka) invites him to manage her rock band and enter their school's upcoming battle of the bands competition. It is all very predictable of course but Todd Graff's fresh and engaging comedy is miles better than the *High School Musical* series. GS

➤ Alyson Michalka, Vanessa Hudgens, Gaelen Connell, Scott Porter, Lisa Kudrow.
➤ *Dir* Todd Graff, *Pro* Elaine Goldsmith-Thomas, Ron Schmidt and Marisa Yeres, *Screenplay* Graff and Josh A Cagan, *Ph* Eric Steelberg, *Pro Des* Jeff Knipp, *Ed* John Gilbert, *Cos* Ernesto Martinez.

Summit Entertainment/Walden Media/Goldsmith-Thomas Productions-Contender Entertainment Group.
111 mins. USA. 2009. Rel: 12 Aug 2009. Cert. PG.

Basement ★

With its six actors and (for the most part) single set, this is like a pretentious, po-faced fringe play given a bare minimum of cinematic gloss. It recalls the underground confinement of infinitely better films like *The Hole* and *Creep*, sending its half-dozen lab rats wandering interminably round excrement-smeared subterranean corridors in pursuit of a supposedly ironic final twist. To wit, the British government is creating a cloned fighting force from the butchered remnants of anti-war protesters. The end product is a terrible slog and features Danny Dyer describing himself as "directionless", which he most certainly is here. JR

▶ Jimi Mistry, Danny Dyer, Kierston Wareing, Emily Beecham, Lois Winstone, Soraya Radford.
▶ *Dir* Asham Kamboj, *Pro* Kamboj, Ish Jalal and Terry Stone, *Screenplay* Ewen Glass, based on a story by Kamboj and Glass, *Pro Des* Byron Broadbent, *Ed* Peter Davies, *M* Amit Kamboj, *Cos* Florence Chow.
Paperknife Productions-Revolver Entertainment.
77 mins. UK. 2010. Rel: 17 Aug 2010. Cert. 18.

Bathory ★★½

This was the part that should have transformed Anna Friel into Catherine Zeta-Jones. Erzsebet Báthory is one of history's most notorious women, a Countess who supposedly bathed in virgins' blood. Set in Slovakia in the late 16th and early 17th centuries, the film attempts to address the mythical balance. While Ms Friel finds it hard to keep up with her director's visual sweep, audiences may appreciate the plentiful nudity and excessive violence. Incidentally, it's one of the costliest movies to come out of Central Europe. CB

▶ Anna Friel, Franco Nero, Karel Roden, Jiri Madl, Vincent Regan, Anthony Byrne.
▶ *Dir* Juraj Jakubisko, *Pro* Thom Mount, Mike Downey and Deana Horvathova, *Screenplay* Jakubisko and John Paul Chappie, *Ph* F A Brabec and Jan Duris, *Pro Des* Karel Vacek, *Ed* Chris Blunden, *M* Simon Boswell, *Cos* Julia Patkos and Jaroslava Pecharova.
Eurofilm Studio/Film and Music Entertainment/ Jakubisko Film Slovakia etc-Metrodome Distribution.
141 mins. Slovakia/Czech Republic/Hungary/UK. 2008. Rel: 3 Dec 2010. Cert. 15.

Battle for Terra ★★★½

Aristomenis Tsirbas' enjoyable animated feature is strikingly designed and looks fabulous in 3D, particularly in the spectacular battle sequences. The story is not dissimilar to the recent *Planet 51* but without the laughs. It takes place on the planet Terra which is facing a vicious attack from the last surviving members of humanity. The dialogue scenes could do with a bit more pacing but overall this is very entertaining. (Original title: *Terra*) GS

▶ Voices of Chad Allen, Mark Hamill, Rosanna Arquette, James Garner, Danny Glover, Brian Cox, Beverly D'Angelo.
▶ *Dir, Ph* and *Pro Des* Aristomenis Tsirbas, *Pro* Keith Calder, Ryan Colucci, Dane Allan Smith and Jessica Wu, *Screenplay* Tsirbas and Evan Spiliotopoulos, from a story by Tsirbas, *Ed* J Kathleen Gibson, *M* Abel Korzeniowski.
MeniThings LLC/Snoot Entertainment-The Works UK Distribution.
85 mins. USA. 2007. Rel: 12 February 2010. Cert PG.

The Be All and End All ★★★★

Liverpudlian teenager Robbie (Josh Bolt) and his best friend Ziggy (Eugene Byrne) have only one thing on their minds – how to lose their virginity. But things take an unexpected turn when one of them is diagnosed with a serious illness... This fresh and original film boasts endearing and confident performances from the young actors. Director Bruce Webb successfully mingles comedy with tragedy and never sinks into sentimentality. GS

▶ Josh Bolt, Eugene Byrne, Neve McIntosh, Kate Henry, Liza Tarbuck.
▶ *Dir* Bruce Webb, *Pro* Webb and John Maxwell, *Screenplay* Tony Owen and Steve Lewis, *Ph* Zillah Bowes, *Pro Des* Tine Jespersen, *Ed* Joe Wilby, *M* Richard Lannoy, *Cos* Lydia Hardiman.
Whatever Pictures-Verve Pictures.
100 mins. UK. 2009. Rel: 3 Dec 2010. Cert. 15.

The Beaches of Agnès ★★★½

This latest film essay by Agnès Varda is in the nature of an autobiographical memoir. As she reaches 80 she looks back on her career and her life,

Sands of time: Agnès Varda in her autobiographical memoir *The Beaches of Agnès*.

American graffiti: a scene from Aaron Rose and Joshua Leonard's inspiring *Beautiful Losers*.

including her devotion to her late husband Jacques Demy who died of AIDS. Those familiar with her work will be intrigued, but sometimes she side-steps and, given comments that have been made about Demy's sexuality, ignoring that aspect of a man so crucial to her life lessens the value of the self-portrait. (Original title: *Les Plages d'Agnès*) MS

▶ With Agnès Varda, Rosalie Varda, Mathieu Demy, Jim McBride, Zalman King.
▶ *Dir, Writer* and *Ed* Agnès Varda, *Ph* Hélène Louvart, Alain Sakot, Varda and others, *Art Dir* Franckie Diago, *M* Joanna Bruzdowicz, Stéphane Vilar and Paule Cornet.

Ciné-Tamaris/ARTE France Cinema/Canal+ etc-Artificial Eye. 113 mins. France. 2008. Rel: 2 Oct 2009. Cert. 18.

Bear ★½

Another marvel from the low-budget digital horror film phenomenon: a marvel that this found its way into a British cinema. Here we have the usual quota of moronic youths who find themselves in a remote area (a Californian forest) faced by an angry force of nature (the eponymous grizzly). The unappealing victims get what's coming to them (one of their number kills the grizzly's cub) and leave one pining for the merits of *The Edge*, *The Bear*, *Grizzly* et al. CB

▶ Brendan Michael Coughlin, Patrick Scott Lewis, Katie Lowes, Mary Alexander Stiefvater.
▶ *Dir* John Rebel, *Pro* Roel Reine, Ethan Wiley, Alicia Martin and Freddie Wong, *Screenplay* Reine and Wiley, *Pro Des* Rose Shawhan, *Ed* Herman P Koerts, *M* Trevor Morris.

Rebel Film BV/Wiseacre Films-Metrodome Distribution. 90 mins. USA. 2010. Rel: 4 June 2010. Cert. 15.

Beautiful Kate ★★★½

Actress Rachel Ward turns director and, in adapting a novel, switches its location from Idaho to Southern Australia. This well-acted movie also elects to reset the tale in recent times with flashbacks to the 1980s. Initially effective, the film's portrait of a dysfunctional family moves increasingly towards the stuff of melodrama. The eponymous Kate is a teenage

Twin set: Maggie Hatcher in Andrew Bujalski's wholly persuasive *Beeswax*.

member of the family, one who had died in a car crash, but the big twist in the story concerns her and if you relish melodrama it will be to your advantage here. MS

‣ Ben Mendelssohn, Bryan Brown, Maeve Dermody, Sophie Lowe, Rachel Griffiths.
‣ *Dir* Rachel Ward, *Pro* Leah Churchill-Brown and Bryan Brown, *Screenplay* Ward, from Newton Thornburg's novel, *Ph* Andrew Commis, *Pro Des* Ian Jobson, *Ed* Veronica Jenet, *M* Tex Perkins and Murray Paterson, *Cos* Ruth De La Lande.

Screen Australia/Showtime Australia/New Town/New Doll etc-Matchbox Pictures.
101 mins. Australia. 2009. Rel: 30 July 2010. Cert. 15.

Beautiful Losers ★★★½

Aaron Rose's art documentary follows a group of unconventional and non-conformist artists who developed their various crafts underground in New York City in the early 1990s. It is a unique group with a diverse mix of skateboarding, surf, punk, hip hop, film and graffiti lovers whose enthusiasm for their art is inspiring. Many artists are featured including film director Harmony Korine, best known as the 19-year-old screenwriter of Larry Clark's *kids* – he met Clark while skateboarding in New York. GS

‣ Thomas Campbell, Shepard Fairey, Jo Jackson, Chris Johanson, Harmony Korine, Margaret Kilgallen.
‣ *Dir* Aaron Rose and Joshua Leonard, *Pro* Jon Barlow, Chris Green, Richard Lim and Noah Khoshbin, *Ph* Tobin Yelland, *Ed* Lenny Mesina, *M* Money Mark.

Sidetrack Films/Back Lake Productions/Perception Media-Revolver Entertainment.
90 mins. USA. 2008. Rel: 7 Aug 2009. Cert. 15.

Beeswax ★★★★

Following *Funny Ha Ha* and *Mutual Appreciation*, Andrew Bujalski's third feature is his best. It's superbly cast and features twins as twins, one of whom, Tilly Hatcher, is confined to a wheelchair both here and in real life. Substitute American authenticity for French and the comparisons with the late Eric Rohmer are more justified than ever. It's a slice of life rather than a story, but wholly persuasive and this time in colour. There's no better screen portrait of a disabled person living her life. MS

‣ Tilly Hatcher, Maggie Hatcher, Alex Karpovsky, Katy O'Connor, David Zellner.
‣ *Dir*, *Screenplay* and *Ed* Andrew Bujalski, *Pro* Dia Sokol and Ethan Vogt, *Ph* Matthias Grunsky.

Funded in part by The Media Arts Fellowships, a programme of Tribeca Film Institute & LEF Moving Image Fund-ICA Films.
100 mins. USA. 2009. Rel: 14 Apr 2010. No Cert.

Swimming for Slovenia: Martin Strel goes undercover in John Maringouin's extraordinary *Big River Man*.

Beyond the Pole ★½

Two losers attempt to become the first carbon neutral, organic vegetarians to reach the North Pole… Juggling environmentalism, slapstick and black comedy, *Beyond the Pole* is a very odd contrivance. While making a mockery of the mockumentary 'genre' (a tired format that fails to bolster the film's credibility), this serves up some predictable comic beats and an all too familiar performance from Stephen Mangan. But its worst fault is that it's not remotely funny and really doesn't make any sense. JC-W

‣ Rhys Thomas, Alexander Skarsgård, Stephen Mangan, Mark Benton, Rosie Cavaliero, Helen Baxendale.
‣ *Dir* David L Williams, *Pro* Williams and Andrew J Curtis, *Screenplay* Williams and Neil Warhurst, *Ph* Stuart Biddlecombe, *Pro Des* Lisa Hall, *Ed* Rob Miller, *M* Guy Michelmore, *Cos* Nikkie Alsford.

Shooting Pictures/Polite Storm-Hanway Films.
87 mins. UK. 2009. Rel: 12 Feb 2010. Cert. 15.

Big River Man ★★★½

This intriguing and well-photographed documentary is a portrait of the Slovenian Martin Strel, a man in his fifties and a great swimmer of rivers, who is here seen attempting his longest venture of all – the 3,375 miles of the Amazon. His son acts as narrator but the cost of family co-operation may have been a commitment not to ask unwelcome questions. Consequently key issues are ducked, but the film is never less than interesting. MS

‣ With Martin Strel, Borut Strel (narrator).
‣ *Dir* John Maringouin with Molly Lynch, *Pro* Maria Florio, Lynch, Maringouin and others, *Screenplay* and *Ed* Maringouin and Lynch, *Ph* Maringouin, *M* Rich Ragsdale.

Self Pictures/Earthworks Films-Revolver Entertainment.
101 mins. USA. 2008. Rel: 4 Sep 2009. Cert. 15.

Going native: Alicélia Batista Cabreira in Marco Bechis's hypnotic and powerful *BirdWatchers*.

BirdWatchers ★★★★

Set in contemporary Brazil, this drama is a comment on the plight of the Guarani-Kaiowá, the native people of South America, told through a family story that incorporates a *Romeo and Juliet* element when a native youth falls in love with the daughter of a white farmer. The high suicide rate amongst the natives evidences their situation in a society that exploits them, and the film is deeply felt. The potential of the narrative is not always realised, however, partly perhaps on account of the decision to use non-professional actors. (Original title: *La terra degli uomini rossi*) MS

▶ Claudio Santamaria, Alicélia Batista Cabreira, Chiara Caselli, Abrisio da Silva Pedro, Ambrósio Vilhalva, Ademilson Concianza Verga (Kiki), Fabiane Pereira da Silva.
▶ *Dir* Marco Bechis, *Pro* Amedeo Pagani, Bechis, Fabiano Gullane and Caio Gullane, *Screenplay* Bechis and Luiz Bolognesi, from a story by Bechis, *Ph* Hélcio 'Alemão' Nagamine, *Art Dir* Clóvis Bueno and Caterina Giargia, *Ed* Jacopo Quadri, *M* Domenico Zipoli and Andrea Guerra, *Cos* Giargia and Valéria Stefani.

Classic/RAI Cinema/Karta Film/Gullane Filmes etc-Artificial Eye.
104 mins. Italy/Brazil. 2008. Rel: 18 Sep 2009. Cert. 15.

Black Death ★★★

Though entirely financed in Germany, this plague-spotted 14th century quest saga has been co-opted into Britain's ongoing horror revival thanks to its director Christopher Smith, who was previously responsible for *Creep* and *Severance*. Vaguely reminiscent of the forgotten *Anazapta*, only without the laughs, here Smith adopts a dour and doom-laden tone that makes the first two-thirds seem a bit of a slog, and not just for the superstitious mercenary band led by grizzled Sean Bean. The third act is much better, showcasing a really potent clash of irrational belief systems worthy of *The Wicker Man*, plus a climactic 'quartering' by straining horses. JR

▶ Sean Bean, Eddie Redmayne, David Warner, Carice van Houten, Tim McInnerny, John Lynch.
▶ *Dir* Christopher Smith, *Pro* Robert Bernstein, Douglas Rae, Phil Robertson and Jens Meurer, *Screenplay* Dario Poloni, *Ph* Sebastian Edschmid, *Pro Des* John Frankish, *Ed* Stuart Gazzard, *M* Christian Henson, *Cos* Petra Wellenstein.

Egoli Tossell Film etc-Revolver Entertainment.
97 mins. Germany. 2010. Rel: 11 June 2010. Cert. 15.

Black Dynamite ★★★★

This lovingly produced blaxploitation spoof of 1970s gangster films is simply hilarious. Ex-CIA commando Black Dynamite (Michael Jai White) begins a long search to find his brother's killers, which leads him to many adventures involving heroin-addicted orphans as well as a manic President Nixon and a kick-ass first lady. I haven't laughed out loud as much for ages, especially in the sequence where they try to solve the mystery by word association that involves Greek mythology, anacondas and chocolate. Great fun. GS

▶ Arsenio Hall, Tommy Davidson, Michael Jai White, Richard Edson, Phil Morris, Kevin Chapman.
▶ *Dir* Scott Sanders, *Pro* Jon Steingart and Jenny Wiener Steingart, *Screenplay* Michael Jai White,

Sanders and Byron Minns, based on a story by Sanders and Minns, *Ph* Shawn Maurer, *Pro Des* Denise Rizzini, *Ed* and *M* Adrian Younge, *Cos* Ruth E Carter.

Ars Nova/Destination Films/Goliath Entertainment/Harbor Entertainment/Six Point Harness-Icon Film Distribution. 84 mins. USA. 2009. Rel: 13 Aug 2010. Cert. 15.

Blind Dating ★★★

Intelligent and attractive Danny (Chris Pine) seems to have everything in life apart from his sight. He is popular with the ladies but is saving his virginity for someone special. He falls for his eye doctor's Indian nurse, the lovely Leeza (Anjali Jay), but she is already promised to someone else in an arranged marriage... Pine has fun with his role but the real revelation is Jay, who delivers a sensitive performance. This is an entertaining film despite the redundant farcical and scatological scenes. GS

▶ Jenny Alden, Chris Pine, Eddie Kaye Thomas, Anjali Jay, Jane Seymour.
▶ *Dir* James Keach, *Pro* Keach, Joy Melling, Costa Theo and David Shanks, *Screenplay* Christopher Theo, *Ph* Julio Macat, *Pro Des* Eric Weiler, *Ed* Larry Bock, *M* Heitor Pereira, *Cos* Cheri Ingle.

Samuel Goldwyn Films/MilCoz Films/Catfish Productions/Blind Guy Films/Theta Film Holdings-The Works. 95 mins. USA. 2006. Rel: 18 Sep 2009. Cert. 15.

The Blind Side ★★½

Michael Oher (Quinton Aaron) is quiet, educationally sub-standard and very, very big. But, boy, he can handle a ball and Wingate High could do with a new star player. *The Blind Side* ticks all the right boxes as an inspirational true-life drama. Sandra Bullock continues her winning streak as a tough mom with no negative characteristics, the supporting cast smiles blandly in secondary roles, and Quinton Aaron struts his stuff as the imposing, troubled Michael Oher. Ultimately, though, it's an anodyne *Precious* with a lot of football thrown in. JC-W

▶ Sandra Bullock, Tim McGraw, Quinton Aaron, Jae Head, Lily Collins, Kathy Bates, Ray McKinnon.
▶ *Dir* and *Screenplay* John Lee Hancock, from the book by Michael Lewis, *Pro* Andrew A Kosove, Gil Netter and Broderick Johnson, *Ph* Alar Kivilo, *Pro Des* Michael Coren Blith, *Ed* Mark Livolsi, *M* Carter Burwell, *Cos* Daniel Orlandi.

Zucker-Netter Productions/Alcon Entertainment-Warner Bros. 129 mins. USA. 2009. Rel: 26 Mar 2010. Cert. 12A.

Bluebeard ★★★½

Bluebeard's legend is revisited but seen here from a different perspective. Two contemporary sisters begin to read the story before the action moves into Bluebeard's castle. A young woman called Anne (Daphné Baiwir) is sent from the convent to become Bluebeard's latest bride and perhaps the notorious wife killer has finally met his match... Catherine Breillat's authentically composed medieval drama works thanks to its simplicity and careful production values that gracefully convey the period. It is in fact so authentic that you can almost smell the banquet and the moist dark corridors. (Original title: *Barbe Bleu*) GS

▶ Dominique Thomas, Lola Créton, Marilou Lopes-Benites, Daphné Baiwir, Lola Giovanetti.
▶ *Dir* and *Screenplay* Catherine Breillat, from the story by Charles Perrault, *Pro* Sylvette Frydman and Jean-François Lepetit, *Ph* Vilco Filac, *Pro Des* Oliver Jacquet, *Ed* Pascale Chavance, *Cos* Rose-Marie Melka.

Flach Films/CB Films/Arte France-New Wave Films. 78 mins. France. 2009. Rel: 16 July 2010. Cert. 15.

Blur: No Distance Left to Run ★★★★

Dylan Southern and Will Lovelace's attractive documentary tells the story of Blur from their early days in Colchester (at the time when the

Beyond belief: Kimberley Nixon in Christopher Smith's dour and doom-laden *Black Death*.

Going Biblical: Denzel Washington in bookish mode in the Hughes brothers' visually striking *The Book of Eli*.

dreaded Thatcher manifesto was taking over suburbia) up until their recent reunion concert in Glastonbury, their first in nine years. It is an honest and highly watchable film told in the band's own words about the highs and lows of Blur – and it is not just for the fans. GS

▶ Damon Albarn, Graham Coxon, Alex James, Dave Rountree, Phil Daniels, Liam Gallagher, Noel Gallagher.
▶ *Dir* Will Lovelace and Dylan Southern, *Pro* Lucas Ochoa, *Ph* Southern and Ross McLennan, *Ed* Southern.
Pulse Films-Arts Alliance Media.
104 mins. UK. 2010. Rel: 19 Jan 2010. Cert. 15.

Bonded by Blood ★

Drug criminals Tony Tucker (Terry Stone), Patrick Tate (Tamer Hassan) and Craig Rolfe (Neil Maskell) have been terrorising Essex for years, but in 1995 they get their comeuppance in Rettendon while waiting in a Range Rover. Sacha Bennett's unimaginative gangster thriller revisits the notorious 1990s Essex drugs case but adds nothing new to an over-familiar genre. It's practically impossible to identify with any of its hugely unsympathetic characters. GS

▶ Terry Stone, Neil Maskell, Tamer Hassan, Dave Legeno, Kierston Wareing, Adam Deacon.
▶ *Dir* Sacha Bennett, *Pro* Daniel Toland and Terry Stone, *Screenplay* Bennett and Graeme Muir, *Ph* Ali Asad, *Pro Des* Matthew Button, *Ed* Kate Evans, *M* Jason Kaye, *Cos* Hayley Nebauer.
Gateway Films/Prime Focus-Revolver Entertainment.
96 mins. UK. 2010. Rel: 3 Sep 2010. Cert. 18.

Boogie Woogie ★★★

A first-rate cast have a tricky time trying to make this satire of the international art scene work smoothly, but they just about succeed. Danny Huston stars as amoral art dealer Art Spindle who employs ambitious Beth Freemantle (Heather Graham) and young roller-skater Paige (Amanda Seyfried). Spindle wants to buy the Mondrian painting of the title from Christopher Lee and his wife Joanna Lumley, but... As a Robert Altman-style character-driven epic parody, it's a bit blunt and obvious, and Danny Moynihan's script lacks true wit and sophistication. But the film and the performances are entertaining enough and it remains quite provocative and amusing. DW

▶ Gillian Anderson, Alan Cumming, Heather Graham, Danny Huston, Christopher Lee, Joanna Lumley, Charlotte Rampling, Amanda Seyfried, Stellan Skarsgård, Jamie Winstone.
▶ *Dir* Duncan Ward, *Pro* Danny Moynihan, Kami Naghdi, Cat Villiers and Christopher Simon, *Screenplay* Danny Moynihan based on his own novel, *Ph* John Mathieson, *Pro Des* Caroline Greville-Morris, *Ed* Kant Pan, *M* Janusz Podrazik, *Cos* Claire Anderson.
Autonomous/Colour Frame/Constance Media/Firefly Muse Productions/S Films/The Works International-Vertigo Films.
94 mins. UK. 2009. Rel: 16 Apr 2010. Cert. 15.

The Book of Eli ★★★★½

In a world ravaged by war, one man ventures west aided by a lethal sword, an iPod and a copy of the King James' Bible. Another week, another post-apocalyptic nightmare. This one, though, takes Cormac McCarthy's *The Road* [qv] and runs with it, injecting healthy doses of pop-cultural allusions and embracing everything from *A Clockwork Orange* to Edward Albee. It's also a visual marvel, stretching the vistas of *The Road* to true cinematic extremes. A mix of *Mad Max* and *I Am Legend*, the film has fun while making a number of valid points about the present state of humanity. JC-W

‣ Denzel Washington, Gary Oldman, Mila Kunis, Ray Stevenson, Jennifer Beals, Evan Jones, Frances de la Tour, Michael Gambon, Tom Waits.
‣ *Dir* Albert and Allen Hughes, *Pro* Joel Silver, Andrew A Kosove, David Valdes and Broderick Johnson, *Screenplay* Gary Whitta, *Ph* Don Burgess, *Pro Des* Gae Buckley, *Ed* Cindy Mollo, *M* Atticus Ross, Leopold Ross and Claudia Sarne, *Cos* Sharen Davis.

Silver Pictures/Alcon Entertainment-Entertainment Film Distributors.
118 mins. USA. 2010. Rel: 15 Jan 2010. Cert. 15.

Born in 68 ★★★½

Covering the period from 1968 to 2007, this French saga follows a group of characters down the years, taking in more than one generation in the process. Compared to Téchiné's *The Witnesses* (2006), which also offered a mix of personal stories in a changing social context, this is more akin to soap opera, but it's all quite watchable and it's something of a triumph that the film so readily sustains its long running time. (Original title: *Nés en '68 Nous nous aimerons jusqu'à la mort*) MS

‣ Laetitia Casta, Yannick Renier, Yann Trégouët, Christine Citti, Sabrina Seyvecou, Théo Frilet, Edouard Collin, Marc Citti, Kate Moran, Alain Fromager, Slimane Yefsah.
‣ *Dir* and *Screenplay* (from an original idea by Guillaume Le Touze) Olivier Ducastel and Jacques Martineau, *Pro* Philippe Martin and Lola Gans, *Ph* Matthieu Poirot-Delpech, *Art Dir* Denis Moutereau, *Ed* Dominique Gallieni, *M* Philippe Miller, *Cos* Catherine Rigault.

Les Films Pelléas/Arte France/France 2 etc-Peccadillo Pictures.
173 mins. France. 2008. Rel: 25 Sep 2009. Cert. 15.

The Bounty Hunter ★

The Bounty Hunter is so inept on so many levels that it's laughable. Sadly, there isn't a chuckle to be found in the entire film. Once again, Jennifer Aniston finds herself in a grievous romantic tangle in which the outcome is inevitable. Gerard Butler plays the hunk who happens to be her ex-husband and is handsomely paid to bring her to justice. Unfortunately, irrationality, chemical vapidity and the year's worst 'funny' music mar any possibilities of enjoyment. It's like a slapdash alloy of *The Defiant Ones* and *Out*

of Sight without the humour of either. JC-W

‣ Jennifer Aniston, Gerard Butler, Gio Perez, Joel Marsh Garland, Matt Malloy, Jason Kolotouros, Christine Baranski.
‣ *Dir* Andy Tennant, *Pro* Neal H Moritz, *Screenplay* Sarah Thorp, *Ph* Oliver Bokelsberg, *Pro Des* Jane Musky, *Ed* Troy Takaki, *M* George Fenton, *Cos* Sophie De Rakoff.

Columbia Pictures/Relativity Media/Original Film etc-Sony Pictures Releasing.
110 mins. USA. 2010. Rel: 17 Mar 2010. Cert. 12A.

The Box ★½

The Box starts promisingly. A married couple are presented with a device with a button, which, should they press it, will guarantee them a million dollars – and the death of a stranger… Had this high-concept adaptation of Richard Matheson's short story been given an iota of style it could have raised some genuine scares. As it is, the characters are solid stereotypes while the plot descends into unbridled absurdity. Intrigue quickly gives way to irritation – and confusion – and we are left feeling decidedly boxed in. JC-W

‣ Cameron Diaz, James Marsden, Frank Langella, James Rebhorn, Holmes Osborne.
‣ *Dir* Richard Kelly, *Pro* Kelly and Dan Lin, *Screenplay* Kelly and Sean McKittrick, based on Richard Matheson's story *Button Button*, *Ph* Stephen Poster, *Pro Des* Alec Hammond, *Ed* Sam Bauer, *M* Win Butler, Régine Chassagne and Owen Pallett, *Cos* April Ferry.

Darico Entertainment/Lin Pictures/Radar Pictures-Icon Film Distribution.
115 mins. USA. 2009. Rel: 4 Dec 2009. Cert. 12A.

A Boy Called Dad ★★½

Kyle Ward plays a 14-year-old who lives on Merseyside and becomes a father. However, the key relationship in the film is that between

This time it's personal: Andy Tennant (centre) discusses sexual politics with Gerard Butler and Jennifer Aniston on the set of his *The Bounty Hunter*.

the boy and his own dad (Ian Hart), who ran out on the family but retains strong paternal feelings even so. Both players are first class, but they can't prevent the film from capsizing due to the plot developing in ways that are totally unbelievable. MS

▶ Ian Hart, Kyle Ward, Charlene McKenna, Sacha Parkinson, Louise Delamere, Steve Evets, Chrissy Rock.
▶ *Dir* Brian Percival, *Pro* Michael Knowles and Stacey Murray, *Screenplay* Julie Rutterford, *Ph* David Katznelson, *Pro Des* John Ellis, *Ed* Kristina Hetherington, *M* Srdjan Kurpjel and Marios Takoushis, *Cos* Lynne Walsh.

EM Media/Northwest Vision/Made Up North etc-Kaleidoscope Home Entertainment.
80 mins. UK. 2009. Rel: 30 April 2010. Cert. 15.

The Boys Are Back ★★

Although its origin lies in a real-life memoir about a father's relationship with his two sons following his second wife's death, this film comes across as a highly fictionalised work. The main setting is Southern Australia and the cast, which is headed by Clive Owen, try hard, but the film is determined to milk the emotions of the audience. It's all so rigged and manipulative that it descends into sheer nonsense. MS

▶ Clive Owen, Emma Booth, Laura Fraser, George MacKay, Nicholas McAnulty, Julia Blake, Chris Haywood.

Poetry in motion: Abbie Cornish and Ben Whishaw in Jane Campion's *Bright Star*.

▶ *Dir* Scott Hicks, *Pro* Greg Brenman and Tim White, *Screenplay* Allan Cubitt, from Simon Carr's memoir, *Ph* Grieg Fraser, *Pro Des* Melinda Doring, *Ed* Scott Gray, *M* Hal Lindes, *Cos* Emily Seresin.

Miramax Films/BBC Films/Screen Australia/Tiger Aspect etc-Buena Vista.
104 mins. Australia/UK/USA/New Zealand. 2009. Rel: 22 Jan 2010. Cert. 12A.

Breathless ★★★

Yang Ik-joon is not only a strong acting presence but also a confident young director. His impressive debut is extremely violent and purposely provocative but grows on you slowly like a drug. He plays Sang-hoon, an emotionally damaged young man who works as a hired thug for his friend's debt collecting firm. His unpredictable explosions of violence and rage are due to his brutal upbringing, but Sang-hoon finds his match when he meets the equally troubled schoolgirl (Kot-bi Kim), who is as fearless as he is. (Original title: *Ddongpari*) GS

▶ Yang Ik-joon, Kot-bi Kim, Man-shik Jeong, Seung-il Hong, Lee Hwan.
▶ *Dir, Pro* and *Screenplay* Yang Ik-joon, *Ph* Yun Jong-ho, *Art Dir* Hon Zi, *Ed* Yang Ik-joon, Jeong and Jung Lee, *M* The Invisible Fish, *Cos* Zib, Jang Sun-jin and Son Seung-hyun.

Mole Film/CJ/CGV Independent Promotions etc-Terracotta Media.
130 mins. South Korea. 2009. Rel: 29 Jan 2010. Cert. 18

Bright Star ★★★★

Jane Campion's film on the last years of poet John Keats is a creditable piece of work. While never aiming too high in the excitement stakes it is nonetheless an artfully made film. Drawn to Fanny Brawne, daughter of a fashionable Hampstead family, perhaps because of her outgoing personality, the poet finally recovers from the death of his brother Tom and becomes fascinated by Miss Brawne. Abbie Cornish is delightful as Fanny, as is Kerry Fox as her mother. Ben Whishaw adds another inspired performance as Keats to his roster of eccentric film roles. MHD

▶ Ben Whishaw, Abbie Cornish, Kerry Fox, Paul Schneider, Edie Martin, Samuel Barnett.
▶ *Dir* and *Screenplay* Jane Campion, *Pro* Jan Chapman, Caroline Hewitt and Mark L Rosen, *Ph* Greig Fraser, *Pro Des* and *Cos* Janet Patterson, *Ed* Alexandre de Franceschi, *M* Mark Bradshaw.

Pathé/Screen Australia/BBC Films/UK Film Council/ New South Wales Film & Television Office/Hopscotch International/Jan Chapman Pictures-Warner Bros.
119 mins. UK/Australia/France. 2009. Rel: 6 Nov 2009. Cert. PG.

brilliantlove ★★★

Ashley Horner's second feature is uneven but decidedly interesting. He gets superb performances from his young leads, Liam Browne and Nancy Trotter Landry. They play a couple whose sexual relationship is depicted almost as explicitly as that in Michael Winterbottom's *9 Songs* (2004). The tale of their passion begins compellingly but the plot development fails to ring true and consequently the film implodes. Unless you object to strong sex on screen it deserves a look all the same. MS

▶ Liam Browne, Nancy Trotter Landry, Michael Hodgson, Stephen Bent.
▶ *Dir* Ashley Horner, *Pro* Horner and Karl Liegis, *Screenplay* Sean Conway, *Ph* Simon Tindall, *Pro Des* Julie Ann Horan and Emma Crossley, *Ed* Ben Wilson, *M* Sol Seppy, *Cos* Mel O'Connor.

Northern Film & Media/Pinball Film-Soda Pictures. 97 mins. UK. 2010. Rel: 12 Nov 2010. No Cert.

Broken Embraces ★★★

Almodóvar's latest is both a love story and a drama set in the film industry showing a director fighting to bring his film to the screen in its proper form. Technically this is as adroit as one would expect, but the film packs in too much and fails to move us due to the miscasting of Lluís Homar as a romantic hero. Penélope Cruz is there to play out the ill-fated romance, but Blanca Portillo's role as a former lover capable of betrayal is far more interesting. (Original title: *Los abrazos rotos*) MS

▶ Penélope Cruz, Lluís Homar, Blanca Portillo, José Luis Gomez, Rubén Ochandiano.
▶ *Dir* and *Screenplay* Pedro Almodóvar, *Pro* Agustin Almodóvar and Esther García, *Ph* Rodrigo Prieto, *Art Dir* Antxón Gómez, *Ed* José Salcedo, *M* Alberto Iglesias, *Cos* Sonia Grande.

El Deseo/an Almodóvar film/Universal Pictures International etc-Pathé Distribution. 128 mins. Spain/UK. 2009. Rel: 28 Aug 2009. Cert. 15.

Brooklyn's Finest ★★★★

Three types of cop pick their way through the battlefield of everyday life in New York's Brooklyn Projects. The complex characterisation of these men – Richard Gere's disillusioned vet, Don Cheadle's morally compromised undercover cop and Ethan Hawke's highly strung family man – provides the film with a fascinating fibre, well realised by credible actors at the top of their form. In the hands of director Fuqua (*Training Day*), the suspense is a given and the tragic outcome inevitable, while the journey there is a sweaty, authentic ride. JC-W

▶ Richard Gere, Don Cheadle, Ethan Hawke, Wesley Snipes, Vincent D'Onofrio, Ellen Barkin.
▶ *Dir* Antoine Fuqua, *Pro* Elie Cohn, John Thompson, John Langley, Avi Lerner and Basil Iwanyk, *Screenplay* Michael C Martin, *Ph* Patrick

Roman-à-clef: Penélope Cruz in Pedro Almodóvar's Hitchcockian *Broken Embraces.*

The war at home: Toby Maguire as Sam and Natalie Portman, as Grace, in Jim Sheridan's complex, devastating *Brothers*.

Murguia, *Pro Des* Thérèse DePrez, *Ed* Barbara Tulliver, *M* Marcelo Zarvov, *Cos* Juliet Polcsa.

Millennium Films/Nu Image/Langley Films Inc./Fuqua Films/Thunder Road Film Productions/Brooklyn's Finest Productions-Momentum Pictures.
132 mins. USA. 2009. Rel: 11 June 2010. Cert. 18.

Brothers ★★★

Those unfamiliar with the original, a Danish film released here in 2005, will have the advantage of not knowing about the plot twists in this story of two brothers, one of whom is captured while serving in Afghanistan and presumed dead. Intercutting between that country and America, where the other brother is attracted to the supposed widow, detracts from the flow, and the finale here seems melodramatic. Look out, though, for fine supporting performances from Mare Winningham and Carey Mulligan, the latter proving already that *An Education* was no flash in the pan. MS

▶ Tobey Maguire, Jake Gyllenhaal, Natalie Portman, Sam Shepard, Carey Mulligan, Mare Winningham.
▶ *Dir* Jim Sheridan, *Pro* Ryan Kavanaugh, Sigurjón Sighvatsson and Michael De Luca, *Screenplay* David Benioff, based on the film *Brødre* by Suzanne Bier and Anders Thomas Jensen, *Ph* Frederick Elmes, *Pro Des* Troy Fanning, *Ed* Jay Cassidy, *M* Thomas Newman, *Cos* Durinda Wood.

Lionsgate/Relativity Media LLC/Sighvatsson Films etc-Lionsgate UK.
104 mins. USA. 2009. Rel: 22 Jan 2010. Cert. 15.

The Brothers Bloom ★★

Made in 2007, this film by Rian Johnson should have been left buried. It's a tale of con-men brothers (Adrien Brody and Mark Ruffalo) and of the eccentric millionairess (Rachel Weisz) who is their target. A work that is centred on the tricks of con-men (even one attempting a marked degree of humour) needs to have just enough conviction to encourage the audience to suspend disbelief. That's impossible here and, despite Weisz's gallant efforts to inject feeling into the romantic sub-plot, the film sinks leaving no survivors. MS

▶ Rachel Weisz, Adrien Brody, Mark Ruffalo, Rinko Kikuchi, Maximilian Schell, Robbie Coltrane, Max Records.
▶ *Dir* and *Screenplay* Rian Johnson, *Pro* Ram Bergman and James D Stern, *Ph* Steve Yedlin, *Pro Des* Jim Clay, *Ed* Gabriel Wrye, *M* Nathan Johnson, *Cos* Beatrix Aruna Pasztor.

Summit Entertainment/Ram Bergman etc-Optimum Releasing.
114 mins. USA. 2008. Rel: 4 June 2010. Cert. 12A.

Brüno ★★★½

After *Ali G* and *Borat* could Sasha Baron Cohen be anyone more outrageous? Brüno, a gay Austrian fashionista, outrages his TV audience and gets the chop. He heads for the US with friend Lutz, but to no avail. Returning, he picks up an African baby to swap for a U2 i-pod then, after a night of sex with Lutz, Brüno decides to go straight with

Catwalk hero: Sacha Baron Cohen in his most outrageous comedy yet, the crass, gobsmacking and offensive *Brüno*.

the aid of Christian gay converters. Later on he does cage fighting with Lutz but they alienate their audience by making love, and once again Cohen has delighted/horrified us with his warped view of the world. MHD

▶ Sacha Baron Cohen, Gustaf Hammarsten, Clifford Banagale, Josh Meyers, Sting, Bono, Chris Martin, Elton John, Snoop Dog.
▶ *Dir* Larry Charles, *Pro* Sacha Baron Cohen, Dan Mazer, Monica Levinson, Jay Rach, *Screenplay* Cohen and Anthony Hines, *Ph* Anthony Hardwick and Wolfgang Held, *Pro Des* Dan Butts, Denise Hudson, David Saenz e Maturana, *Ed* Scott M Davids, Eric Kissack and James Thomas, *M* Erran Baron Cohen, *Cos* Jason Alper.

Universal Pictures/Media Rights Capital/Four by Two/ Everyman Pictures-Universal Pictures International. 81 mins. USA. 2009. Rel: 10 July 2009. Cert. 18.

Budrus ★★★★

Julia Bacha's powerful documentary tells the inspirational story of the Budrus villagers in the West Bank as they make an unarmed and peaceful stand against the Israeli army in an attempt to save their land. The Israeli bulldozers are ready to uproot thousands of olive trees in this Palestinian territory in order to build a wall running through the cemetery right next to their school, but the villagers, especially the young women, are not giving up the battle. It is a deeply moving and stirring film that needs to be seen. GS

▶ *Dir* and *Screenplay* Julia Bacha, *Pro* Bacha, Ronit Avri and Rula Salamen, *Ph* Bacha and Mohammed Fawzi, *Ed* Bacha and Geeta Gandbhir, *M* Kareem Roustom.
Just Vision Films-Dogwoof Pictures.

78 mins. Israel/Occupied Palestinian Territory/USA. 2009. Rel: 24 Sep 2010. Cert. PG.

Bunny and the Bull ★★★★

The eccentric and agoraphobic Steven Turnbull (Edward Hogg) eats the same food and watches the same television programmes every day until he is forced to change his habits when his flat is overtaken by mice. He then begins to reflect on his past at the time when he was travelling around Europe with his best friend Bunny (Simon Farnaby), an irresponsible womaniser who leads Steven into many disastrous adventures... The film is fresh, original and beautifully designed. Writer/ director Paul King is definitely a talent to watch. GS

▶ Edward Hogg, Simon Farnaby, Veronica Echegui, Noel Fielding, Waleed Khalid.

Man on wire: A scene from Julia Bacha's deeply moving and stirring *Budrus*.

> *Dir* and *Screenplay* Paul King, *Pro* Mary Burice, Mark Herbert and Robin Gutch, *Ph* John Sorapure, *Pro Des* Gary Williamson, *Ed* Mark Everson, *M* Ralfe Band, *Cos* Sam Perry.

Screen Yorkshire/Warp X-Optimum Releasing. 101 mins. UK. 2009. Rel: 27 Nov 2009. Cert. 15.

Buried ★★★½

Here's an oddity. There's only one man on screen (the accomplished Ryan Reynolds) and he regains consciousness at the start to find that he is buried alive. He's somewhere in Iraq and at least he has a cell-phone to call for help. The Catch-22 is that if you suffer from claustrophobia you will hate this film, and if you don't the single enclosed setting may feel like a limitation. However, *Buried* is very well made and the ending is highly persuasive. MS

> Ryan Reynolds, José Luis García Pérez, Rob Patterson, Samantha Mathis.
> *Dir* and *Ed* Rodrigo Cortés, *Pro* Adrián Guerra and Peter Safran, *Screenplay* Chris Sparling, *Ph* Eduard Grau, *Art Dir* Maria de la Cámara and Gabriel Paré, *M* Victor Reyes, *Cos* Elisa de Andrés.

Working as a waitress in a cocktail bar: Christina Aguilera in Steven Antin's likeable and energetic *Burlesque*.

Versus Entertainment/The Safran Company/Dark Trick Films etc-Icon Film Distribution.
95 mins. Spain/USA. 2009. Rel: 29 Sep 2010. Cert. 15.

Burke & Hare ★½

A grisly saga of 1820s Edinburgh, the director of *An American Werewolf in London*, and a host of Britain's top-class comedy talent… Promising ingredients, you might think. Unfortunately, the result is a witless stodge in which two of history's most despicable serial killers are presented as jolly Jack-the-lads. There's some stunt casting (Michael Winner, Christopher Lee), though only Ronnie Corbett emerges with any credit. (He's also one of the few genuine Scots in the cast.) After this and their dismal *Dorian Gray* reboot, the revived Ealing would be well advised to leave such subjects to the revived Hammer. JR

> Simon Pegg, Andy Serkis, Isla Fisher, Jessica Hynes, Tom Wilkinson, Bill Bailey, Tim Curry, Christopher Lee, Ronnie Corbett, Reece Shearsmith, Jenny Agutter.
> *Dir* John Landis, *Pro* Barnaby Thompson, *Screenplay* Piers Ashworth and Nick Moorcroft, *Ph* John Mathieson, *Pro Des* Simon Elliot, *Ed* Mark Everson, *M* Joby Talbot, *Cos* Deborah Nadolman.

Ealing Studios/Aegis Film Fund/Fragile Films/Prescience-Entertainment Film Distributors. 91 mins. UK. 2010. Rel: 29 Oct 2010. Cert. 15.

Burlesque ★★★

Small-town girl Ali (Christina Aguilera) arrives in Los Angeles hoping to hit the big time as a singer but ends up working as a cocktail waitress at the Burlesque Lounge instead. However, she gets her chance to impress the club's proprietor Tess (Cher) when one of the artists becomes pregnant… This likeable and energetic show takes you on a phantasmagorical journey using every cliché in the book, with strong reference to both *Chicago* and *Cabaret* but with unmemorable songs. GS

> Cher, Christina Aguilera, Alan Cumming, Peter Gallagher, Kristen Bell, Stanley Tucci.
> *Dir* and *Screenplay* Steven Antin, *Pro* Donald De Line, *Ph* Bojan Bazelli, *Pro Des* Jon Gary Steele, *Ed* Virginia Katz, *M* Christophe Beck, *Cos* Michael Kaplan.

De Line Pictures-Sony Pictures Releasing. 119 mins. USA. 2010. Rel: 17 Dec 2010. Cert. 12A.

Burlesque Undressed ★★½

In this naughty but fun documentary the myth behind the burlesque phenomenon is unveiled. Modern diva of the genre, Immodesty Blaize, narrates the story aided by a series of interviews with legendary performers from the past. Blaize is an intelligent and highly watchable performer but is also the producer – so inevitably her rather unbalanced film gives more time to her own overextended stage act than it does to those of her veteran colleagues. GS

▷ Marc Almond, Satan's Angel, Kalani Kokonuts, Immodesty Blaize, April March, Catherine D'Lish, Teri Geary (Kitten De Ville).
▷ *Dir* and *Written by* Alison Grist, *Executive Pro* Anthony Caulfield and Nicola Woodroff, *Ph* Barrie Dodd, *Ed* Steve Paton.

Nightfall Films-More2 Screen.
88 mins. UK. 2010. Rel: 22 Jan 2010. Cert. 15.

Burma VJ Reporting from a Closed Country ★★★★½

In this film Danish film-maker Anders Østergaard sets out to show the hidden truth about conditions in Burma through images taken secretly by video journalists including one VJ, here called 'Joshua', who acts as narrator. There are reconstructions too, but everywhere a sense of authenticity reigns. The fate of those like Aung San Suu Kyi and others campaigning for democracy is presented at slightly too great a length for maximum effect, but even so the film is intensely powerful and a document of historical importance. Seek it out. MS

▷ With Joshua, Ko Maung, Tun Zaw. Aung Win.
▷ *Dir* Anders Østergaard, *Pro* Lise Lense-Møller, *Screenplay* Østergaard and Jan Krogsgaard, *Ph* Simon Plum and others, *Ed* Janus Billeskov Jansen and Thomas Papapetros , *M* Conny C-A Malmqvist.

Magic Hour Films/WG Film/Mediamente- Dogwoof Pictures.
89 mins. Denmark/Sweden/Italy/UK/Germany/ Netherlands/Norway/Israel/Spain/Belgium. 2008. Rel: 17 July 2009. Cert. 12A.

Bustin' Down the Door ★★★★

Despite the recent rush of surfing films, Jeremy Gosch's celebration of the Australian and South African surfers is a winner. His illuminating documentary focuses on the Hawaiian winter of 1975 when a group of young surfers risked almost everything to become the best in the world. It is narrated by Edward Norton and features interviews with such greats as Kelly Slater and Rob Machado plus some amazing surfing sequences. GS

▷ Wayne Bartholomew, Edward Norton, Mark Richards, Kelly Slater, Tom Curren, Ian Cairns.
▷ *Dir* Jeremy Gosch, *Pro* Monika Gosch, Shaun Tomson and Robert Traill, *Screenplay* Jeremy and Monika Gosch, *Ph* Gary Rohan, *Ed* Danny Bresnik, *M* Stuart Michael Thomas.

Fresh and Smoked-Screen Media Films.
96 mins. USA. 2008. Rel: 4 Sep 2009. Cert. 15.

The Calling ★

Joanna (Emily Beecham) is a spoilt rich young woman who believes she has a calling to become a nun despite objections from her best friend, mother and boyfriend. When she finally gets to the convent she is taken under the wing of the politically active Novice Sister Ignatious (Brenda Blethyn). The script is implausible and the acting is mostly wrongly pitched in Jan Dunn's below-average drama. Sadly, the psychotic Mother Superior was the last film role of the great Susannah York. A waste of talent. GS

▷ Brenda Blethyn, Amanda Donohoe, Emily Beecham, Chloe Sirene, Susannah York, Rita Tushingham, Pauline McLynn, Corin Redgrave.
▷ *Dir* Jan Dunn, *Pro* Elaine Wickham, *Screenplay* Jan Dunn, *Ph* Ole Bratt Birkeland, *Pro Des* Stevie Stewart, *Ed* Emma Collins, *M* Janette Mason, *Cos Supervisor* Rae Donnelly.

MEDB Films/Kent County Council/Maidstone Studios/ Courtyard Studios/Screen South-Guerilla Films.
109 mins. UK. 2009. Rel: 23 Apr 2010. Cert. 15.

Cameraman: The Life and Work of Jack Cardiff ★★★★★

Craig McCall's brilliant tribute to British cinematographer and director Jack Cardiff took 17 years to make and was only released after Cardiff's death, aged 94, in 2009. His work for Powell and Pressburger on *A Matter of Life and Death*, *Black Narcisssus* and *The Red Shoes* produced some of British cinema's finest work. Cardiff was admired by actors, directors and cinematographers alike, many of whom (Martin Scorsese, Lauren Bacall, Charlton Heston, John Mills, Freddie Francis, Alan Parker, Christopher Challis et al) pay tribute here. This is an exemplary film biography illustrated by pristine clips of some of Cardiff's astonishing work. MHD

▷ Jack Cardiff (archive footage), Martin Scorsese, Kirk Douglas, Lauren Bacall, Thelma Schoonmaker, Christopher Challis, Kim Hunter, Alan Parker, Peter Yates etc.
▷ *Dir* and *Pro* Craig McCall, *Ph* Steven Chivers, Ricardo Coll, Simon Fanthorpe, Nicholas Hoffman, Jonathan Rho, Ian Salvage, John Walker, James Welland and Bob Williams, *Pro Des* Miles Glyn, *Ed* Dan Roberts, *M* Mark Sayer-Wade.

Modus Operandi Films-Optimum Releasing.
90 mins. UK. 2010. Rel: 7 May 2010. No Cert.

Capitalism: A Love Story ★★★

If documentaries have now taken on a new lease of life in cinemas it's largely down to Michael Moore, but his quirkily humorous approach, once so delightful, has now come to define a too-familiar persona as on-screen personality

Big shot: Édgar Ramírez as Ilich Ramírez Sánchez aka *Carlos* in Olivier Assayas' film of the same name.

and voice-over. Self-indulgence has set in too, as evidenced by this film lasting 127 minutes. It's a shame because, alongside contrived moments in this vein, are criticisms of various features of a capitalist society well deserving of exposure. MS

▶ With Michael Moore.
▶ *Dir* and *Screenplay* Michael Moore, *Pro* Anne and Michael Moore, *Ph* Daniel Marracino and Jayme Roy, *Ed* John Walter, Conor O'Neill and Pablo Proenza, *M* Jeff Gibbs.

Paramount Vantage/Overture Films/The Weinstein Company/Dog Eat Dog Films-Paramount Pictures UK. 127 mins. Canada/USA. 26 Feb 2010. Rel: 2009. Cert. 12A.

Carlos ★★★★

This huge and impressive biopic about Carlos the Jackal was made for television, but it's good that the longer version which I saw has gained a cinema release in addition to the shorter one (334 minutes as opposed to 165). It's not the stuff of which a masterpiece is made but it is intelligent, varied and well made, and it boasts a first-class performance from Edgar Ramirez. Anybody ready to commit to such a long work is unlikely to feel let down by what director and co-writer Olivier Assayas has achieved. MS

▶ Edgar Ramirez, Alexander Scheer, Nora Von Waldstätten, Sarajeanne Drillaud.
▶ *Dir* Olivier Assayas, *Pro* Daniel Leconte, *Screenplay* Assayas and Don Franck, from Leconte's idea, *Ph* Yorick Le Saux and Denis Lenoir, *Art Dir* François-Renaud Labarthe, *Ed* Luc Barnier and Marion Monnier, *Cos* Jürgen Doering and others.

Canal+/ARTE France/Egoli Tossell Film/Film en

Stock etc-Optimum Releasing. 334 mins or 165 mins. France/Germany/Belgium. 2010. Rel: 22 Oct 2010. Cert. 15.

Carriers ★★★½

Four seemingly carefree friends are driving across the south-western US hoping to reach a secluded beach in the Gulf of Mexico. At first it seems they are on holiday but we soon realise that they are running away from a deadly virus that is spreading fast all over America... The Pastor Brothers make an impressive debut with this engaging thriller. Their script could have afforded to be a bit sharper but they show enough flair and style to make the recent overexposed virus genre look fresh and original. GS

▶ Lou Taylor Pucci, Chris Pine, Piper Perabo, Emily VanCamp, Christopher Meloni.
▶ *Dir* and *Screenplay* Alex Pastor and David Pastor, *Pro* Ray Angelic, Anthony Bregman and Robert Veló, *Ph* Benoit Debie, *Pro Des* Clark Hunter, *Ed* Craig McKay, *M* Peter Nashel, *Cos* Jill Newell.

Paramount Vantage/Likely Story/This Is That Productions/Ivy Boy Productions-Paramount Vantage Distributors. 84 mins. USA. 2009. Rel: 11 Dec 2009. Cert. 15.

Case 39 ★½

A 'family services specialist', Emily Jenkins (Renée Zellweger), suspects that little Lillith Sullivan is the victim of child abuse. However, she cannot convince her boss that this is the case, so decides to get down and personal with the girl's strange and threatening parents. Had this been a thriller

about child abuse, it might have been very, very scary. As it is, the film's change of tack to full-out psychological horror loses its effect due to just too many implausibilities, not to mention a surplus of sudden knocks and loud bangs. JC-W

▶ Renée Zellweger, Jodelle Ferland, Ian McShane, Kerry O'Malley, Callum Keith Rennie, Bradley Cooper, Adrian Lester.
▶ *Dir* Christian Alvart, *Pro* Kevin Misher, *Screenplay* Ray Wright, *Ph* Hagen Bogdanski, *Pro Des* John Willett, *Ed* Mark Goldblatt, *M* Michl Britsch, *Cos* Monique Prudhomme.

Paramount Pictures/Mischer Films/Anonymous Content-Paramount Pictures.
109 mins. USA/Canada. 2009. Rel: 5 Mar 2010. Cert. 15.

Catfish ★★★½

This is a teaser of a film. It's presented as a documentary about the dangers of accepting internet communications at face value. But what about the film's own face value? Just how authentic it is has been the subject of much debate and what happens in it does carry echoes of *The Night Listener* (2006). Whatever the truth, *Catfish* does succeed in making viewers ask questions about the internet, even if we also query some aspects of the movie. MS

▶ With Yaniv 'Nev' Schulman, Angela Wesselman-Pierce, Ariel Schulman, Henry Joost.
▶ *Dir* Ariel Schulman and Henry Joost, *Pro* Andrew Jarecki, Marc Smerling, Joost and Schulman, *Ph* Joost, Ariel Schulman and Yaniv Schulman, *Ed* Zac Stuart-Pontier, *Animation* Andrew Zuchero.

Supermarché/Hit the Ground Running-Momentum Pictures.
87 mins. USA. 2010. Rel: 17 Dec 2010. Cert. 12A.

Cats and Dogs: The Revenge of Kitty Galore ★

This inept sequel to 2001's likeable kiddie effects actioner *Cats and Dogs* isn't saved by numerous James Bond jokes. Rogue M.E.O.W.S. agent Galore poses such a threat that the talking cats and dogs actually join forces here to defeat her. That's as bad an idea as it sounds and the film goes downhill from there. 3D in selected cinemas. JC

▶ Voices of Bette Midler, Christina Applegate, Jack McBrayer, Nick Nolte, Neil Patrick Harris, Wallace Shawn, Roger Moore, with Chris McDonnell.
▶ *Dir* Brad Peyton, *Pro* Andrew Lazar, *Screenplay* Ron J Friedman and Steve Bencich based on characters by John Requa and Glenn Ficarra, *Ph* Steven Poster, *Pro Des* Rusty Smith, *Ed* Julie Rogers, *M* Christopher Lennertz, *Cos* Tish Monaghan.

CD2 Films/Mad Chance/Polymorphic Pictures/Village Road Show Pictures-Warner Bros.
82 mins. USA. 2010. Rel: 4 Aug 2010. Cert. U.

Cemetery Junction ★★★★

Considering its multiple thematic strands, Merchant-Gervais' first feature film snaps neatly together. At times mercilessly uncomfortable in its examination of early 1970s middle-England, and at others sweet and conventional, *Cemetery Junction* delivers on its name – a picture of cosy working-class values as a moral morgue every bit as awful as David Brent's present-day Slough. And Anne Reid channelling Dandy Nichols' Else Garnett is something else. Sweet, acidic and actually rather moving. JC-W

▶ Christian Cooke, Tom Hughes, Jack Doolan, Felicity

Head case: Renée Zellweger in Christian Alvart's laughable *Case 39.*

Jones, Anne Reid, Ralph Fiennes, Emily Watson, Matthew Goode, Ricky Gervais, Stephen Merchant.
‣ *Dir* and *Screenplay* Ricky Gervais and Stephen Merchant, *Pro* Sue Baden-Powell, Charlie Hanson, Gervais and Merchant, *Ph* Remi Adefarasin, *Pro Des* Anna Higginson, *Ed* Valerio Bonelli, *M* Tim Atack, *Cos* Ruth Myers.

Sony International Motion Picture Production Group-Sony Pictures Releasing.
95 mins. UK. 2010. Rel: 14 Apr 2010. Cert. 15.

Centurion ★★

Michael Fassbender, Dominic West and a bunch of Roman Centurions are in the good old UK of 117AD, where life is nasty, brutish and short. Can they survive the Picts and get back to life under the Tuscan sun? Director Neil Marshall brings his horror movie sensibilities to bear on what could have been a jolly, exciting saga, betraying entertainment value for a kind of battle hyper-realism of non-stop slashings, choppings, hackings, gougings, stabbings etc. This sadistic stuff is vile and the film's entertainment value is further reduced by spatterings of present-day four-letter words. Fassbender is rather good and so is Imogen Poots as healing outsider Arian. DW

‣ Michael Fassbender, Dominic West, Olga Kurylenko, Imogen Poots, Noel Clarke, David Morrissey, J J Field, Axelle Carolyn, Rachael Stirling.
‣ *Dir* and *Screenplay* Neil Marshall, *Pro* Christian Colson and Robert Jones, *Ph* Sam McCurdy, *Pro Des* Simon Bowles, *Ed* Chris Gill, *M* Ilan Eshkeri, *Cos* Keith Madden.

Celador Films-Pathé.
97 mins. UK. 2010. Rel: 23 Apr 2010. Cert. 15.

Certified Copy ★★★★

Any suggestion that Abbas Kiarostami is here making a more commercial movie is emphatically misguided despite the fact that it stars Juliette Binoche. A man and a woman meet in Tuscany (not in Marienbad) and, as we observe their day together, we ponder whether they are strangers or a formerly married couple. The man, convincingly incarnated by the singer William Shimell, is an author and lecturer and issues about values in art (what about copies?) are debated. Essentially it's a film for those who like to discuss afterwards the meaning and significance of what they have just seen. (Original title: *Copie conforme*) MS

‣ Juliette Binoche, William Shimell, Jean-Claude Carrière, Gianna Giachetti.
‣ *Dir* Abbas Kiarostami, *Pro* Marin Karmitz, Nathanaël Karmitz, Charles Gilbert and Angelo Barbagallo, *Screenplay* Kiarostami with Caroline Eliacheff and Massoumeh Lahidji, *Ph* Luca Bigazzi, *Art Dir* Giancarlo Basili and Ludovica Ferrario, *Ed* Bahman Kiarostami, *Cos Supervisor* Sandra Berrebi.

MK2/BiBi Film/France 3 Cinéma etc-Artificial Eye.
107 mins. France/Italy/Belgium. 2009. Rel: 3 Sep 2010. Cert. 12A.

Charles Dickens's England ★

Julian Richards' dull and unintentionally funny documentary is a laborious journey around the country which highlights the various locations where Dickens found the inspiration to write his famous stories. Dickens deserves better treatment and Derek Jacobi makes an awkward presenter,

Enigma variation: Juliette Binoche in Abbas Kiarostami's provocative and puzzling *Certified Copy*.

Lost weekend:
Rupert Grint,
Kimberley Nixon
and Robert
Sheehan in Lisa
Barros D'Sa and
Glenn Leyburn's
Cherrybomb.

with his smug delivery, endless posing, overacting and over-enthusiasm. Instead of celebrating his subject's work, this has the opposite effect. From the evidence of this you would never know that he was an acclaimed actor. GS

▶ Lee Ault, Thelma Grove, Roy Hattersley, Derek Jacobi, Tony Pointon, Adrian Wootton.
▶ *Dir* Julian Richards, *Pro* David Wilkinson, *Screenplay* Charles Dickens, Emily Price and David Wilkinson, *Ph* Alan M Trow, *Ed* Simon Cox, *M* Chris Smith, *Cos* Amy Roberts.

Boz Films/Sky Arts-Guerilla Flms
120 mins. UK. 2009. Rel: 24 July 2009. Cert. U.

Chatroom ★★½

While *The Social Network* and *Catfish* [both qv] vie for being the best film about the internet, this effort (British-made despite being helmed by Japan's Hideo Nakata) falls way behind. Here, by utilising chatrooms set up on the internet, a troubled man seeks to mislead and dominate others, but the unconvincing dialogue and an uneasy attempt at stylisation sink the project. All that Nakata can do is to give the film a certain visual flourish. MS

▶ Aaron Johnson, Imogen Poots, Matthew Beard, Hannah Murray, Daniel Kaluuya.
▶ *Dir* Hideo Nakata, *Pro* Laura Hastings-Smith, Alison Owen and Paul Trijbits, *Screenplay* Enda

Walsh, from his play, *Ph* Benoît Delhomme, *Pro Des* Jon Henson, *Ed* Masahiro Hirakubo, *M* Kenji Kawai, *Cos* Julian Day.

Film 4/UK Film Council/West End Films etc-Revolver
Entertainment.
97 mins. UK. 2010. Rel: 22 Dec 2010. Cert. 15.

Cherrybomb ★★★★

Two teenage mates in Northern Ireland become rivals for a girl who encourages their competitiveness. That doesn't sound like the greatest of stories but, even so, Daragh Carville's screenplay is admirably detailed and persuasive while the two debutant directors do well. However, it is the exceptional performances that make this film memorable: Kimberley Nixon as the provocative yet unsure Michelle, Robert Sheehan as the cocky, worldly-wise Luke and Rupert Grint as the more sympathetic Malachy, staking a claim to an impressive post-Harry Potter future. MS

▶ Rupert Grint, Kimberley Nixon, Robert Sheehan, James Nesbitt, Lalor Roddy.
▶ *Dir* Lisa Barros D'Sa and Glenn Leyburn, *Pro* Mark Huffam, Michael Casey, Brian Kirk and Simon Bosanquet, *Screenplay* Daragh Carville, *Ph* Damien Elliott, *Pro Des* David Craig, *Ed* Nick Emerson, *M* David Holmes and Stephen Hilton, *Cos* Hazel Webb-Crozier.

Generator Entertainment/Green Park Films etc-Blue
Dolphin Film & Video.
86 mins. UK/Ireland, 2008. Rel: 23 Apr 2010. Cert. 15.

Ghetto blaster: Denis Moschitto in Özgür Yildirim's *Chiko.*

Cherry Tree Lane ★★★½

The third feature from Paul Andrew Williams of *London to Brighton* is not, as has been suggested, some kind of semi-horror film but a work of social comment. That's so despite it being about a well-off couple threatened by strangers who invade their house and count as the have-nots. Stereotyping is avoided and there's food for thought here, although the film is not without unconvincing moments. MS

▶ Rachael Blake, Tom Butcher, Jumayn Hunter, Ashley Chin, Sonny Muslim, Tom Kane.
▶ *Dir* and *Screenplay* Paul Andrew Williams, *Pro* Ken Marshall, *Ph* Carlos Catalan, *Pro Des* Alison Butler, *Ed* Tom Hemmings, *M* UNKLE, *Cos* Marianne Agertoft.
UK Film Council/MoliFilms/Steel Mill Pictures etc-Metrodome Distribution.
77 mins. UK. 2010. Rel: 3 Sep 2010. Cert. 18.

Chevolution ★★★½

This documentary can be regarded as a footnote to Steven Soderbergh's films about Che Guevara since it is an investigation of the most famous picture of Che, the one taken in 1960 by the photographer known as 'Korda'. Its subsequent history, both as a symbol for the oppressed and as merchandise (the latter meaning that capitalism turned it into a source of profit), is well presented but not without a certain amount of repetition. MS

▶ With Michael Casey, Diana Diaz, José A Figueroa, Antonio Banderas, Gael García Bernal. Narration by Miguel Najera.
▶ *Dir* Trisha Ziff and Luis Lopez, *Pro* Ziff, *Writers* Sylvia Stevens, Ziff, etc *Ph* Jan Pester, *Ed* Lopez, *M* Joseph Julian Gonzalez.
Red Envelope Entertainment/212Berlin Film/Facton Films etc-ICA Films
85 mins. USA/Mexico/UK. 2008. Rel: 18 Sep 2009. No Cert.

Chico & Rita ★★★★

Chico is a pianist and Rita a singer and theirs is a love story set mainly in Havana and New York. More than mere background is the music of the 1940s and 50s, which pays homage to such jazz giants as Charlie Parker and Dizzy Gillespie. The surprise, though, is that this is an animated feature for adults, a labour of love devoid of computer effects. The result is an engaging and genuinely romantic tale told in a way that's truly groundbreaking. MS

▶ With the voices of Limara Meneses, Eman Xor Oña, Bebo Valdés, Idania Valdés.
▶ *Dir* Fernando Trueba, Javier Mariscal and Tono Errando, *Pro* Santi Errando, Cristina Huete, Martin Pope and Michael Rose, *Screenplay* Trueba and Ignacio Martínez de Pisón, *Ed* Arnau Quiles, *M* Bebo Valdés, *Animation Dir* Manolo Galiana.
Fernando Trueba P.C./Estudio Marsical/Magic Light Pictures/Cinema NX, Isle of Man Film etc-CinemaNX Distribution.
93 mins. Spain/UK. 2010. Rel: 19 Nov 2010. Cert. 15.

Chiko ★★½

Like Fatih Akin, who produces here but does not direct, Özgür Yildirim is a Turk born in Germany. This first feature is promising technically. However, although he has declared that he was seeking to portray contemporary life in a suburban ghetto of Hamburg with authenticity, his story of youths involved with drug-dealing and prostitution increasingly defies belief. He invites us to compare this with *Scarface* but, if so, it's De Palma's over-the-top remake that comes to mind. MS

▶ Denis Moschitto, Moritz Bleibtreu, Volkan Özcan, Reyhan Sahin, Lilay Huser.
▶ *Dir* and *Screenplay* Özgür Yildirim, *Pro* Fatih Akin, Klaus Macek, Andreas Thiel and Ann-Kristin Demuth, *Ph* Matthias Boliger, *Art Dir* Iris Trescher and Kim Porr, *Ed* Sebastian Thümler, *M* Darko Krezic, *Cos* Lore Tesch.
A Corazón International, NDR co-production/Dorje Film etc-Vertigo Films
92 mins. Germany/Italy. 2007. Rel: 21 Aug 2009. Cert. 18.

Chloe ★★★

It's usually very successful French films that get remade and emerge as Hollywood movies. But here we have the independent film-maker Atom Egoyan choosing to work from a screenplay by Erin Cressida Wilson which is an English language version of Anne Fontaine's unmemorable *Nathalie*. Julianne Moore is on fine form as the wife who hires a prostitute to check out her doubts about her husband's fidelity, but what begins stylishly ends up as more melodramatic than the original. Adding lesbianism to the tale leads nowhere. MS

▶ Julianne Moore, Liam Neeson, Amanda Seyfried, Max Thierot.
▶ *Dir* Atom Egoyan, *Pro* Ivan Reitman, Joe Medjuck and Jeffrey Clifford, *Screenplay* Erin Cressida Wilson, based on the film *Nathalie*, *Ph* Paul Sarossy, *Pro Des* Phillip Barker, *Ed* Susan Shipton, *M* Mychael Danna, *Cos* Debra Hanson.

StudioCanal/Montecio Picture Company etc-Optimum Releasing.
96 mins. France/USA/Canada. 2009. Rel: 5 Mar 2010. Cert. 15.

The Chronicles of Narnia: The Voyage of the Dawn Treader ★★★½

Andrew Adamson gives way to Michael Apted as director and Disney yields to Fox as distributor with this third instalment of the Narnia tales by C S Lewis. Once again the children are transported to Narnia for fresh adventures. This time those adventures are more succinctly presented (good) but less memorable (for example, Tilda Swinton's White Witch makes the briefest of appearances). There are excellent special effects and a sense of affection for the tales is happily preserved. MS

▶ Georgie Henley, Skandar Keynes, Ben Barnes, Will Poulter, Tilda Swinton and the voices of Simon Pegg and Liam Neeson.
▶ *Dir* Michael Apted, *Pro* Mark Johnson, Andrew Adamson and Philip Steuer, *Screenplay* Christopher Markus, Stephen McFeely and Michael Petroni, from the book by C S Lewis, *Ph* Dante Spinotti, *Pro Des* Barry Robison, *Ed* Rick Shaine, *M* David Arnold, *Cos* Isis Mussenden.

Fox 2000 Pictures/Walden Media/Dune Entertainment etc-20th Century Fox.
113 mins. USA/Australia. 2010. Rel: 9 Dec 2010. Cert. PG.

Cirque du Freak: The Vampire's Assistant ★★

The tale of a teen-turned-vampire (Chris Massoglia) who hits the road with a travelling freak show of theatrical blood-suckers, this colourful screen adaptation of the Darren Shan best-sellers is an adequate time-waster for kids, a pre-pre-teen fantasy with a vague *Twilight*-y vibe. It's white bread stuff though, with John C Reilly not particularly well cast as a charismatic blood sucker, and a lifeless supporting cast including Salma Hayek as Reilly's girlfriend, as if that would ever happen. Let's just say the movie lacks bite and leave it there. MJ

▶ John C Reilly, Josh Hutcherson, Chris Massoglia,

Jessica Carlson, Willem Dafoe, Jane Krakowski.
▶ *Dir* Paul Weitz, *Pro* Ewan Leslie and Lauren Shuler Donner, *Screenplay* Weitz and Brian Helgeland, from the books by Darren Shaw, *Ph* J Michael Muro, *Pro Des* William Arnold, *Ed* Leslie Jones, *M* Steven Trask, *Cos* Judianna Makovsky.

Universal Pictures/Relativity Media/Donners' Company/ Depth of Field Productions-Universal Studios
109 mins. USA. 2009. Rel: 23 Oct 2009. Cert. 12A.

City Island ★★★½

This film won an Audience Award at the Tribeca Film Festival and will appeal to those who like dramas which, not without humour, feature a family and offer intertwined plot threads for each of its members. Here they are New Yorkers and the sentimental ending will appeal to American taste. It's pleasant enough but too lightweight to do more than provide an acceptable but forgettable evening's diversion. MS

▶ Andy Garcia, Julianna Margulies, Steven Strait, Alan Arkin, Emily Mortimer, Dominik Garcia-Lorido, Ezra Miller.
▶ *Dir* and *Screenplay* Raymond De Felitta, *Pro* Andy Garcia, De Felitta, Zachary Matz and Lauren Versel, *Ph* Vanja Cernjul, *Pro Des* Franckie Diago, *Ed* David Leonard, *M* Jan A.P. Kaczmarek, *Cos* Tere Duncan.

Anchor Bay Films/CineSon Productions/Medici Entertainment/Lucky Monkey Pictures etc-Anchor Bay Entertainment UK.
104 mins. USA/Poland. 2009. Rel: 23 July 2010. Cert. 12A.

Little and large: Reepicheep befriends a dragon in Michael Apted's *The Chronicles of Narnia: The Voyage of the Dawn Treader.*

City of Life and Death ★★★★

China's Lu Chuan was revealed as a master of screen images in his second feature *Mountain Patrol*. Now comes this very different piece about the slaughter of 300,000 people in Nanking in 1937 after the capital city had fallen to Japanese troops. The film-maker's stance in this anti-war work is evidenced by his making central to it a young Japanese soldier obliged to carry out orders yet viewed sympathetically. Not everything is perfectly judged but the film combines commanding visuals with a depth of feeling that recalls Wajda's *Katyń*. (Original title: *Nanjing! Nanjin!*) MS

▶ Liu Ye, Gao Yuanyuan. Nakaizumi Hideo, Fan Wei, Yao Di, John Paisley, Qin Lan.
▶ *Dir* and *Screenplay* Lu Chuan, *Pro* Han Sanping, Qin Hong, Zhou Li and others, *Ph* Cao Yu, *Pro Des* Hao Yi and Lin Chaoxiang, *M* Liu Tong.
Beijing Film Studio/China Film Group Corporation/ Stellar Mega Films etc-High Fliers Distribution. 135 mins. People's Republic of China/Hong Kong. 2009. Rel: 16 Apr 2010. Cert. 15.

City of War: The Story of John Rabe ★★★½

It's fascinating to compare this able but occasionally fictionally toned film with the Chinese feature on the same subject, *City of Life and Death* [qv]. Both films portray the bloodbath in Nanking for which the Japanese army was responsible in 1937, but here the focus is on the German John Rabe, who heroically stayed to help the citizens. Ulrich Tukur is persuasive but, by placing his character screen centre, the film misses the tragic depths achieved by the rival movie. (Original title: *John Rabe*) MS

▶ Ulrich Tukur, Daniel Brühl, Anne Consigny, Dagmar Manzel, Steve Buscemi.
▶ *Dir* Florian Gallenberger, *Pro* Mischa Hofmann, Jan Mojto and Benjamin Herrmann, *Screenplay*

Gallenberger, from a concept by Orkun Ertener, inspired by *John Rabe. Der gute Deutsche von Nanking* edited by Erwin Wickert, *Ph* Jürgen Jürges, *Pro Des* Tu Juhua and Tu Xin Ran, *Ed* Hansjörg Weißbrich, *M* Laurent Petitgirard and Annette Focks, *Cos* Lisy Christl.
Hofmann & Voges Entertainment/EOS Entertainment/ Majestic Filmproduktion etc-Metrodome Distribution. 134 mins. Germany/France/People's Republic of China/ Spain/Italy. 2009. Rel: 2 Apr 2010. Cert. 15.

Clash of the Titans ★

As much as we love the movies blessed by Ray Harryhausen's stop-motion effects, few would argue that those films had much worth beyond their incredible visuals. What we have here, then, is a Harryhausen adventure minus the Harryhausen, which renders it pointless. A soulless fantasy from director Louis Leterrier, a master of unnecessary arts, this sees a bunch of ancient Greeks battle unconvincing, computer-generated beasties while weak actors struggle even more desperately with a leaden screenplay. Boo to James Cameron's *Avatar* for making a star of Sam Worthington, and shame on Liam Neeson for his Zeus. Unleash the Kraken, indeed. MJ

▶ Sam Worthington, Liam Neeson, Ralph Fiennes, Jason Flemyng, Gemma Arterton, Alexa Davalos, Pete Postlethwaite, Elizabeth McGovern, Danny Huston.
▶ *Dir* Louis Leterrier, *Pro* Basil Iwanyk and Kevin De La Noy, *Screenplay* Travis Beacham, Matt Manfredi and Phil Hay, based on Beverley Cross' 1981 screenplay, *Ph* Peter Menzies Jr, *Pro Des* Martin Laing, *Ed* Vincent Tabaillon, David Freeman and Martin Walsh, *M* Ramin Djawadi, *Cos* Lindy Hemming.
The Zanuck Company/Warner Bros Pictures/Legendary Pictures/Thunder Road Film-Warner Bros. 106 mins. UK/USA. 2010. Rel: 2 Apr 2010. Cert. 12A.

A Closed Book ★★★½

Tom Conti is on top form as an author and critic blinded in a car crash. He's in need of help from an amanuensis in the form of Jane (Darryl Hannah), who proves to have her own agenda. Adapted by Gilbert Adair from his own book, it offers intelligent dialogue but it still plays like a cross between *Sleuth* and *Misery* that is decidedly short of action, even if the denouement shows that it is not short of ideas. MS

▶ Tom Conti, Daryl Hannah, Miriam Margolyes, Elaine Paige, Simon MacCorkindale.
▶ *Dir* Raoul Ruiz, *Pro* Nick Napier-Bell, Duncan Napier-Bell, Romain Schroeder and others, *Screenplay* Gilbert Adair, from his novel, *Ph* Ricardo Aronovitch, *Pro Des* Keith Slote, *Ed* Valeria Sarmiento, Adrian Murray and Sean Barton, *Cos* Kate O'Farrell.

Autumnal passions: Horst Westphal and Ursula Werner in Andreas Dresen's surprisingly frank Cloud 9.

Eyeline Entertainment/Atlantic Film Distributors/
Kaleidoscope Centurion etc-Eyeline Entertainment.
88 mins. UK. 2009. Rel: 19 Feb 2010. Cert. 15.

Cloud 9 ★★★★½

This undervalued film, which boasts some
of the best acting to be seen in recent years,
features one of the most unusual romantic
triangles in cinema history. That's because
the woman concerned is 63 and the men in
her life, her husband and her new lover, are
in their seventies. Sexually candid but never
for sensation's sake, it is a moral drama about
fulfilling one's own life even if that hurts others.
One might prefer a different resolution, but this
is thought-provoking and heartfelt and deserves
to be sought out. (Original title: *Wolke 9*) MS

▶ Ursula Werner, Horst Rehberg, Horst Westphal,
Steffi Kühnert, Werner Schmidt.
▶ *Dir* Andreas Dresen, *Pro* Peter Rommel, *Story
Development* Dresen, Cooky Ziesche, Laila Stieler
and Jörg Hauschild, *Ph* Michael Hammon, *Art Dir*
Susanne Hopf, *Ed* Hauschild, *Cos* Sabine Greunig.

**Rommel Film/RBB - Rundfunk Berlin-Brandenburg/ARTE
etc-Soda Pictures.**
100 mins. Germany. 2008. Rel: 10 July 2009. Cert. 15.

Cloudy with a Chance of Meatballs ★★

Flint Lockwood had always dreamed of making
his mark through a unique invention. Having
failed with his spray-on shoes and monkey
translator, he sets about turning water into food.
The title is not exactly encouraging and, indeed,
this 3D 'toon turns out to be an ugly, strident
affair beating a very loud drum. It screams in 90
minutes what *WALL-E* drolly slipped into the
conversation. Here, we're treated to the sight
of American gluttony on an apocalyptic scale.
While there is some visual wit, there's no charm,
subtlety or that much originality – but an awful
lot of food. JC-W

▶ Voices of Bill Hader, Anna Faris, James Caan,
Andy Samberg, Bruce Campbell, Mr T.
▶ *Dir* and *Screenplay* Phil Lord and Chris Miller,
based on the book by Judi and Ron Barrett,
Pro Pam Marsden, *Pro Des* Justin Thompson,
M Mark Mothersbaugh.

Sony Pictures Animation-Sony Pictures Releasing.
90 mins. USA. 2009. Rel: 18 Sep 2009. Cert. U.

Coco Before Chanel ★★★★

A box-office hit here, this French biopic about
the early life of designer Coco Chanel is too
superficial to be a significant film but, as a
popular-style romantic period drama that side-
steps any dubious aspects in the life of its heroine,

Heaven scent:
Anna Mouglalis
excels herself
in Jan Kounen's
cinematic and
stylish *Coco
Chanel & Igor
Stravinsky.*

it is tailor-made for its audience. It's also well
mounted and offers the star presence of Audrey
Tautou, whose admirers will not be disappointed.
(Original title: *Coco avant Chanel*) MS

▶ Audrey Tautou, Benoît Poelvoorde, Alessandro
Nivola, Marie Gillain, Emmanuelle Devos.
▶ *Dir* Anne Fontaine, *Pro* Caroline Benjo, Carole
Scotta, Philippe Carcassonne and Simon Arnal,
Screenplay Anne and Camille Fontaine with
Christopher Hampton and Jacques Fieschi, from
L'irrégulière ou mon itinéraire Chanel by Edmonde
Charles-Roux, *Ph* Christophe Beaucarne,
Art Dir Olivier Radot, *Ed* Luc Barnier, *M* Alexandre
Desplat, *Cos* Catherine Leterrier.

**Haut & Court/Ciné @/Warner Bros/France 2 Cinéma
etc-Optimum Releasing.**
110 mins. France/Belgium. 2008. Rel: 31 July 2009.
Cert. 12A.

Coco Chanel & Igor Stravinsky ★★★

This is, in effect, a sequel to the Audrey Tautou
movie *Coco avant Chanel*, picking up her story
from where the earlier film left off. Now Anna
Mouglalis is Coco Chanel. There's a good sense of
period, starting with a recreation of the notorious
premiere of *The Rite of Spring*, but the attempt to

Message in a bottle: Paul Giamatti as another of his grumpy eccentrics in Sophie Barthes' decidedly original *Cold Souls*.

suggest that Stravinsky (Mads Mikkelsen) was the love of her life is unpersuasive and the film is all style and very little substance. MS

▷ Mads Mikkelsen, Anna Mouglalis, Elena Morozova, Grigori Manoukov.
▷ *Dir* Jan Kounen, *Pro* Claudie Ossard and Chris Bolzli, *Screenplay* Chris Greenhalgh with Carlo De Boutiny and Kounen, from the novel *Coco & Igor* by Greenhalgh, *Ph* David Ungaro, *Art Dir* Marie-Hélène Sulmoni, *Ed* Anny Danché, *M* Gabriel Yared, *Cos* Chattoune & Fab.

Eurowide Film Production/Hexagon Pictures/Canal+/ TPS Star/Wild Bunch etc-Soda Pictures.
119 mins. France/Switzerland/Japan. 2009. Rel: 6 Aug 2010. Cert. 15.

Coffin Rock ★★★★

When an emotionally unstable young man discovers that an older woman is trying to conceive a child, he decides to help out… Unimaginatively billed as being 'from the producer of *Wolf Creek*,' *Coffin Rock* at least shares a geographical moniker with the former. But whereas *Wolf Creek* was a full-out horror film, this is an Australian thriller in the vein of *Fatal Attraction* – and highly effective thanks to its credible characters. Making the most of its stark, wintry locale, this is a handsomely executed and genuinely unnerving film that neither tricks nor cheats its audience. JC-W

▷ Lisa Chappell, Terry Camilleri, Robert Taylor, Sam Parsonson, Joseph Del Re.
▷ *Dir* and *Screenplay* Rupert Glasson, *Pro* Ayisha Davies and David Lightfoot, *Ph* David Foreman, *Pro Des* Tony Cronin, *Ed* Adrian Rostirolla, *M* John Gray, *Cos* Theo Benton.

Head Gear Films/Ultra Films-Bankside Films.
92 mins. UK/Australia. 2009. Rel: 4 Sep 2009. Cert. 15.

Cold Souls ★★★

Nothing if not individual, Sophie Barthes' comedy/drama is about an actor who is called Paul Giamatti and who takes advantage of a service in New York which extracts souls from those burdened by them. Having taken this step the actor changes his mind but, as with drugs, there is worldwide trafficking in souls, as he finds out when he sets out to recover his own soul, which has been sent to Russia. Giamatti is sound in the lead role, David Strathairn even better, but the curious concept never generates the power to sustain a feature film. MS

▷ Paul Giamatti, David Strathairn, Dina Korzun, Emily Watson, Sergey Kolesnikov.
▷ *Dir* and *Screenplay* Sophie Barthes, *Pro* Dan Carey, Elizabeth Giamatti, Andrij Parekh and others, *Ph* Parekh, *Pro Des* Elizabeth Mickle, *Ed* Andrew Mondshein, *M* Dickon Hinchcliffe, *Cos* Erin Benach.

Two Lane Pictures/Winner Arts Limited/Journeyman Pictures/Touchy Feely Films etc-The Works.
101 mins. USA/France. 2008. Rel: 13 Nov 2009. Cert. 12A.

Colin ★½

While wiping the blood off his hands in his kitchenette, Colin is attacked – and bitten – by a zombie… If this film hadn't allegedly cost £45, it wouldn't have found the publicity to land a distributor. However, for a homemade movie it is impressive, particularly its use of sound and virtual abandonment of dialogue. But it's also *so* cheap that much of the imagery is lost in an under-lit blur and for much of the time it's hard to know exactly what's going on. In the event, not a lot *does* seem to be happening, at least in a narrative sense. JC-W

▷ Alastair Kirton, Daisy Atkins, Tat Whalley, Leanne Pammen, Kate Alderman, Justin Mitchell Davey, Kerry Owen, Leigh Crocombe.
▷ *Dir*, *Pro*, *Screenplay*, *Ph*, *Ed* Marc (Vincent) Price, *M* Dan Weekes, Jack Elphick, Simon Bevan, Spencer McGarry Season.

Nowhere Fast Films-Kaleidoscope Entertainment (UK).
97 mins. UK. 2009. Rel: 23 Oct 2009. Cert. 18.

Collapse ★★★★

Chris Smith's fascinating documentary features Michael C Ruppert, a former Los Angeles police officer turned reporter who predicted the current financial crisis. The film works well despite the fact that this is practically a monologue from the highly intelligent and articulate Ruppert, who expertly reports about global issues including oil and financial crises. This honest piece of work is cleverly edited around a series of interviews with Ruppert and is a satisfying experience despite its bleak and pessimistic outlook. GS

▶ Michael C Ruppert.
▶ *Dir* Chris Smith, *Pro* Smith and Kate Noble, *Screenplay* Michael C Ruppert, based on his book *A Presidential Energy Policy*, *Ph* Smith, Ed Lachman and Max Makin, *Pro Des* Andrew Resnick, *Ed* Barry Poltermann, *M* Didier Leplae, Noisola and Joe Wong.

Blue Mark Productions-Dogwoof Pictures.
82 mins. USA. 2009. Rel: 1 Oct 2010. No Cert.

The Collector ★★½

Marcus Dunstan, who makes his directorial debut here, has been heavily involved with the *Saw* franchise, having scripted four of the sequels. He recycles many of the latter's gory ideas in this slice of torture porn in which a resourceful thief finds himself trapped in a house of horrors. There is some ingenuity here, but ultimately Dunstan settles for sadism over suspense. CB

▶ Josh Stewart, Michael Reilly Burke, Andrea Roth, Juan Fernández, Danielle Alonso.
▶ *Dir* Marcus Dunstan, *Pro* Patrick Rizzotti, Brett Forbes and Julie Richardson, *Screenplay* Dunstan and Patrick Melton, *Ph* Brandon Cox, *Pro Des* Emanno Di Febo-Orsini, *Ed* Howard E Smith, James Mastracco and Alex Luna, *M* Jerome Dillon, *Cos* Ashlyn Angel.

Liddell Entertainment/Fortress Features/Imaginarium Entertainment Group-Icon Film Distribution.
90 mins. USA. 2009. Rel: 25 June 2010. Cert. 18.

The Concert ★★

If you take the view that a feel-good film need not have anything about it that is credible, then this tale of a Russian conductor conniving to reform his old orchestra and eventually triumphing against the odds at a concert. in Paris might be just the thing for you. It's utterly unbelievable and the fact that central to it is the suffering of Jewish musicians in the Brezhnev years adds insult to injury. At least it should introduce some viewers to Tchaikovsky's Violin Concerto! MS

▶ Alexeï Guskov, Dimitri Nazarov, Mélanie Laurent, François Berléand, Miou Miou.
▶ *Dir* Radu Mihaileanu, *Pro* Alain Attal, *Screenplay* Mihaileanu, from a story by Hector Cabello Reyes and Thierry Degrandi, *Ph* Laurent Daillant, *Art Dir* Cristian Niculescu, *Ed* Ludo Troch, *M* Armand Amar, *Cos* Viorica Petrovici.

Les Productions du Trésor/Oï Oï Oï Productions/France 3 Cinéma etc-Optimum Releasing.
123 mins. France/Romania/Belgium/Italy. 2009. Rel: 16 July 2010. Cert. 15.

Confucius ★★½

China in 500 BC. When wise commoner Kong Fe (Confucius) is made Minister of Law, he inspires the leader of the ancient Kingdom of Lu to rise to new heights but also causes him to become a target for the warlike nation of Qi... Chow Yun-fat is a strong presence and plays the title role with his usual authority, but the confusing plot is far too complex to make this enjoyable despite the superb production values. GS

▶ Chow Yun-fat, Zhou Xun, Lu Yi, Chen Jian-bin, Ren Quan, Yao Lu.
▶ *Dir* Hu Mei, *Pro* Hu Mei and San-ping Han, *Screenplay* Chan Khan, Jiang Qitao, He Yanjiang and Hu Mei, *Ph* Peter Pau, *Ed* Zhan Haihong, *M* Zhao Jiping, *Cos* Chung-man Yee.

Beijing Dadi Century Ltd/Dadi Film Group-China Film Group.
125 mins. China. 2010. Rel: 24 Sep 2010. Cert. 15.

Bolshy orchestra: Miou-Miou in Radu Mihaileanu's César-winning *The Concert*.

Cop Out ★

Originally titled *A Couple of Dicks*, which would have meant this movie delivered at least one laugh, the aptly retitled *Cop Out* comes from director Kevin Smith, working with the studios for once and with a screenplay he didn't write. Suffice to say, things did not work out. This flat, laboured, cop-themed buddy comedy, starring Bruce Willis and *30 Rock*'s Tracy Morgan as crime fighters, starts weak and hurtles downhill from there. MJ

▶ Bruce Willis, Tracy Morgan, Juan Carlos Hernández, Cory Fernandez, Ana de la Reguera, Jason Hunt, Jeff Lima.
▶ *Dir* and *Ed* Kevin Smith, *Pro* Marc Platt and Michael Tadross, *Screenplay* Rob Cullen and Mark Cullen, *Ph* David Klein, *Pro Des* Michael Shaw, *M* Harold Faltermeyer, *Cos* Juliet Polcsa.
Warner Bros Pictures/Marc Platt Productions-Warner Bros.
107 mins. USA. 2010. Rel: 16 Apr 2010. Cert. 15.

Couples Retreat ★

It is difficult to find anything positive to say about this lame comedy apart from its stunning location. On an exotic island four midwestern couples embark on a dream holiday but they soon begin to re-examine their relationships when therapy is imposed on arrival. It is difficult to care about these unlikeable and stereotypical characters despite the talented cast, who are simply wasted here. The situation and dialogue never ring true and ultimately it is a total waste of time. GS

▶ Vince Vaughn, Jason Bateman, Faizon Love, Jon Favreau, Kristen Bell, Malin Akerman, Peter Serafinowicz, Jean Reno, Charlotte Cornwell.
▶ *Dir* Peter Billingsley, *Pro* Vaughn and Scott Stuber, *Screenplay* Vaughn and Favreau, *Ph* Eric Edwards, *Pro Des* Shepherd Frankel, *Ed* Dan Lebenthal, *M* A R Rahman, *Cos* Susan Matheson.
Universal Pictures/Relativity Media/Wild West Picture Show Productions/Stuber Productions-Universal Pictures International.
113 mins. USA. 2009. Rel: 14 Oct 2009. Cert. 15.

The Cove ★★★★

This powerful documentary has all the strength of a fictional thriller as it follows the attempts of Ric O'Barry and others to uncover evidence of the annual slaughter of dolphins in Japan, despite the efforts of the authorities to hide what is going on. Both stylistically and factually you can quibble over minor details, but this is a forceful work that carries the viewer with it. MS

▶ With Ric O'Barry.
▶ *Dir* Louie Psihoyos, *Pro* Paula DuPré Pesmen and Fisher Stevens, *Screenplay* Mark Monroe, *Ph* Brook Aitken, *Ed* Geoffrey Richman, *M* J Ralph.
Oceanic Preservation Society/Diamond Docs/Quickfire Films/Fish Films-Vertigo Films.
91 mins. USA. 2009. Rel: 23 Oct 2009. Cert. 12A.

Cracks ★★★½

Like *The Prime of Miss Jean Brodie*, the setting is a 1930s girls' school where the students have a thing going for their glamorous swimming instructor, Miss G (Eva Green). When a new pupil arrives in the shape of the Spanish Fiamma (Maria Valverde), Miss G becomes increasingly preoccupied with the new girl on the block, the green-eyed monster rears its pretty little head and all hell breaks loose in this

Saving Flipper: Ric O'Barry in Louie Psihoyos's forceful, Oscar-winning documentary *The Cove*.

Zombie practice: Radha Mitchell takes aim in Breck Eisner's reasonably engrossing remake, *The Crazies*.

hothouse of schoolgirl intrigue and manipulation. Nicely shot, if a tad too melodramatic for comfort, but with some glamorous contributions by the young female cast. MHD

▷ Eva Green, Juno Temple, Maria Valverde, Imogen Poots, Sinead Cusack.
▷ *Dir* Jordan Scott, *Pro* Kwesi Dickson and Andrew Lowe, *Screenplay* Scott, Ben Court and Caroline Ip, *Ph* John Mathieson, *Pro Des* Ben Scott, *Ed* Valerio Bonelli, *M* Javier Navarrete, *Cos* Alson Byrne.

HandMadeFilms/Scott Free Productions/Antenna 3 Films/Future Films/Killer Films/John Wells Productions etc-Optimum Releasing.
104 mins. UK/Ireland/Spain/France/Switzerland. 2009. Rel: 4 Dec 2009. Cert. 15.

The Crazies ★★★

As zombie fests and horror remakes jostle for breathing space in the marketplace, George A Romero's walking dead mini-classic of 1973 gets predictably disinterred. Sophomore director Breck Eisner (*Sahara*) gives it a naturalistic spin, partly by reining in the excesses of the genre and by casting halfway decent actors. There's more tension here than full-out terror (although there are two stand-out scenes involving a garden fork and a car wash), but it's all reasonably engrossing, albeit devoid of a funny bone. JC-W

▷ Timothy Olyphant, Radha Mitchell, Joe Anderson, Danielle Panabaker, Christie Lynn Smith.
▷ *Dir* Breck Eisner, *Pro* Michael Aguila, Rob Cowan, Dean Georgaris, *Screenplay* Scott Kosar and Ray Wright, based on George A Romero's 1973 film, *Ph* Maxime Alexandre, *Pro Des* Andrew Menzies,

Ed Billy Fox, *M* Mark Isham, *Cos* George L Little.

Overture Films/Participant Media/Penn Station/Road Rebel etc-Momentum Pictures.
101 mins. USA/United Arab Emirates. 2010. Rel: 26 Feb 2010. Cert. 15.

Crazy Heart ★★★½

Jeff Bridges has a tailor-made role here as a singer of country songs past his prime at 57. He provides a firm centre to this first feature by Scott Cooper. However, the film is less than sure-footed as its tone switches from an easy admiration for its chief character to a more tragic view of his life. Ardent fans of Bridges will relish this and the songs (Bridges himself sings) are good, but personal taste will decide just how much you get out of this movie. MS

▷ Jeff Bridges, Maggie Gyllenhaal, Robert Duvall, Colin Farrell, Tom Bower.
▷ *Dir* and *Screenplay* (from the novel by Thomas Cobb) Scott Cooper, *Pro* Cooper, Robert Duvall, Judy Cairo and others, *Ph* Barry Markowitz, *Pro Des* Waldemar Kalinowski, *Ed* John Axelrad and Jeffrey Ford, *M* Stephen Bruton and T Bone Burnett, *Cos* Doug Hall.

Fox Searchlight Pictures/Informant Media/Butcher's Run Films-20th Century Fox.
112 mins. USA. 2009. Rel: 19 Feb 2010. Cert. 15.

Creation ★★

Towards the end of this biopic about Charles Darwin the audience is led almost literally up the garden path by being invited to believe that the flames of an outdoor bonfire are burning up his as

Persecución inminente: Harrison Ford grapples with some foreign bodies in Wayne Kramer's gripping and undervalued *Crossing Over.*

yet unpublished book *On the Origin of Species*. This gross manipulation of the audience's emotions insultingly assumes ignorance of the book's publication! Choosing too to present Darwin's dead daughter as a ghost, the film struck me as inept in every department, save for Bill Paterson's persuasive cameo. Many seem to take a different view so you may wish to check it out for yourself. MS

▶ Paul Bettany, Jennifer Connelly, Jeremy Northam, Martha West, Toby Jones, Benedict Cumberbatch, Jim Carter, Bill Paterson.
▶ *Dir* Jon Amiel, *Pro* Jeremy Thomas, *Screenplay* John Collee, from a story by Amiel and Collee, based on Randal Keynes' book *Annie's Box*, *Ph* Jess Hall, *Pro Des* Laurence Dorman, *Ed* Melanie Oliver, *M* Christopher Young, *Cos* Louise Stjernsward.

Ocean Pictures/BBC Films/Hanway Films/Recorded Picture Company etc-Icon Film Distribution.
108 mins. UK. 2009. Rel: 25 Sep 2009. Cert. PG.

The Crimson Wing ★★★½

Those who recall the Disney True Life Adventures of the 1950s will be interested to discover that this release by British film-makers is presented by a new set-up, Disneynature (sic). Aimed at children as well as adults and seeking to educate as well as to entertain, this particular film is about the flamingos of Northern Tanzania. The film is not without weaknesses, including its commentary, but the images are great and it's the

wonders of nature rather than scientific detail that the film emphasises. MS

▶ With Ngaiye Mungazia Mollel. Narration by Mariella Frostrup.
▶ *Dir* Matthew Aeberhard and Leander Ward, *Pro* Paul Webster, Ward and Aeberhard, *Screenplay* Melanie Finn, *Ph* Aeberhard, *Ed* Nicolas Chaudeurge, *M* The Cinematic Orchestra.

Disneynature/a Natural Light Films and Kudo Pictures production-Buena Vista International (UK).
78 mins. USA/UK/France. 2008. Rel: 25 Sep 2009. Cert. PG.

Crossing Over ★★★½

Like Paul Haggis' over-praised *Crash* (2004), this is an American drama that presents interlinking personal stories that reflect contemporary American society. Central, however, are issues concerning immigrants and, while it lacks the quality of Ken Loach's *Bread and Roses* or Tom McCarthy's *The Visitor*, this movie deserved a wider audience than it found. It's not always persuasive, but it does entertain and invites the audience to draw their own conclusions on the question of immigration. MS

▶ Harrison Ford, Ray Liotta, Ashley Judd, Jim Sturgess, Alice Eve, Alice Braga.
▶ *Dir* and *Screenplay* Wayne Kramer, *Pro* Frank Marshall and Kramer, *Ph* James Whitaker, *Pro Des*

Toby Corbett, *Ed* Arthur Coburn, *M* Mark Isham, *Cos* Kristin M. Burke.

The Weinstein Company/a Kennedy/Marshall Company and a Movie Prose production-Entertainment Film Distributors.
113 mins. USA. 2008. Rel: 31 July 2009. Cert. 18.

Crude ★★★½

Following his study of the rock band Metallica, Joe Berlinger here turns to another kind of documentary, one of an increasingly popular sort that questions the irresponsibility of oil companies – in this instance in Ecuador and around the Amazon. Being over-long and sometimes repetitive, it's not the very best example of its kind but nevertheless it's good, strong stuff and such exposés are to be encouraged. MS

❧ With Pablo Fajardo, Steven Donziger, Trudie Styler, Sting.
❧ *Dir* Joe Berlinger, *Pro* Berlinger, Michael Bonfiglio and others, *Ph* Juan Diego Pérez, *Ed* Alyse Ardell Spiegel, *M* Wendy Blackstone.

Red Envelope Entertainment/an Entendre Films production etc-Dogwoof Pictures
105 mins. USA, 2009. Rel: 15 Jan 2010. No Cert.

Crying With Laughter ★★★

Stephen McCole is excellent as the star of this darkly comic psychological thriller set in Edinburgh. He plays a reckless stand-up comedian whose life unravels after he runs into an old school friend with a secret agenda. Taking the BAFTA Scotland Best Feature Film Award in 2009, Scots writer-director Justin Molotnikov's debit film is neatly done, with more than enough creepy atmosphere and mounting tension to keep it gripping throughout. DW

❧ Stephen McCole, Niall Greig Fulton, Jo Hartley, Tom Jude, Laura Keenan, Andrew Neil.
❧ *Dir* and *Screenplay* Justin Molotnikov, *Pro* Rachel Robey, Claire Mundell and Alastair Clark, *Ph* Martin Radich, *Pro Des* Mike McLoughlin, *Ed* Gary Scott, *M* Lorne Balfe, *Cos* Anna Robbins.

Synchronicity Films/Wellington Films-Brit Films.
93 mins. UK. 2009. Rel: 16 Apr 2010. Cert. 18.

Cuckoo ★★

This attempt at a psychological drama set in London seems half way between *Gaslight* and *Repulsion* as it presents us with a central figure who appears to hear voices and noises in her head. This is poor Laura Fraser, but in pitying her I am thinking not of her character's stress but of the banal dialogue and the film's fatal lack of intensity. It amounts to nothing very much at all. MS

❧ Laura Fraser, Antonia Bernath, Richard E Grant, Adam Fenton, Tamsin Greig.
❧ *Dir* and *Screenplay* Richard Bracewell, *Pro* Tony and Richard Bracewell, *Ph* Mark Partridge, *Pro Des* Simon Scullion, *Ed* Craig M. Cotterill, *M* Andrew Hewitt, *Cos* Susie Phillips.

Verve Pictures/Cuckoo Films etc-Verve Pictures.
89 mins. UK. 2010. Rel: 17 Dec 2010. Cert. 15.

Cyrus ★★★½

Those kings of 'Mumblecore' Jay and Mark Duplass retain their style in this more expensive

Oil on troubled waters? A scene from Joe Berlinger's solidly disturbing *Crude*.

Everything was beautiful at the ballet: a scene from Frederick Wiseman's *La Danse: The Paris Ballet Opera.*

tragi-comedy with a strong cast. A divorcee (John C Reilly) finds his chance of fresh happiness with Molly (Marisa Tomei) threatened by her manipulative 21-year-old son Cyrus (Jonah Hill). Catherine Keener at her considerable best is also on hand, but the happy ending seems too contrived to work. MS

➤ John C Reilly, Jonah Hill, Marisa Tomei. Catherine Keener, Matt Walsh.
➤ *Dir* and *Screenplay* Jay and Mark Duplass, *Pro* Michael Costigan, *Ph* Jas Shelton, *Pro Des* Annie Spitz, *Ed* Jay Deuby, *M* Michael Andrews, *Cos* Roemehl Hawkins.

Fox Searchlight Pictures/Scott Free etc-20th Century Fox. 91 mins. USA. 2010. Rel: 10 Sep 2010. Cert. 15.

Dance Flick ★

Megan (Shoshana Bush) gives up her dream to become a dancer after her mother is killed in a car accident. She moves to another city and joins Musical High instead of going to Juilliard. In this lazy and utterly unfunny spoof of the dance movie genre the plot is practically nonexistent and the script feels as if the actors are making it up as they go along. The only scene that manages to raise a feeble smile is the *Fame* send-up. Avoid! GS

➤ Shoshana Bush, Damon Wayans Jr, Essence Atkins, Affion Crockett, Luis Dalmasy, Amy Sedaris.
➤ *Dir* Damien Dante Wayans, *Pro* Rick Alvarez, Keenan Ivory Wayans, Marlon Wayans and Shawn Wayans, *Screenplay* Damien Dante Wayans, Keenan Ivory Wayans, Marlon Wayans, Craig Wayans and Shawn Wayans, *Ph* Mark Irwin, *Pro Des* Aaron Osborne, *Ed* Scott Hill, *Music Supervisor* Lisa Brown, *Cos* Judy L Ruskin.

**Paramount Pictures/MTV Films/Wayans Brothers-Paramount Pictures.
83 mins. USA. 2009. Rel: 21 Aug 2009. Cert. 15.**

La Danse: The Paris Ballet Opera ★★★½

Frederick Wiseman is the doyen of documentary in America and this piece is characteristic of his work; that is to say, it's very long, acutely observed but without any commentary. The film covers all strands in the ballet company at the Paris Opera, but not knowing which ballets are being prepared and who is involved is frustrating. For that reason balletomanes will appreciate the film more than those who enjoy ballet without being quite so knowledgeable. The artistic director Brigitte Lefèvre is an engaging figure. MS

➤ With Brigitte Lefèvre, Wayne McGregor, Marie-Agnès Gillot, Angelin Preljocaj.
➤ *Dir* Frederick Wiseman, *Pro* Françoise Gazio, Pierre-Olivier Bardet and Wiseman, *Ph* John Davey, *Ed* Wiseman and Valérie Pico.

**Produced in co-production with L'Opéra National de Paris in association with Public Broadcasting Service PBS etc-Soda Pictures.
159 mins. France/USA/Japan/Finland, 2009. Rel: 23 Apr 2010. Cert. PG.**

Date Night ★★

Steve Carrell and Tina Fey play a married couple whose relationship has gone flat. To spice it up, they go on a date night, pinch a no-show's table at an upscale NY restaurant, and are catapulted into an unsettling netherworld of dubious deals and gangster intrigue. Despite terrific work from its two leads, Shawn Levy's comedy proves less than satisfying. JC

▶ Steve Carell, Tina Fey, Mark Wahlberg, Taraji P Henson, Jimmi Simpson, Kristen Wiig, Mark Ruffalo.
▶ *Dir* Shawn Levy, *Pro* Levy and Tom McNulty, *Screenplay* John Klausner, *Ph* Dean Semler, *Pro Des* David Gropman, *Ed* Dean Zimmerman, *M* Christophe Beck, *Cos* Marlene Stewart.

Twentieth Century Fox/21 Laps/Media Magik Entertainment-20th Century Fox.
88 mins. USA. 2010. Rel: 21 Apr 2010. Cert. 15.

Daybreakers ★★★½

Frightening, smart and thrilling with a wicked sense of humour, this paints a unique, near-futuristic portrait of a world overrun by vampires who are famished for blood and mutating into something nightmarish. A compelling vision of society transformed – starring Ethan Hawke as a 'can't we all just get along' vamp scientist, Willem Dafoe as a 'no we can't' human freedom fighter and Sam Neill as an evil 'I'll drink every last one of you dry' business vamp – it's creative, exciting, atmospheric and packed full of fascinating detail. MJ

▶ Ethan Hawke, Sam Neill, Willem Dafoe, Harriet Minto-Day, Jay Laga'Aia, Damen Garvey, Sahaj Dumpleton.
▶ *Dir* and *Screenplay* Michael and Peter Spierig, *Pro* Chris Brown, Brian and Sean Furst, *Ph* Ben Nott, *Pro Des* and *Cos* George Liddle, *Ed* Matt Villa, *M* Christopher Gordon.

Lionsgate Films/Paradise/Pacific Film and TV Commission/Film Finance Corporation Australia/Furst Films-Lionsgate.
98 mins. Australia/USA. 2009. Rel: 6 Jan 2010. Cert. 15.

Dead Man Running ★★★

Ex-con Nick (Tamer Hassan) tries to go straight but finds himself in trouble when he is unable to pay his debts to the fearless shark Mr Thigo (50 Cent). He has only 24 hours to find the money

and puts not only his life in jeopardy but also that of his wheelchair-bound mother (Brenda Blethyn). Alex De Rakoff's energetic gangster thriller benefits from Hassan's committed performance and from Blethyn's unexpected turn but doesn't add anything new to an over-familiar genre. GS

▶ Danny Dyer, 50 Cent, Tamer Hassan, Monet Mazur, Brenda Blethyn, Blake Ritson, Philip Davis.
▶ *Dir* Alex De Rakoff, *Pro* Pikki Fearon, *Screenplay* De Rakoff and John Luton, from a story by Luton, *Ph* Ali Asad, *Pro Des* Matthew Button, *Ed* Alan Strachan, *M* Mark Sayfritz, *Cos Supervisor* Shirley Nevin.

Next Generation TV & Film/P & T Productions-Revolver Entertainment.
92 mins. UK. 2009. Rel: 30 Oct 2009. Cert. 15.

Dear John ★★★

Lasse Hallström-directed part war movie, part romantic drama in which Amanda Seyfried falls for soldier on leave Channing Tatum, who must then return to a war zone with his Special Forces. An unexpectedly engaging subplot features Richard Jenkins as the soldier's housebound father. Nothing special, but likeable in its own way. JC

▶ Channing Tatum, Amanda Seyfried, Henry Thomas, Scott Porter, Richard Jenkins.

Below left: Channing Tatum in Lasse Hallström's likeable *Dear John*.

Below: Sam Neill in Michael and Peter Spierig's thrilling and atmospheric *Daybreakers*.

❯ *Dir* Lasse Hallström, *Pro* Ryan Kavanaugh, Marty Bowen and Wyck Godfrey, *Screenplay* Jamie Linden, based on the novel by Nicholas Sparks, *Ph* Terry Stacey, *Pro Des* Kara Lindstrom, *Ed* Kristina Boden, *M* Deborah Lurie, *Cos* Dana Campbell and Kathryn Langston.

Relativity Media/Temple Hill-Paramount Pictures. 108 mins. USA. 2010. Rel: 14 Apr 2010. Cert. 12A.

The Death and Life of Charlie St Cloud ★★★

Charlie (Zac Efron) becomes inconsolable after his younger brother's death in a car accident. However, Charlie has the ability to see his brother and to meet up with him every evening. In the meantime he falls for a young woman called Tess (Amanda Crew)... The story isn't bad and has a clever twist but this sentimental film feels over-extended. It is beautifully shot but the manipulative score gets in the way. (Original title: *Charlie St Cloud*) GS

❯ Zac Efron, Kim Basinger, Ray Liotta, Charlie Tahan, Amanda Crew, Augustus Prew.
❯ *Dir* Burr Steers, *Pro* Michael Fottrell and Mark Platt, *Screenplay* Craig Pearce and Lewis Colick, based on the novel by Ben Sherwood, *Ph* Enrique Chediak, *Pro Des* Ida Random, *Ed* Padraic McKinley, *M* Rolfe Kent, *Cos* Denise Wingate.

Universal Pictures/Relativity Media/Mark Platt Productions/Charlie Film Productions-United International Pictures. 99 mins. USA/Canada. 2010. Rel: 8 Oct 2010. Cert. 12A.

The first Japanese feature to win the Oscar for Best Foreign Language Film: Masahiro Motoki in Yôjirô Takita's Departures.

Death at a Funeral ★★★★★

This is a US reboot of the 2007 British comedy with Peter Dinklage reprising his role as the dwarf

and an otherwise all-new cast. Transplanting the proceedings shot by shot to California and populating it with a largely black cast (headed by Chris Rock, Martin Lawrence and Keith David) works wonders for director Neil LaBute: the result is far funnier than the original. JC

❯ Peter Dinklage, Danny Glover, Martin Lawrence, James Marsden, Tracy Morgan, Chris Rock, Zoe Saldana, Luke Wilson, Loretta Devine.
❯ *Dir* Neil LaBute, *Pro* Sidney Kimmel, Laurence Malkin, Share Stallings and William Horberg, *Screenplay* Dean Craig, *Ph* Rogers Stoffers, *Pro Des* Jon Gary Steele, *Ed* Tracey Wadmore-Smith, *M* Christophe Beck, *Cos* Maya Lieberman.

Parabolic Pictures Inc/Screen Gems/Sidney Kimmel Entertainment/Stable Way Entertainment/Wonderful Films-Sony Pictures Releasing. 92 mins. USA. 2010. Rel: 4 June 2010. Cert. 15.

Departures ★★★

An Oscar-winner it may be but this competently made Japanese film is far inferior to those which lost out (*The Class*, *Waltz with Bashir* etc). It's the story of a musician who, forced to take another job, finds himself working for undertakers. There are sensitive moments about the handling of the dead but the film veers from the comic (itself involving conflicting tones) to the sentimental. Ultimately it's a slushy weepie adeptly done for those who like that kind of thing – which includes Americans who vote for Oscar's Best Foreign Language Film. (Original title: *Okuribito*) MS

❯ Motoki Masahiro, Hirosue Ryoko, Yamazaki Tsutomu, Yo Kimiko, Yoshiyuki Kazuko.
❯ *Dir* Takita Yôjirô, *Pro* Nakazawa Toshiaki and Watai Toshihisa, *Screenplay* Koyama Kundo, *Ph* Hamada Takeshi, *Pro Des* Ogawa Fumio, *Ed* Kawashima Akimasa, *M* Hisaishi Joe, *Cos* Kitamura Katsuhiko.

Departures Film Partners-Arrow Film Distrubutors. 130 mins. Japan. 2008. Rel: 4 Dec 2009. Cert. 12A.

The Descent Part 2 ★★½

In Jon Harris' sequel the story begins as Sarah Carter (Shauna Macdonald) emerges from the Appalachian cave without her five friends. A rescue team is ready to go back into the cave in order to find the missing women – and a rather confused Sarah is thrown back into another nightmare. The new characters are not introduced properly after a rather rushed prologue in this déjà vu scenario but Macdonald proves again what a strong heroine she can be. GS

❯ Shauna Macdonald, Natalie Jackson Mendoza, Krysten Cummings, Gavan O'Herlihy, Joshua Dallas, Douglas Hodge.
❯ *Dir* and *Ed* Jon Harris, *Pro* Christian Colson and Ivana Mackinnon, *Screenplay* J Blakeson, James Watkins and

James McCarthy, *Ph* Sam McCurdy, *Pro Des* Simon Bowles, *M* David Julyan, *Cos* Nancy Thompson.

Celador Films-Lionsgate.
94 mins. UK. 2009. Rel: 2 Dec 2009. Cert. 18.

Despicable Me ★★½

'Gru' relishes the prospect of being the world's Greatest Villain of All Time. So, from the bowels of his suburban home, he plots a way to steal the moon… While taking a leaf out of Roald Dahl's legacy, *Despicable Me* borrows liberally from the template of *The Incredibles* and *Lemony Snicket* and knocks up a predictable tale of malevolence vs family. The details are funny and the 3D effects are put to good use, but the peculiar ugliness of the human characters is depressingly mainstream American. JC-W

▶ Voices of Steve Carell, Jason Segel, Russell Brand, Julie Andrews, Will Arnett, Kristen Wiig.
▶ *Dir* Pierre Coffin and Chris Renaud, *Pro* John Cohen, Janet Healy and Chris Meledandri, *Screenplay* Cinco Paul and Ken Daurio from a story by Sergio Pablos, *Pro Des* Yarrow Cheney, *Ed* Gregory Perletz and Pam Zielenhagen, *M* Heitor Pereira.

Universal Pictures/Illumination Entertainment-Universal Pictures International.
95 mins. USA. 2010. Rel: 15 Oct 2010. Cert. U.

Devil ★★½

From the brain of M Night Shyamalan (and isn't that a disheartening way to start a review?) comes the first in a series of creepy mindbenders, conceived and produced by Shyamalan but co-written and directed by promising nobodies.

Collected under catch-all banner *The Night Chronicles*, *Devil* is the first of these *Twilight Zone*-style tales and, although it brings nothing new to the table, it's a fun, easy and slightly spooky watch. Following the fate of five strangers stuck in an elevator, one of whom turns out to be the Devil, it's a brisk mid-budget chiller aimed squarely at horror fans. MJ

▶ Chris Messina, Jacob Vargas, Carole Dhavernas, Bokeem Woodbine, Matt Craven, Joe Cobden.
▶ *Dir* John Erik Dowdle, *Pro* M Night Shayamalan and Sam Mercer, *Screenplay* Shayamalan and Brian Nelson, from a story by Shayamalan, *Ph* Tak Fujimoto, *Pro Des* Martin Whist, *Ed* Elliot Greenberg, *M* Fernando Velázquez, *Cos* Erin Benach.

Media Rights Capital/Night Chronicles-United International Pictures.
80 mins. USA. 2010. Rel: 17 Sep 2010. Cert. 15.

Diary of a Wimpy Kid ★½

In spite of the efforts of four scriptwriters – two called Jeff – this trawl through the travails of middle-school one-upmanship is obvious, glib and shockingly unamusing. This is the story of a schoolboy who, tormented by his older brother (and ignored by his parents), is unable to find any friends. Based on the book by Jeff Kinney (no relation to the scriptwriters), it makes one yearn for the comic ingenuity of *Home Alone 3*. JC-W

▶ Zachary Gordon, Robert Capron, Rachael Harris, Steve Zahn, Connor Fielding, Owen Fielding.
▶ *Dir* Thor Freudenthal, *Pro* Nina Jacobson, Ethan Smith and Bradford Simpson, *Screenplay* Gabe Sachs, Jeff Judah, Jackie Filgo and Jeff Filgo, based

Villains, Inc.: Vector seems unperturbed by Gru's gruesomeness in Pierre Coffin and Chris Renaud's enormously successful *Despicable Me*.

on books by Jeff Kinney, *Ph* Jack Green, *Pro Des* Brent Thomas, *Ed* Wendy Greene Bricmont, *M* Theodore Shapiro, *Cos* Monique Prudhomme.

Dayday Films/Color Force/Dune Entertainment III-20th Century Fox.
94 mins. USA. 2010. Rel: 20 Aug 2010. Cert. PG.

Did You Hear About the Morgans? ★½

Successful Manhattan couple Paul and Meryl Morgan (Hugh Grant and Sarah Jessica Parker) are on the brink of a divorce, but when they accidentally witness a murder they also become a target for the contract killer. Under the police protection plan they are sent into the middle of nowhere in a tiny town in Wyoming. Despite the potentially fun premise this fails to engage and is not helped by the actors' lack of chemistry and a lame script. GS

▶ Hugh Grant, Sarah Jessica Parker, Natalie Klimas, Vincenzo Amato, Elizabeth Moss, Sam Elliott, Wilford Brimley, Mary Steenburgen.
▶ *Dir* and *Screenplay* Mark Lawrence, *Pro* Liz Glotzer and Martin Shafer, *Ph* Florian Ballhaus, *Pro Des* Kevin Thompson, *Ed* Susan E Morse, *M* Theodore Shapiro, *Cos* Christopher Peterson.

Columbia Pictures/Relativity Media/Castle Rock Entertainments/Banter Films-Sony Pictures Releasing.
103 mins. USA. 2009. Rel: 1 Jan 2010. Cert. PG.

Died Young, Stayed Pretty ★★½

There have been a lot of good documentaries lately but this is not one of them. The film-maker, Eileen Yaghoobian, spent four years filming underground graphic artists best known for alternative-style posters, some promoting pop bands. Their output is related to both punk and porn, but all we get is an uncritical shapeless mass of material haphazardly put together. When music doesn't drown out the comments, the talk to be heard reveals nothing of interest. MS

Street Creed: Gemma Arterton in her bravest performance yet, in J Blakeson's smart, suspenseful The Disappearance of Alice Creed.

▶ With Brian Chippendale, Art Chantry, Bryce McCloud, Rob Jones, Jay Ryan.
▶ *Dir, Pro, Ph, Ed* Eileen Yaghoobian, *M* Mark Greenberg.

Norotomo Productions/Canada Council for the Arts-ICA Films.
94 mins. Canada. 2008. Rel: 9 Oct 2009. No Cert.

Dinner for Schmucks ★★

On the verge of big things, financial analyst Tim Conrad finds that his life, career, flat, Porsche and imminent fiancée are threatened by a chance encounter with a decidedly odd little man... The original *Le dîner de cons* was a dark, deadpan, superbly acted and above all bitingly funny adaptation of Francis Veber's play. The inevitable American remake – long in the works – harvests the embarrassment of the original and drains the humour out of it. Sadly, this is yet another case of a French soufflé curdled into American suet. JC-W

▶ Steve Carell, Paul Rudd, Stephanie Szostak, Zach Galifianakis, Jemaine Clement, Lucy Punch, David Walliams.
▶ *Dir* Jay Roach, *Pro* Roach, Walter F Parkes and Laurie MacDonald, *Screenplay* Michael Handelman and David Guion, based on Francis Veber's film *Le dîner de cons*, *Ph* Jim Denault, *Pro Des* Michael Corenblith, *Ed* Alan Baumgarten and Jon Poll, *M* Theodore Shapiro, *Cos* Mary E Vogt.

Paramount Pictures/DreamWorks Pictures/Parkes-MacDonald/Spyglass Entertainment/Everyman Pictures-United International Pictures.
114 mins. USA. 2010. Rel: 28 Aug 2010. Cert. 15.

Dirty Oil ★★★★

Following *A Crude Awakening* and *Crude* [qv], here is yet another documentary concerned with oil companies and the environment. This one, a distinguished example of the genre, focuses on Alberta, Canada in particular, makes its points well and sensibly refrains from outstaying its welcome. The director, Leslie Iwerks, has done an admirable job. *H2Oil* [qv] is a comparable work. MS

▶ With Andrew Nikiforuk, Dr John O'Connor, Lester Brown. Narrated by Neve Campbell.
▶ *Dir, Ed* and *Screenplay* Leslie Iwerks, *Pro* Philip Alberstat, Mark Cranwell and Randy Bradshaw, *Ph* Suki Medencevic and Steven D Smith, *M* Stu MacQuarrie and Mike Shields.

Babelgum/49 North Inc. etc-Dogwoof Pictures.
76 mins. Canada/Iceland. 2009. Rel: 19 Mar 2010. Cert. U.

The Disappearance of Alice Creed ★★★★

This British kidnapping drama replete with plot twists may well offend some viewers, especially those who feel that it's a work that plays on the

exploitation of a woman. Even so, this is an inherently cinematic treatment of a piece that might well have come across as theatrical, the surprises work well, and both Martin Compston and Eddie Marsan (the latter steals the acting honours) give it their all. MS

▶ Gemma Arterton, Martin Compston, Eddie Marsan.
▶ *Dir* and *Screenplay* J Blakeson, *Pro* Adrian Sturges, *Ph* Philipp Blaubach, *Pro Des* Ricky Eyres, *Ed* Mark Eckersley, *M* Marc Canham, *Cos* Julian Day.
CinemaNX/Isle of Man Film-CinemaNX.
100 mins. UK. 2009. Rel: 30 April 2010. Cert. 18.

Disgrace ★★

Based on the Booker Prize-winning novel of 1999 by J M Coetzee, this is a dramatic tale which initially suggests a companion piece to 2007's *Elegy*, as it shows a professor with an eye for his pupils. Soon, however, it converts into a tale about the professor's lesbian daughter being abused by black youths. The whole thing may be a symbolic tale about South Africa's race relations but I found it highly unlikely in its details and felt distant from it. Admirers of the book may disagree. MS

▶ John Malkovich, Jessica Haines, Eriq Ebouaney, Fiona Press, Antoinette Engel.
▶ *Dir* Steve Jacobs, *Pro* Anna-Maria Monticelli, Emile Sherman and Jacobs, *Screenplay* Monticelli, from J M Coetzee's novel, *Ph* Steve Arnold, *Pro Des* Mike Berg and Annie Beauchamp, *Ed* Alexandre de Franceschi, *M* Antony Partos, *Cos* Diana Cilliers.
Film Finance Corporation Australia/Wild Strawberries/

Sherman Pictures etc-ICA Films.
119 mins. Australia/USA/Netherlands/South Africa. 2007. Rel: 4 Dec 2009. Cert. 15.

Disney's A Christmas Carol ★★★

The animated layering used by Robert Zemeckis in *The Polar Express* is combined here with state-of-the-art 3D. As a telling of Charles Dickens' famous Christmas story, the film is no more than passable and it frequently pauses in the narrative to dwell on effects set up for 3D. Jim Carrey is Scrooge but the piece can only be recommended to those looking for a 3D sideshow rather than a memorable recreation of a classic tale. MS

▶ Jim Carrey, Gary Oldman, Colin Firth, Bob Hoskins, Robin Wright Penn.
▶ *Dir* and *Screenplay* (from the novel by Charles Dickens) Robert Zemeckis, *Pro* Steve Starkey, Zemeckis and Jack Rapke, *Ph* Robert Presley, *Pro Des* Doug Chiang, *Ed* Jeremiah O'Driscoll, *M* Alan Silvestri, *Visual Effects Supervisor* George Murphy.
Walt Disney Pictures/ImageMovers Digital-Buena Vista.
96 mins. USA. 2009. Rel: 4 Nov 2009. Cert. PG.

District 9 ★★★★½

Twenty years ago an alien spaceship docked above Johannesburg, its cargo of creatures proving to be both helpless and irritable. Rounded up and put into camps, the visitors adopt a liking for cat food and anti-social behaviour. Eventually, a plan is hatched to move the aliens out of the city – a plan that

Outer spacism: Sharlto Copley in Neill Blomkamp's thrilling, no-holds-barred *District 9*.

Local colour: Elodie Yung in Patrick Alessandrin's violent and beautifully choreographed *District 13: Ultimatum*.

goes disastrously awry. Loosely disguised as a mockumentary, this South African-New Zealand co-production is a thrilling, no-holds-barred slice of sci-fi escapism with a political edge. Combining elements of *Transformers*, *The Fly* and *Tsotsi*, it is at once a powerful piece of social commentary and delirious B-movie cinema. JC-W

▶ Sharlto Copley, Jason Cope, Nathalie Boltt, Sylvaine Strike, William Allen Young.
▶ *Dir* Neill Blomkamp, *Pro* Carolyne Cunningham and Peter Jackson, *Screenplay* Blomkamp and Terri Tatchell, *Ph* Trent Opalach, *Pro Des* Philip Ivey, *Ed* Julian Clarke, *M* Clinton Shorter, *Cos* Dianna Cilliers.
Tri-Star Pictures/WingNut Films/Key Creatives/QED International-Sony Pictures Releasing.
112 mins. USA/New Zealand/Canada/South Africa. 2009. Rel: 4 Sep 2009. Cert. 15.

District 13: Ultimatum ★★★★

The time now is 2013, three years after the French government promised but failed to clean up the notorious District 13. Resident hero Leito (David Belle) rejoins forces with undercover agent Tomaso (Cyril Raffaelli) in an attempt to expose the corrupt cops and government officials' plan to cause civil unrest in the district and cash in on its redevelopment. This sequel is as thrilling as the original with wonderful set pieces – very violent, of course, but beautifully choreographed in a graphic novel fashion. (Original title: *Banlieue 13 – Ultimatum*) GS

▶ Cyril Raffaelli, David Belle, Philippe Torreton, Daniel Duval, Eloide Yung.
▶ *Dir* Patrick Alessandrin, *Pro* and *Screenplay* Luc Besson, *Ph* Jean-François Hensgens, *Pro Des* Hugues Tissandier, *Ed* Julien Ray, *M* Track Invaders, Charlie Nguyen Kim, *D A* Octopus, *Cos* Thierry Delettre.
Europa Corp/TF1 Films Production/CiBy 2000/Canal +/ Cinécinema/Sofica Eurocorp-Momentum Pictures.
101 mins. France. 2009. Rel: 2 Oct 2009. Cert. 15.

Dog Pound ★★★

This Canadian movie is set in a facility for juvenile offenders and, like *A Prophet* [qv], shows the corrupting effect of prison life on the less criminal inmates. There's a sense of déjà vu here, some rather exaggerated drama and even the odd moment that proves unintentionally comic. However, the film's perfectly judged ending adds to our appreciation of what a good job has been done by the director Kim Chapiron. MS

▶ Adam Butcher, Shane Kippel, Mateo Morales, Slim Twig, Taylor Poulin.
▶ *Dir* Kim Chapiron, *Pro* Georges Bermann and Sam Grana, *Screenplay* Jeremie Delon and Chapiron, based on Ray Minton's screenplay for *Scum*, *Ph* André Chemetoff, *Ed* Benjamin Weill, *M* K'naan and Nikkfurie of La Caution, *Cos* Brenda McLeese and Chris O'Neil.
Partizan Films/Grana Productions Inc./Mars Films etc-Optimum Releasing.
91 mins. France/Canada. 2009. Rel: 27 Aug 2010. Cert. 18.

Dogging: A Love Story ★

Simon Ellis' debut feature follows the adventures of young unemployed journalist Dan (Luke Treadaway) who is looking for the perfect story in order to hit the big time. He gets inspired by his cousin Rob's (Richard Riddell) free thinking when it comes to sex and believes that investigating couples having sex in car parks may be the answer. The script is never convincing and it is neither funny nor strong enough on satire – and ultimately it is rather boring. GS

▶ Luke Treadaway, Richard Riddell, Terry A Johnson, Michael Groom, Justine Glenton, Sammy Dobson.
▶ *Dir* and *Ed* Simon Ellis, *Pro* Jane Hooks, Allan Niblo, James Richardson and Brock Norman Brock, *Screenplay* Brock, *Ph* Robert Hardy, *Pro Des* Sami Khan, *M* Tom Bailey, *Cos* Jo Mapp.

Vertigo Films-Vertigo Films.
108 mins. UK. 2009. Rel: 28 Dec 2009. Cert. 18.

Dogtooth ★★½

Like *Home* [qv], this is a stylised work and its characters seem to exist solely to serve the thesis that the patriarchal family is deadly dangerous and deforms us. The film has won awards but it's so busy being sexually explicit that it never develops its ideas in a way that enables us to become involved in its unreal metaphorical world. It's often obscure, sometimes shocking and far too distancing – but feel free to disagree. (Original title: *Kynodontas*) MS

▶ Christos Stergioglou, Michelle Valley, Aggeliki Papoulia, Christos Passalis, Mary Tsoni.

▶ *Dir* Yorgos Lanthimos, *Pro* Yorgos Tsourgiannis, *Screenplay* Lanthimos and Efthimis Filippo, *Ph* Thimios Bakatakis, *Art Dir* and *Cos* Elli Papageorgakopoulou, *Ed* Yorgos Mavropsaridis.

Boo Productions/Greek Film Center/Yorgos Lanthimos/ Horsefly Productions-Verve Pictures.
97 mins. Greece. 2009. Rel: 23 April 2010. Cert. 18.

Dorian Gray ★★★

Having filmed a couple of Oscar Wilde's plays, Oliver Parker now turns to his novel *The Picture of Dorian Gray*. He retains some of the Wildean dialogue but chooses to treat the story of the man whose portrait ages while he himself does not as a Gothic horror tale. Handled thus, this aspect of the film recalls the heyday of Hammer. The result is a clash of styles reconciled only by Colin Firth as Dorian's mentor. MS

▶ Ben Barnes, Colin Firth, Ben Chaplin, Rebecca Hall, Rachel Hurd-Wood, Fiona Shaw.
▶ *Dir* Oliver Parker, *Pro* Barnaby Thompson, *Screenplay* Toby Finlay, from Oscar Wilde's novel *The Picture of Dorian Gray*, *Ph* Roger Pratt, *Pro Des* John Beard, *Ed* Guy Bensley, *M* Charlie Mole, *Cos* Ruth Myers.

Ealing Studios/Alliance Films/UK Film Council/Fragile etc-Momentum Pictures.
112 mins. UK/Cayman Islands/Canada. 2009. Rel: 9 Sep 2009. Cert. 15.

Double Take ★★½

Hitchcock becomes his own McGuffin in this avant-garde exercise by Johan Grimonprez; at the 2009 London Film Festival it was screened under the heading 'Experimenta'. I am totally

Beyond its shelf life: Ben Barnes in the title role of Oliver Parker's *Dorian Gray*.

unpersuaded by this essay film's thesis that Hitchcockian suspense in the 1960s was on a par with that era's political manipulation. As for footage of Hitch from film trailers and TV introductions, it only confirms that he was a one-off with no convincing double. The film is a genuine oddity but hardly more than that. MS

▷ With Ron Burrage, Delfine Bafort and the voice of Mark Perry.
▷ *Dir* and *Screenplay* Johan Grimonprez, *Pro* Emmy Oost and Grimonprez, *Story by* Tom McCarthy, inspired by the essay *24 August 1983* by Jorge Luis Borges, *Ph* Martin Testar and Hans Buyse, *Art Dir* Pol Heyvaert, *Ed* Dieter Diependaele and Tyler Hubby, *M* Christian Halten, *Cos* Nathalie Lermitte.
Zapomatik/Nikovantastic Film/Volya Films etc-Soda Pictures.
83 mins. Belgium/Germany/The Netherlands/Italy/France/USA/UK. 2009. Rel: 2 Apr 2010. Cert. 12A.

Down Terrace ★★★★

This daring gangster drama is a cross between Mike Leigh and *The Royle Family* with a touch of Jacobean tragedy. When Karl (Robin Hill) gets acquitted, his father Bill (Robert Hill) wants to know who grassed him up to the police. It is compelling stuff where it is difficult to know whom to trust. There are some amazing performances, particularly from Julia Deakin as Maggie – Karl's deceptively sweet mother – who may be capable of much tougher things than just making a cup of tea. GS

▷ Robin Hill, Robert Hill, Julia Deakin, David Schaal, Tony Way, Kitty Blue.
▷ *Dir* Ben Wheatley, *Pro* Andrew Starke, *Screenplay*

Wheatley and Robin Hill, *Ph* Laurie Rose, *Ed* Wheatley and Robin Hill, *M* Jim Williams.
Baby Cow Productions/Boum Productions-Magnet Releasing.
89 mins. UK. 2009. Rel: 30 July 2010. Cert. 15.

Dragon Hunters ★★

While French animation sealed its standing with *Belleville rendez-vous* and *The Illusionist*, this CG fantasy hardly ups the ante. Unable to compete with the fantastical magic of Japan's Hayao Miyazaki or the entertainment value of, say, Hollywood's *How to Train Your Dragon*, this slim tale follows the fortunes of a girl determined to best a fearsome dragon known as the World Gobbler. Good for her. Unfortunately, neither the characterisation nor the plotting can match the visuals, while the film's derivative disposition (think *Mulan* meets *Avatar*) is disappointing (Original title: *Chasseurs de dragons*) CB

▷ Voices of Forest Whitaker, John DiMaggio, Jess Harnell, Nick Jameson, Mary Matilyn Mouser, Rob Paulsen.
▷ *Dir* Guillaume Ivernel and Arthur Qwak, *Pro* Philippe Delarue, *Screenplay* Qwak and Frédéric Lenoir, *Ed* Soline Guyonneau, *M* Klaus Badelt.
Luxanimation/Futurikin/Trixter Film-Stealth Media Group.
80 mins. UK/France/Germany/USA/Italy/Spain etc. 2008. Rel: 24 Sep 2010. Cert. PG.

Dream Home ★★★½

This extremely violent satire on the ruthless housing market in Hong Kong claims to be based on a true story. Cheng (Josie Ho) dreams

Keep off the grass: Kitty Blue and Michael Smiley in Ben Wheatley's compelling, well acted Down Terrace.

Home improvement: Ho-cheung Pang's stylish, extremely violent *Dream Home.*

of buying a luxurious apartment with a sea view but even with two jobs she is still unable to afford it as its value keeps rapidly increasing. Then she dreams of the perfect plan but it requires her to resort to extreme measures... Ho-cheung Pang's stylish horror is certainly not for the squeamish, particularly a sequence with a pregnant woman. (Original title: *Wai doe lei ah yut ho*) GS

▶ Josie Ho, Eason Chan, Michelle Ye, Juno Mak, Norman Chu, Chu-chu Zhou.
▶ *Dir* Ho-cheung Pang, *Pro* Pang, Conroy Chan, Subi Wang and Chi-chung, *Screenplay* Pang, Kwok-cheung Tsang and Chi-man Wan, from a story by Pang, *Ph* Nelson Yu Lik-wai, *Pro Des* Lim Chung Man, *Ed* Wenders Li, *M* Gabriele Roberto.
852 Films/Making Film-Network Releasing.
96 mins. Hong Kong. 2010. Rel: 19 Nov 2010. Cert. 18.

Driving Aphrodite ★★

Rom-com with Nia (*My Big Fat Greek Wedding*) Vardalos as Georgia, an unlucky-in-love, reluctant tour guide in Athens, whose American visitors want nothing more than a run round the souvenir shops. Her fellow guide (Alistair McGowan) gets the more intelligent Canadians. An encounter with Irv, an older US tourist (Richard Dreyfuss), leads Georgia in another direction romantically as she finds love where she least expects it. This is a fairly stone-faced comedy saved only by the photogenic surroundings of sunny Athens in what could be called *My Big Fat Unfunny Movie.* (Original title: *My Life in Ruins*) MHD

▶ Nia Vardalos, Richard Dreyfuss, Maria Adanez, Sheila Bernette, Mario Botto, Rachel Dratch, Alexis Georgoulis, Ralph Nossek, Bernice Stegers, Alistair McGowan, Harland Williams, Ian Ogilvy.
▶ *Dir* Donald Petrie, *Pro* Michelle Chydzik Sowa and Nathalie Marciano, *Screenplay* Mike Reiss, *Ph* José Luis Alcaine, *Pro Des* David Chapman, *Ed* Patrick J Don Vito, *M* David Newman, *Cos* Lala Huete and Lena Mossum.
Warner Bros Pictures/Echo Bridge Entertainment/26 Films/Kanzaman Productions etc-Warner Bros.
95 mins. USA/Spain. 2009. Rel: 2 Oct 2009. Cert. 12A.

Due Date ★★★

Peter (Robert Downey Jr) is running out of time if he is to reach Los Angeles for his baby's birth and, after he is thrown off a plane, he is forced to share a car with Ethan (Zach Galifianakis), an aspiring actor who turns everything he touches into disaster... It is a fun premise but there are not as many gags and surprises as in Todd Phillips' earlier film *The Hangover.* It is mildly entertaining and Galifianakis works well with Downey, confirming his rising star status. GS

▶ Robert Downey Jr, Zach Galifianakis, Michelle Monaghan, Jamie Foxx, Juliette Lewis.
▶ *Dir* Todd Phillips, *Pro* Phillips and Daniel Goldberg, *Screenplay* Phillips, Alan R Cohen, Alan Freedland and Adam Sztykiel, from a story by Cohen and Freedland, *Ph* Lawrence Sher, *Pro Des* Bill Brzeski, *Ed* Debra Neil-Fisher, *M* Christophe Beck, *Cos* Louise Mingenbach.
Warner Bros Pictures/Legendary Pictures/Green Hat Films-Warner Bros.
95 mins. USA. 2010. Rel: 5 Nov 2010. Cert. 15.

Easier with Practice ★★★½

Brian Geraghty gives one of the best performances of recent years in this sexually frank road movie, said to be based on fact. It concerns a writer travelling through New Mexico with his brother and becoming obsessed with a stranger whose unsolicited call has led to telephone sex. It's an intriguing work of some quality but, whatever the origins of the piece, the crucial twist in the tail is not persuasive. MS

▶ Brian Geraghty, Kel O'Neill, Marguerite Moreau, Jeanette Brox, Eugene Byrd.
▶ *Dir* Kyle Patrick Alvarez, *Pro* Cookie Carosella and Alvarez, *Screenplay* Alvarez, based on the true story by Davy Rothbart, *Ph* David Morrison, *Pro Des* Brooke Peters, *Ed* Fernando Collins, *Cos* Tom Soluri.

Forty Second Productions-Axiom Films.
100 mins. USA. 2009. Rel: 3 Dec 2010. Cert. 15.

Easy A ★★★★

In order to impress her best friend, Olive (Emma Stone) lies that she had a date with a fantasy man. The news soon spreads around their high school and Olive becomes a 'scarlet' woman... The script is a little gem in Will Gluck's charming and highly original film. There are fun references to Nathaniel Hawthorne's book *The Scarlet Letter* and its two film versions: "I like the original, not the version with Demi Moore and her fake British accent," Olive claims. Stone delivers a star-making performance and is well supported by a tremendous cast, particularly by Stanley Tucci and Patricia Clarkson as her eccentric parents. GS

▶ Emma Stone, Thomas Haden Church, Penn Badgley, Dan Byrd, Patricia Clarkson, Lisa Kudrow, Malcolm McDowell, Stanley Tucci.
▶ *Dir* Will Gluck, *Pro* Gluck and Zane Devine, *Screenplay* Bert V Royal, *Ph* Michael Grady, *Pro Des* Marcia Hinds, *Ed* Susan Littenberg, *M* Brad Segal, *Cos* Mynka Draper.

Screen Gems/Olive Bridge Entertainment-Sony Pictures Releasing.
92 mins. USA. 2010. Rel: 22 Oct 2010. Cert. 15.

Eat Pray Love ★★★½

True to its title, this big and broad adaptation of Elizabeth Gilbert's true-life bestseller has eating, praying and a whole lotta lovin'. More importantly, these activities are represented by the infinitely picturesque Italy, India and Indonesia, each country lit up by the high-wattage smile of Julia Roberts in her biggest role since *Erin Brockovich*. And Ms Roberts give good smile. Her director, Ryan Murphy, does good travelogue and here infuses Ms Gilbert's well-thumbed, soul-searching pages with vibrancy, warmth, poetry, humour and passion. JC-W

▶ Julia Roberts, Javier Bardem, Richard Jenkins, Billy Crudup, Viola Davis, James Franco.
▶ *Dir* Ryan Murphy, *Pro* Dede Gardner, *Screenplay*

Travel slickness: Julia Roberts in Ryan Murphy's vibrant and glossy *Eat Pray Love*.

Murphy and Jennifer Salt based on the book by Elizabeth Gilbert, *Ph* Robert Richardson, *Pro Des* Bill Groom, *Ed* Brad Buecker, *M* Dario Marianelli, *Cos* Michael Dennison.

Columbia Pictures/Red Om Films/Syzygy Productions/ Plan B Entertainment/India Take One-Sony Pictures Releasing.
133 mins. USA. 2010. Rel: 24 Sep 2010. Cert. PG.

Eccentricities of a Blonde-haired Girl ★★★★

Portuguese film-maker Manoel de Oliveira is now a centenarian. This film of his may be slight and of specialised appeal but how beautifully crafted it is. Told in flashback, it's the story of a young man who seeks his fortune abroad in order to impress the mother of a girl who has taken his eye to the point of obsession. The sensual eroticism of the tale is spellbinding, yet the film displays the utmost artistic refinement. MS

➤ Ricardo Trêpa, Catarina Wallenstein, Diogo Dória, Júlia Buisel, Leonor Silveira.
➤ *Dir* Manoel de Oliveira, *Pro* François D'Artémare, Maria João Mayer, Luis Miñarro etc, *Screenplay* Oliveira, from the story by Eça de Queiroz, *Ph* Sabine Lancelin, *Art Dir* Christian Marti and José Pedro Penha, *Ed* Oliveira and Catherine Krassovsky, *Cos* Adelaide Maria Trêpa.

Filmes do Tejo II (Portugal)/Les Films de l'Après-Midi (France)/Eddie Saeta S.A. (Spain) etc-New Wave Films.
63 mins. Portugal/France/Spain/Germany. 2009. Rel: 6 Aug 2010. Cert. U.

Echoes of Home ★★★

A documentary about yodelling in the Swiss Alps may not be such an attractive prospect but surprisingly Stefan Schwietert's eccentric film grows on you. He follows three vocal artists through the magnificent Alpine landscape and examines the origin of their music. Christian Zehnder is performing in popular concerts and collaborating with Mongolian throat singing legends Huun Huur Tu, while the Swiss-American vocal and performance artist Ericka Stucky provides welcome light relief. In addition, Noldi Alder, the youngest member of a legendary family dynasty, is now in his fifties and still experiments with more innovative yodelling styles. (Original title: *Heimatklänge*) GS

➤ Erika Stucky, Noldi Alder, Christian Zehnder, Huun Huur Tu.
➤ *Dir* and *Screenplay* Stefan Schwietert, *Pro* Brigtte Hofer and Cornelia Seitler, *Ph* Pio Corradi and Ueli Nüesch, *Ed* Stephan Krumbiegel and Calle Overweg, *M* Knut Jensen.

Maximage GmbH/Schweizer Fernsehen/Zerofilm GmbH-ICA Films.
82 mins. Switzerland/Germany. 2007. Rel: 10 July 2009. No Cert.

Eclipse: see **Twilight Saga: Eclipse**

Edge of Darkness ★★★

As one who never saw the TV piece from which this is derived, I can declare this to be an unexceptional but adequate thriller in which a company is the arch villain. The central figure is Mel Gibson's investigating policeman who loses his daughter (the highly promising Bojana Novakovic) in a shooting incident. Despite a sentimental conclusion, the film plays up the violence to a sometimes laughable extent, but in general it's both watchable and utterly unmemorable. MS

➤ Mel Gibson, Ray Winstone, Danny Huston, Bojana Novakovic, Shawn Roberts.
➤ *Dir* Martin Campbell, *Pro* Graham King, Tim Headington and Michael Wearing, *Screenplay* William Monahan and Andrew Bovell, based on the TV series written by Troy Kennedy Martin, *Ph* Phil Méheux, *Pro Des* Tom Sanders, *Ed* Stuart Baird, *M* Howard Shore, *Cos* Lindy Hemming.

GK Films/BBC Films/Icon Productions-Icon Film Distribution.
117 mins. USA/UK. 2010. Rel: 29 Jan 2010. Cert. 15.

An Education ★★★★½

Danish director Lone Scherfig and writer Nick Hornby have turned Lynn Barber's memoir of 1960s teenage seduction into a credible period film. Innocent Jenny can't wait to explore the world of art, French films and recitals with David, the smart but smarmy older man who picks her up. Carey Mulligan is a delight as Jenny and Peter Sarsgaard decidedly creepy as the seducer offering her excitements culminating in a trip to Paris.

After seven years away from the big screen, Mel Gibson returns in Martin Campbell's utterly unmemorable Edge of Darkness.

Learning curve:
Carey Mulligan in
her Oscar-nominated
performance as Jenny
in Lone Scherfig's
shocking, funny
and moving
An Education.

Good support by Alfred Molina as Jenny's gauche father, Dominic Cooper as David's friend and Rosamund Pike as his ditsy co-conspirator in this marvellous evocation of an innocent escaping suburban ordinariness. MHD

▶ Peter Sarsgaard, Alfred Molina, Rosamund Pike, Dominic Cooper, Olivia Williams, Emma Thompson, Carey Mulligan, Sally Hawkins, Cara Seymour.
▶ *Dir* Lone Scherfig, *Pro* Amanda Posey and Fiona Dwyer, *Screenplay* Nick Hornby, based on the memoir by Lynn Barber, *Ph* John de Borman, *Pro Des* Andrew McAlpine, *Ed* Barney Pilling, *M* Paul Englishby, *Cos* Odile Dicks-Mireaux.

BBC Films/Finola Dwyer Productions/Wildgaze Films etc-E1 Entertainment.
100 mins. UK. 2009. Rel: 30 Oct 2009. Cert. 12A.

Embodiment of Evil ★★½

Brazilian cult director José Mojica Marins also plays Coffin Joe, the loathsome character he created in *At Midnight I'll Take Your Soul* (1963). Coffin Joe is still looking for the woman who will deliver him the perfect son and, again as in the earlier films in the series, the over-enthusiastic but mostly amateurish acting is very loud. The film is a hallucinatory cocktail of gory horror scenes involving snakes, spiders and brutal killings. It is badly re-voiced, repetitive but curiously addictive. (Original title: *Encarnação do demônio*) GS

▶ José Mojica Marins, Jece Valadão, Adrano Stuart,

Milhem Cortaz, Rui Resende.
▶ *Dir* José Mojica Marins, *Pro* Caio Gullane, Fabiano Gullane, Débora Ivanov and Paulo Sacramento, *Screenplay* Marins and Dennison Ramalho, *Ph* José Roberto Eliezer, *Pro Des* Cássio Amarante, *Ed* Paulo Sacramento, *M* André Abujamra and Marcio Nigro, *Cos* David Parizotti.

Gullane Filmes/Olhos de Cão Produções Cinematográficas-Anchor Bay Entertainment.
94 mins. Brazil. 2008. Rel: 4 July 2009. Cert. 18.

Enemies of the People ★★★★

One could ask for some tightening of the material here but this is undoubtedly a humane historical document of real value. Thet Sambath, one of the film-makers, lost his family in the killing fields of Cambodia and is here seen devoting himself to tracing and talking to the man who, following the death of Pol Pot, became the most prominent figure in that regime to survive. Sambath comes to see this monster as someone who is also a human being and reconciliation is an issue tackled by this very fine film. MS

▶ With Thet Sambath, Nuon Chea, Khoun, Suon.
▶ *Dir*, *Pro*, *Ph* and *Screenplay* Rob Lemkin and Thet Sambath, *Ed* Stefan Ronowicz, *M* Daniel Pemberton.

Old Street Films/Thet Sambath etc-Dogwoof Pictures.
93 mins. UK/Cambodia/USA. 2009. Rel: 10 Dec 2010. No Cert.

Enter the Void ★★½

That great provocateur, Gaspar Noé, knocks you for six with astounding visuals in Scope and a stunning sense of cinema. But even the shorter version released here lasts all of 142 minutes and Noé's story about a drug dealer and his sister in Tokyo loses interest and clarity all too soon. The characters are people for whom one has no sympathy but the film is something of an acid trip and may well become a cult. But some will find it so self-indulgent that in the end they'll be praying for it to end. MS

▶ Paz de la Huerta, Nathaniel Brown, Cyril Roy, Olly Alexander, Massato Tanno.
▶ *Dir* Gaspar Noé, *Pro* Brahim Chioua, Vincent Maraval, Olivier Delbosc, etc, *Screenplay* Noé with Lucile Hadzihalilovic, *Ph* Benoît Debie, *Pro Des* Kikuo Ohta and Jean Carrière, *Ed* Noé, Marc Boucrot and Jerome Pesnel, *Cos* Tony Crosbie and Nicoletta Massone.
Wild Bunch/Fidélité/BUF/Les Cinémas de la Zone etc-Trinity Filmed Entertainment.
142 mins. France/USA/Germany/Italy/Japan/Canada. 2010. Rel: 24 Sep 2010. Cert. 18.

Erasing David ★★½

David Bond is determined to prove in this egocentric documentary that there is no such thing as privacy these days, especially in England, which is the third most intrusive surveillance state in the world. He hires two private investigators to track him down as he attempts to disappear, leaving his pregnant wife and young child behind. Bond's film verges on paranoia as he claims that even Facebook is a CIA invention in order to keep tabs on us. GS

▶ Frank M Ahearn, David Bond, Cameron Gowlett, Duncan Mee.
▶ *Dir* David Bond and Melinda McDougall, *Pro* Ashley Jones, *Ph* Annemarie Lean-Vercoe, *Ed* Steve Barclay and Wojciech Duczmal, *M* Michael Nyman and Andy Simms.
Green Lions-Channel 4.
80 mins. UK. 2009. Rel: 29 Apr 2010. No Cert.

Everybody's Fine ★★½

Robert De Niro here gives one of his better performances of recent years, but it's wasted on a remake of an Italian movie of the same title made by Giuseppe Tornatore in 1990. As before, but even more emphatically now, we have a totally improbable family tale about a harsh father adjusting his attitude to his grown children following his wife's death. Despite the efforts of its cast, it's sentimental, bogus and a waste of time. MS

▶ Robert De Niro, Drew Barrymore, Kate Beckinsale, Sam Rockwell, Melissa Leo.
▶ *Dir* and *Screenplay* (from Giuseppe Tornatore's film *Stanno tutti bene*) Kirk Jones, *Pro* Gianni Nunnari, Ted Field, Vittorio Cecchi Gori and Glynis Murray, *Ph* Henry Braham, *Pro Des* Andrew Jackness, *Ed* Andrew Mondshein, *M* Dario Marianelli, *Cos* Aude Bronson-Howard.
Miramax Films/Radar Pictures/Hollywood Gang Productions-Buena Vista.
99 mins. USA. 2009. Rel: 26 Feb 2010. Cert. 12A.

Exam ★★★★

Far better than you might expect, this modest but ambitious British drama concentrates on eight people vying for a job by taking an enigmatic test paper in an enclosed and guarded room. It's a film of game-playing but adroitly made, despite the limited setting, and written so as to provide a metaphor about how we choose to react to others. Neatly done, it makes Stuart Hazeldine, the man behind it, a name to look out for. MS

▶ Nathalie Cox, Jimi Mistry, Chuk Iwuji, Colin Salmon, Luke Mably, Gemma Chan.
▶ *Dir* and *Screenplay* (from a story by Simon Garrity and himself) Stuart Hazeldine, *Pro* Hazeldine and Gareth Unwin, *Ph* Tim Wooster, *Pro Des* Patrick

Family man: Robert De Niro with Kate Beckinsale in Kirk Jones' predictable and mawkish remake, *Everybody's Fine*.

Bill, *Ed* Mark Talbot-Butler, *M* Stephen Barton, *Cos* Rebecca Gore.

Hazeldine Films/Bedlam Productions-Hazeldine Films. 101 mins. UK. 2009. Rel: 8 Jan 2010. Cert. 15.

Examined Life ★★★★

One of the best of recent documentaries, this film by Astra Taylor offers a well-designed opportunity for nine philosophers to talk in a non-daunting way about their attitudes to life. Taylor presents it in segments which have a real cinematic feel to them since they utilise walks and other settings to provide a varied and relevant background. You won't take to all the contributors equally, but that's a matter of personal taste and this is an admirably intelligent and considered film. MS

▶ With Cornel West, Judith Butler, Kwame Anthony Appiah, Peter Singer, Slavoj Zizek.
▶ *Dir* and *Screenplay* Astra Taylor, *Pro* Bill Imperial and Lea Marin, *Ph* John M. Tran, *Ed* Robert Kennedy.

Sphinx Productions/National Film Board of Canada etc-ICA Films.
97 mins. Canada. 2008. Rel: 2 Nov 2009. No Cert.

Exit Through the Gift Shop
★★★★★

Disconnected: A scene from Banksy's mischievous *Exit Through the Gift Shop.*

Graffiti artist Banksy perpetuates the mystery behind his fame with this entertaining documentary which follows the story of Thierry Guetta, the eccentric French shopkeeper and amateur film enthusiast whose quest to find and befriend Bansky becomes an obsession. But Bansky turns his camera on Guetta instead... The film has a mischievous and wicked sense of fun not dissimilar to Banksy's outrageous work, and the sequence where he smuggles a life-size statue of a Guantanamo Bay detainee into Disneyland is to be treasured. GS

▶ Banksy, Shepard Fairey, Thierry Guetta, Rhys Ifans, Space Invader, Joshua Levine.
▶ *Dir* Banksy, *Pro* James Gay-Rees, Jaimie D'Cruz and Holly Cushing, *Ph* Jerry Henry, *Ed* Chris King.

Paranoid Pictures-Revolver Entertainment.
87 mins. USA/UK. 2010. Rel: 5 Mar 2010. Cert. 15.

The Expendables ★½

There is a certain morbid fascination in watching a gang of ol' boys past their sell-by date getting together for one last shoot-'em-up. But there's no Tarantino script to inspire thoughts of career re-invention and so a whole forest of dead wood do what they've always done, only with bigger guns and more liver spots. Mindless and offensive, the film follows the pursuits of a bunch of ageing mercenaries – and the 37-year-old Jason Statham – as they single-handedly destroy an entire country somewhere in South America. JC-W

▶ Sylvester Stallone, Jason Statham, Jet Li, Eric Roberts, Dolph Lundgren, Mickey Rourke.

▶ *Dir* Sylvester Stallone, *Pro* Kevin King, John Thompson, Avi Lerner etc, *Screenplay* Stallone and David Callaham, from a story by Callaham, *Ph* Jeffrey Kimball, *Pro Des* Franco-Giacomo Carbone, *Ed* Ken Blackwell and Paul Harb, *M* Brian Tyler, *Cos* Lizz Wolf.

Millennium Films/Nu Image/Rogue Marble-Lionsgate. 103 mins. USA. 2010. Rel: 19 Aug 2010. Cert. 15.

Extract ★★★★

Beavis & Butthead creator Mike Judge continues to mine the workplace for comedy. *Office Space* took on the plight of white-collar workers; *Extract* casts Jason Bateman as the factory owner with industrial relations problems and more. Judge seems very much at home in this territory, which he appears to be making all his own. It's also very, very funny – but with an underlying human warmth. JC

▶ Jason Bateman, Mila Kunis, Kristen Wiig, Ben Affleck, J K Simmons, Gene Simmons.
▶ *Dir* and *Screenplay* Mike Judge, *Pro* John Altschuler and Michael Rotenberg, *Ph* Tim Suhrstedt, *Pro Des* Maher Ahmad, *Ed* Julia Wong, *M* George S Clinton, *Cos* Alix Friedberg.

Ternion Pictures/F & A Productions/3 Arts Entertainment-Paramount Pictures. 92 mins. USA. 2009. Rel: 23 Apr 2010. Cert. 15.

Extraordinary Measures ★★

Behind the soapy dynamics of this 'disease of the week' clunker is a fascinating story. Informed that both his son and daughter are terminally ill with the rare Pompe disease, businessman John Crowley refuses to accept the inevitable – and sets out to change medical history. It's an empowering premise but is reduced to trite simplicity in this slick, one-dimensional treatment. Frankly, Brendan Fraser lacks the emotional complexity to trace Crowley's psychological journey while Andrea Guerra's ghastly score reduces the whole thing to formulaic bathos. JC-W

▶ Brendan Fraser, Harrison Ford, Keri Russell, Meredith Droeger, Diego Velazquez, Sam M Hall, Jared Harris.
▶ *Dir* Tom Vaughan, *Pro* Stacey Sher, Michael Shamberg and Carla Santos Shamberg, *Screenplay* Robert Nelson Jacobi, from the book *The Cure: How a Father Raised $1 Million – and Bucked the Medical Establishment – in a Quest to Save His Children* by Geeta Anand, *Ph* Andrew Dunn, *Pro Des* Derek R Hill, *Ed* Anne V Coates, *M* Andrea Guerra, *Cos* Deena Appel.

CBS Films/Double Feature Films-Sony Pictures Releasing. 106 mins. USA. 2010. Rel: 26 Feb 2010. Cert. PG

Eyes Wide Open ★★★½

This story of gay love in Israel is ably acted and the director, Haim Tabakman, displays a very special skill in telling stories by distinctively visual means. In dramatic terms there's a striking

Unorthodox Orthodox: Ran Danker (right) strays from the gospel in Haim Tabakman's *Eyes Wide Open.*

moral conflict in the situation of a butcher who is a married man with children yet comes to realise that he is basically gay and can only fulfil his true nature by hurting those close to him. However, despite an unnecessarily bleak ending, the film fails to capture to the full the intensity of the dilemma. (Original title: *Einaym pkuhot*) MS

▶ Zohar Strauss, Ran Danker, Tinkerbell, Tzahi Grad, Isaac Sharry, Avy Grayinik.
▶ *Dir* Haim Tabakman, *Pro* Rafael Katz, Michael Eckelt, Isabelle Attal and David C Barrot, *Screenplay* Merav Doster, *Ph* Axel Schneppat, *Art Dir* Avi Fahima, *Ed* Dov Steuer, *M* Nathaniel Mechaly, *Cos* Yam Brusilovsky.

Pimpa Film Productions/Rafael Katz Company/Riva Filmproduktion GmbH etc-Peccadillo Pictures. 96 mins. Israel/Germany/France. 2009. Rel: 14 May 2010. Cert. 12A.

F ★

Here, at last, is a film brave enough to address the issue of hoodies and their supposed threat to society. Sadly, this just proves to be an excuse to produce a low-budget, low-IQ horror quickie featuring a cast of seemingly deaf and idiotic teachers and pupils. In fact, *F* – the fateful grade given to an incompetent student – is a film so meaningless, monotonous and inept that it really doesn't deserve to be written about. JC-W

▶ David Schofield, Eliza Bennett, Ruth Gemmell, Juliet Aubrey, Tom Mannion, Emma Cleasby.
▶ *Dir* and *Screenplay* Johannes Roberts, *Pro* Paul Blacknell and Ernest Riera, *Ph* Tim Sidell, *Pro Des* Malin Lindholm, *Ed* John Palmer, *M* Neil Stemp, *Cos* Anna-Louise Day.

Black Robe/Gatlin Pictures-Optimum Releasing. 79 mins. UK. 2010. Rel: 17 Sep 2010. Cert. 18.

Fame ★½

This is a redundant remake of Alan Parker's 1980 musical which was by no means faultless

Family film: Louis-Do de Lencquesaing and Alice de Lencquesaing in Mia Hansen-Løve's splendid *Father of My Children*.

but looks like a masterpiece compared to this. The original was fun and engaging, with strong dancing and exciting songs, whereas this is dull and uninspiring despite the strong presence of Debbie Allen, Charles S Dutton, Kelsey Grammer, Megan Mullaly and Bebe Neuwirth as the school's instructors. Again a group of young hopefuls join New York City High School of Performing Arts seeking fame but, finally, who cares? GS

▶ Kay Panabaker, Kherington Payne, Megan Mullally, Charles S Dutton, Debbie Allen, Kelsey Grammer, Naturi Naughton, Bebe Neuwirth, Asher Book.
▶ *Dir* Kevin Tancharoen, *Pro* Mark Canton, Richard S Wright, Tom Rosenberg and Gary Lucchesi, *Screenplay* Allison Burnett based on the 1980 screenplay by Christopher Gore, *Ph* Scott Kevan, *Pro Des* Paul Eads, *Ed* Myron I Kerstein, *M* Mark Isham, *Cos* Dayna Pink.

Lakeshore Entertainment/Metro-Goldwyn-Mayer Pictures/United Artists-Entertainment Film Distributors. 107 mins. USA. 2009. Rel: 25 Sep 2009. Cert. PG.

Fantastic Mr. Fox ★★★★

Wes Anderson turns to animation by way of adapting Roald Dahl's book about a fox, his family and their fight against crafty farmers. It's a surprise coming from this director, but it's also a labour of love and that shows. As an engaging work likely to appeal to both children and adults, it invites comparison with Nick Park's *Chicken Run*. There's expert voicing of the characters by the likes of George Clooney, Meryl Streep and – as the big British villain of the piece – Michael Gambon. MS

▶ With the voices of George Clooney, Meryl Streep, Jason Schwartzman, Bill Murray, Michael Gambon, Willem Dafoe, Owen Wilson, Jarvis Cocker, Wes Anderson.
▶ *Dir* Wes Anderson, *Pro* Alison Abbate, Scott Rudin, Anderson and Jeremy Dawson, *Screenplay* Anderson and Noah Baumbach, based on the book by Roald Dahl, *Ph* Tristan Oliver, *Pro Des* Nelson Lowry, *Ed*

Ralph Foster and Stephen Perkins, *M* Alexandre Desplat, *Animation Dir* Mark Gustafson.

Twentieth Century Fox/Indian Paintbrush/Regency Enterprises/American Empirical -20th Century Fox. 87 mins. USA. 2009. Rel: 23 Oct 2009. Cert. PG.

Father of my Children ★★★★

The first half of Mia Hansen-Løve's acclaimed film portrays marvellously the hectic life of a film producer in Paris who believes in cinema as an art form. It is, in fact, a story that echoes the life of just such a man, Humbert Balsan, who committed suicide in 2005. In the key role Louis-Do de Lencquesaing is superb, but the second half is paler by far and lacks a sense of direction. However, there is much here that is splendid. (Original title: *Le Père de mes enfants*) MS

▶ Louis-Do de Lencquesaing, Chiara Caselli, Alice de Lencquesaing, Alice Gautier.
▶ *Dir* and *Screenplay* Mia Hansen-Løve, *Pro* Philippe Martin and David Thion, *Ph* Pascal Auffray, *Art Dir* Mathieu Menut, *Ed* Marion Monnier, *M* Christian Garcia, *Cos* Bethsabée Dreyfus.

Les films Pelléas/27 Films/Arte France Cinéma & Acte II etc-Artificial Eye. 111 mins. France/Germany. 2009. Rel: 5 Mar 2010. Cert. 12A.

Fathers of Girls ★★

The promising dramatic notion here is to tell a story about the special bond between fathers and daughters. The chosen context is that of a lawyer (Ray Winstone) coming to terms with his child's death from a drug overdose. But as written and directed the piece proves both dull and inept. Indeed, one gets the impression, however erroneous, that one is watching the kind of home movie that is the cinematic equivalent of vanity publishing in the book world. MS

▶ Ray Winstone, Chloe Howman, Glen Murphy, Lois Winstone, Luke Kempner.
▶ *Dir* and *Screenplay* Karl Howman and Ethem Çetintas, *Pro* Riza Nur Paçalioglu, *Ph* Digby Elliott, *Pro Des* Neil Pollard, *Ed* Ash Mills, *M* Stuart Roslyn, *Cos* Julie Evans.

Silver Productions/Linefilm/FoG Films-Soda Pictures. 76 mins. UK. 2010. Rel: 19 Nov 2010. Cert. 15.

Fezeka's Voice ★★★★

This heartfelt documentary follows a choir of South African teenagers from the Fezeka High School in Gugulethu outside Cape Town as they prepare for a trip to Salisbury Cathedral in order to take part in an international concert. These talented kids are trying to succeed against all odds and are blessed with choirmaster Phumi Tsewu, whose dedication in honing their gift is hugely admirable. It is powerful, moving and a work of great dignity. GS

▶ With Fezeka High School Choir, Phumi Tsewu etc.
▶ *Dir, Ph* and *Ed* Holly Lubbock, *Pro* Katherine Crawley and Joanne Fishburn.

Ciel Productions/All Living Things-Ciel Productions. 80 mins. UK/South Africa. 2009. Rel: 12 Nov 2010. No Cert.

The Final ★★

A group of high school students are being continually bullied, so it is time to turn the tables and take revenge on their tormentors. They join forces and organise a fancy dress party in a remote farmhouse where they drug the guests and begin the torture... Joey Stewart's debut horror takes its time to introduce his characters and that enables us to root for the victims. Sadly, as the film develops credibility is lost and so is our interest in the plight of these people. GS

▶ Marc Donato, Jascha Washington, Whitney Hoy, Lindsay Seidel, Julin.
▶ *Dir* Joey Stewart, *Pro* and *Screenplay* Jason Kabolati, *Ph* Dave McFarland, *Pro Des* Eric Whitney, *Ed* Bill Marcellus, *M* Damon Criswell, *Cos* Stephen M Chudej.

Agora Entertainment-Chelsea Films. 93 mins. USA. 2010. Rel: 13 Aug 2010. Cert. 18.

The Final Destination ★★★★

The fourth of this successful but predictable series begins in a car-racing stadium. Nick (Bobby Campo) has the horrific premonition that the racing cars will crash into the spectators and he and his friends will meet a terrible death. He convinces his friends to leave before his premonition comes true. But death feels cheated and demands to take each one of the survivors in the most bizarre situations... David R Ellis' predictable horror works thanks to the cleverly constructed set-pieces and terrific use of 3D effects. GS

▶ Bobby Campo, Shantel VanSanten, Nck Zano, Haley Webb, Krista Allen.
▶ *Dir* David R Ellis, *Pro* Craig Perry and Warren Zide, *Screenplay* Eric Bress, based on characters by Jeffrey Reddick, *Ph* Glen MacPherson, *Pro Des* Jaymes Hinkle, *Ed* Mark Stevens, *M* Brian Tyler, *Cos* Claire Breaux.

New Line Cinema/FlipZide Pictures/Practical Pictures/ Parallel Zide-Entertainment Film Distributors. 82 mins. USA. 2009. Rel: 28 Aug 2009. Cert. 15.

Fireball ★★★½

The story of two brothers both played by Thai rock star Preeti 'Bank' Barameeanat. When Tai gets released from prison he finds his twin brother Tan in hospital, deep in a coma following a brutal attack. Tai, determined to find those responsible for his brother's condition, poses as Tan and gains

entry into the deadly underground sport called Fireball, a combination of basketball with the brutal Muay Thai fighting. It is yet another revenge story but has masses of energy and imaginative action – but some very violent sequences. GS

▶ Preeti Barameeanat, Khanutra Chuchuaysuwan, Kumpanat Oungsoongnern, Phuthant Prombandal, 9 Million Sam, Arucha Tosawat.
▶ *Dir* Thanakorn Pongsuwan, *Pro* Adirek Wattaleela, *Screenplay* Pongsuwan and Jiat Sansanandana, *Ph* Teerawat Rujintham, Suntipong Waiwong and Wardhana Vunchuplou, *Pro Des* Sippapas Pucare, *Ed* Pongsuwan, Wattaleela and Saknakorn Neteharn, *M* Giant Wave, *Cos* Kaseya Kongsamram.

Bangkok Film Studio/Forfilms-Lionsgate. 94 mins. Thailand. 2009. Rel: 8 Jan 2010. Cert. 15.

Fired Up! ★½

This lame and silly teenage comedy follows the story of two randy friends, Shawn Colfax (Nicholas D'Agosto) and Nick Brady (Eric Christian Olsen), who instead of football camp decide to join a cheerleader summer camp in order to bed as many attractive girls as possible. They are having the time of their lives until Shawn falls in love. It's all rather harmless but don't expect any big surprises. GS

▶ Nicholas D'Agosto, Eric Christian Olsen, Sarah Roemer, Molly Sims, Danneel Harris.
▶ *Dir* Will Gluck, *Pro* Matthew Gross, Peter Jaysen and Charles Weinstock, *Screenplay* Freedom Jones, *Ph* Thomas E Ackerman, *Pro Des* Marcia Hinds, *Ed* Tracey Wadmore-Smith, *M* Richard Gibbs, *Cos* Mynka Draper.

Screen Gems/Moving Pictures DPI/Gross Entertainment/ Weinstock Productions-Sony Pictures Releasing. 90 mins. USA. 2009. Rel: 10 July 2009. Cert. 12A.

The Firm ★★

Nick Love's flashy film revisits familiar territory but adds nothing new to an overcrowded genre. This is a loose remake of Alan Clarke's

Joining the club: Daniel Mays in Nick Love's flashy but all-too-familiar *The Firm*.

groundbreaking 1989 TV drama which tells the story of Dom (Calum MacNab), an impressionable young man who is lured into the dangerous world of football hooliganism. It is stylishly shot but has the feeling of déjà vu all over it and doesn't come anywhere near Clarke's masterpiece. GS

▶ Daniel Mays, Doug Allen, Camille Coduri, Paul Anderson, Calum MacNab.
▶ *Dir* Nick Love, *Pro* Allan Niblo and James Richardson, *Screenplay* Al Ashton, adaptation by Nick Love, *Ph* Matt Gray, *Pro Des* Eve Stewart, *Ed* Stuart Gazzaro, *M* Laura Rossi, *Cos* Andrew Cox.
Vertigo Films-Warner Bros.
90 mins. UK. 2009. Rel: 18 Sep 2009. Cert. 18.

The First Day of the Rest of Your Life ★★★

A hit in France, this is a family tale told by looking at specific days between 1988 and 2000, each of which is presented from the viewpoint of a different member of the family. At times we have comedy in an exaggerated vein and elsewhere drama that indulges sentimentality. Consequently it suggests not so much real life as a kind of soap opera. If that's what you are looking for, you will find it competently done. (Original title: *Le premier jour du reste de ta vie*) MS

▶ Jacques Gamblin, Déborah François, Zabou Breitman, Marc-André Grondin, Pio Marmaï.
▶ *Dir* and *Screenplay* Rémi Bezançon, *Pro* Isabelle Grellat, Éric Altmayer and Nicolas Altmayer, *Ph* Antoine Monod, *Art Dir* Maamar Ech-Cheikh, *Ed* Sophie Reine, *M* Sinclair, *Cos* Marie-Laure Lasson.
Mandarin Cinéma/StudioCanal/France 2 Cinéma

etc-Metrodome Distribution.
113 mins. France. 2008. Rel: 20 Nov 2009. Cert. 15.

The First Movie ★★★★

Mark Cousins' terrific documentary visits a remote Kurdish village in Iraq during Ramadan where all the adults are fasting indoors while the children are out playing in the sun. Cousins wants to introduce cinema to these kids and, after giving them cameras, he urges them to make their first movie. It is a charming film lovingly told, with Cousins effortlessly conveying his passion for the cinema to these innocent souls who have never seen a film in their lives. GS

▶ *Dir, Pho* and *Screenplay* Mark Cousins, *Pro* Trish Dolman and Gill Parry, *Ed* Timo Langer, *M* Melissa Hui.
CONNECTfilm/Screen Siren Pictures-More4 TV.
76 mins. UK/Canada. 2009. Rel: 1 Oct 2010. Cert. 12A.

Fish Story ★★★★

This genuine oddity from Japan could become a cult movie like *Donnie Darko*. Featuring an unacclaimed song recorded by a pop group ahead of its time back in 1975, it moves on to 1982, 2009 and 2012 but not in that order. It brings together humour, action, sensitivity, unease and a climax in which the world is on the brink of disaster. Just how the song links all sections of the film is revealed fully only in a flourish provided by a final montage. Doubtless not to everybody's taste, it's nevertheless individual in a good way. MS

▶ Atsushi Ito, Kengo Kora, Mikako Tabe, Gaku Hamada, Omori Nao.

Déborah François in Rémi Bezançon's hugely successful *The First Day of the Rest of Your Life*.

Dir Nakamura Yoshihiro, *Pro* Utagawa Yasushi and Endo Hitosh, *Screenplay* Hayashi Tamio, from the novel by Isaka Kotaro, *Ph* Komatsu Takashi, *Pro Des* Nakamae Tomoharu, *Ed* Eisuke Ohata, *M* Sasaki Tsugihiko.

DUB/Planning Partner Company: Shinchosha-Third Window Films.
112 mins. Japan. 2009. Rel: 28 May 2010. No Cert.

Fish Tank ★★★★

Everyone has rightly praised newcomer Katie Jarvis for her acting here as a troubled 15-year-old in Essex who falls for her mother's boyfriend. But Michael Fassbender in the latter role matches her naturalistic performance perfectly and, although the tale is bleak (one questions Andrea Arnold's assumption that her film would have been loved by multiplex audiences had they seen it), some critics failed to recognise the positive nature of the ending, in which the girl starts to learn from her experiences. MS

▶ Katie Jarvis, Michael Fassbender, Kierston Wareing, Harry Treadaway, Rebecca Griffiths.
▶ *Dir* and *Screenplay* Andrea Arnold, *Pro* Kees Kasander and Nick Laws, *Ph* Robbie Ryan, *Pro Des* Helen Scott, *Ed* Nicolas Chaudeurge, *Cos* Jane Petrie.

BBC Films/UK Film Council/Limelight etc-Artificial Eye.
123 mins. UK. 2009. Rel: 11 Sep 2009. Cert. 15.

Fit ★★★

This film has nothing to do with art and everything to do with promotion. But that is,

perhaps, understandable because Rikki Beadle-Blair is here presenting a film version of his play, which toured around schools to encourage discussions with pupils about homophobia and sexuality. As a cinema attraction this offering is a dubious proposition, but as a DVD for educational use linked to discussion it certainly serves a useful function. MS

▶ Rikki Beadle-Blair, Sasha Frost, Duncan MacInnes, Ludvig Bonin, Stephen Hoo.
▶ *Dir* Rikki Beadle-Blair, *Pro* Carleen Beadle, Diane Shorthouse and Beadle-Blair, *Screenplay* Beadle-Blair, from his play, *Ed* Edmund Swabey.

Team Angelica/Stonewall/The Shorthouse Organisation-Peccadillo Pictures.
108 mins. UK. 2009. Rel: 5 Nov 2010. Cert. 12A.

(500) Days of Summer ★★★

By beginning at the end, this sophisticated American romantic comedy invites us to look back on various days which reveal the growth and decay of the relationship between Joseph Gordon-Levitt's Tom and Zooey Deschanel's Summer. Each of the days is enumerated but they appear out of chronological order. Much of this is neat and engaging but it seems over-long (jumping back and forth in time is no help in shaping a structure). Also, fine actor though he is, Gordon-Levitt seems made for drama rather than comedy. MS

▶ Joseph Gordon-Levitt, Zooey Deschanel, Geoffrey Arend, Chloë Grace Moretz.

Katie Jarvis in Andrea Arnold's gritty and ultimately optimistic *Fish Tank*.

Seasonal greetings: Joseph Gordon-Levitt and Zooey Deschanel listen to the wise words of Marc Webb on the set of *(500) Days of Summer.*

▶ *Dir* Marc Webb, *Pro* Jessica Tuchinsky, Mark Waters, Mason Novick and Steven J Wolfe, *Screenplay* Scott Neustadter and Michael H Weber, *Ph* Eric Steelberg, *Pro Des* Laura Fox, *Ed* Alan Edward Bell, *M* Mychael Danna and Rob Simonsen, *Cos* Hope Hanafin.

Fox Searchlight Pictures/Watermark etc-20th Century Fox. 95 mins. USA. 2009. Rel: 2 Sep 2009. Cert. 12A.

Food, Inc. ★★★★

Featuring author Eric Schlosser, whose book *Fast Food Nation* was oddly treated on film by Richard Linklater, this is a superior work, a very fine documentary about food production in America. From comments on the use of cheap illegal labour and the conditions in slaughterhouses to the benefits of organic food, this film has much to say and there's a warning here that George Orwell would have approved. MS

▶ With Eric Schlosser, Richard Lobb, Barbara Kowalcyk, Michael Pollan.
▶ *Dir* Robert Kenner, *Pro* Kenner and Elise Pearlstein, *Screenplay* Kenner, Pearlstein and Kim Roberts, *Ph* Richard Pearce, *Ed* Roberts, *M* Mark Adler.

Participant Media/River Road Entertainment etc-Dogwoof Pictures. 84 mins. USA. 2008. Rel: 12 Feb 2010. Cert. PG.

For Colored Girls ★★

This is based on the 1974 play by Ntozake Shange, *For Colored Girls Who Have Considered Suicide When The Rainbow Is Enuf*, which tells the story of nine different women mixing poetry, dance and music. This cinematic version starts well with the crème de la crème of black actresses. But it soon sinks into melodrama with every cliché in the book under Tyler Perry's heavy-handed and utterly humourless direction. GS

▶ Janet Jackson, Anika Noni Rose, Whoopi Goldberg, Kerry Washington, Thandie Newton, Macy Gray.
▶ *Dir* and *Screenplay* Tyler Perry, from the play *For Colored Girls Who Have Considered Suicide When The Rainbow Is Enuf* by Ntozake Shange, *Pro* Perry, Paul Hall and Roger M Bobb, *Ph* Alexander Gruszynski, *Pro Des* Ina Mayhew, *Ed* Maysie Hoy, *M* Aaron Zigman, *Cos* Johnetta Boone.

34th Street Films/Tyler Perry Company/FCG Productions/Lionsgate-Eagle Films. 133 mins. USA. 2010. Rel: 10 Dec 2010. Cert. 15.

44 Inch Chest ★½

Ray Winstone plays Colin, a villain who kidnaps the geezer who's shagging his missus, Liz (Joanne Whalley). She's hitched up with a waiter (Melvil Poupaud), so Colin's cronies lock Loverboy in a wardrobe while they discuss how to dispose of this French ponce. Most of the film is set in a derelict house which gives the film the look and, in Louis Mellis and David Scinto's elliptical script, the feel of a play. A wasted cast, including Ian McShane, John Hurt, Tom Wilkinson and Stephen Dillane as Colin's mates, fail to bring even the foul language of the screenplay to life. MHD

▶ Ray Winstone, Ian McShane, John Hurt, Tom Wilkinson, Stephen Dillane, Joanne Whalley, Steven Briggs, Edna Doré, Steven Berkoff.
▶ *Dir* Malcolm Venville, *Pro* Richard Brown and Steve Golin, *Screenplay* Louis Mellis and David Scinto,

Ph Dan Landin, *Pro Des* John Stevenson, *Ed* Rick
Russell, *M* Angelo Badalamenti, *Cos* Caroline Harris.

Prescience Media/Omni Films/Twilight Production
and Entertainment/I M Global/Anonymous Content/
Passenger-Momentum Pictures.
95 mins. UK. 2009. Rel: 15 Jan 2010. Cert. 18.

Four Lions ★★★★½

Four Lions is an ironic title as Chris Morris'
protagonists are more like pussy cats, a quartet
of Yorkshire jihadists out to make martyrs of
themselves. Having failed to graduate from a
Pakistan fundamentalist training camp, they
set about blowing themselves up at the London
Marathon, wearing explosives under their fancy
dress costumes. Their plans consistently backfire,
however, as one by one they are picked off and
packed off to paradise. The film is hilarious
because these would-be terrorists are just twits.
Morris may not be making a very serious
statement but, despite the subject matter, his
little lions do make entertaining company. MHD

▶ Kayvan Novak, Riz Ahmed, Nigel Lindsay,
Benedict Cumberbatch, Chris Wilson, Julia Davis.
▶ *Dir* Christopher Morris, *Pro* Mark Herbert and
Derrin Schlesinger, *Screenplay* Morris, Simon
Blackwell, Sam Bain and Jesse Armstrong, *Ph* Lol
Crawley, *Pro Des* Dick Lunn, *Ed* Billy Sneddon,
Music Supervisor Phil Canning, *Cos* Charlotte Walter.

Film Four/Wild Bunch/Ward Films-Optimum Releasing.
101 mins. UK. 2010. Rel: 7 May 2010. Cert. 15.

4.3.2.1. ★★½

Although stolen diamonds are involved, this is less
a thriller than a quartet of interconnected dramas
involving four girls who are friends. Writer/director
Noel Clarke leaves his comfort zone as established
in *Kidulthood* and *Adulthood* only to come a cropper,
since too much of this drama seems wholly fictional
in the worst sense. On occasion you hope that some
absurdity is meant to be comic, but the unearned
sentimental moments suggest not. MS

▶ Emma Roberts, Tamsin Egerton, Ophelia
Lovibond, Shanika Warren-Markland, Adam Deacon,
Noel Clarke, Sean Pertwee, Adam Gillen, Mandy
Patinkin, Kevin Smith, Eve.
▶ *Dir* Noel Clarke and Mark Davis, *Pro* Damon
Bryant, Dean O'Toole, Clarke and Davis, *Screenplay*
Clarke, *Ph* Francesco Pezzino, *Pro Des* Murray
McKeown, *Ed* Mark Everson, *M* Adam Lewis and
Barnaby Robson, *Cos* Andy Blake.

Universal Pictures/Magna Films/Unstoppable
Entertainment/Retro-Juice etc-The Works.
117 mins. UK. 2010. Rel: 2 June 2010. Cert. 15.

The Fourth Kind ★★

Presented in a semi-documentary style with bursts
of disturbing sci-fact drama, this is an odd but
not unwatchable attempt to get us nervous about
alien abduction. Presented by Milla Jovovich,
the movie references Spielberg's *Close Encounters*
but takes a far darker path. Set in a small Alaskan
town that's rife with body-stealing, mind-messing
ETs, along with the requisite government cover-
up, it builds to a number of strange, vaguely
nerve-jangling sequences that just might rattle
you a little, as long as you can switch off your
inner cynic. Otherwise it's total nonsense. MJ

▶ Milla Jovovich, Will Paton, Hakeem Kae-Kazim,
Corey Johnson, Elias Koteas.
▶ *Dir* Olatunde Osunsanmi, *Pro* Paul Brooks, Joe
Carnahan and Terry Robbins, *Screenplay* Osunsanmi,
from a story by Osunsanmi and Terry Lee Robbins,
Ph Lorenzo Senatore, *Pro Des* Carlos Silva Da Silva, *Ed*
Paul Covington, *M* Alti Örvarsson, *Cos* Johnetta Boone.

Gold Circle Films/Dead Crocs Productions/Focus Films/
Fourth Kind Productions/Chambara Pictures-Universal
Pictures.
98 mins. USA/UK. 2009. Rel: 6 Nov 2009. Cert. 15.

Freakonomics ★★★★

This fascinating documentary is based on the
book by Steven D Levitt and Stephen J Dubner,
who also act as narrators. It is divided into
different sections with various filmmakers

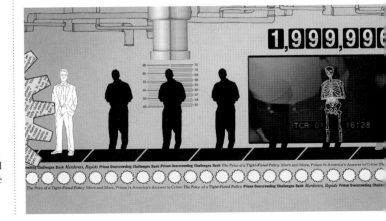

Gunning for Sarkozy: John Travolta in Pierre Morel's instantly gratifying *From Paris With Love.*

contributing, including Morgan Spurlock, who directs the amusing segment about baby names and the repercussions they face later on in life, and Alex Gibney, whose segment exposes the truth behind Sumo wrestling and its corruption. This documentary is a true original and reveals answers you thought you knew to questions you never thought to ask. GS

▶ James Ransone, Zoe Sloane, Jade Viggiano, Sammuel Soifer, Steven D Levitt, Grey Crowe, Stephen J Dubner.
▶ *Dir* Heidi Ewing, Seth Gordon, Morgan Spurlock, Rachel Grady and Eugene Jarecki, *Pro* Dan O'Meara, Chris Romano and Chad Troutwine, *Screenplay* Ewing and Grady, Gibney and Peter Bull, Spurlock and Jeremy Chilnick, Jarecki and Gordon, based on a book by Levitt and Dubner, *Ph* Rob VanAlkemade, Junji Aoki, Tony Hardmon, Darren Lew, Derek Hallquist and Daniel Marracino, *Pro Des* Joe Posner, *Ed* Douglas Blush, Sloane Klevin, Nelson Ryland, Michael Taylor and Tova Goodman, *M* Paul Brill, Michael Furjanic, Human, Michael Wandmacher, Peter Nashel, Jon Spurney and Mike McAllister.
Chad Troutwine Films/Jigsaw Productions/Cold Fusion Media Group/Green Film Company/Human Worldwide/Loki Films-Celsius Entertainment.
93 mins. USA. 2010. Rel: 3 Dec 2010. Cert. U.

Fred: The Movie ★

This is not only one of the worst films of the year but it is also certainly the most irritating. Lucas Cruikshank created the dreadful character of teenage Fred, who has surprisingly become a YouTube phenomenon. In his first movie (and let us hope his last), the nerdy Fred is in love with his next-door neighbour Judy, but first he has to

fight his nemesis Kevin. The screeching voice of Fred will drive you to distraction. Avoid! GS

▶ Lucas Cruikshank, Jennette McCurdy, Jake Weary, John Cena, Pixie Lott, Siobhan Fallon Hogan.
▶ *Dir* Clay Weiner, *Pro* Gary Binkow, Sharla Sumpter and Evan Weiss, *Screenplay* David A Goodman, *Ph* Scott Henriksen, *Pro Des* Joshua Locy, *Ed* Ned Bastille, *M* Roddy Bottum, *Cos* Lydia Paddon.
Derf Films/Varsity Pictures-Lionsgate.
83 mins. USA. 2010. Rel: 17 Dec 2010. Cert. 12A.

Free Jimmy ★★★

There are some enchanting characters in this weird and slightly wonderful Norwegian CGI animated feature for adults, notably the heroin-addicted elephant Jimmy (voice of Jeremy Price) that four stoners, five vegans, three Lapp Mafia mobsters and four drunken hunters want to set free. Jimmy is the star attraction at a run-down Russian circus and he causes no end of bother and chasing around when he decides to go on the lam with a valuable secret: a huge stash of smack is surgically sewn under his hide. With the peculiarly crazy Norwegian sense of humour to the fore, this is not your average cartoon and might even bewilder some non-Scandinavian audiences. Nevertheless, it's eye-catching and quite a lot of quirky fun, with some genuinely big laughs, and the seemingly eccentrically chosen English language voices add a useful layer of oddball entertainment. DW
(Note: This review appeared in *Film Review* number 65 in truncated form. It now appears here in full.)

▶ Voices of Woody Harrelson, Jeremy Price, Simon Pegg, Emilia Fox, Phil Daniels, David Tennant, Jay

Simpson, Kyle MacLachlan, Samantha Morton, Jim Broadbent, Kris Marshall.

‣ *Dir* Christopher Nielsen, *Pro* Lars Andreas Hellebust, *Screenplay* Nielsen and Pegg (English screenplay), *Pro Des* Mikael Holmberg, *Ed* Alastair Reid, *M* Simon Boswell.

AnimagicNet A/S/Free Jimmy Productions/Modelink/ Storm Studio-Break Thru Films.
86 mins. Norway/UK. 2006. Rel: 17 Oct 2008. Cert. 15.

Freestyle ★

Kolton Lee's project may come from the heart but it fails to convince in almost every department. The unrealistic dialogue, inept plot and thinly drawn characters are matched by equally superficial acting in this clichéd story about a beautiful teenager called Ondene (Lucy Konadu) whose dreams of going to Oxford are put on hold when she meets Leon (Arinze Kene), a charming student who introduces her to freestyle basketball. GS

‣ Chris Wilson, Arinze Kene, Suzann McLean, Lucy Konadu, Wolfgang Mwanje.
‣ *Dir* Kolton Lee, *Pro* Lincia Daniel, *Screenplay* Michael Maynard, *Ph* Steve Gray, *Pro Des* Dan Taylor, *Ed* Dominic Strevens, *M* Matt Constantine, *Cos* Miss Molly.

Big Media/Film London/Microwave-Revolver Entertainment.
86 mins. UK. 2010. Rel: 26 Feb 2010. Cert. 12A.

From Paris With Love ★★★½

A personal aide to the US Ambassador in France finds his life turned upside down when he's paired with a reckless cop from the States. Two pairs of the most penetrating eyes in the business illuminate the City of Light in another Luc Besson spectacle. This is formulaic stuff, but it moves at the speed of light and John Travolta enjoys himself enormously, whether annihilating half of the Paris underworld or scoffing a Royale with cheese. And, like the aforementioned hamburger, this is fast, take-away and immediately satisfying. JC-W

‣ John Travolta, Jonathan Rhys Meyers, Kasia Smutniak, Richard Durden, Yin Bing, Eric Godon, François Bredon, Amber Rose Revah.
‣ *Dir* Pierre Morel, *Pro* Luc Besson, India Osborne and Virginie Silla, *Screenplay* Adi Hasak, from a story by Besson, *Ph* Michel Abramowicz, *Pro Des* Jacques Bufnoir, *Ed* Frédéric Thoraval, *M* David Buckley, *Cos* Olivier Bériot.

EuropaCorp/M6 Films/Grive Productions/Apipoulaï Productions/Canal +/TPS Star/JTP Films etc-Warner Bros.
92 mins. France. 2010. Rel: 26 Feb 2010. Cert. 15.

Frontier Blues ★★★½

Golestan in Northern Iran is the location for Babak Jalali's debut feature. The early suggestion that this is a film about heartbreak and tractors sets the tone. Concerned with individuals unable to break away from this remote region, there's humour and pathos here: it's a quiet, gentle work of some appeal, even if the storylines remain slight in themselves. MS

‣ Mahmoud Kalteh, Khajeh Araz Dordi, Abolfazi Karimi, Bezhad Shahrivari, Karima Adebibe, Hossein Shams.

Border burro: life in the slow lane (in Golestan) in Babak Jalali's *Frontier Blues*.

Life in the snow lane: Melissa Leo in the performance that won her her first Oscar nomination, in Courtney Hunt's absorbing, chilling *Frozen River*.

▶ *Dir* and *Screenplay* Babak Jalali, *Pro* Ginevra Elkann and Saadi Soudavar, *Ph* Shahriar Assadi, *Art Dir* Marjan Golzar, *Ed* Jalali and Kambiz Saffari, *M* Noaz Deshe.

Caspian Films/Cinéfondation-Artificial Eye.
97 mins. UK/France. 2010. Rel: 30 July 2010. Cert. 12A.

Frownland ★★

Ronald Bronstein's odd film debut tells the story of Keith Sontag (Dore Mann), a neurotic and manipulative New Yorker who has problems communicating with people, especially with his roommate who wants him out – pronto. The film has its moments but it is almost impossible to sympathise with such an unlikeable character. Ultimately this oddity is far too eccentric for its own good and becomes rather tiresome, especially towards the end. GS

▶ Dore Mann, Paul Grimstead, David Sandholm, Carmine Marino, Mary Wall, Paul Grant.
▶ *Dir, Screenplay* and *Ed* Ronald Bronstein, *Pro* Mark Raybin, *Ph* Sean Price Williams, *M* Paul Grimstad.

Frownland-Factory 25.
106 mins. USA. 2007. Rel: 9 July 2010. No Cert.

Frozen ★★★½

Adam Green's chilling film is strong on atmosphere and is a worthy cinematic experience despite its static nature. Most of the action takes place on an open chairlift as three friends are left stranded in the freezing snow after a ski resort closes for a week. The premise is not dissimilar to *Open Water* – just think skiing instead of scuba diving – and the result is equally disturbing. GS

▶ Shawn Ashmore, Emma Bell, Kevin Zegers, Ed Ackerman, Chris York, Rileah Vanderbilt.
▶ *Dir* and *Screenplay* Adam Green, *Pro* Peter Block and Cory Neal, *Ph* Will Barratt, *Pro Des* Bryan McBrian, *Ed* Ed Marx, *M* Andy Garfield, *Cos* Barbara Nelson.

A Bigger Boat/ArieScope Pictures-Momentum Pictures.
93 mins. USA. 2010. Rel: 24 Sep 2010. Cert. 15.

Frozen River ★★★★

Unsentimental but warmly engaging, Courtney Hunt's drama is set on the border between Canada and America, the river of the title being the St Lawrence. Oscar-nominated Melissa Leo is a mother deserted by her husband who, in desperation, resorts to raising money by helping immigrants get into the USA. However, this is not just a suspense drama but a story illustrating the bonds that can develop between people from different worlds. Misty Upham is Leo's equal as the Mohawk woman who against the odds becomes her friend. MS

▶ Melissa Leo, Misty Upham, Charlie McDermott, Michael O'Keefe, Michael Sky.
▶ *Dir* and *Screenplay* Courtney Hunt, *Pro* Heather Rae and Chip Hourihan, *Ph* Reed Dawson Morano, *Pro Des* Inbal Weinberg, *Ed* Kate Williams, *M* Peter Golub and Shahzad Ali Ismaily, *Cos* Abby O'Sullivan.

Harwood Hunt Productions/Cohen Media Group/ Offhollywood Pictures-Axiom Films.
97 mins. USA. 2008. Rel: 17 July 2009. Cert. 15.

Funny People ★★★

Former stand-up comic and now big Hollywood
star George Simmons (Adam Sandler) is forced
to re-examine his life after being diagnosed
with an incurable disease. He tells no one about
his condition apart from his new assistant,
struggling comedian Ira (Seth Rogen), who
encourages George to share his secret with
his family and friends. The story is not as
grim as it sounds but is not that funny either.
Judd Apatow's engaging but rather overlong
bittersweet comedy works thanks to the honesty
of the performances and that of his writing.
Sandler is brilliantly used as the insensitive and
arrogant star. GS

▶ Adam Sandler, Seth Rogen, Leslie Mann, Eric
Bana, Jonah Hill.
▶ *Dir* and *Screenplay* Judd Apatow, *Pro* Apatow,
Barry Mendel and Clayton Townsend, *Ph* Janusz
Kaminski, *Pro Des* Jefferson Sage, *Ed* Craig Alpert
and Brent White, *M* Michael Andrews and Jason
Schwartzman, *Co* Betsy Heimann and Nancy Steiner.
**Universal Pictures/Columbia Pictures/Relativity Media/
Apatow Productions/Company-Universal Studios.
146 mins. USA. 2009. Rel: 28 Aug 2009. Cert. 15.**

Furry Vengeance ★

A group of animals led by a clever raccoon join
forces in order to save their peaceful Oregon
forest from Dan Sanders (Brendan Fraser) and
his latest redevelopment that threatens to ruin
their environment. Despite the hilarious opening
sequence, it is sadly downhill all the way
thereafter. The furry protagonists are adorable but
the less said about the overacting of the humans,
especially Brendan Fraser, the better. GS

▶ Brendan Fraser, Ricky Garcia, Eugene Cordro, Patrice
O'Neal, Jom Norton, Brooke Shields, Wallace Shawn.
▶ *Dir* Roger Kumble, *Pro* Keith Gldberg and Robert
Simonds, *Screenplay* Michael Carnes and Josh
Gilbert, *Ph* Peter Lyons Collister, *Pro Des* Stephen
Lineweaver, *Ed* Lawrence Jordan, *M* Edward
Shearmur, *Cos* Alexandra Welker.
**Imagenation Abu Dhabi FZ/Participant Media/Summit
Entertainment-E1 Entertainment.
92 mins. USA/United Arab Emirates. 2010. Rel: 7 May
2010. Cert. PG.**

G Force 3D ★★

James Bond meets The Chipmunks in this utterly
routine, in-one-eye-and-out-the-other, Disneyfied
spy-themed adventure featuring computer-
generated guinea pigs with skills and gadgets who
embark upon a particularly predictable world-saving
mission. Playing the human science nerd who
cares for them, Zach Galifianakis is uncommonly
ordinary, while voice stars Penélope Cruz, Steve
Buscemi, Sam Rockwell and Nicolas Cage add
at least a thin layer of sparkle to the routine
screenplay. Are you ready for moderate fun, kids? MJ

▶ Bill Nighy, Sam Rockwell, Will Arnett, Jon Favreau,
Zach Galifianakis, Nicolas Cage, Penélope Cruz,
Steve Buscemi.
▶ *Dir* Hoyt Yeatman Jr, *Pro* Jerry Bruckheimer,
Screenplay Cormac Wibberley and Marianne
Wibberley, from a story by Yeatman, *Ph* Bojan Bazelli,
Pro Des Deborah Evans, *Ed* Mark Goldblatt and Jason
Hellmann, *M* Trevor Rabin, *Cos* Ellen Mirojnick.

The highest
paid man in
Hollywood:
Adam Sandler in
Judd Apatow's
engaging but
rather overlong
Funny People.

Jerry Bruckheimer Films/Walt Disney Pictures/Whamafram Productions-Walt Disney Studios Motion Pictures.
88 mins. USA. 2009. Rel: 2009. 31 July 2009. Cert. PG.

Gainsbourg ★★★

The accomplished Eric Elmosnino plays the singer Serge Gainsbourg in this stylised film about his life. Surreal elements and animation feature, and it's a far cry from a standard biopic. Since Gainsbourg's music is featured his admirers may be caught up by it, but characters come and go in a manner which suggests scenes from a life rather than a clear, convincing overall view. The movie is unconventional enough for reactions to it to be a matter of taste. MS

▶ Eric Elmosnino, Lucy Gordon, Laetitia Casta, Mylène Jampanoï, Anna Mouglalis, Doug Jones, Yolande Moreau, Claude Chabrol.
▶ *Dir* and *Screenplay* Joann Sfar, *Pro* Marc Du Pontavice and Didier Lupfer, *Ph* Guillaume Schiffman, *Art Dir* Christian Marti, *Ed* Maryline Monthieux, *M* Olivier Daviaud, *Cos* Pascaline Chavanne.

One World Films/Studio 37/Focus Features International/France 2 Cinéma/Xilam Films/Lilou Films etc-Optimum Releasing.
135 mins. France/UK. 2010. Rel: 30 July 2010. Cert. 15.

Gamer ★

This is a boring and utterly redundant futuristic thriller about a computer game that involves Death Row prisoners. They are controlled by having chips implanted in their brains but one man tries to break free. It is directed by Mark Neveldine and Brian Taylor, the team behind the vastly superior *Crank* films, but this one lacks their energy and sheer sense of fun. Also, the one-dimensional Gerard Butler is a poor substitute for Jason Statham. GS

▶ Gerard Butler, Amber Valletta, Michael C Hall, Kyra Sedgwick, Alison Lohman, Ludakris.
▶ *Dir* and *Screenplay* Mark Neveldine and Brian Taylor, *Pro* Gary Lucchesi, Tom Rosenberg, Skip Williamson and Richard S Wright, *Ph* Ekkehart Pollack, *Pro Des* Jerry Fleming, *Ed* Peter Amundson, Doobie White and Fernando Villena, *M* Rob Williamson and Geoff Zanelli, *Cos* Alix Friedberg.

Lionsgate/Lakeside Entertainments-Entertainment Film Distributors.
95 mins. USA. 2009. Rel: 16 Sep 2009. Cert. 18.

Gangster's Paradise: Jerusalema ★★★★

Lucky Kunene (Rapulana Seiphemo) is a young man determined to escape from the poor shanty town of Soweto by any means possible during the last years of Apartheid. He begins by stealing cars for a local drug lord before he grows into a sophisticated crime boss. Director Ralph Ziman creates a violent world in this epic true story while Rapulana Seiphemo is a towering presence. Johannesburg is an extremely violent city and

Ziman's excellent set-pieces never shy away from highlighting this fact. (Original title: *Jerusalema*) GS

▶ Rapulana Seiphemo, Daniel Buckland, Robert Hobbs, Kevon Kane, Kenneth Nkosi, Ronnie Nyakale.
▶ *Dir* and *Screenplay* Ralph Ziman, *Pro* Ziman and Tendeka Matatu, *Ph* Nic Hofmeyer, *Pro Des* Flo Ballack, *Ed* David Helfand and Bert Lovitt, *M* Alan Ari Lazar, *Cos* Natalie Lundon.

Muti Films-Anchor Bay Entertainment UK.
119 mins. South Africa. 2008. Rel: 9 July 2010. Cert. 15.

Gay Sex in the 70s ★★★½

The sex here is all American as well as all gay, the emphasis being on New York in a decade when its backrooms and bath-houses made it a sexual mecca. Towards the end of this documentary AIDS looms but the film's tone is celebratory. That does not prevent it from possessing historical worth, but it would have been a more valuable document had it taken a broader sociological approach and considered also the possible downside of a freedom that encouraged promiscuity. MS

▶ Robert Alvarez, Alvin Baltrop, Barton Benes, Larry Kramer.
▶ *Dir* Joseph F Lovett, *Pro* and *Ph* Michael Sean Kaminsky and Lovett, *Ed* Jason Szabo, *M* Art Labriola.

Lovett Productions/Frameline/Heartlove Productions-Peccadillo Pictures.
67 mins. USA. 2005. Rel: 2 July 2010. Cert. 18.

Gentlemen Broncos ★★★

This is the kind of film where you wonder, 'How did this ever get made?' A celebration of cult sci-fi is a minority taste, but some will treasure its silly and affectionate laughs. Michael Angarano plays a teenager at a creative fantasy writing convention who finds his sci-fi novel ripped off by oily teacher and dried-up author Dr Ronald Chevalier (Jemaine Clement). Meanwhile, Angarano meets budding romantic novelist Tabatha (Halley Feiffer), and creepy filmmaker Lonnie (Hector Jimenez) and lets them adapt his story into a no-budget movie. Not just quirky but truly oddball, it is genuinely affectionate and funny. DW

▶ Michael Angarano, Halley Feiffer, Hector Jimenez, Jemaine Clement, Jennifer Coolidge.
▶ *Dir* Jared Hess, *Pro* Mike White and John J Kelly, *Screenplay* Jared and Jerusha Hess, *Ph* Munn Powell, *Pro Des* Richard A Wright, *Ed* Yuka Ruell, *M* David Wingo, *Cos* April Napier.

Rip Cord Productions-Fox Searchlight Pictures.
90 mins. USA. 2009. Rel: 30 Apr 2010. Cert. 12A.

Get Him to the Greek ★★★

A devotee of the British rock group Infant Sorrow, Aaron Green (Jonah Hill) finds his love sorely tested when he's hired to escort the band's frontman to Los Angeles. Beneath the predictable comic riffs of this Judd Apatow orgy of sex, drugs and rock 'n' roll (and vomit, booze and anal rape) is a serious contemplation on fame and substance abuse. Building on the character he created in *Forgetting Sarah Marshall*, Russell Brand is as indomitable as ever, proving he can pass muster as a stadium rocker. It's a hit-and-miss affair but with enough belly laughs to pass the time most amiably. JC-W

▶ Jonah Hill, Russell Brand, Elisabeth Moss, Colm Meaney, Rose Byrne, Sean 'Diddy' Combs.
▶ *Dir* Nicholas Stoller, *Pro* Stoller, Judd Apatow, David Bushell and Rodney Rothman, *Screenplay* Stoller, based on characters created by Jason Segal, *Ph* Robert D Yeoman, *Pro Des* Jan Roelfs, *Ed* William Kerr and Michael L Sale, *M* Lyle Workman, *Cos* Leesa Evans.

Universal Pictures/Relativity Media/Apatow/Spyglass Entertainment-Universal Studios.
109 mins. USA. 2010. Rel: 25 June 2010. Cert. 15.

The Ghost ★★★

Any links to Tony and Cherie Blair in this political thriller adapted by Robert Harris from his own novel are hardly important. This is a well-acted but conventional, slow and rather old-fashioned suspense piece about a writer who, called in to ghost a former Prime Minister's memoirs, uncovers dangerous secrets. It is certainly not up to Polanski's best work and the ending is particularly ludicrous. But it passes the time and Olivia Williams adds to her already considerable reputation as a fine actress. MS

▶ Ewan McGregor, Pierce Brosnan, Kim Cattrall, Olivia Williams, Tom Wilkinson, Eli Wallach, Timothy Hutton.

Antler motive: Sam Rockwell in Jared Hess's affectionate and funny *Gentlemen Broncos*.

Cause célèbre: Catherine Deneuve in André Téchiné's *The Girl on the Train*.

> *Dir* Roman Polanski, *Pro* Polanski, Robert Benmussa and Alain Sarde, *Screenplay* Robert Harris and Polanski, from Harris' novel, *Ph* Pawel Edelman, *Pro Des* Albrecht Konrad, *Ed* Hervé de Luze, *M* Alexandre Desplat, *Cos* Dinah Colin.

R.P. Films/France 2 Cinéma/ELFTE Babelsberg Film GmbH etc-Optimum Releasing.
128 mins. France/Germany/UK. 2009. Rel: 16 Apr 2010. Cert. 15.

G.I. Joe: The Rise of Cobra ★

An all-action feature adaptation of the perennial toy line from *Mummy* director Stephen Sommers, this is exactly the kind of film that gives summer blockbusters a bad name. Devoid of any vestige of personality or style, drowned by a deluge of cheesy computerised effects, horribly written without an ounce of wit or intelligence, and played by a dead-eyed cast with all the charm of a zombie apocalypse, it's a painful yawn-fest from start to finish. MJ

> Adewale Akinnuoye-Agbaje, Christopher Eccleston, Joseph Gordon-Levitt, Dennis Quaid, Byung-hun Lee, Sienna Miller, Jonathan Pryce.
> *Dir* Stephen Sommers, *Pro* Sommers, Lorenzo di Bonaventura and Bob Ducsay. *Screenplay* Stuart Bettie, David Elliott and Paul Lovett, from a story by Sommers, Beattie and Michael B Gordon, *Ph* Mitchell Amundsen, *Pro Des* Ed Verreaux, *Ed* Ducsay and Jim May, *M* Alan Silvestri, *Cos* Ellen Mirojnick.

Paramount Pictures/Spyglass/Entertainment/Hasbro/Di Bonaventura Pictures-Paramount Pictures.
118 mins. USA/Czech Republic. 2009. Rel: 7 Aug 2009. Cert. 12A.

The Girlfriend Experience ★★½

This offbeat study of a high-class Manhattan call-girl finds Steven Soderbergh in his experimental vein. Despite starring porn star Sasha Grey, it's a documentary-style work without strong sex scenes. It suggests a more distanced variant on Godard's *Vivre sa vie*, but without a star presence or any ability to hold the audience mesmerised. The film does reflect America at the time of the 2008 presidential election but it all seems pretty pointless. MS

> Sasha Grey, Chris Santos, Philip Eytan, Glenn Kenny, David Levien, Timothy Davis.
> *Dir* Steven Soderbergh, *Pro* Gregory Jacobs, *Screenplay* David Levien and Brian Koppelman, *Ph* Peter Andrews (i.e. Soderbergh), *Art Dir* Carlos Moore, *Ed* Mary Ann Bernard, *M* Ross Godfrey, *Cos* Christopher Peterson.

Magnolia Pictures/2929 Productions/Extension 765-Revolver Entertainment.
77 mins. USA. 2009. Rel: 4 Dec 2009. Cert. 15.

The Girl on the Train ★★★

An astonishing real-life event involving a bogus claim to have been assaulted on a train in Paris in an anti-Semitic attack has become the basis of this drama from André Téchiné. Émilie Dequenne from *Rosetta* is most persuasive as the girl but you expect Téchiné to have more ideas to express that might explain her actions. Viewers who favour bringing their own ideas to enigmatic material will be more responsive than others. (Original title: *La Fille du RER*) MS

> Émilie Dequenne, Catherine Deneuve, Michel Blanc, Nicolas Duvauchelle, Mathieu Demy, Ronit Elkabetz.
> *Dir* André Téchiné, *Pro* Saïd Ben Saïd, *Screenplay* Téchiné, Odile Barski and Jean-Marie Besset, based on Besset's play *RER*, *Ph* Julien Hirsch, *Art Dir* Michèle Abbe, *Ed* Martine Giordano, *M* Philippe Sarde, *Cos* Khadija Zeggaï.

UGC/SBS Films/France2 Cinéma etc-Soda Pictures.
101 mins. France. 2009. Rel: 4 June 2010. Cert. 15.

The Girl who Kicked the Hornets' Nest ★★★★

Without equalling the impact of the first piece, *The Girl with the Dragon Tattoo* [qv], this film version of the last instalment of Stieg Larsson's acclaimed trilogy is a thriller that works well. Noomi Rapace as the put-upon heroine is once again first class and, if the movie is a shade over-long, it nevertheless comes across as a solid genre piece not without social comment by way of an extra. (Original title: *Luftslottet som sprängdes*) MS

> Michael Nyqvist, Noomi Rapace, Annika Hallin, Lena Endre, Mikael Spreitz.

▶ *Dir* Daniel Alfredson, *Pro* Søren Staermose, *Screenplay* Ulf Ryberg, from the Millennium series by Stieg Larsson, *Ph* Peter Mokrosinski, *Art Dir* Maria Hååd and Jan Olof Ågren, *Ed* Håkan Karlsson, *M* Jacob Groth, *Cos* Cilla Rörby.

Yellow Bird/Sveriges Television/ZDF Enterprises/Nordisk Film etc-Momentum Pictures.
147 mins. Sweden/Denmark/Germany. 2009. Rel: 26 Nov 2010. Cert. 15.

The Girl who Played with Fire
★★★½

This, the middle instalment of the trilogy which makes up the Lisbeth Salander story, is by far the weakest, with Daniel Alfredson taking over as director from the superior Niels Arden Oplev. It recaps on *The Girl with the Dragon Tattoo* but will work best if you have already seen the earlier film. The acting remains strong, but even for a thriller the plot goes way over the top, this time with a ludicrous final section. But if you've invested in the trilogy you will forgive this low point. (Original title: *Flickan som lekte med elden*) MS

▶ as per *The Girl who Kicked the Hornets' Nest*, plus Per Oscarsson, Peter Andersson.
▶ *Dir, Pro Ph, Pro Des, M* and *Cos* see *The Girl who Kicked the Hornets' Nest*,
Screenplay Jonas Frykberg, from the Millennium series by Steig Larsson, *Ed* Mattias Morheden.

Production and distribution as per The Girl who Kicked the Hornets' Nest.
129 mins. Sweden/Denmark/Germany. 2009. Rel: 27 Aug 2010. Cert. 15.

The Girl with the Dragon Tattoo ★★★★

Superior to both *The Ghost* and *Shutter Island* [both qv], those other recent long thrillers adapted from best-selling novels, this Swedish film – first of a trilogy (see above) – deals with an inquiry into a 40-year-old disappearance that might be murder. An investigative journalist teams up with the helpful titular figure, a

Lapp of honour: Noomi Rapace in Niels Arden Oplev's The Girl Who Kicked the Hornet's Nest.

The Man With No Pain: Mikael Spreitz in the final instalment of the Stieg Larsson trilogy, The Girl Who Played With Fire.

Hair today: Chris Rock (right) turns trichologist in Jeff Stilson's rather endearing *Good Hair.*

bisexual tattooed computer hacker with a ring in her nose – thus 1940s *film noir* meets 21st century trends. One rape scene is too disturbing for its context, but with a great lead actress in Noomi Rapace this will surely be better by far than the projected Hollywood remake. (Original title: *Män som hatar kvinnor*) MS

‣ Noomi Rapace, Michael Nyqvist, Sven-Bertil Taube, Peter Haber, Peter Andersson, Ewa Fröling, Lena Endre, Gunnel Lindblom.
‣ *Dir* Niels Arden Oplev, *Pro* Søren Staermose, *Screenplay* Nicolaj Arcel and Rasmus Heisterberg, from the novel by Stieg Larsson, *Ph* Eric Kress, *Pro Des* Niels Sejer, *Ed* Anne Østerud, *M* Jacob Groth, *Cos* Cilla Rörby and Maria José Contreras.
Yellow Bird/ZDF Enterprises/Sveriges Television/Nordisk Film etc-Momentum Pictures.
153 mins. Sweden/Denmark/Germany. 2009. Rel: 12 Mar 2010. Cert. 18.

Give Me Your Hand ★★★

In this French road movie twins appear as twins, but the story by writer/director Pascal-Alex Vincent posits the notion that the sometimes uneasy bond between siblings can create even greater tensions when one is gay and the other straight. The journey they take as hitchhikers to their mother's funeral in Spain makes for a very episodic and fragmented narrative. It doesn't always convince, although it is watchable if never deeply involving. The landscapes add visual appeal and there's some neat animation at the start. (Original title: *Donne-moi la main*) MS

‣ Alexandre Carril, Victor Carril, Anaïs Demoustier, Samir Harrag, Katrin Sass.
‣ *Dir* Pascal-Alex Vincent, *Pro* Nicolas Brévière, Marcelo Busse and Markus Halberschmidt, *Screenplay* Vincent and Martin Drouot, from an

idea by Olivier Nicklaus and Vincent, *Ph* Alexis Kavyrchine, *Pro Des* François Sacré, *Ed* Dominique Pétrot, *M* Tarwater, Bernd Jestram and Ronald Lippock, *Cos* Marie-Prune Houdayer.
Local Films/Adam Productions/Busse & Halberschmidt/ CinéCinéma etc-Peccadillo Pictures.
76 mins. France/Germany/Netherlands. 2008. Rel: 16 Apr 2010. No Cert.

Glorious 39 ★★

This conspiracy drama by Stephen Poliakoff has been promoted by him as a significant portrait of England in 1939 and of the desire in some quarters to appease and support Hitler. In fact it's a would-be Hitchcockian rigmarole which the master would have disdained for its improbabilities and its lack of cunning. (One can spot the villain a mile off.) Good players are involved but, frankly, it's a totally inglorious occasion. MS

‣ Romola Garai, Bill Nighy, Eddie Redmayne, Julie Christie, Juno Temple, Hugh Bonneville, Jeremy Northam, Christopher Lee, Corin Redgrave, Muriel Pavlow, Jenny Agutter, David Tennant, Charlie Cox, Toby Regbo.
‣ *Dir* and *Screenplay* Stephen Poliakoff, *Pro* Barney Reisz and Martin Pope, *Ph* Danny Cohen, *Pro Des* Mark Leese, *Ed* Jason Krasucki, *M* Adrian Johnston, *Cos* Annie Symons.
BBC Films/UK Film Council/Talkback Thames etc-Momentum Pictures.
129 mins. UK. 2009. Rel: 20 Nov 2009. Cert. 12A.

Going the Distance ★★★

This cute romantic comedy tells the story of Erin (Drew Barrymore), a young woman who returns home to San Francisco for a new job but is still determined to make her relationship work with her New York lover Garrett (Justin Long) – despite the long distance. There are no surprises here but there is a likeable chemistry and enough sparkle between the two leads to make this quite watchable. GS

▶ Drew Barrymore, Justin Long, Ron Livingston, Charlie Day, Christina Applegate.
▶ *Dir* Nanette Burstein, *Pro* Jennifer Gibgot and Garrett Grant, *Screenplay* Geoff LaTulippe, *Ph* Eric Steelberg, *Pro Des* Kevin Kavanaugh, *Ed* Peter Teschner, *M* Mychael Danna, *Cos* Catherine Marie Thomas.
New Line Cinema/Offspring Entertainment-New Line Cinema.
102 mins. USA. 2010. Rel: 10 Sep 2010. Cert. 15.

Good Hair ★★½

Fancy a documentary on Afro-American hairstyles? If you like Chris Rock, the co-producer, co-writer and host of *Good Hair*, then you could warm to it. Rock, whose own daughters' interest in the subject drove him to this pass, travels to India to see why women sacrifice their locks, talks to scientists and celebrities and attends the International Hair Show in Atlanta. Giving the whole thing a socio-political-sexual slant, he has helped to create a rather endearing if lightweight diversion. CB

▶ Chris Rock, Tracie Thoms, Maya Angelou, Al Sharpston, Ice-T.
▶ *Dir* Jeff Stilson, *Pro* Stilson, Jenny Hunter and Kevin O'Donnell, *Screenplay* Stilson, Chris Rock, Lance Crouther and Chuck Sklar, *Ph* Cliff Charles and Mark Henderson, *Ed* Paul Marchand and Greg Nash, *M* Marcus Miller.
HBO Films/Chris Rock Entertainment-Icon Film Distribution.
96 mins. USA. 2009. Rel: 25 June 2010. Cert. 12A.

Goodbye Solo ★★★★

Brilliantly acted, and close to being a two-hander, this concerns a Senegalese taxi driver living in America and a passenger who hires him for a forthcoming one-way drive into the mountains; this could well be for a planned suicide. Some aspects of the story seem improbable, but in its almost minimalistic way the film is both compelling and thought-provoking, marking an advance for its creator Raman Bahani and featuring two of the best performances of the year. MS

▶ Souléymane Sy Savané, Red West, Diana Franco Galindo, Carmen Leyva.
▶ *Dir* and *Ed* Ramin Bahrani, *Pro* Jason Orans and Bahrani, *Screenplay* Bahareh Azimi and Bahrani, *Ph* Michael Simmonds, *Pro Des* Chad Keith, *M* M. Lo.
Gigantic Pictures/Noruz Films/Lucky Hat Entertainment etc-Axiom Films.
91 mins. USA. 2008. Rel: 9 Oct 2009. Cert. 15.

The Goods: Live Hard, Sell Hard ★★

When a used car lot faces bankruptcy, its owner calls on a team of crack salesmen to save the day. The methods employed by Don 'The Goods' Ready may be unconventional, but he does appear to know what he's doing. There are a few smart moves in this broad, crude comedy, but they're all in the first half. Having set up its roster of wacky, colourful characters – memorably led by Jeremy Piven's charismatic Don Ready – the film slips into a neutral, generic gear. Worse, it succumbs to sentimentality and loses the whiplash bite of its earlier promise. JC-W

▶ Jeremy Piven, Ving Rhames, James Brolin, David Koechner, Kathryn Hahn.
▶ *Dir* Neal Brennan, *Pro* Will Ferrell and Chris Henchy, *Screenplay* Andy Stock and Rick Stempson, *Ph* Daryn Okada, *Pro Des* Stefania Cella, *Ed* Michael Jablow and Kevin Tent, *M* Lyle Workman, *Cos* Mary Jane Fort.
Gary Sanchez Productions-Paramount Vantage.
89 mins. USA. 2009. Rel: 23 Oct 2009. Cert. 15.

Greek Pete ★★★★

Andrew Haigh's fascinating and occasionally very explicit documentary follows a year in the life of rent boy Peter Pittaros, or Greek Pete to his clients. Pete may not be the brightest but he is certainly very charming and the film benefits tremendously from his honesty and relaxed manner in front of the camera. However, the film could have been much stronger and less one-sided if Haigh had managed to interview Pete's conservative Cypriot parents as well as some of his acquaintances. GS

▶ Peter Pittaros, Lewis Wallis, Robert Day, Tristan Field, Barry Robinson, Liam Thompson, Rachel Whitbread.
▶ *Dir*, *Pro*, *Screenplay*, *Ph* and *Ed* Andrew Haigh, *M* James Edward Barker.
Elmbourne Films-Peccadillo Pictures.
75 mins. USA. 2009. Rel: 4 Sep 2009. Cert. 18.

On the road: Souléymane Sy Savané in Ramin Bahrani's compelling and thought-provoking *Goodbye Solo*.

On target: Matt Damon in Paul Greengrass's high-octane if one-dimensional *Green Zone*.

Green Zone ★★★½

With absolute honesty, Paul Greengrass has declared that this is a gamble – an attempt to offer a commercial action drama starring Matt Damon that also underlines Greengrass' concern over the politicians' lies regarding Iraq's possession of weapons of mass destruction in 2003. It is least successful in its over-extended chase finale and its distracting use of hand-held camera for Scope images, but it's not too far off-target. MS

‣ Matt Damon, Greg Kinnear, Brendan Gleeson, Amy Ryan, Khalid Abdalla, Jason Isaccs.
‣ *Dir* Paul Greengrass, *Pro* Tim Bevan, Eric Fellner, Lloyd Levin and Greengrass, *Screenplay* Brian Helgeland, inspired by the book *Imperial Life in the Emerald City* by Rajiv Chandrasekaran, *Ph* Barry Ackroyd, *Pro Des* Dominic Watkins, *Ed* Christopher Rouse, *M* John Powell, *Cos* Sammy Sheldon.

Universal Pictures/Studio Canal/Relativity Media/
Working Title etc-Universal Pictures International.
115 mins. USA/UK/Spain/Japan/France. 2009. Rel: 12 Mar 2010. Cert. 15.

Greenberg ★★

Having tackled marital breakdown and sibling rivalry with excoriating observation in *The Squid and the Whale* and *Margot at the Wedding*, Noah Baumbach now takes on mental illness. But the trouble is that casting Ben Stiller as his loony does bring with it an anticipation of comedy – yet Stiller's Roger Greenberg is a very, very sad man. The film, which is devoid of narrative form, begs to be darker, more passionate, more savage even, but what we get is embarrassment-lite (with two or three laughs). JC-W

‣ Ben Stiller, Greta Gerwig, Jennifer Jason Leigh, Chris Messina, Juno Temple, Rhys Ifans.
‣ *Dir* Noah Baumbach, *Pro* Jennifer Jason Leigh and Scott Rudin, *Screenplay* Baumbach and Leigh, based on their own story, *Ph* Harris Savides, *Pro Des* Ford Wheeler, *Ed* Tom Streeto, *M* James Murphy, *Cos* Mark Bridges.

Scott Rudin Productions/Twins Financing LLC-Universal Pictures International.
107 mins. USA. 2010. Rel: 11 June 2010. Cert. 15.

Grown Ups ★

This is a totally unfunny comedy with a lot of talent simply wasted. Five childhood friends get together with their families on the Fourth of July for the first time in 30 years following their basketball coach's funeral. There is a plethora of abysmal gags that never induce even a smile, just plenty of groans, while Rob Schneider wins the close contest for worst performance. Avoid at all costs because it's really not even worth one star. GS

‣ Adam Sandler, Chris Rock, Steve Buscemi, Salma Hayak, Kevin James, Rob Schneider, David Spade, Maria Bello, Joyce Van Patten.
‣ *Dir* Dennis Dugan, *Pro* Sandler and Jack Giarraputo, *Screenplay* Sandler and Fred Wolf, *Ph* Theo van de Sande, *Pro Des* Perry Andelin Blake, *Ed* Tom Costain, *M* Rupert Gregson-Williams, *Cos* Ellen Lutter.

Happy Madison Productions/Relativity Media-Sony Pictures Releasing.
102 mins. USA. 2010. Rel: 27 Aug 2010. Cert. 12A.

Gulliver's Travels ★½

There is so much awry with Rob Letterman's *Gulliver's Travels* that it's hard to know where to begin. Easier, then, to alight on its merits: the CGI is pretty accomplished, Princess Emily Blunt looks like she could be the daughter of Queen Catherine Tate, and Chris O'Dowd is mildly amusing in what should've been the Christopher Guest part. But the notion of Jack Black recycling his cowardly loser schtick as a modern-day version of Lemuel Gulliver was a bad, bad idea. Let's just hope the kiddies connect with the material. JC-W

▶ Jack Black, Emily Blunt, Jason Segel, Amanda Peet, Billy Connolly, Chris O'Dowd, James Corden, Catherine Tate.
▶ *Dir* Rob Letterman, *Pro* Jack Black, Ben Cooley, Gregory Goodman and John Davis, *Screenplay* Joe Stillman and Nicholas Stoller, from the book by Jonathan Swift, *Ph* David Tattersall, *Pro Des* Gavin Bocquet, *Ed* Nicholas De Toth, Dean Zimmerman, Alan Edward Bell and Maryann Brandon, *M* Henry Jackman, *Cos* Sammy Sheldon.

Twentieth Century Fox/Davis Entertainment Company/ Electric Dynamite-20th Century Fox. 85 mins. USA. 2010. Rel: 26 Dec 2010. Cert. PG.

Hachi – A Dog's Tale ★★★

Based on the 1987 Japanese film *Hachiko monogatari*, the story is now transported to America where college professor Parker (Richard Gere) finds a lost puppy (Hachi) and adopts him over his wife Cate's (Joan Allen) objections. Soon Hachi and Parker become inseparable in a friendship that will last for years. There is not a lot of action in this likeable but sentimental film. It's not helped by an obtrusive over-orchestrated score, while Gere's generous performance gives more emphasis to his highly watchable canine co-star. (Original title: *Hachiko: A Dog's Story*) GS

▶ Richard Gere, Joan Allen, Cary-Hiroyuki Tagana, Sarah Roemer, Jason Alexander, Erick Avari.
▶ *Dir* Lasse Hallström, *Pro* Richard Gere, Bill Johnson and Vicki Shigekuni Wong, *Screenplay* Stephan P Lindsey, based on Kaneto Shindô's 1987 screenplay *Hachiko monogatari*, *Ph* Ron Fortunato, *Pro Des* Chad Detwiller, *Ed* Kristina Boden, *M* Jan A P Kaczmarek, *Cos* Deborah Newhall.

Inferno Production/Grand Army Entertainment/ Opperman Viner Chrystyn Entertainment/Scion Films-Entertainment Film Distributors. 93 mins. USA/UK. 2009. Rel: 12 Mar 2010. Cert. U.

Halloween II ★★

Dancer and model Sheri Moon Zombie returns from her husband's 2007 *Halloween* remake as mum Deborah Myers. Scout Taylor-Compton is back too as Laurie Strode, now in hospital after apparently killing Michael Myers, but the mask-wearing monster (Tyler Mane again) is still alive and soon murderously rampaging once more. Rob Zombie's ethos is the more gore and more women-abusing sadism the merrier – to hell with convincing dialogue, suspense, subtlety, good acting or decent story. Malcolm McDowell is dreadful again as Dr Loomis and Brad Dourif's sheriff is pretty ripe. Note: this is not a remake of 1981's *Halloween II* but a continuation of Rob Zombie's own part one. DW

▶ Sheri Moon Zombie, Chase Vanek, Tyler Mane, Scout Taylor-Compton, Brad Dourif, Malcolm McDowell, Margot Kidder.
▶ *Dir* and *Screenplay* Rob Zombie, *Pro* Rob Zombie, Andy Gould and Malek Akkad, *Ph* Brandon Trost, *Pro Des* Gareth Stover, *Ed* Glenn Garland and Joel Pashby, *M* Tyler Bates, *Cos* Mary McLeod.

Dimension Films/Spectacle Entertainment GP/Trancas International Films-Entertainment Film Distributors. 105 mins. USA. 2009. Rel: 9 Oct 2009. Cert. 18.

The Happiest Girl in the World ★★★

This minimalist Romanian movie centres on a schoolgirl who wins a car and with it the chance to promote the sponsors in a commercial shot in Bucharest. Exploited by her father, she is a victim of patriarchy in a country that appears to offer her nothing. The cast – especially the lead actress, Andreea Bosneag – are fine. But it's the bleakest comedy imaginable, while the lack of dramatic momentum prevents it from becoming an emotionally involving tragi-comedy. MS

▶ Andreea Bosneag, Vasile Muraru, Violetta Haret, Serban Pavlu, Andi Vasluianu.
▶ *Dir* Radui Jude, *Pro* Ada Solomon, *Screenplay* Augustina Stanciu and Jude, *Ph* Marius Panduru, *Art Dir* and *Cos* Stanciu, *Ed* Catalin F Cristutiu.

Sponsored bliss: Andreea Bosneag in Radui Jude's rather bleak comedy *The Happiest Girl in the World*.

Hi Film Productions/Circe Films/Centrului National al Cinematografiei România etc- Soda Pictures.
103 mins. Romania/Netherlands. 2009. Rel: 28 May 2010. Cert. 15.

Happy Ever Afters ★½

As Maura (Sally Hawkins) marries an African immigrant for money, Freddie (Tom Riley) finds his own wedding reception spilling into Maura's. It's a sad state of affairs when the extras in a film look more appealing than the principals. In this ineptly edited, flatly photographed farce, Sally Hawkins is miscast in the Meg Ryan part, while only Ariyon Bakare exhibits a shred of likeability – as a man from 'Loco' in Africa. The film's concept certainly has potential but desperately needs some basis in reality to engage an audience. JC-W

➤ Sally Hawkins, Tom Riley, Ariyon Bakare, Charley Boylan, Gary Cooke, Simon Delaney.
➤ *Dir* and *Screenplay* Stephen Burke, *Pro* Alex Ward and Lesley McKimm, *Ph* Jonathan Kovel, *Pro Des* Owen Power, *Ed* Guido Krajewski, *M* Sponge Music, *Cos Supervisor* Mary Fox.

Newgrange Pictures-Verve Pictures.
104 mins. Ireland. 2009. Rel: 19 Mar 2010. Cert. 15.

Harry Brown ★★★★

Ex-Army old-timer Harry Brown (Michael Caine), having witnessed sickening violence and drug dealing on a south London estate, wreaks revenge on the scumbags who killed his friend Leonard (David Bradley). He follows the perpetrators to their drug-fuelled lair to literally beat the living daylights out of them. Caine gives a superbly restrained performance and director Daniel Barber does full justice to Gary Young's spare, almost Pinteresque screenplay. Visually the film conjures up a dark, doomy atmosphere in Martin Ruhe's cinematography. A supporting cast (Joseph Gilgun, Jack O'Connell, Sean Harris etc) couldn't make these misfits more believable in this impressive piece of filmcraft. MHD

➤ Michael Caine, Emily Mortimer, Charlie Creed-Miles, David Bradley, Iain Glen.
➤ *Dir* Daniel Barber, *Pro* Keith Bell, Matthew Brown, Kris Thykier and Matthew Vaughn, *Screenplay* Gary Young, *Ph* Martin Ruhe, *Pro Des* Kave Quinn, *Ed* Joe Walker, *M* Ruth Barrett and Martin Phipps, *Cos* Jane Petrie.

Marv Partners/Hanway Films/UK Film Council/ Prescience/Framestore Features-Lionsgate.
103 mins. UK. 2009. Rel: 11 Nov 2009. Cert. 18.

Harry Potter and the Deathly Hallows Part 1 ★★★★

For all the studio's monetary intentions, the decision to divide J K Rowling's seventh book into two movies does pay off creatively. For the first time the viewer is permitted the luxury of spending quality time with Harry, Ron and Hermione as living, breathing teenagers, without all the distractions of CGI indigestion. At this stage in the game, who would have thought that *HP7* would end up being the second strongest episode – after Alfonso Cuarón's thrilling and supremely cinematic *Prisoner of Azkaban*? JC-W

➤ Daniel Radcliffe, Emma Watson, Rupert Grint, Julie Walters, Alan Rickman, Bill Nighy, Richard Griffiths, Jason Isaacs, Ralph Fiennes, Michael Gambon, Fiona

In arm's way: Michael Caine (right) with arms dealer Joseph Gilgun in Daniel Barber's terrifying *Harry Brown*.

Shaw, Robbie Coltrane, Brendan Gleeson.
▶ *Dir* David Yates, *Pro* David Heyman and David Barron, *Screenplay* Steve Kloves from the book by J K Rowling, *Ph* Eduardo Serra, *Pro Des* Stuart Craig, *Ed* Mark Day, *M* Alexander Desplat, *Cos* Jany Temime.

Warner Bros Pictures/Heyday Films-Warner Bros. 146 mins. UK/USA. 2010. Rel: 19 Nov 2010. Cert. 12A.

Harry Potter and the Half-Blood Prince ★★½

Each new episode in the *Harry Potter* franchise is more contrived than the last. There's the new professor, the major plot twist, a death or two and, of course, the inevitable cliffhanger. Only Potter devotees could really embrace this sixth chapter, although it does look sensational. But boasting a budget of $250m, *The Half-Blood Prince* should supply more than teenage sexual politics and a link to the seventh instalment. Incidentally, the film's most amazing sequence is over in the first five minutes – the next two-and-a-half hours are merely the post-coital cigarette. JC-W

▶ Daniel Radcliffe, Rupert Grint, Emma Watson, Michael Gambon, Robbie Coltrane, Alan Rickman, Jim Broadbent, Timothy Spall, Helena

Bonham Carter, Julie Walters.
▶ *Dir* David Yates, *Pro* David Barron and David Heyman, *Screenplay* Steve Kloves, based on the book by J K Rowling, *Ph* Bruno Delbonnel, *Pro Des* Stuart Craig, *Ed* Mark Day, *M* Nicholas Hooper, *Cos* Jany Temime.

Warner Bros Pictures/Heyday Films-Warner Bros. 153 mins. UK/USA. 2009. Rel: 15 July 2009. Cert. 12A.

The Headless Woman ★

Although admired by some, and effective enough visually and in its use of sound, this film from Argentina's Lucrecia Martel strikes me as pretentious, ill-judged and inconsiderate to the audience. Told from the viewpoint of a totally unsympathetic female dentist responsible for a car accident which may have killed a youth, it has no point of engagement and it doesn't even bother to clarify who the subsidiary characters are. As social comment, J B Priestley did it all so much better in *An Inspector Calls*! (Original title: *La mujer sin cabeza*) MS

▶ María Onetto, Claudia Cantero, Inés Efrón, César Bordón, Daniel Genoud, Maria Vaner.
▶ *Dir* and *Screenplay* Lucrecia Martel, *Pro* Pedro Almodóvar, Agustín Almodóvar, Esther Garcia, Martel

Rowling on: Daniel Radcliffe, Rupert Grint and Emma Watson in the penultimate *Harry Potter and the Deathly Hallows Part 1*.

and others, *Ph* Bárbara Alvarez, *Art Dir* María Eugenia Sueiro, *Ed* Miguel Schverdfinger, *Cos* Julio Suárez.

Aquafilms/El Deseo/Slot Machine/Teodora Film etc-New Wave Films.

89 mins. Argentina/Spain/France/Italy. 2008. Rel: 19 Feb 2010. Cert. 12A.

Heart of Fire ★★★★

Inevitably grim but heartfelt, this is a film about child soldiers in Eritrea in the 1980s centred on the tale of one little girl who, forced into this position by her father, tries to rebel. The film, shot in Kenya since Eritrea itself could not be used, is loosely based on a true story and the non-professional cast, largely refugees from Eritrea, are wholly committed. The director is Luigi Falorni, who here has material admirably contrasted to *The Story of the Weeping Camel*, on which he was co-director. (Original title: *Feuerherz*) MS

❯ Letekidan Micael, Solomie Micael, Seble Tilahun, Daniel Seyoum, Mekdes Wegene.
❯ *Dir* Luigi Falorni, *Pro* Andreas Bareiss, Sven Burgemeister, Gloria Burkert and Bernd Burgemeister, *Screenplay* Falorni and Gabriele Kister, freely adapted from the life story of Senait G Mehan, *Ph* Judith Kaufmann, *Art Dir* Vittoria Sogno, *Ed* Anja Pohl, *M* Andrea Guerra, *Cos* Brigitta Lohrer-Horres.

Burkert Bareiss/TV60Film/Senator Film Produktion etc-Metrodome Distribution.

89 mins. Germany/Austria/Kenya. 2008. Rel: 25 Sep 2009. No Cert.

Heartbreaker ★★★★

A sure-footed French rom-com, *Heartbreaker* is about a trickster named Alex (Romain Duris)

whose seductive appeal is available for hire in order to break up unwelcome romances. Consequently the father of Juliette (Vanessa Paradis) employs him to prevent her from going through with a marriage to an Englishman regarded by Dad as not being a satisfactory son-in-law. Inevitably Alex falls for Juliette, who then discovers that he was employed by her father. Monaco makes an ideal location, it's well paced and the stars have chemistry. In short, it's a lightweight piece that knows exactly what it is doing. (Original title: *L'arnacoeur*) MS

❯ Romain Duris, Vanessa Paradis, Andrew Lincoln, Julie Ferrier, François Damiens.
❯ *Dir* Pascal Chaumeil, *Pro* Nicolas Duval Adassovsky, Yann Zenou and Laurent Zeitoun, *Screenplay* Zeitoun, Jeremy Doner and Yoann Gromb, from Zeitoun's idea, *Ph* Thierry Arbogast, *Art Dir* Hervé Gallet, *Ed* Dorian Rigal Ansous, *M* Klaus Badelt, *Cos* Charlotte Betaillole.

Quad Films/Script Associés/Universal/Chaocorp etc-Revolver Entertainment.

105 mins. France/UK. 2010. Rel: 2 July 2010. Cert. 15.

Heartless ★★

A shy photographer with a disfiguring birthmark makes a Faustian pact with the Devil. To transpose the Faust legend to London's East End is something of a tall order and writer-director Philip Ridley just doesn't get the mood right. Not so much multi-levelled as multi-toned, this bizarre offering shifts from social realism to horror to black comedy to fantasy like a possessed gearbox. Still, any film with Eddie Marsan in a hilarious and chilling cameo is not a total waste of time. JC-W

A soldier's life for her: Letekidan Micael in Luigi Falorni's heartfelt *Heart of Fire*.

A *feinte* romance: Vanessa Paradis and Romain Duris in Pascal Chaumeil's hugely successful *Heartbreaker*.

▶ Jim Sturgess, Luke Treadaway, Clémence Poésy, Justin Salinger, Timothy Spall, Noel Clarke, Ruth Sheen, Eddie Marsan.
▶ *Dir* and *Screenplay* Philip Ridley, *Pro* Pippa Cross and Richard Raymond, *Ph* Matt Gray, *Pro Des* Ricky Eyres, *Ed* Chris Gill and Paul Knight, *M* David Julyan, *Cos* Jo Thompson.

Cross Day Productions/Richard Raymond Films/May 13/Regent Capital/Cinema Two/Matador Pictures/ CinemaNX-Lionsgate.
114 mins. UK. 2009. Rel: 21 May 2010. Cert. 18.

The Heavy ★

Poor dialogue, unbelievable plotting and some weak acting pull down this ropey British crime thriller starring boxer turned actor Gary Stretch as ex-con 'Boots' Mason who, after serving seven years in jail, gets a job working for dodgy businessman Stephen Rea. The clichés pile high after it turns out a contract has been put on the life of Boots' brother, rising politician Christian Mason (Adrian Paul)... Even with Vinnie Jones as a bent copper, Christopher Lee and Jean Marsh as the brothers' estranged parents, alongside Sadie Frost and Lee Ryan from Blue, this is none too interesting, involving or exciting. DW

▶ Gary Stretch, Vinnie Jones, Stephen Rea, Adrian Paul, Lee Ryan, Shannyn Sossamon, Christopher Lee, Jean Marsh, Sadie Frost.
▶ *Dir* and *Screenplay* Marcus Warren, *Pro* John Cairns, *Pro Des* Marcus Wookey, *Ed* David Head, *M* Paul Oakenfold, *Cos* Andrew Cox.

Heavy Productions/Contraption Ltd-Parkland Pictures.
102 mins. UK/USA. 2010. Rel: 16 Apr 2010. Cert. 18.

Henri-Georges Clouzot's Inferno ★★★½

This is a documentary to intrigue admirers of the French director Clouzot and/or the actress Romy Schneider, since it resurrects the remains of the uncompleted drama *Inferno*, which they set out to make in 1964. It fascinates both for Clouzot's attempt to join the avant-garde and for the echoes of his more familiar style. New and old interviews are included, together with surviving test shots, silent footage of the film itself and actors reading from the screenplay. Fascinating indeed, but also a bit over-extended. (Original title: *L'Enfer d'Henri-Georges Clouzot*) MS

▶ With Romy Schneider, Serge Reggiani, Cathérine Allegret, Inès Clouzot, William Lubtchansky, Costa-Gavras, Jacques Gamblin, Bérénice Béjo.
▶ *Dir* Serge Bromberg and Ruxandra Medrea Annonier, *Pro* Bromberg, *Ph* Irina Lubtchansky and

Freeze frame: Henri-Georges Clouzot and Romy Schneider as seen in *Henri-Georges Clouzot's Inferno*.

Gap year: Nathan Gamble, Haley Bennett and Chris Massoglia in Joe Dante's spooky *The Hole*.

that every touch suggests not the character's experience but the director's manipulation. MS

▶ Elena Anaya, Bea Segura, Miriam Correa, Kaiet Rodríguez, Mar Sodupe.
▶ *Dir* Gabe Ibáñez, *Pro* Alvaro Augustin, Jesus de La Vega, *Screenplay* Javier Gullón, *Ph* Alejandro Martinez, *Art Dir* Patrick Salvador, *Ed* Enric García i Vilà and Enrique Garcia, *M* Zacarías M de la Riva, *Cos* Patricia Martinez.

Madrugada Films/Telecinco Cinema/Roxbury Pictures etc-Optimum Releasing
89 mins. Spain/France. 2009. Rel: 18 June 2010. Cert. 12A.

The Hole ★★★½

After moving to a new neighbourhood, brothers Dane (Chris Massoglia) and Lucas (Nathan Gamble) discover a hole in their basement. Along with their neighbour Julie (Haley Bennett), they enter the hole but they soon begin to regret their decision... Joe Dante is a master in creating atmosphere and here his likeable adventure is suitably spooky and dark, with decent 3D effects, but it never attempts to enter into major Grand Guignol territory. GS

▶ Chris Massoglia, Haley Bennett, Nathan Gamble, Teri Polo, Bruce Dern, Quinn Lord.
▶ *Dir* Joe Dante, *Pro* Claudio Faeh, Vicki Sotheran, David Lancaster, Michael Litvak, *Screenplay* Mark L Smith, *Ph* Theo van de Sande, *Pro Des* Brentan Harron, *Ed* Marshall Harvey, *M* Javier Navarrete, *Cos* Kate Main.

Bold Films/The Hole/Bender Spink/Paradise F X Corp-E1 Entertainment.
92 mins. USA. 2009. Rel: 24 Sep 2010. Cert. 12A.

Jérôme Krumenacker, *Art Dir* Valérie Massadian, *Ed* Janice Jones, *M* Bruno Alexiu.

Lobster Films/France 2 Cinéma etc-Park Circus.
100 mins. France. 2009. Rel: 6 Nov 2009. Cert. 15.

Hierro ★½

Lead actress Elena Anaya does her best here but Gabe Ibáñez's first feature is disastrously unpersuasive. Hoping to be as atmospheric as *The Orphanage* or *Pan's Labyrinth*, it invites us to share the stress of a mother whose young son has gone missing on a holiday trip to the Spanish island of El Hierro. Is there a conspiracy or is she delusional? So self-conscious is the film-making

Highway blues: Adélaïde Leroux in Ursula Meier's surreal, extraordinary *Home*.

Holy Water ★★★

When the central comic concept is about stolen Viagra getting into the water supply of an Irish village, it's wise not to set one's hopes high. This movie doesn't defy expectations yet even so it has been too readily dismissed. There are lots of genuine echoes of Ealing comedies (*Whisky Galore!, The Maggie*) and there's an engagingly warm comic player in Cornelius Clark. It's not that good admittedly, but more interesting than you might suppose. MS

▷ John Lynch, Cian Barry, Cornelius Clark, Linda Hamilton, Susan Lynch, Deirdre Mullins.
▷ *Dir* Tom Reeve, *Pro* Nick Napier-Bell, Duncan Napier-Bell, Romin Schroeder and Frank Konigsberg, *Screenplay* Caroline O'Meara and Reeve, from Michael O'Mahony's story, *Ph* Joost van Starrenburg, *Pro Des* Keith Slote, *Ed* Adrian Murray and Sean Barton, *M* Franco Tortora and Tom Batoy, *Cos* Kate O'Farrell.

Eyeline Entertainment/Atlantic Film Distributors/Idiom Films etc-Kaleidoscope Home Entertainment.
93 mins. UK/USA. 2009. Rel: 5 Feb 2010. Cert. 15.

Home ★★½

Ursula Meier's first feature stars Isabelle Huppert and is a very odd piece about a family whose rural house is beside a road that is designated a motorway. Home becomes hell but mother especially is determined to stay put. It starts as comedy, with Tati-like satire on the heartlessness of modern life, but it turns increasingly to drama as bleak as the world of Samuel Beckett. There's novelty aplenty but nothing much to sustain a full-length feature film. It's left to the audience to make of it what they will. MS

▷ Isabelle Huppert, Olivier Gourmet, Adelaïde Leroux, Kacey Mottet Klein.
▷ *Dir* Ursula Meier, *Pro* Elena Tatti, Thierry Spicher, Denis Freyd and Denis Delcampe, *Screenplay* Meier, Antoine Jaccoud, Raphaëlle Valbrune and others, *Ph* Agnès Godard, *Art Dir* Ivan Niclass, *Ed* Susana Rossberg, *Cos* Anna van Bree.

Box Productions/Archipel 35/Need Productions etc-Soda Pictures.
98 mins. Switzerland/France/Belgium. 2008. Rel: 7 Aug 2009. Cert. 15.

The Horde ★★★½

A group of police officers attack a suburban high-rise apartment block in order to avenge their colleague's murder. But the raid goes wrong and soon, instead of being the attackers, they become the victims. Yannick Dahan and Benjamin Rocher's nasty and brutal horror gives a new lease of life to a tired genre. Their energetic zombies have more appetite for flesh than all the recent living dead films. The plot doesn't make much sense but that's hardly relevant when the extremely violent action takes over. (Original title: *La horde*) GS

▷ Claude Perron, Jean-Pierre Martins, Eriq Ebouaney, Jo Prestia, Yves Pignot, Aurélien Recoing, Antoine Oppenheim.
▷ *Dir* Yannick Dahan and Benjamin Rocher, *Pro* Raphaël Rocher, *Screenplay* Dahan, Benjamin Rocher, Arnaud Bordas and Stéphane Moïssakis, *Ph* Julien Meurice, *Pro Des* Jérémie Streliski, *Ed* Dimtri Amar, *M* Christopher Lennertz, *Cos* Priscilla Van Sprengel.

Capture Films/Le Pacte/Coficup/Canal +/CinéCinéma-Momentum Pictures.
90 mins. France. 2009. Rel: 17 Sep 2010. Cert. 18.

The Horseman ★★★★

Christian (Peter Marshall) begins a long journey through Northern Queensland, determined to find those responsible for his daughter's death. She was heavily into drugs and was led to her death while making porno films. Kastrissios' compelling film debut doesn't shy away from its dark subject matter and fully explores

Attacking the block: Eriq Ebouaney in Yannick Dahan and Benjamin Rocher's nasty and brutal *The Horde*.

the situation in this brutal and extremely violent film, aided by a terrifically committed performance from Marshall, who never loses sympathy despite all the atrocities. GS

▶ Peter Marshall, Caroline Marohasy, Brad McMurray, Jack Henry, Evert McQueen.
▶ *Dir, Screenplay* and *Ed* Steven Kastrissios, *Pro* Kastrissios and Rebecca Dakin, *Ph* Mark Broadbent, *Pro Des* Amanda Broomhall, *M* Ryan Potter, *Cos* Kelly Pasek.

Kastle Films-Kaleidoscope Film Distribution. 96 mins. Australia. 2008. Rel: 30 Oct 2009. Cert. 18.

Horses ★★★★

This documentary from Liz Mermin is a triumph of editing as she selects from footage that covers a year in the life of a show-jumping stable in County Wexford. The horses, affectionately viewed, steal the film from their trainers and jockeys. Horse-lovers will rightly revel in it. MS

▶ With Paul Nolan, James Nolan.
▶ *Dir* and *Screenplay* Liz Mermin, *Pro* Aisling Ahmed, *Ph* Ken O'Mahony and Ciarán Tanham, *Ed* Bert Hunger, *M* James Burrell.

West Park West/BBC/RTÉ etc-DCD Media. 87 mins. UK/Ireland. 2009. Rel: 28 Feb 2010. No Cert.

Hot Tub Time Machine ★½

The oeuvre of gross-out comedy – think projectile vomiting, dog shit and misplaced semen – is given a new twist in this farce produced by John Cusack. Here, the three protagonists hung over from middle-age find themselves transported back to 1986 – via, um, a magic hot tub. It's a one-joke premise reinforced by cultural references to everybody from Michael Jackson to Miley Cyrus via Mötley Crüe. Can John Cusack, a one-note charmer, have really sunk this low? JC-W

▶ John Cusack, Clark Duke, Crispin Glover, Craig Robinson, Rob Corddry, Sebastian Stan, Chevy Chase.

▶ *Dir* Steve Pink, *Pro* John Cusack, John Morris, Grace Loh and Matt Moore, *Screenplay* Morris, Sean Anders and Josh Heald, based on a story by Heald, *Ph* Jack Green, *Pro Des* Bob Ziembicki, *Ed* George Folsey Jr and James Thomas, *M* Christophe Beck, *Cos* Dayna Pink.

Metro-Goldwyn-Mayer Pictures/United Artists/New Crime-20th Century Fox. 99 mins. USA. 2010. Rel: 7 May 2010. Cert. 15.

The House of the Devil ★★★★

Desperate for cash, college student Sam (Jocelin Donahue) begins to regret deeply her decision to work as a babysitter when she answers an ad placed by a mysterious man who lives in the middle of nowhere. A total lunar eclipse is approaching and the creepy Mr and Mrs Ulman (Tom Noonan and Mary Woronov) have different plans for Sam... Ti West's assured direction creates a very believable 1980s setting with a terrific soundtrack. He may be using all the tricks of the genre but he does it with great flair and imagination. GS

▶ Jocelin Donahue, Tom Noonan, Dee Wallace, Mary Woronov, Greta Gerwig, A J Bowen.
▶ *Dr, Ed* and *Screenplay* Ti West, *Pro* Josh Braun, Peter Phok, Roger Kass and Larry Essenden, *Ph* Eliot Rockett, *Pro Des* Jade Healy, *M* Jeff Grace, *Cos* Robin Fitzgerald.

MPI Media Group/RingTheJing/Entertainment/ Construction Vision/Glass Eye Pictures-Metrodome Distribution. 95 mins. USA. 2009. Rel: 19 Mar 2010. Cert. 18.

How to Train Your Dragon
★★★★★

Harnessing the old-fashioned values of story-telling and strong characterisation onto extraordinary visuals and 3D spectacle, *How to Train Your Dragon* is simply a delirious experience. With its pictorial wit, sharp dialogue and inversion of the Beowulf template, the cartoon transports the viewer to a wonderland of virile

Dragon art: Hiccup rides his Night Fury into battle in Chris Sanders and Dean DeBlois' witty and delirious *How To Train Your Dragon*.

Sitting for Satan: Jocelin Donahue in Ti West's stylish *The House of the Devil.*

Vikings (with Scottish accents) and dreadful dragons. Only the artless title itself – drawn from Cressida Cowell's book – lets the side down. JC-W

▶ Voices of Jay Baruchel, Gerard Butler, Craig Ferguson, America Ferrera, T J Miller, Kristen Wiig, Ashley Jensen.
▶ *Dir* Dean DeBlois and Chris Sanders, *Pro* Bonnie Arnold, *Screenplay* DeBlois, Sanders and William Davies, based on the novel by Cressida Cowell, *Pro Des* Kathy Altieri, *Ed* Maryann Brandon and Darren T Holmes, *M* John Powell.

DreamWorks Animation/Mad Hatter Entertainments/ Mad Hatter Films/Vertigo Entertainment-Paramount Pictures.
98 mins. USA. 2010. Rel: 31 Mar 2010. Cert. PG.

H2Oil ★★★★

Pertinent as the issue is, it's strange to have three documentary films on release about the devastating effects of oil operations in the tar sands of Alberta, Canada. Where *Petropolis* [qv] provides an essentially visual experience, *H2Oil* and *Dirty Oil* [also qv] are similar in approach and even share detailed comments from the same people. All three films are very able so you needn't worry about taking your pick. MS

▶ With Dr John O'Connor, Chief Allan Adam, Aaron and Cathy Mathers, Ivy Simpson.
▶ *Dir* and *Screenplay* Shannon Walsh, *Pro* Sergeo Kirkby and Sarah Spring, *Ph* Alan Kohl and others, *Ed* Étienne Gagnon and Sophie Leblond, *M* Rebecca Foon, Ian Ilavsky and Eric Craven.

Loaded Pictures/Canwest Media etc-Dogwoof Pictures
76 mins. Canada 2009. Rel: 11 June 2010. Cert. 12A.

The Human Centipede (First Sequence) ★★½

Posited as the grossest film of the year, this is actually a rather coy addition to the 'torture porn' genre. A mad scientist who has spent his career separating Siamese twins has elected to 'create' the first Siamese triplets. This ambition involves surgically connecting an alimentary canal through the bodies of three unwitting tourists. The trouble with Tom Six's curious film is that its characters – the quarry and the police – are so dim-witted. The result, then, is neither scary not funny and only mildly revolting. JC-W

▶ Dieter Laser, Ashley C Williams, Ashlyn Yennie, Akihiro Kitamura, Andreas Leupold, Peter Blankenstein.
▶ *Dir* and *Screenplay* Tom Six, *Pro* Tom and Ilona Six, *Ph* Goof de Koning, *Pro Des* Thomas Stefan, *Ed* Nigel de Hond, *M* Patrick Savage and Holeg Spies.

Six Entertainment-Bounty Films.
92 mins. Netherlands. 2009. Rel: 2 Aug 2010. Cert. 18.

Humpday ★★★½

Unexpectedly memorable despite its title, Lynn Shelton's film is in the American mumblecore tradition of cheap independent film-making with much talk. It features two heterosexual men – one married, the other drawn to a bohemian lifestyle – who, when drunk, agree to have gay sex together in a porn film. Instead of being silly or cheap, this well-acted film is genuinely insightful about men's concerns over their male image and about sexuality generally. The movie's final section is not its strongest but the piece is well worth a look. MS

➤ Mark Duplass, Alycia Delmore, Joshua Leonard, Lynn Shelton, Trina Willard.
➤ *Dir*, *Pro* and *Screenplay* Lynn Shelton, *Ph* Benjamin Kasulke, *Pro Des* Jasminka Vukcevic, *Ed* Nat Sanders, *M* Vinny Smith.

Made with support from 4Culture, Northwest Film Forum etc-Vertigo Films.
94 mins. USA. 2009. Rel: 18 Dec 2009. Cert. 15.

The Hunter ★★½

Rafi Pitts is the Iranian film-maker who made his mark with the beautiful 2006 film *It's Winter*. Here he doesn't repeat himself but he disappoints, perhaps because this new work doesn't travel. It would have far more meaning for an Iranian audience but, as it is, it invites us unsuccessfully to care about a bereaved husband and father who goes berserk and shoots people. An actor with magnetism might have involved us more but unfortunately circumstances forced Pitts to take on the leading role himself. (Original title: *Shekarchi*) MS

➤ Rafi Pitts, Mitra Hajjar, Ali Nicksaulat, Hassan Ghalendi, Saba Yaghoobi.
➤ *Dir* and *Screenplay* Rafi Pitts, *Pro* Thanassis Karathanos, *Ph* Mohammad Davudi, *Art Dir* Malak Jahan Khazai, *Ed* Hassan Hassandoost.

Twenty Twenty Vision Filmproduktion GmbH/Aftab Negaran Film etc-Artificial Eye.
92 mins. Germany/Iran. 2010. Rel: 29 Oct 2010. Cert. 15.

Loose cannon: Jeremy Renner in his Oscar-nominated performance as Sgt William James in Kathryn Bigelow's incredibly suspenseful, shocking and eye-opening The Hurt Locker.

The Hurt Locker ★★★★

Superbly crafted by Kathryn Bigelow, this is not a political drama but a heart-stopping suspense drama about American soldiers in Baghdad whose job is to defuse bombs. The central character is a brave but alarming sergeant (Jeremy Renner) whose risk-taking often endangers his own men. You feel that you are there, but, in contrast to the Powell & Pressburger classic *The Small Back Room* which made you care for the people carrying out such work, this is a macho action movie, brilliant but heartless. MS

➤ Jeremy Renner, Anthony Mackie, Brian Geraghty, Ralph Fiennes, Guy Pearce.
➤ *Dir* Kathryn Bigelow, *Pro* Bigelow, Mark Boal, Nicolas Chartier and Greg Shapiro, *Screenplay* Boal, *Ph* Barry Ackroyd, *Pro Des* Karl Júlíusson, *Ed* Bob Murawski and Chris Innis, *M* Marco Beltrami and Buck Sanders, *Cos* George Little and Vicki Mulholland.

Voltage Pictures/First Light/Kingsgate Films etc-Optimum Releasing.
130 mins. USA. 2008. Rel: 28 Aug 2009. Cert. 15.

I Am Love ★★★½

What starts off as a drama about inheritance and the future of an industrial empire owned by a Milanese family then side-steps disconcertingly into a story about the rebellion through love of a Russian outsider (Tilda Swinton) who has

Welsh dresser: Robert Carlyle in Justin Kerrigan's undervalued *I Know You Know.*

married into it. The film is erratic (the family scenes use space to denote wealth quite superbly but there's an over-the-top kitschy sex scene), yet it's certainly interesting. Supporting actress Alda Rohrwacher is new to me and an actress to watch. (Original title: *Io sono l'amore*) MS

▶ Tilda Swinton, Flavio Parenti, Edoardo Gabbriellini, Alba Rohrwacher, Pippo Delbono, Diane Fleri, Maria Paiato, Gabriele Ferzetti.
▶ *Dir* Luca Guadagnino, *Pro* Guadagnino, Tilda Swinton, Alessandro Usai and others, *Screenplay* Barbara Alberti, Ivan Cotroneo, Walter Fasano and Guadagnino, from his story, *Ph* Yorick Le Saux, *Pro Des* Francesca di Mottola, *Ed* Fasano, *M* John Adams, *Cos* Antonella Cannarozzi.

First Sun/Mikado Film/RAI Cinema/Dolcevita Productions etc-Metrodome Distribution.
119 mins. Italy. 2009. Rel: 9 April 2010. Cert. 15.

I Know You Know ★★½

It's a great shame that this film fails to convince because the writer/director, *Human Traffic*'s Justin Kerrigan, has undertaken a very personal project and in this portrayal of a father and his 11-year-old son Robert Carlyle and Arron Fuller are excellent. The boy takes it that his father is working for MI5 but the truth (which should not be revealed) proves to be otherwise. Unfortunately, we have lost all belief in what seems to be happening long before the plot twist belatedly explains things. MS

▶ Robert Carlyle, Arron Fuller, David Bradley, Karl Johnson, Valerie Lilley, Daniel Flynn.
▶ *Dir* and *Screenplay* Justin Kerrigan, *Pro* Sally Hibbin, *Ph* Ed Wild, *Pro Des* Christina Casali,

Ed Stuart Gazzard, *M* Guy Farley, *Cos* Sian Jenkin.

The Little Film Company/Wales Creative IP Fund/ Parallax East etc-Network Releasing
79 mins. UK/USA/Germany. 2008. Rel: 9 Apr 2010. No Cert.

I Love You, Beth Cooper ★

Hayden Panettiere glows as 18-year-old high-school girl Beth Cooper, for whom Paul Rust suddenly declares his love. Panettiere has a boyfriend and doesn't care. This could have prompted some decent laughs, but the script and direction blow it by taking the silly slapstick route. Though talented, Rust seems too old and charmless to be the romantic lead in this slack teen romcom. Panettiere is cute and Jack T Carpenter makes skilful headway as Rust's best buddy, who may be gay or not or bi (who cares?). You want to like it, but the struggling script has only half a dozen really funny lines. DW

▶ Hayden Panettiere, Paul Rust, Jack T Carpenter, Lauren London, Lauren Storm, Shawn Roberts.
▶ *Dir* Chris Columbus, *Pro* Columbus, Michael Barnathan and Mark Radcliffe, *Screenplay* Larry Doyle, based on his novel, *Ph* Phil Abraham, *Pro Des* Howard Cummings, *Ed* Peter Honess, *M* Christophe Beck, *Cos* Karen L Matthews.

Fox Atomic/1492 Pictures/The Bridge Studios/Bece Canada Productions/Dune Entertainment III/Ingenious Film Partners-20th Century Fox.
102 mins. Canada/USA. 2009. Rel: 21 Aug 2009. Cert. 15.

I Love You Phillip Morris ★★★★

Ex-cop Steven Russell decides to come out of the closet and turn con man to pay for his new lifestyle. Ending up behind bars, he meets fellow gay Phillip

Morris: they fall in love, set up home and try to live happily ever after. But with Steven that's not possible… The film is more wacky gay rom-com than gay drama and, as odd as the allegedly true plot is, it's mostly played for laughs. Jim Carrey as Steven is unusually restrained while Ewan McGregor as Phillip is rather sweet. It's very entertaining, although US audiences were not that amused. MHD

‣ Jim Carrey, Ewan McGregor, Leslie Mann, Rodrigo Santorp, Ted Alderman, Nicholas Alexander.
‣ *Dir* and *Screenplay* Glenn Ficarra and John Requa, from the book by Steven McVicker, *Pro* Andrew Lazar and Far Shariat, *Ph* Xavier Pérez Grobet, *Pro Des* Hugo Luczyc-Wyhowski, *Ed* Thomas J Nordberg, *M* Nick Urata, *Cos* David C Robinson.
EuropaCorp/Mad Chance-E1 Entertainment.
102 mins. France/USA. 2009. Rel: 17 Mar 2010. Cert. 15.

Ice Age 3 ★★½

As the mammoths Manny and Ellie prepare for the birth of their first child, Sid the sloth gets paternal feelings of his own. Meanwhile, a whole new world is discovered beneath the ice – where dinosaurs still rule. After the improvement of the last sequel, this totally redundant follow-up is given a 3D boost to little creative gain. There is some inventive imagery, but no thanks to the extra dimension. There are also a handful of good-ish jokes ('Do my ankles look fat?' 'What ankles?') and the pace is helter-skelter – but there are no guffaws, let alone any charm. (Original title: *Ice Age: Dawn of the Dinosaurs*) JC-W

In prison, out of the closet: Ewan McGregor as PM in Glenn Ficarra and John Requa's I Love You Phillip Morris.

‣ Voices of Eunice Cho, Karen Disher, Harrison Fahn, Maile Flanagan, Bill Hader, Queen Latifah, Denis Leary, John Leguizamo, Simon Pegg.
‣ *Dir* Carlos Saldanha and Mike Thurmeier, *Pro* John C Donkin and Lori Forte, *Screenplay* Peter Ackerman, Yoni Brenner, Michael Berg and Mike Reiss, from a story by Jason Carter Eaton, *Pro Des* Mike Knapp, *Ed* Harry Hitner and James Palumbo, *M* John Powell.
Blue Sky Studios-20th Century Fox.
94 mins. USA. 2009. Rel: 1 July 2009. Cert. U.

Ichi ★★★★

Fumihiko Sori's stylish epic tells the story of Ichi (Haruka Ayase), a blind musician and martial arts expert who begins a journey in search of the swordsman, also blind, who raised her as a child. She encounters many dangers but she is always ready to draw her sword and kill those that threaten to take advantage of her disability. The production values are superb and Ayase is a stunning presence in the first female version of the classic *Zatoichi* series of films and TV shows. GS

‣ Haruka Ayase, Shido Nakamura, Yôsuke Kubozuka, Takao Ôsawa.
‣ *Dir* Fumihiko Sori, *Pro* Toshiaki Nakazawa, Sumio Kiga, Yshio Irie, Yasushi Umemura etc, *Screenplay* Kan Shimosawa, *Ph* Keiji Hashimoto, *Pro Des* Sasaki Hisashi, *Ed* Mototaka Kusakabe, *M* Michael Edwards and Lisa Gerard.
ICHI Film Partners-Manga Entertainment.
120 mins. Japan. 2008. Rel: 10 July 2009. Cert. 15.

The Illusionist ★★★½

Sylvain Chomet's animated feature is a labour of love based on an unfilmed screenplay by Jacques Tati about a magician still touring in the 1950s

Breakfast is interrupted by a magician's bunny in Sylvain Chomet's *The Illusionist.*

but finding the music halls taken over by rock 'n' roll acts. Relocated in the main to Edinburgh, it evokes that city beautifully, but I found the tale fey and unconvincing in its treatment of the near father/daughter relationship between the magician and a young girl, while some of the humour lacks Tati's subtlety. But many took a different view and loved this film. MS

▶ With the voices of Jean-Claude Donda, Eilidh Rankin, Duncan MacNeil.
▶ *Dir, Ed* and *M* Sylvain Chomet, *Pro* Bob Last and Sally Chomet, *Screenplay* Jacques Tati, adapted by Sylvain Chomet, *Art Dir* Bjarne Hansen.

Pathé/Django Films/Ciné B/France 3 Cinéma etc-Warner Bros.
80 mins. UK/France. 2010. Rel: 20 Aug 2010. Cert. PG.

I'm Still Here ★★

When Joaquin Phoenix announced his retirement from acting to become a rap star, he became the butt of Hollywood. To spotlight his fall from grace, Joaquin has collaborated with his brother-in-law Casey Affleck (husband of Summer Phoenix) to produce this navel-gazing home movie, warts and all. And so Affleck and Phoenix reveal the star as monster: a bloated, shaggy, foul-mouthed, chain-smoking, coke-snorting travesty of the earnest young artiste he once was. Part *Borat* without the laughs, part *Raging Bull* without the artistry, this is a new kind of film, masochistic catharsis posing as mockumentary. JC-W

▶ Joaquin Phoenix, Jack Nicholson, Antony Langdon, Larry McHale, Billy Crystal, Danny Glover, Bruce Willis, Danny DeVito, Jamie Foxx, Ben Stiller.
▶ *Dir* Casey Affleck, *Pro* Affleck, Phoenix and Amanda White, *Screenplay* Affleck and Phoenix, *Ph* Affleck and Magdalena Górka, *Ed* Dody Dorn, *M* Marty Fogg.

They Are Going To Kill Us Productions-Optimum Releasing.
106 mins. USA. 2010. Rel: 17 Sep 2010. Cert. 15.

The Imaginarium of Doctor Parnassus ★★★½

Here's a fantasy film that will be remembered as the work completed after Johnny Depp, Jude Law and Colin Farrell took over to show different aspects of the character Heath Ledger was playing at the time of his tragic death. However, it's not an actors' film but a Faustian tale memorable for the imagination and visual imagery of its creator Terry Gilliam. It may not build to a satisfactory climax but along the way it fascinates and nobody else could have made it. MS

▶ Heath Ledger, Christopher Plummer, Verne Troyer, Andrew Garfield, Lily Cole, Tom Waits, Johnny Depp, Colin Farrell, Jude Law.
▶ *Dir* Terry Gilliam, *Pro* William Vince, Amy Gilliam, Samuel Hadida and Terry Gilliam, *Screenplay* Terry Gilliam and Charles McKeown, *Ph* Nicola Pecorini, *Pro Des* Anastasia Masaro, *Ed* Mick Audsley, *M* Mychael and Jeff Danna, *Cos* Monique Prudhomme.

In memoriam: Heath Ledger's final performance, in Terry Gilliam's *The Imaginarium of Doctor Parnassus.*

Samuel Hadida/Infinity Features Entertainment/Poo Poo Pictures etc-Lionsgate UK.
123 mins. UK/Canada/France. 2009. Rel: 16 Oct 2009. Cert. 12A.

Imagine That ★

In this no-concept film, Eddie Murphy, who looks totally uninterested in the project and his fellow actors, plays a successful financial executive who has no time for anybody, just his business. He doesn't even try to act, so it's left to little Yara Shahidi, who plays his mischievous seven-year-old daughter, to bring some energy and much-needed intelligence to this unfortunate project. This is a strong contender for the worst film of the year! GS

❦ Eddie Murphy, Martin Sheen, Thomas Haden Church, Ronny Cox, Yara Shahidi, Vanessa Williams, Michael Vorhaus.
❦ *Dir* Karey Kirkpatrick, *Pro* Lorenzo di Bonaventura and Ed Solomon, *Screenplay* Solomon and Chris Matheson, *Ph* John Lindley, *Pro Des* William Arnold, *Ed* David Moritz, *M* Mark Mancina, *Cos* Ruth E Carter.
Paramount Pictures/Nickelodeon Movies/Di Bonaventura Pictures/Goldcrest Pictures etc-Paramount Pictures.
107 mins. USA. 2009. Rel: 14 Aug 2009. Cert. PG.

I'm Gonna Explode ★★½

What makes me want to explode is that a brilliant start is frittered away in this unsympathetic story of empty-headed rebellious teenagers. It runs out of steam but not out of footage. Yet for part of the time the film is riveting, not just for an admirer's nod to Godard but for sequences that equal the French director's best. That it plummets and dies out is infuriating. The setting is Mexico and the director is Gerardo Naranjo. (Original title: *Voy a explotar*) MS

❦ María Deschamps, Juan Pablo de Santiago, Daniel Giménez Cacho, Rebecca Jones.

❦ *Dir* and *Screenplay* Gerardo Naranjo, *Pro* Pablo Cruz, Naranjo, Hunter Gray and Alain de la Mata, *Ph* Tobias Datum, *Pro Des* Claudio Castelli, *Ed* Yibrán Asuad, *Music Supervisor* Lynn Fainchtein, *Cos* Annaí Ramos Maza and Amanda Cárcamo.
Cancana/Cinematográfica Revolcadero etc-Artificial Eye.
103 mins. Mexico/USA. 2008. Rel: 1 Jan 2010. Cert. 15.

In Our Name ★★★

The excellent Joanne Froggatt plays a woman soldier newly back from Iraq whose husband is unable to understand the traumas she is undergoing due to linking in her mind a child killed in the fighting with her own daughter who is of the same age. Writer/director Brian Welsh is properly committed to his theme, but his sincerity cannot conceal the fact that the film's second half tries to manipulate the emotions of the audience and goes off the rails in the process. MS

❦ Joanne Froggatt, Mel Raido, Chloe-Jayne Wilkinson, Andrew Knott, Janine Leigh.
❦ *Dir* and *Screenplay* Brian Welsh, *Pro* Michelle Eastwood, *Ph* Sam Care, *Pro Des* Anna Lavelle, *Ed* Hazel Baillie, *M* Stuart Earl, *Cos* Kate Eccles.
Curzon Artificial Eye/NFTS/Escape Films/A10 Films etc-Artificial Eye.
93 mins. UK. 2010. Rel: 10 Dec 2010. Cert. 18.

In the Land of the Free ★★★½

This documentary does well to draw attention to the appalling situation in many American prisons where inmates are kept in solitary in the most confined spaces. This wider point emerges during the film's enquiry into three such prisoners in one jail in Louisiana who became known as the Angola 3. It's a pity, though, that film-maker Vadim Jean uses music and contrived images to underline the drama when the facts are eloquent in themselves. The exaggerated style of the presentation irritates. MS

❦ With Robert King, Scott Fleming, Teenie Verrett. Narrated by Samuel L Jackson.
❦ *Dir* and *Screenplay* Vadim Jean, *Pro* Jean, Paul Brooks, Ian Sharples and Claudia Morris, *Ph* Michael Fox and Adam Stone, *Ed* David Charap, *M* David Buckley.
The Mob Film Company/Gold Circle Films/Yesterday Films-Mob Film Company.
84 mins. UK/USA. 2009. Rel: 26 Mar 2010. Cert. 15.

Inception ★★★½

The special effects are marvellous and, as director, Christopher Nolan handles the material with masterly panache. As writer, however, he presents us with dream worlds and a plot about the possibility of implanting ideas in the brain. It results in a narrative so complex that it probably takes several viewings to unravel it. But given Leonardo DiCaprio as the star and some stunning action scenes many have relished the challenge. Does some great film-making justify such impenetrability? MS

▶ Leonardo DiCaprio, Ken Watanabe, Joseph Gordon-Levitt, Marion Cotillard, Ellen Page, Tom Hardy, Cillian Murphy, Tom Berenger, Michael Caine, Pete Postlethwaite.
▶ *Dir* and *Screenplay* Christopher Nolan, *Pro* Emma Thomas and Nolan, *Ph* Wally Pfister, *Pro Des* Guy Hendrix Dyas, *Ed* Lee Smith, *M* Hans Zimmer, *Cos* Jeffrey Kurland.
Warner Bros. Pictures/Legendary Pictures/Syncopy-Warner Bros.
148 mins. USA/UK. 2010. Rel: 16 July 2010. Cert. 12A.

The Infidel ★★

Mahmud Nasir (Omid Djalili) is a dedicated Muslim family man who gets the shock of his life when he discovers that he was adopted at birth and that his real name is Solly Shimshillewitz. He wants to know more about his Jewishness but also tries to keep it a secret, especially from his son's future father-in-law, the fanatical Muslim cleric Arshad-El-Masri (Igal Naor). It's a fun idea but David Baddiel's script feels like an overextended television sketch, while Josh Appignanesi's rather indifferent direction is not helped by Djalili's overblown performance. GS

▶ Archie Panjabi, Matt Lucas, Richard Schiff, Omid Djalili, Chris Wilson, Miranda Hart, Paul Kaye, Tracy-Ann Oberman, David Schneider, Igal Naor.
▶ *Dir* Josh Appignanesi, *Pro* Djalili, David Baddiel, Arvind Ethan David, Uzma Hasan and Stewart Le Marechal, *Screenplay* David Baddiel, *Ph* Natasha

Braier, *Pro Des* Erik Rehl, *Ed* Kim Gaster, *M* Erran Baron Cohen, *Cos* Marianne Agertoft.
Met Film/Slingshot Productions-Revolver Entertainments.
105 mins. UK. 2010. Rel: 5 May 2010. Cert. 15.

The Informant! ★★★

Matt Damon is at his very best in this true story of an unreliable whistleblower. Perhaps through being aware of the quality of a not dissimilar tale told by Michael Mann in 2000 in *The Insider*, Steven Soderbergh took on this project only after it had been decided to play it for comedy. Unfortunately, a comic take quickly fades into insignificance and the piece is instantly forgettable, save for Damon's performance and the pristine colour photography of Soderbergh under his regular alias of Peter Andrews. MS

▶ Matt Damon, Scott Bakula, Joel McHale, Melanie Lynskey, Lucas Carroll, Eddie Jemison.
▶ *Dir* Steven Soderbergh, *Pro* Michael Jaffe, Howard Braunstein, Kurt Eichenwald and others, *Screenplay* Scott Z Burns, based on the book by Eichenwald, *Ph* Peter Andrews (i.e. Soderbergh), *Pro Des* Doug Meerdink, *Ed* Stephen Mirrione, *M* Marvin Hamlisch, *Cos* Shoshana Rubin.
Warner Bros Pictures/Participant Media/Section Eight/Groundswell Productions/Jaffe/Braunstein Enterprise-Warner Bros.
108 mins. USA. 2009. Rel: 20 Nov 2009. Cert. 15.

The Informers ★★

Los Angeles; 1983. A network of degenerates from the worlds of music, television and film go about their business of abusing each other and

Telling tales: Matt Damon reveals all in Steven Soderbergh's misconceived *The Informant!*

A dirty war:
Brad Pitt rather
overdoes it in
Quentin Tarantino's
impudent and
allusive *Inglourious
Basterds*.

themselves. For inexplicable reasons a stellar cast of actors coast along in familiar roles – Kim Basinger is distant and distressed, Mickey Rourke sleazy and weird – in an ensemble pieced together from a short story collection by Bret Easton Ellis. So, is this depressing social commentary or a well-told sick joke without a punch line? JC-W

❯ Kim Basinger, Mickey Rourke, Rhys Ifans, Billy Bob Thornton, Winona Ryder, Jon Foster, Austin Nichols, Amber Heard, Lou Taylor Pucci, Mel Raido.
❯ *Dir* Gregor Jordan, *Pro* Marco Weber, *Screenplay* Bret Easton Ellis and Nicholas Jarecki, from the novel by Ellis, *Ph* Petra Korner, *Pro Des* Cecilia Montiel, *Ed* Robert Brakey, *M* Christopher Young, *Cos* Sophie Carbonell.
Senator Entertainment Company-Entertainment Film Distributors.
98 mins. USA/Germany. 2008. Rel: 17 July 2009. Cert. 15.

Inglourious Basterds ★★★★½

It's difficult to understand just how Tarantino juggles violence and humour to such good effect without falling flat on his face. Here he has a Jewish girl out to avenge the killing of her family, while a gung-ho US soldier leads his band of scalphunters in search of Nazis in order to literally lop their locks. Screamingly funny at times despite its subject matter, and often visually beautiful, *Inglourious Basterds* wins hands down. Over-the-top performances by Brad Pitt and the Oscar-winning Christoph Waltz make the film more like an opera than a movie, but it's none the worse for that. MHD

❯ Brad Pitt, Christoph Waltz, Eli Roth, Michael Fassbender, Diane Kruger, Mélanie Laurent, Daniel Brühl.

❯ *Dir* and *Screenplay* Quentin Tarantino, *Pro* Lawrence Bender, *Ph* Robert Richardson, *Pro Des* David Wasco, *Ed* Sally Menke, *Music Supervisor* Mary Ramos, *Cos* Anna B Sheppard.
Universal Pictures/The Weinstein Company/A Band Apart/Zehnte Babelsberg Film/Visiona Romantica-Universal Pictures International.
153 mins. USA/Germany. 2009. Rel: 19 Aug 2009. Cert. 18.

Into Eternity ★★

There have been many impressive documentaries lately but this is not one of them. It deals with the storage underground of nuclear waste and that's a valid concern with its potential threat for future generations. However, with much repetition and views that can only be surmised, it is as though what would have made a good half-hour TV programme has in a decidedly effortful way been extended to 75 minutes. MS

❯ With Michael Madsen, Tímo Äikäs, Peter Wikberg, Timo Seppälä, Wendla Paile.
❯ *Dir* and *Writer* Michael Madsen, *Pro* Lise Lense-Møller, *Ph* Heikki Färm, *Ed* Daniel Dencik and Stefan Sundlöf.
Magic Hour Films/Mouka Filmi/Atmo/Film i Väst etc-Dogwoof Pictures.
75 mins. Denmark/Finland/Sweden. 2009. Rel: 12 Nov 2010. No Cert.

The Invention of Lying ★★½

In a small American town everybody from politicians to advertisers speaks the truth, while down-on-his-luck scriptwriter Mark Bellison (Ricky Gervais) begins to tell lies in order to save his job and apartment as well as to impress Anna

(Jennifer Garner), who thinks he is fat and ugly. This new invention brings him unexpected fame and riches. The first half is very funny but, when it starts dealing with religion and life after death, it becomes a much darker affair that doesn't entirely suit the style of the film. GS

‣ Ricky Gervais, Jennifer Garner, Rob Lowe, Tina Fey, Jonah Hill, Louis C K, Jeffrey Tambor, Fionnula Flanagan.
‣ *Dir* and *Screenplay* Ricky Gervais and Matthew Robinson, *Pro* Gervais, Dan Lin, Lynda Obst and Oly Obst, *Ph* Tim Suhrstedt, *Pro Des* Alec Hammond, *Ed* Chris Gill, *M* Tim Atack, *Cos* Susie DeSanto.

Focus Features International/Radar Pictures/Media Rights Capital/Lynda Obst Productions/Lin Pictures/ Wintergreen Productions-Universal Pictures. 99 mins. USA. 2009. Rel: 2 Oct 2009. Cert. 12A.

Invictus ★★★

Clint Eastwood's energy in old age is admirable but this latest directorial work of his is far from being his best. It tells of Nelson Mandela's ploy to champion the Springboks as a team with a fresh image epitomising the new united South Africa. Morgan Freeman plays well but this Attenborough-style movie endorsing unity lacks dramatic depth and you have to be a sporting enthusiast to relish over half an hour devoted to the 1995 World Cup Final. To his credit Eastwood insisted that the film use real South African locations. MS

‣ Morgan Freeman, Matt Damon, Tony Kgoroge, Patrick Mofokeng, Matt Stern.
‣ *Dir* Clint Eastwood, *Pro* Eastwood, Lori McCreary, Robert Lorenz and Mace Neufeld, *Screenplay* Anthony Peckham, from John Carlin's book *Playing the Enemy*, *Ph* Tom Stern, *Pro Des* James J Murakami, *Ed* Joel Cox and Gary D Roach, *M* Kyle Eastwood and Michael Stevens, *Cos* Deborah Hopper.

Warner Bros. Pictures/Spyglass Entertainment/Malpaso etc-Warner Bros. 133 mins. USA/South Africa. 2009. Rel: 5 Feb 2010. Cert. 12A.

Involuntary ★★★½

A film from Sweden which isn't a thriller, this is an offbeat movie that incorporates five distinct stories with a largely non-professional cast. The range of human behaviour within these anecdotes suggests the mix of comedy and sadness found in the films of Roy Andersson. His work, however, seems more precisely judged, as this film is uneven. It's quite interesting all the same. (Original title: *De ofrivilliga*) MS

‣ Villmar Bjorkman, Lola Ewerlund, Maria Lundqvist, Henrik Vikman, Cecilia Milocco.
‣ *Dir* and *Ed* Ruben Ostlund, *Pro* Eric Hemmendorff, *Screenplay* Ostlund and Hemmendorff, *Ph* Marius

Dybwad Brandrud, *Art Dir* Pia Aleborg and Vanja Sandell Billström, *M* Benny Andersson, *Cos* Pia Aleborg.

Plattform Produktion/Coproduction Office/Film i Väst/ Sveriges Television etc-Trinity Filmed Entertainment. 102 mins. Sweden/Norway/France. 2008. Rel: 29 Oct 2010. Cert. 15.

Ip Man ★★★★

This is a biopic of Ip Man (Donnie Yen), founder of the Wing Chun martial arts school and (after the period covered in the film) the teacher of Bruce Lee. Taking considerable liberties with history, it showcases unexpected acting prowess from Yen alongside predictably impressive action scenes. Sammo Hung's Hong Kong film award for Best Action Choreography is well deserved. Compelling subplots involve Ip Man's family life and the Second Sino-Japanese War. Also features impressive period production design. (Original title: *Yip Man*) JC

‣ Donnie Yen, Simon Yam, Siu-Wong Fan, Ka Tung Lam, Yu Xing Chan Zi.
‣ *Dir* Wilson Yip, *Pro* Bak-Ming Wong, *Screenplay* Edmond Wong, *Ph* Sing-Pui O, *Ed* Ka-Fai Cheung, *M* Kenji Kawai.

Beijing ShengShi HuaRei Film Investment & Management Company/China Film Co-Production Corporation/Shanghai Film Group etc-Mandarin Film Distribution Company. 106 mins. Hong Kong. 2008. Rel: 2 Oct 2009. Cert. 15.

Iron Man 2 ★★½

Iron Man is one of the greatest superhero movies ever made. Smart, fun and exciting, with a great lead, memorable villain and incredible action. *Iron Man 2*, however, is a major fail. Chalk that up to a grotesque over-egging of every element that made the first successful. You like one villain? Take three. You like heroes? Here's a

Stark staring: Robert Downey Jr returns to the red suit in Jon Favreau's *Iron Man 2*.

Rock royalty:
Jack White,
Jimmy Page and
The Edge in David
Guggenheim's
It Might Get Loud.

bunch more. Needlessly busy, the movie's so keen to get on with the next subplot and introduce the next new character that nothing and no one gets the attention they deserve, and it all ends up as a big, sickly blur. The only thing there should have been more of is action. MJ

❯ Robert Downey Jr, Don Cheadle, Scarlett Johansson, Gwyneth Paltrow, Sam Rockwell, Garry Shandling, Mickey Rourke, Samuel L Jackson.
❯ *Dir* Jon Favreau, *Pro* Kevin Feige, *Screenplay* Justin Theroux, from the Marvel comic book by Stan Lee, Jack Kirby, Larry Lieber and Don Heck, *Ph* Matthew Libatique, *Pro Des* J Michael Riva, *Ed* Dan Lebental and Richard Pearson, *M* John Debney, *Cos* Mary Zophres.

Paramount Pictures/Marvel Entertainment/Marvel Studios/Fairview Entertainment-Paramount Pictures. 124 mins. USA. 2010. Rel: 30 Apr 2010. Cert. 12A.

The Island ★★★½

There's a very Russian flavour to this religious drama about a war-time coward who, rescued by monks, then chooses to live with them and to become a monk himself. He's an eccentric who over the years gains fame as a holy man, a cross between a Holy Fool and Christ at his most abrasive. How to interpret this is often left up to the individual viewer and the intensity of Robert Bresson is missing, but Pavel Lounguine's film is highly cinematic in its use of black and white Scope. (Original title: *Ostrov*) MS

❯ Pyotr Mamonov, Viktor Sukhorukov, Dmitry Dyuerv, Viktoria Isakova, Nina Usatova.
❯ *Dir* and *Pro* Pavel Lounguine, *Screenplay* Dmitry

Sobolev, *Ph* Andrey Zhegalov, *Art Dir* Igor Kotsarev and Alexander Tolkachev, *Ed* Albina Antipenko, *M* Vladimir Martynov, *Cos* Ekaterina Dyminskaya.

Pavel Lounguine Studio/TV Channel Russia-Artificial Eye. 112 mins. Russia (Republic). 2006. Rel: 5 Feb 2010. Cert. PG.

It Might Get Loud ★★★★

The award-winning director of *The Inconvenient Truth*, Davis Guggenheim, has recruited three generations of electric guitar experts for this entertaining documentary. Jimmy Page, the Led Zeppelin veteran, joins forces with The Edge from U2 and Jack White from The White Stripes for a once in a lifetime event on an empty soundstage. They share stories about the ways they developed their unique styles before they start making music together. Their immense passion and enthusiasm for their work is infectious. GS

❯ Jimmy Page, The Edge, Jack White, and archive footage of Bono, Michael McKean, Robert Plant, Larry Mullen Jr, Meg White.
❯ *Dir* Davis Guggenheim, *Pro* Guggenheim, Thomas Tull, Lesley Chilcott and Peter Afterman, *Ph* Guillermo Navarro and Erich Roland, *Pro Des* Donald Graham Burt, *Ed* Greg Finton, *Music Supervisor* Margaret Yen.

Thomas Tull Productions-Blue Dolphin. 98 mins. USA. 2008. Rel: 5 Jan 2010. Cert. PG.

It's Complicated ★★★

After a decade of divorce, successful baker Jane Adler (Meryl Streep) finds herself being courted by her married ex (Alec Baldwin)... In the vein of Nancy Meyers' *Something's Gotta Give*, this genial farce tackles the complications of middle-aged love and sex. Recalling the shenanigans of Leo McCarey's classic *The Awful Truth*, the film plays for broad comedy in the land of divorcees-in-love – although Baldwin's Jake is too sleazy to root for. Better is Steve Martin in an understated performance, embracing his real age for once (64). And Streep is magnificent. JC-W

‣ Meryl Streep, Steve Martin, Alec Baldwin, John Krasinski, Lake Bell, Mary Kay Place.
‣ *Dir* and *Screenplay* Nancy Meyers, *Pro* Meyers and Scott Rudin, *Ph* John Toll, *Pro Des* John Hutman, *Ed* Joe Hutshing and David Moritz, *M* Heitor Pereira and Hans Zimmer, *Cos* Sonia Grande.

Universal Pictures/Relativity Media/Waverly Films/Scott Rudin Productions-Universal Pictures International.
120 mins. USA. 2009. Rel: 8 Jan 2010. Cert. 15.

It's a Wonderful Afterlife ★★★

There's real warmth in the film-making of Gurinder Chadha (a quality much rarer than it should be). Here she's created a rather silly story about an Indian mother in London who takes lethal revenge on people who have hindered her daughter's chances of marriage. It's a comedy that occasionally recalls superior works such as *The Ladykillers* and *Blithe Spirit*, and it's endearing despite its many misjudgments. In any case, Shabana Azmi and Goldy Notay do Chadha proud. MS

‣ Shabana Azmi, Goldy Notay, Sendhil Ramamurthy, Sally Hawkins, Sanjeev Baskar, Jimi Mistry, Zoë Wanamaker, Mark Addy.

‣ *Dir* and *Pro* Gurinder Chadha, *Screenplay* Chadha and Paul Mayeda Berges, *Ph* Dick Pope, *Po Des* Nick Ellis, *Ed* Oral Norrie Ottey, *M* Craig Pruess, *Cos* Jill Taylor.

Bend It Films/Indian Films/Studio 18-Icon Films Distribution.
100 mins. UK. 2009. Rel: 21 April 2010. Cert. 12A.

Ivul ★★

Andrew Kötting's work is surely an acquired taste and that's especially true of this, his third feature, the first made in French with subtitles. It shows a family in decline: a Russian patriarch, his French wife and their children, including a son sexually drawn to his sister. This youth reacts against his father by choosing to live in the treetops. It's bizarre but boring and the characters lack the depth to make us feel any involvement. MS

‣ Aurélia Petit, Jean-Luc Bideau, Adelaïde Leroux, Jacob Auzanneau, Xavier Tchili.
‣ *Dir* Andrew Kötting, *Pro* Emilie Blézat etc, *Screenplay* John Cheetham. Kötting and Andrew Mitchell, *Ph* Nick Gordon Smith and Gary Parker, *Ed* Baptiste Evrard and David Dusa, *M* Christian García, *Cos* Leila McMillan.

Sciapode/Box Productions/CinéCinema etc-Artificial Eye.
101 mins. France/Switzerland/UK. 2009. Rel: 23 July 2010. Cert. 15.

Jack Said ★

This low-budget British thriller is based on the graphic novel by Paul Tanter and tells the story

Tree hugger: Jacob Auzanneau in Andrew Kötting's bizarre and one-of-a-kind *Ivul.*

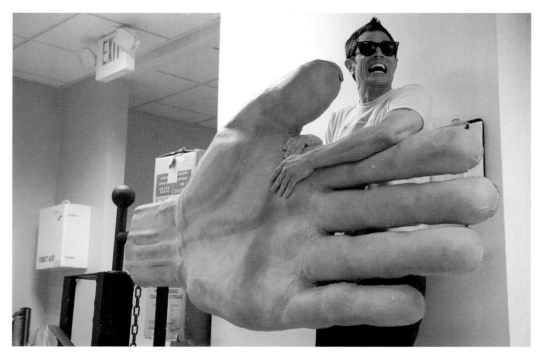

Another handful: Johnny Knoxville in Jeff Tremaine's scatological *Jackass 3D*.

of Nathan (Danny Dyer yet again), a gangster working for the notorious Guv'nor and his psychotic daughter, who is befriended by Jack (Simon Phillips) an undercover cop. The amateur production values, the grainy black and white photography and the dispirited performances contribute to a thoroughly dull experience. Even Dyer's presence can't save this. GS

▶ Danny Dyer, David O'Hara, Simon Phillips, Ashlie Walker, Terry Stone, Julian Lee.
▶ *Dir* Lee Basannavar, *Pro* Toby Meredith, *Screenplay* Paul Tanter, based on characters created by Piers Pereira, *Ph* Bob Komar, *Pro Des* Sophie Wyatt, *Ed* Richard Colton, *M* Warren Bennett, *Cos* Suzy Peters.
**Fourth Turning Productions/Goliath Productions/Kali Masu Productions/Lord Gadsby Films/Lucky Strike Productions/Paleface Pictures-Optimum Releasing.
101 mins. UK. 2009. Rel: 25 Sep 2009. Cert. 18.**

Jackass 3D ★★★

This third outing is more ambitious than ever but the 3D doesn't add much to these scatological exercises in poor taste. There's no doubt that this group of masochists enjoy pain but they also have masses of fun and their enjoyment is surprisingly infectious. There are more excrement gags than before, such as one with a portable toilet that needs a strong stomach – so make sure you don't eat before you watch it. GS

▶ Johnny Knoxville, Steve-O, Ryan Dunn, Jason 'Wee Man' Acuña, Bam Margera, Spike Jonze.
▶ *Dir* Jeff Tremaine, *Pro* Tremaine, Knoxville and Jonze, *Screenplay* Preston Lacy, *Ph* Lance Bangs, Rick Kosick and Dimitry Elyashkevich, *Pro Des* James Peter

Blackmon and Seth Meisterman, *Ed* Seth Casriel, Mat Kosinski and Matt Probst.
**MTV Films/Dickhouse Productions/Paradise F X Corp-Paramount Pictures.
94 mins. USA/Romania. 2010. Rel: 5 Nov 2010. Cert. 18.**

Jackboots on Whitehall ★★★

The action of this eccentric puppet animation feature takes place in a small Kentish village in 1940. The villagers are unaware of the impending Nazi invasion of England while farmer Chris (Ewan McGregor) is annoyed that he cannot join the army because of his large hands. However, he soon proves that he has more than it takes when it comes to bravery... McGregor is perfectly cast in this crazy film but it is Timothy Spall's somewhat demented Churchill who steals the show. GS

▶ Voices of Ewan McGregor, Rosamund Pike, Richard E Grant, Tom Wilkinson, Alan Cumming, Timothy Spall, Pam Ferris, Stephen Merchant, plus Dominic West.
▶ *Dir* and *Screenplay* Edward McHenry and Rory McHenry, *Pro* Karl Richards and Patrick Scoffin, *Pro Des* David McHenry, *Ed* Chris Blunden, *M* Guy Michelmore, *Cos* Elizabeth Marcussen.
**E-Motion/McHenry Bros/Swipe Films/Cinema Four etc-Vertigo Films.
91 mins. UK. 2010. Rel: 8 Oct 2010. Cert. 15.**

Jasper, Penguin Explorer ★★½

This likeable German animation feature is based on the 'Jasper Penguin' series. Jasper is a curious penguin who, unlike his fellow penguins, believes that the world is not flat. One day he meets a brightly coloured parrot who is desperate to find his missing eggs. Together this unlikely couple board an ocean liner, determined to sail around the globe and find the eggs. The dubbing is terrible but the colourful animation will keep younger children entertained. (Original title: *Jasper: Journey to the End of the World*) GS

▶ Voices of Rick Adams, Rob Rackstram, Steve Hudson, Kate Rawlings.
▶ *Dir* Eckart Fingberg and Kay Delventhal, *Pro* Sunita Struck, *Screenplay* Fingberg, John Chambers and Michael Mädel, *Ed* Reiko Pfeiffer, *M* Florian Tessloff.
Amuse Films/Toons 'n' Tales-Soda Pictures. 82 mins. Germany. 2008. Rel: 23 July 2010. Cert. U.

Je veux voir ★★★½

As in 2007's *Under the Bombs*, we have here a comment on the human tragedy to be found in war-torn Lebanon; each film involves a journey out of Beirut by car on roads where land mines are a threat. There's a great sense of physical presence together with the novelty of Catherine Deneuve playing an actress – in effect herself – who is there to help fund-raising. The earlier film is the greater but this is undoubtedly sincere. (aka *I Want to See*) MS

▶ Catherine Deneuve, Rabih Mroué, Brigitte Curmi, Joseph Silva.
▶ *Dir* Joana Hadjithomas and Khalil Joreige, *Pro* Anne-Cécile Berthomeau, Farès Ladjimi and others, *Ph* Julien Hirsch, *Ed* Enrico Gattolini, *M* Scrambled Eggs.
Mille et Une Productions/Abbout Productions/Tony Arnoux etc-Soda Pictures. 75 mins. France/Lebanon/Netherlands. 2008. Rel: 18 Sep 2009. Cert. 12A.

Jennifer's Body ★½

After hanging out with a self-centred indie rock band, Jennifer Check is not what she used to be. In fact, she's switched over from being 'high school evil' to really, really evil… Whatever *Jennifer's Body* aspires to, it's not funny and it's not scary. It does have some spicy dialogue, which one might expect from the Oscar-winning scribe of *Juno*. However, Megan Fox lacks the personality to drive the film's emotional engine and the result is a bland generic offshoot of *Carrie* and *The Hottie and the Nottie*. JC-W

▶ Megan Fox, Amanda Seyfried, Johnny Simmons, Adam Brody, Sal Cortez, Ryan Levine, Juan Riedinger, Chris Pratt.
▶ *Dir* Karyn Kusama, *Pro* Daniel Dubecki, Mason Novick and Jason Reitman, *Screenplay* Diablo Cody, *Ph* M David Mullen, *Pro Des* Arvinder Grewal, *Ed* Plummy Tucker, *M* Stephen Barton and Theodore Shapiro, *Cos* Katia Stano.

Fox Atomic/Dune Entertainment/Hard C-20th Century Fox. 102 mins. USA. 2009. Rel: 4 Nov 2009. Cert. 15.

Jetsam ★★½

This British thriller has been likened to Christopher Nolan's *Memento*, which is fair enough in terms of complexity but not quality. Simon Welsford's debut as writer and director does show a real eye for images, but the characters lack depth and as a contemporary drama of spying and surveillance it is not so much enigmatic as downright confusing. MS

▶ Alex Reid, Jamie Draven, Shauna Macdonald, Adam Shaw, Cal MacAninch.
▶ *Dir* and *Screenplay* Simon Welsford, *Pro* Sonny DeVille and Welsford, *Ph* Zac Nicholson, *Art Dir* Julian Nagel, John Pearce and Katie Welsford, *Ed* Ned Baker, *M* Mat Davidson.
Skyman Films-Jinga Films. 84 mins. UK. 2007. Rel: 28 Aug 2009. No Cert.

Johnny Mad Dog ★★★

Like *Heart of Fire* [qv], this is a grim view of youngsters forced to become soldiers. It's a powerful generalised comment (the location is African but non-specific) presented in a modern, confrontational manner that younger audiences may find compelling. Even so, I'm inclined to think that this is a work that preaches to the converted, while the 15-year-old titular character is a pitiful figure yet one without the ability to stir the emotions of the audience, as the young heroine of *Heart of Fire* does. MS

▶ Christophe Minie, Daisy Victoria Vandy, Dagbeh Tweh, Careen Moore, Barry Chernoh.

Shore leave: Alex Reid in Simon Welsford's complex and somewhat confusing *Jetsam*.

Food, inc: Meryl Streep as Julia Child in Nora Ephron's vivid and delightful *Julie & Julia.*

have a home to die for, while teenage kids Amber Heard and Ben Hollingsworth quickly become the envy of their high school. Gotta-have-it neighbours Gary Cole and Glenne Headley struggle to keep up materialistically. But the Joneses are not what they seem. A clever screenplay well cast, this packs a real punch and deserves to be seen. JC

➤ Demi Moore, David Duchovny, Gary Cole, Glenne Headley, Lauren Hutton, Amber Heard, Ben Hollingsworth.
➤ *Dir* and *Screenplay* Derrick Borte, *Pro* Borte, Andrew Spaulding, Kristi Zea and Doug Manoff, *Ph* Yaron Orbach, *Pro Des* Kristi Zea, *Ed* Janice Hampton, *M* Nick Urata, *Cos* Renee Ehrlich Kalfus.
Echo Lake Productions/The Joneses/Premiere Picture-E1 Entertainment.
96 mins. USA. 2009. Rel: 23 Apr 2010. Cert. 15.

Journey to Mecca ★★★½

The IMAX format ensures that there are great images to be found here. That will satisfy many, but the storyline offered, a reconstruction of a real-life pilgrimage undertaken in the 14th century by Ibn Battista, a young law student, suffers from feeble dramatisation that brings to mind Universal-International features of the early 1950s. However, the shots of Mecca itself and of the landscapes en route are suitably impressive. MS

➤ Chems Eddine Zinoun, Hassam Chancy, Nabil Elouhabi.
➤ *Dir* Bruce Neibaur, *Pro* Taran Davies, Dominic Cunningham-Reid and Jonathan Barker, *Screenplay* Neibaur, Tahir Shah and Carl Knutson, *Ph* Matthew Williams and others, *Pro Des* Mike Fowlie, *Ed* Jean-Marie Drot, *M* Michael Brook, *Cos* Emmanuel Belloq.
SK Films/National Geographic/Cosmic Picture/Eagle Vision Media Group/Desert Door Productions-SK Films.
46 mins. USA/Morocco/Kuwait/Canada 2009. Rel: 18 June 2010. Cert. PG.

Julie & Julia ★★★★

In this delightfully entertaining movie two narratives are ingeniously intertwined. One tells of Julia Child, the cook and TV personality who became famous for her French cooking (this story extends from the 1940s into the 1960s), and the other shows how one Julie Powell made her name by attempting all of Julia's recipes and recording her endeavours on the internet and in a book. Amy Adams is Julie and Meryl Strep is Julia and neither of them could be bettered. MS

➤ Meryl Streep, Amy Adams, Stanley Tucci, Chris Messina, Linda Emond, Jane Lynch.
➤ *Dir* and *Screenplay* (based on the book of the same title by Julie Powell and on *My Life in France* by Julia Child with Alex Prud'homme) Nora Ephron, *Pro* Laurence Mark, Ephron, Amy Robinson and Eric

➤ *Dir* Jean-Stéphane Sauvaire, *Pro* Mathieu Kassovitz and Benoît Jaubert, *Screenplay* Sauvaire and Jacques Fieschi, from the book *Johnny chien méchant* by Emmanuel Dongala, *Ph* Marc Koninckx, *Art Dir* Alexandre Vivet, *Ed* Stéphane Elmadjian, *M* Jackson Tennessee Fourgeaud, *Cos* Jean-Philippe Ricci.
MNP Enterprise/Explicit Films/Scope Pictures etc-Momentum Pictures.
98 mins. France/Belgium/Liberia. 2008. Rel: 23 Oct 2009. Cert. 15.

Jonah Hex ★★

This is based on the comic book series and tells the story of Jonah Hex (Josh Brolin), a civil war veteran who must now face his own personal war against the evil Quentin Turnball (John Malkovich), the man who killed his family and scarred his face. Jimmy Hayward's moderately entertaining and stylish film is ultimately a mess. The plot is far too muddled to make sense, while the strong cast is wasted. GS

➤ Josh Brolin, Megan Fox, John Malkovich, Michael Fassbender, Will Arnett, Tom Wopat.
➤ *Dir* Jimmy Hayward, *Pro* Akiva Goldsman and Andrew Lazar, *Screenplay* Marc Neveldine and Brian Taylor, based on a story by Neveldine, Taylor and William Farmer, from the DC Comics characters by John Albano and Tony De Zuniga, *Ph* Mitchell Amundsen, *Pro Des* Tom Meyer, *Ed* Kent Beyda, Tom Lewis, Dan Hanley, Fernando Villena, *M* Marco Beltrami and Mastodon, *Cos* Michael Wilkinson.
Warner Bros Pictures/Legendary Pictures/Mad Chance/ Weed Road/DC Entertainment-Warner Bros.
81 mins. USA. 2010. Rel: 3 Sep 2010. Cert. 15.

The Joneses ★★★★

The perfect family move in next door. Designer-clad parents Demi Moore and David Duchovny

Steel, *Ph* Stephen Goldblatt, *Pro Des* Mark Ricker, *Ed* Richard Marks, *M* Alexandre Desplat, *Cos* Ann Roth.

Columbia Pictures/Easy There Tiger Productions/Scott Rudin Productions etc-Sony Pictures Releasing. 123 mins. USA. 2009. Rel: 11 Sep 2009. Cert. 12A.

Just Another Love Story ★★

The title of this Danish film is misleading since it is not really so much a love story as just another preposterous thriller that leaves credibility far behind. Love enters in, but the context is that of an almost blinded car crash victim, Julia, who is encouraged by the man who caused the accident to believe that he is in fact somebody else, namely a man she had loved in Cambodia. The latter is supposedly dead but, of course, he isn't. In *Nightwatch* (1994), director Ole Bornedal drew us in so we could suspend disbelief, but he fails to do that here. (Original title: *Kaerlighed på film*) MS

❧ Anders W Berthelsen, Rebecka Hemse, Nikolaj Lie Kaas, Charlotte Fich, Dejan Cukic.
❧ *Dir* and *Screenplay* Ole Bornedal, *Pro* Michael Obel, *Ph* Dan Laustsen, *Art Dir* Anders Engelbrecht, *Ed* Anders Villadsen, *M* Joachim Holbek, *Cos* Jane Whittaker.

Thura Film/Thura Fiction K/S/DR-Danmarks Radio etc-Revolver Entertainment. 104 mins. Denmark/Norway/Sweden. 2007. Rel: 24 July 2009. Cert. 18.

Just for the Record ★

This is a terrible, low-budget independent spoof documentary about the making of a terrible, low-budget independent British film. It's composed mainly of heads talking to camera, from the outrageously pretentious director to the job-lot of actors who find themselves trapped in a spiral of movie-making that's going nowhere. This terrible idea is presumably meant as a satirical exercise on how not to waste your money and talent in the British film industry. Those involved (no names, to protect the guilty) should have given the budget to charity instead. The best thing about it is the imagination displayed in the opening credits. MHD

❧ Pete Morgan, Karen Anderson, Barry Austin, Steven Berkoff, Phil Davis, Danny Dyer, Craig Fairbrass, Rik Mayall, Jamie Foreman, Sean Pertwee, Billy Murray.
❧ *Dir* Steven Lawson, *Pro* Lawson and Jonathan Sothcott, *Screenplay* Lawson, Ben Shillito and Phillip Barron, *Ph* James Friend, *Pro Des* Sophie Wyatt, *Ed* Lawson and Will Gilbey, *Cos* Alice Woodward.

Black and Blue Films/Raw Film Productions/Raw Production-Metrodome Distribution. 79 mins. UK. 2009. Rel: 7 May 2010. Cert. 18.

Just Wright ★★

Leslie Wright (Queen Latifah) is a physical therapist in a rehabilitation centre and is dreaming of the perfect partner. But when she falls for the basketball player (Common) she is helping recover from an injury, she first has to compete with her super-attractive cousin Morgan (Paula Patton)... Queen Latifah is always a charismatic and highly watchable performer, but she needs a better script and a stronger director

A killer romance: Nikolaj Lie Kaas and Rebecka Hemse in Ole Bornedal's wildly imaginative and darkly comic Just Another Love Story.

The can-do kendo: Jaden Smith and Jackie Chan in Harald Zwart's *The Karate Kid* remake.

than Sanaa Hamri to make this predictable rom-com work. GS

▶ Queen Latifah, Common, Paula Patton, Pam Grier, James Pickens Jr.
▶ *Dir* Sanaa Hamri, *Pro* Latifah, Debra Martin Chase and Shakim Compere, *Screenplay* Michael Elliot, *Ph* Terry Stacey, *Pro Des* Stephanie Carroll and Nicholas Lundy, *Ed* Melissa Kent, *M* Lisa Coleman and Wendy Melvoin, *Cos* David C Robinson.

Fox Searchlight Pictures/Flavor Unit-20th Century Fox. 100 mins. USA. 2010. Rel: 17 Sep 2010. Cert. PG.

Kakera – A Piece of Our Life ★★★½

Momoko Andô's film debut is adapted from a famous manga comic. Haru, a timid college student, has an unpleasant boyfriend who uses her just for sex. She meets Riko, a female prosthetics artist who creates body parts lost through accident or disease and tries to cure her patients' psychological traumas. She believes Haru needs emotional help and a relationship ensues, but the journey is not an easy one. There is some prejudice here against Japanese men, who are presented as generally revolting. The two leading actors, Hikari Mitsushima and Eriko Nakamura, are admirable but their story loses momentum well before the end. (Original title: *Kakera*) MHD

▶ Hikari Mitsushima, Eriko Nakamura, Ken Mitsuishi, Tasuku Nagaoka, Rino Katase, Toshie Negishi.
▶ *Dir* Momoko Andô, *Pro* Keiko Watanabe and Sakura Momoyama, *Screenplay* Andô, with manga scenes by Erika Sakurazawa, *Ph* Kôichi Ishii, *Pro Des* Yuji Takamura, *Ed* Jun'chi Masunaga, *M* James Iha, *Cos* Nohara Hidenon.

Pictures Department/Zero Pictures Company-Third Window Films.
107 mins. Japan. 2009. Rel: 2 Apr 2010. No Cert.

The Karate Kid ★★½

Twelve-year-old Dre (Jaden Smith) has to leave Detroit when his mother gets a new job in China. He soon becomes the object of intense bullying until Mr Han (Jackie Chan), the maintenance man, intervenes. He is secretly a kung fu master and begins training Dre in preparation for a kung fu tournament. There are no surprises in this remake while the story is not dissimilar to *Kung Fu Panda* but without the gags. However, the exciting set-pieces and the superb production values will certainly entertain, despite the film's length. GS

▶ Jackie Chan, Jaden Smith, Taraji P Henson, Wenwen Han, Rongguang Yu.
▶ *Dir* Harald Zwart, *Pro* James Lassiter, Will Smith, Jerry Weintraub, Jada Pinkett Smith and Ken Stovitz, *Screenplay* Christopher Murphey, from a story by Robert Mark Kamen, *Ph* Roger Pratt, *Pro Des* François Séguin, *Ed* Joel Negron, *M* James Horner, *Cos* Han Feng.

Columbia Pictures/China Film Group/Jerry Weintraub Productions/Overbrook Entertainment-Columbia Pictures. 140 mins. USA/China. 2010. Rel: 28 July 2010. Cert. PG.

Katalin Varga ★★★

With great daring Peter Strickland, an English writer/director from Reading, has opted for a first feature with subtitles, set in Transylvania. Aided by his photographer Márk Györi, he has created a film with a truly European flavour. Katalin Varga is a wife, raped prior to her marriage, who is cast out 11 years on when her husband discovers that the child born to her had not been his. The film becomes a tale of revenge on the abuser pitched halfway between harsh reality and fable. As such it lacks the resonance of a contemporary Greek tragedy and the sureness of tone found in Bergman's *The Virgin Spring*. MS

▶ Hilda Péter, Norbert Tankó, László Mátray, Tibor Palfy, Melinda Kántor.
▶ *Dir*, *Pro* and *Screenplay* Peter Strickland, *Ph* Márk Györi, *Ed* Mátyás Fekete, *M* Steven Stapleton and Geoff Cox.

Libra Film-Artificial Eye.
85 mins. UK/Romania. 2009. Rel: 9 Oct 2009. Cert. 15.

Kick-Ass ★★★★★

There have been various revisions of the superhero genre but none as anarchic, smart, stylish, outrageous and just plain entertaining as this. Grounding the genre in a contemporary reality that most teens will relate to, *Kick-Ass* takes the rough parameters of the genre and constantly subverts them; and precisely because of this it keeps the audience on the edge of its seat. Adapted from the Marvel comic, it not only presents a credible, vulnerable teenager as the eponymous crime fighter but also introduces a foul-mouthed 11-year-old girl as his masked nemesis. And Nicolas Cage is perfect as Big Daddy, a ruthless vigilante who really loves his little girl. JC-W

▶ Aaron Johnson, Deborah Twiss, Garrett M Brown, Clark Duke, Mark Strong, Nicolas Cage, Elizabeth McGovern, Evan Peters, Lyndsy Fonseca.
▶ *Dir* Matthew Vaughn, *Pro* Vaughn, Adam Bohling, Brad Pitt, Tarquin Pack, David Reid and Kris Thykier, *Screenplay* Vaughn and Jane Goldman, from the comic book by Mark Millar and John S Romita Jr, *Ph* Ben Davis, *Pro Des* Russell De Rozario, *Ed* Eddie Hamilton, Jon Harris and Pietro Scalia, *M* Marius De Vries, Henry Jackman, John Murphy and Ilan Eshkeri, *Cos* Sammy Sheldon.

Marv Films/Plan B Entertainment-Universal Pictures International.
117 mins. USA/UK 2010. Rel: 26 Mar 2010. Cert. 15.

Kicks ★★½

Having a woman writer and a woman director, this starts off most persuasively as a study of two teenage girls in Liverpool obsessed by a handsome local footballer. Unfortunately the second half, when they kidnap their idol because he plans to leave England to play for Madrid, lacks all conviction. There's strikingly individual colour photography from Eduard Grau but not even the two leading players, Kerrie Hayes and Nichola Burley, can sustain belief beyond the halfway point. MS

▶ Kerrie Hayes, Nichola Burley, Jamie Doyle, Laura Wallace, Sarah Jane Buckley.
▶ *Dir* Lindy Heymann, *Pro* Andy Stebbing, *Screenplay* Leigh Campbell, from a story by Laurence Coriat, *Ph* Eduard Grau, *Pro Des* Grant Armstrong, *Ed* Kant Pan, *M* Daniel Glendining, *Cos* Julian Day.

Northwest Vision/Media and Digital Departures/ Starstruck Films etc-New Wave Films.
84 mins. UK. 2008. Rel: 4 June 2010. Cert. 15.

The Kid ★★½

Based on the best-selling memoirs of Kevin Lewis, the first half of this film deals with his childhood and the second with his adult espousal of self-help and entrepreneurship as encouraged by

A kick above: Chloë Grace Moretz reinvents the 11-year-old in Matthew Vaughn's anarchic, smart and outrageous *Kick-Ass*.

The pulp master: Casey Affleck as the deputy sheriff in Michael Winterbottom's controversial adaptation of Jim Thompson's *The Killer Inside Me.*

and a work that should be readily appreciated by heterosexual audiences, since they can identify with many of the issues presented in this particular context. MS

▶ Julianne Moore, Annette Bening, Mark Ruffalo, Mia Wasikowska, Josh Hutcherson.
▶ *Dir* Lisa Cholodenko, *Pro* Gary Gilbert, Jeffrey Levy-Hinte, Celine Rattray etc, *Screenplay* Cholodenko and Stuart Blumberg, *Ph* Igor Jadue-Lillo, *Pro Des* Julie Berghoff, *Ed* Jeffrey M Werner, *M* Carter Burwell, *Cos* Mary Claire Hannan.
Focus Features/Antidote Films/Mandalay Vision/Gilbert-Universal.
106 mins. USA/France. 2010. Rel: 29 Oct 2010. Cert. 15.

The Killer Inside Me ★★★½

Like *The Grifters*, this is a Jim Thompson story set in America but directed by a Brit. Here we have a study of a compulsive killer who happens to be a policeman. His violence to women is horrifying. Since the depiction of it terrifies, letting it be shown is a matter for the censor rather than for the critic. The acting is strong, the piece powerful, but the sometimes operatic tone prevents the film from closing in effectively on the tragedy of the last victim. MS

▶ Casey Affleck, Jessica Alba, Kate Hudson, Ned Beatty, Elias Koteas, Bill Pullman.
▶ *Dir* Michael Winterbottom, *Pro* Chris Hanley, Bradford L Schlei and Andrew Eaton, *Screenplay* John Curran, from the novel by Jim Thompson, *Ph* Marcel Zyskind, *Pro Des* Rob Simons and Mark Tildesley, *Ed* Mags Arnold, *M* Melissa Parmenter and Joel Cadbury, *Cos* Lynette Meyer.
Stone Canyon/Muse/Revolution/Wild Bunch/Curiously Bright Entertainment/Indion Entertainment Group etc-Icon Film Distribution.
109 mins. USA/UK/Sweden/France. 2010. Rel: 4 June 2010. Cert. 18.

Killers ★½

Katherine Heigl is repeatedly proving that she is no Katharine Hepburn or Carole Lombard. Here, she falls for the chiselled charms of Ashton Kutcher and marries him in the blink of an eye. It turns out he's an assassin determined to put his past behind him. But we've seen this kind of movie before. This one is particularly noisy, asinine and tiresome – and determined to over-distend its audience's patience and credulity. CB

▶ Katherine Heigl, Ashton Kutcher, Tom Selleck, Catherine O'Hara, Kevin Sussman, Katheryn Winnick.
▶ *Dir* Robert Luketic, *Pro* Kutcher, Mike Karz, Jason Goldberg, Scott Aversano etc, *Screenplay* Bob DeRosa and Ted Griffin, from a story by DeRosa,

Margaret Thatcher. It may be based on fact, but as told on screen it has little sense of veracity and the soundtrack (with its self-conscious use of classical music) is an irritant. The players struggle but those who loved the books may be hooked regardless. MS

▶ Rupert Friend, Augustus Prew, Natascha McElhone, Ioan Gruffudd, Bernard Hill, Jodie Whittaker, David O'Hara, Ralph Brown, James Fox.
▶ *Dir* Nick Moran, *Pro* Judith Hunt, *Screenplay* Kevin Lewis, from his books *The Kid* and *The Kid Moves On*, *Ph* Peter Wignall, *Pro Des* Russell De Rozario, *Ed* Trevor Waite, *M* Ilan Eshkeri, *Cos* Stephanie Collie.
Intandem Films/Tin House Films-Revolver Entertainment.
111 mins. UK. 2009. Rel: 17 Sep 2010. Cert. 15.

The Kids Are All Right ★★★★½

Lisa Cholodenko's best film, this is a superbly acted piece partly about parents whose established relationship suddenly seems to be at risk but also about the responses of their teenage children. It so happens that the parents are a lesbian couple and the father, a sperm donor, is a man whom the children want to meet. It's a dramatic story but not without humour and, even if its conclusion lacks weight, it is nevertheless both an excellent lesbian movie

Ph Russell Carpenter, Pro Des Missy Stewart, Ed Richard Francis-Bruce and Mary Jo Markey, M Rolfe Kent, Cos Johanna Argan.

Lionsgate/Aversano Films/Katalyst Films-Lionsgate. 100 mins. USA. 2010. Rel: 16 June 2010. Cert. 12A.

Kisses ★★★½

Irish writer/director Lance Daly deserves to be noted. This tale of two youngsters, children adrift in the modern world, blends the often harsh reality of a Ken Loach film with a true poetic sense (Daly is his own photographer). The realism of the piece is undermined by a contrived climax but at its best the film is magical. It may be imperfect but it's well worth a look. MS

▶ Shane Curry, Kelly O'Neill, Paul Roe, Stephen Rea, Cathy Malone, Neilí Conroy.
▶ Dir, Screenplay and Ph Lance Daly, Pro MacDara Kelleher and Daly, Pro Des Waldemar Kalinowski, Ed J Patrick Duffner, M Go Blimps Go, Cos Leonie Prendergast.

Fastnet Films/Bord Scannán na hÉireann (Irish Film Board) etc-Optimum Releasing. 75 mins. Ireland/Sweden. 2008. Rel: 17 July 2009. Cert. 15.

Knight and Day ★★½

A car enthusiast (Cameron Diaz) is befriended by a gun devotee on a trip from Wichita to Boston. And she ends up fleeing for her life… This is not a film for snobs or cineastes. It's a Big Mac of a movie: a juicy slab of instant escapism with some salt but not a lot of turmeric. It's certainly not in the same class as North by Northwest or Charade, nor is Tom Cruise a latterday Cary Grant. And while Tom and Cameron strive for an ounce of chemistry, the locations of Salzburg, Seville and Jamaica outclass them at every turn. JC-W

▶ Tom Cruise, Cameron Diaz, Peter Sarsgaard, Jordi Mollà, Viola Davis, Maggie Grace, Paul Dano, Marc Blucas.
▶ Dir James Mangold, Pro Cathy Konrad, Todd

Garner and Steve Pink, Screenplay Patrick O'Neill, Ph Phedon Papamichael, Pro Des Andrew Menzies, Ed Quincy Z Gunderson and Michael McCusker, M John Powell, Cos Arianne Phillips.

Twentieth Century Fox/Regency Enterprises/Pink Machine-20th Century Fox. 109 mins. USA. 2010. Rel: 6 August 2010. Cert 12A.

The Kreutzer Sonata ★★★½

This 2010 release may have marked the centenary of Tolstoy's death but, as a contemporary American-set variation on his novella, its emphasis on sex and violence will shock most admirers of the original, and not in a meaningful way. The performers in this portrayal of a man's obsession with the possible infidelity of his wife are good, but ultimately the treatment is more sensational than rewarding. It's powerful but it never evokes pity for its central character. MS

▶ Danny Huston, Elisabeth Röhm, Matthew Yang King, Stella Huston, Anjelica Huston.
▶ Dir, Ph and Ed Bernard Rose, Pro Naomi Despres and Lisa Enos, Screenplay Enos and Rose, based on the novel by Leo Tolstoy.

Animandala/Giant Door/Independent-Axiom Films. 100 mins. USA/UK. 2008. Rel: 12 Mar 2010. Cert. 18.

On the run: Kelly O'Neill and Shane Curry in Lance Daly's poetic and arresting Kisses.

Tuning Tolstoy: Matthew Yang King in Bernard Rose's parabolic The Kreutzer Sonata.

Lala Pipo ★★★

This is another distinct and quite original project from Masayuki Miyano, the director of *Kamikaze Girls* and *Memories of Matsuko*. The script is based on a collection of seemingly unconnected stories dealing with the Japanese porn industry and the title comes from a character's mispronounced observation that Tokyo has 'a lot of people'. It takes a while to get into the eccentric style of the film and to care about its oddball characters but, once you surrender to it, it's fun. GS

▹ Saori Hara, Sayuki Matsumotom Tomoko Murakami, Hiroki Narimiya.
▹ *Dir* Masayuki Miyano, *Pro* Yuki Ishida and Michiyo Satô, *Screenplay* Tetsuya Nakashima, from short stories by Okuda Hideo, *Ph* Ozawa Atsushi, *Pro Des* Tsuzuki Yuji, *Ed* Toyama Chiaki, *M* Sasamoto Yasushi.

DesperaDo/Nikkatsu-Third Window Films.
120 mins. Japan. 2009. Rel: 13 Nov 2009. Cert. 18.

Land of the Lost ★

Ashley Bell in Daniel Stamm's clever and surprising *The Last Exorcism*.

Dr Rick Marshall (Will Ferrell) finds himself in the land of the lost after he gets sucked through a space-time vortex along with his research assistant Holly (Anna Friel) and redneck Will (Danny McBride). They all relish the idea of a new adventure until a giant T. Rex begins to pursue them for his lunch. The actors give energetic performances but seem to be making up the lazy script as they go along in Silberling's unimaginative gross-out comedy. GS

▹ Will Ferrell, Anna Friel, Danny McBride, Jorma Taccone, John Boylan, Matt Lauer.
▹ *Dir* Brad Silberling, *Pro* Sid Krofft, Marty Krofft and Jimmy Miller, *Screenplay* Chris Henchy and Dennis McNicholas, based on the television series by Sid and Marty Krofft, *Ph* Dion Beebe, *Pro Des* Bo Welch, *Ed* Peter Teschner, *M* Michael Giacchino, *Cos* Mark Bridges.

Universal Pictures/Relativity Media/Sid & Marty Krofft Pictures/Mosaic-Universal Studios.
102 mins. USA. 2009. Rel: 31 July 2009. Cert. 12A.

The Last Airbender 3D ★

This hugely disappointing film is a lame attempt to cash in on films like the Narnia franchise. The Fire Nation still demands domination over its fellow tribal nations of Air, Water and Earth, but things are about to change when a young boy with airbending skills named Aang (Noah Ringer) arrives on the scene. The dialogue is flat and occasionally laughable – for example, "We don't like benders in our village" – and the 3D effects are very poor. A worthy winner for the turkey of the year! GS

▹ Noah Ringer, Dev Patel, Nicola Peltz, Jackson Rathbone, Cliff Curtis, Katharine Houghton.
▹ *Dir* and *Screenplay* M Night Shyamalan, *Pro*

Shyamalan, Scott Aversano, Sam Mercer and Frank Marshall, *Ph* Andrew Lesnie, *Pro Des* Philip Messina, *Ed* Conrad Buff, *M* James Newton Howard, *Cos* Judianna Makovsky.

Paramount Pictures/Nickelodeon Movies/Blinding Edge Pictures/The Kennedy-Marshall Company-United International Pictures.
103 mins. USA. 2010. Rel: 13 Aug 2010. Cert. PG.

The Last Exorcism ★★★★

When a documentary crew sets out to make a film about his activities, evangelical preacher Cotton Marcus (Patrick Fabian), who has been performing bogus exorcisms for many years, feels it's time to set the record straight. There is an opportunity for one last exorcism in Louisiana, when farmer's daughter Nell (Ashley Bell) begins to act strangely... Daniel Stamm's clever film wisely takes its time in introducing the characters in a mock documentary style before it explodes in the most unexpected manner. A treat for horror lovers! GS

▶ Patrick Fabian, Ashley Bell, Iris Bahr, Louis Herthum, Caleb Landry Jones.
▶ *Dir* Daniel Stamm, *Pro* Mark Abraham, Eli Roth, Eric Newman and Thomas A Bliss, *Screenplay* Huck Botko and Andrew Gurland, *Ph* Zoltan Honti, *Pro Des* Andrew W Bofinger, *Ed* Shilpa Sahi, *M* Nathan Barr, *Cos* Shauna Leone.

Strike Entertainment/Louisiana Media Productions/Studio Canal/Arcade Pictures-Optimum Releasing.
87 mins. USA/France. 2010. Rel: 3 Sep 2010. Cert. 15.

The Last Seven ★

It is difficult to find anything positive to say about this abysmal post-apocalyptic film. A man wakes up and remembers nothing in a completely deserted London. He struggles to make sense of what has happened and to stay alive against all odds. There are only seven survivors and the Angel of Death (the inevitable Danny Dyer) waits to get them. But who cares anyway? GS

▶ Tamer Hassan, Danny Dyer, Simon Phillips, Daisy Head, Ronan Vibert.
▶ *Dir* Imran Nagvi, *Pro* Simon Phillips, Toby Meredith and Patricia Rybarczyk, *Screenplay* John Stanley, *Ph* David Mackie, *Pro Des* Stuart Kearns, *Ed* Jasdip Sagar, *M* Matthew Williams, *Cos* Natalie Egleton.

Goliath Productions/Nightshade Productions/Press On Features/Vesuvius Film Partners-ILC Group.
84 mins. UK. 2010. Rel: 27 Aug 2010. Cert. 18.

The Last Song ★★★

Miley Cyrus' estranged dad Greg Kinnear is dying of cancer, but, never mind, there's a Greek god (Liam Hemsworth – Josh Taylor in *Neighbours*) hanging around on the beach. Leaving *Hannah Montana* way behind, the 17-year-old Miley does a

Teasing Tolstoy: Helen Mirren in a rare moment of levity in Michael Hoffman's *The Last Station*.

fair bit of acting, but she's not nearly as much fun as when she's all singing all dancing. She has to hide her likeability as an obnoxious teen through the first half of this concocted romantic drama for teenage girls. The Disney version of a parent's death is as you'd imagine – a kids' fairy tale – but the film entertains enough in an escapist way. DW

▶ Miley Cyrus, Greg Kinnear, Bobby Coleman, Liam Hemsworth, Kelly Preston, Carly Chaikin.
▶ *Dir* Julie Ann Robinson, *Pro* Jennifer Gibgot and Adam Shankman, *Screenplay* Nicholas Sparks and Jeff Van Wie, from the book by Sparks, *Ph* John Lindley, *Pro Des* Nelson Coates, *Ed* Nancy Richardson, *M* Aaron Zigman, *Cos* Louise Frogley.

Touchstone Pictures/Offspring Entertainment-Walt Disney Studios Motion Pictures.
107 mins. USA. 2010. Rel: 30 Apr 2010. Cert. PG.

The Last Station ★★★

Released a few weeks before the Tolstoy-derived *The Kreutzer Sonata* [qv], this film wastes the obvious screen potential of Tolstoy's last months, a time when his close bond with his wife became ever more conflicted through differences over religion and the novelist's wish to disinherit his family in furtherance of his socialist principles. The film misguidedly places Tolstoy's secretary (a miscast James McAvoy) screen centre and gives him a romance, when a more detailed focus on the Tolstoys was needed. But thanks to Christopher Plummer and Helen Mirren the film is not a total disaster. MS

▶ Helen Mirren, Christopher Plummer, James McAvoy, Paul Giamatti, Kerry Condon, Anne-Marie Duff, John Sessions.
▶ *Dir* and *Screenplay* (based on the novel by Jay Parini) Michael Hoffman, *Pro* Chris Curling, Jens Meurer and Bonnie Arnold, *Ph* Sebastian Edschmid, *Pro Des* Patrizia von Brandenstein, *Ed* Patricia Rommel, *M* Sergey Yevtushenko, *Cos* Monica Jacobs.

Egoli Tossell Film Halle/Zephyr Films/Andrei Konchalovsky Production Center etc-Optimum Releasing. 113 mins. Germany/Russia (Republic)/UK. 2009. Rel: 19 Feb 2010. Cert. 15.

Late Autumn ★★★★

Never before released in this country, this splendid example of Ozu's Japanese family tales is a film dating from 1960. It's often been seen as a variation on the earlier *Late Spring* but is, I believe, the finer work. It portrays touchingly but also with a great deal of humour the plans to marry off a daughter before her prospects fade. The great Setsuko Hara is the mother and the film is full of details that confirm just how meaningfully Ozu used the minutiae of everyday life. Being a late work it is in colour and it's immensely satisfying. (Original title: *Akibiyori*) MS

▶ Setsuko Hara, Yoko Tsukasa, Mariko Okada, Keiji Sada, Chishû Ryû, Shin Saburi.
▶ *Dir* Yasujiro Ozu, *Pro* Shizuo Yamanouchi, *Screenplay* Ozu and Kogo Noda, based on the novel by Ton Satomi, *Ph* Yûharu Atsuta, *Art Dir* Tatsuo

End of the line: Kristin Scott Thomas in *Leaving*, for which she was nominated for a César.

Hamada, *Ed* Yoshiyasu Hanamura, *M* Kojun Saitô, *Cos* Toshikazu Sugiyama.

Shochiku/Ofuna-British Film Institute. 128 mins. Japan. 1960. Rel: 29 Jan 2010. Cert. PG.

Law Abiding Citizen ★★★

With actors like Jamie Foxx, Viola Davis and Colm Meaney involved you might expect a decent film. But while this thriller wants to be another *The Silence of the Lambs* (it features a vengeful killer operating from inside a jail in Philadelphia), in fact it is totally preposterous. However, it's also fun should you be in the mood for it. It may be tosh, but it's efficient, fast-moving tosh. MS

▶ Jamie Foxx, Gerard Butler, Colm Meaney, Viola Davis, Bruce McGill, Leslie Bibb.
▶ *Dir* F Gary Gray, *Pro* Lucas Foster, Gerard Butler, Kurt Wimmer and others, *Screenplay* Wimmer, *Ph* Jonathan Sela, *Pro Des* Alex Hajdu, *Ed* Tariq Anwar, *M* Brian Tyler, *Cos* Jeffrey Kurland.

The Film Department/Warp Films/Evil Twins (I)-Momentum Pictures. 109 mins. USA/UK. 2009. Rel: 27 Nov 2009. Cert. 18.

Le Donk & Scor-Zay-Zee ★★★★

Although shot quickly and cheaply to prove that it can be done, this film ought not to be underestimated. With film-maker Shane Meadows appearing as himself, it plays like a mockumentary as we see him filming the attempt by 'Le Donk' (Paddy Considine) to use his connections in the music field to promote rap artist Dean Palinczuk, who calls himself 'Scor-Zay-Zee'. But the film is more than it sounds: comic but also touching, it's a warm-hearted movie that's never condescending and ranks high in Meadows' work. MS

▶ Paddy Considine, Dean Palinczuk, Olivia Coleman, Richard Graham, Shane Meadows.
▶ *Dir* Shane Meadows, *Pro* Mark Herbert, *Devised by* Paddy Considine and Meadows, *Ph* Dean Rogers and Meadows, *Art Dir* Alex Collins, *Ed* Richard Graham, *M* Scor-Zay-Zee.

Warp Films/Big Arty Productions etc-Verve Pictures. 72 mins. UK. 2009. Rel: 9 Oct 2009. Cert. 15

Leap Year ★½

A real estate decorator from Boston (Amy Adams) decides to propose to her boyfriend while he's attending a conference in Dublin. But first she must get there… In an ideal world, romantic comedies should be romantic and funny, yet this is neither – and there isn't a shred of credibility to rub any comic sparks off. Offensively, Randy Edelman's score tells us when to laugh while the platitudes of rural Irish life feel heated-up from an earlier, more innocent time. JC-W

▶ Amy Adams, Matthew Goode, Adam Scott, John Lithgow, Noel O'Donovan, Tony Rohr, Pat Laffan, Alan Devlin, Ian McIlhenney.

▶ *Dir* Anand Tucker, *Pro* Roger Birnbaum, Jonathan Glickman, Jake Weiner, Chris Bender and Gary Barber, *Screenplay* Deborah Kaplan and Harry Elfont, *Ph* Newton Thomas Siegel, *Pro Des* Mark Geraghty, *Ed* Nick Moore, *M* Randy Edelman, *Cos* Eimer Ni Mhaoldomhnaigh.

Universal Pictures/Spyglass Entertainment/BenderSpink/Birnbaum-Barber/Octagon Films-Optimum Releasing. 100 mins. USA/France. 2010. Rel: 26 Feb 2010. Cert. PG.

Leap Year ★★★

This drama made in Mexico by Australia's Michael Rowe is not to be confused with the Hollywood offering of the same name. It couldn't be more different, for this minimalistic piece is a serious work about a sado-masochistic relationship. A novel covering the same ground might provide insights by putting the reader inside the mind of one of the central characters. On screen, however, despite an enormously impressive performance from lead actress Mónica del Carmen, there's nothing to be learnt. (Original title: *Año bisiesto*) MS

▶ Mónica del Carmen, Gustavo Sánchez Parra, Marco Zapata.

▶ *Dir* Michael Rowe, *Pro* Edher Campos and Luis Salinas etc, *Screenplay* Rowe and Lucía Carreras, *Ph* Juan Manuel Sepúlveda, *Art Dir* Alisarine Ducolomb, *Ed* Óscar Figueroa Jara, *Cos* Adolfo Cruz Mateo.

Machete Producciones/Instituto Mexicano de Cinematografia etc-Axiom Films. 92 mins. Mexico. 2010. Rel: 26 Nov 2010. Cert. 18.

Leaving ★★★★

Rightly acclaimed, Kristin Scott Thomas once again gives an outstanding performance in this French drama. It's about a married woman who unexpectedly finds herself deeply in love with a Spanish builder (the excellent Sergi López). Told in flashback after a shot has been fired, the story keeps us guessing and is well constructed. However, it may be felt that we are expected to sympathise too readily with a woman who is prepared to desert her children. (Original title: *Partir*) MS

▶ Kristin Scott Thomas, Sergi López, Yvan Attal, Bernard Blancan, Aladin Reibel.

▶ *Dir* Catherine Corsini, *Pro* Fabienne Vonier, *Screenplay* Corsini with Gaëlle Macé, *Ph* Agnès Godard, *Art Dir* Laurent Ott, *Ed* Simon Jacquet, *Cos* Anne Schotte.

Pyramide Productions/Caméra One/VMP/Solaire Production/Canal + etc-Metrodome Distribution. 86 mins. France. 2008. Rel: 9 July 2010. Cert. 15.

Lebanon ★★★★½

Samuel Maoz's film was born of his own traumatic experiences as a young man caught up in the First Lebanon War in 1982. This acclaimed work puts us inside a tank with its crew of four and no other film has so directly confronted its audience with someone's discovery of what being in a war

Head case:
a hard rock
legend revealed
in *Lemmy*.

is really like. Nothing else quite equals the impact established by the first third of the film, but it's all done with an apparent simplicity, an authenticity and a power that make it unforgettable. MS

❧ Yoav Donat, Itay Tiran, Oshri Cohen, Michael Moshonov, Zohar Strauss, Dudu Tasa.
❧ *Dir* and *Screenplay* Samuel Maoz, *Pro* Moshe Edery, Loen Edery, Einat Bikel and others, *Ph* Giora Bejach, *Pro Des* Ariec Roshko, *Ed* Arik Lahav-Leibovich, *M* Nicolas Becker, *Cos* Hila Bargiel.

United King Films/Arte France/Filmstiftung Nordhein-Westfalen etc-Metrodome Distribution. 93 mins. Israel/France/Germany. 2009. Rel: 14 May 2010. Cert. 15.

Legend of the Fist: The Return of Chen Zhen ★★★★

The action in this superbly produced and directed epic takes place in Shanghai in the 1920s. A mysterious stranger (Donnie Yen) returns from abroad and befriends the notorious mafia boss of the city, while by night he disguises himself in a cape and begins to eliminate the city's underworld. This is a thrilling martial arts adventure featuring the character Chen Zhen, originally played by Bruce Lee in *Fist of Fury* and later on by Jet Li in *Fist of Legend*. (Original title: *Jing wu feng yun: Chen Zhen*) GS

❧ Donnie Yen, Qi Shu, Anthony Wong Chau-sang, Karl Dominik, Siyuan Huo.

❧ *Dir* Wai-keung Lau, *Pro* Wai-keung Lau and Gordon Chan, *Screenplay* Chan, *Ph* Andrew Lau and Man-ching Ng, *Pro Des* Eric Lam, *Ed* Azrael Chung, *M* Kwong Wing Chan, *Cos* Dora Ng.

Media Asia Films/Enlight Pictures/Basic Pictures/ Shanghai Film Media Asia-Metrodome Distributors. 105 mins. Hong Kong/China. 2010. 3 Dec 2010. Cert. 18.

Legends of the Guardians: The Owls of Ga'Hoole ★★★

Young owl Soren (Jim Sturgess) is fascinated by his father's stories and longs to meet the brave owl warriors of Ga'Hoole. Meanwhile his jealous brother Kludd (Ryan Kwanten) is hungry for power and finds his opportunity to fulfil his purpose when the evil Pure Ones offer him the chance... The opening and climactic sequences of this striking animated feature are magnificent. But there are far too many characters and subplots which make the story confusing. GS

❧ Voices of Emily Barclay, Abbie Cornish, Helen Mirren, Bill Hunter, Miriam Margolyes, Sam Neill, Ryan Kwanten, Jim Sturgess, Hugo Weaving, Geoffrey Rush.
❧ *Dir* Zack Snyder, *Pro* Zareh Nalbadian, *Screenplay* John Orloft and Emil Stern, based on Kathryn Lasky's series of novels *Guardians of Ga'Hoole*, *Pro Des* Simon Whiteley, *Ed* David Burrows, *M* David Hirschfelder.

Warner Bros Pictures/Village Roadshow Pictures/Animal Logic-Warner Bros. 97 mins. USA/Australia. 2010. Rel: 22 Oct 2010. Cert. PG.

120   FILM REVIEW 2010-2011

Legion ★½

God's lost his faith in mankind and, based on this disappointing action fantasy, I'm not surprised. A supernatural actioner in which Paul Bettany's Archangel Michael battles to save mankind from hordes of avenging angels in a middle-of-nowhere US diner, *Legion* should have been awesome. Angels with Uzis, old lady demons, Bettany and Quaid (Dennis not Randy): it sounded so good. The trailer was a laugh. But did the movie come together? No. Was it as exciting as it looked? No. It *was* a lot dumber, though. MJ

▶ Paul Bettany, Lucas Back, Dennis Quaid, Tyrese Gibson, Kevin Durand, Adrianne Palicki.
▶ *Dir* Scott Stewart, *Pro* David Lancaster and Michel Litvak, *Screenplay* Stewart and Peter Schink, *Ph* John Lindley, *Pro Des* Jeff Higinbotham, *Ed* Steven Kemper, *M* John Frizzelli, *Cos* Wendy Partridge.
Bold Films-Sony Pictures Releasing.
100 mins. USA. 2010. Rel: 5 Mar 2010. Cert. 15.

Lemmy ★★★½

This fascinating documentary follows the remarkable Lemmy Kilmister, the rock'n'roll phenomenon, who formed Motorhead in 1975 when he was sacked from Hawkwind. It's an honest portrayal of this eccentric man, who now lives in Los Angeles and has been declared 'The Greatest Living Englishman'. He comes clean about his drug and alcohol abuse, talks about his fascination with Nazi memorabilia, and explains that he is not a Nazi sympathiser despite the accusations. But the most affecting scene is when he proudly plays music with his son. GS

▶ Music documentary with Alice Cooper, Dave Brock, Mikkey Dee, Phil Campbell, David Grohl, East Eddie Clarke, Jarvis Cocker, Joan Jett, Ozzie Ozbourne and with Lemmy Kilmister.
▶ *Dir* and *Pro* Greg Olliver and Wes Orshoski, *Ph* and *Ed* Greg Olliver, *Music Clearance* Chris Robertson.
Damage Case Films and Distribution/Secret Weapon Films/Stay Free Films-E1 Entertainment.
116 mins. USA. 2010. Rel: 10 Dec 2010. Cert. 15.

Let Me In ★★★

The first theatrical release for the resurrected Hammer Film Productions, Matt Reeves' stylish remake of the stunning Swedish film *Let the Right One In* boasts almost identical set-pieces despite the fact that the action has been transported to Los Alamos in New Mexico. Owen (Kodi Smit-McPhee) is an introverted 12-year-old who gets bullied repeatedly at school. He forms an unlikely friendship with the mysterious Abby (Chloë Grace Moretz) when she moves next door – a 12-year-old unlike any other girl her age who has a deep secret and a hunger for blood. GS

▶ Kodi Smit-McPhee, Chloë Grace Moretz, Richard Jenkins, Cara Buono, Elias Koteas, Sasha Barese.
▶ *Dir* and *Screenplay* Matt Reeves, based on the novel and screenplay *Låt den rätte komma in* by John Ajvide Lindqvist, *Pro* Alex Brunner, Simon Oakes, Donna Gigliotti, Carl Molinder, Guy East, Tobin Armbrust and John Nordling, *Ph* Greig Fraser, *Pro Des* Ford Wheeler, *Ed* Stan Salfas, *M* Michael Giacchino, *Cos* Melissa Brunning.
Hammer Film Productions/EFTI/Goldcrest Post Production London/Overture Films-Icon Film Distribution.
116 mins. UK/USA. 2010. Rel: 5 Nov 2010. Cert. 15.

Letters to Juliet ★★

When aspiring writer Sophie Hall visits Verona with her fiancé, she stumbles across a letter addressed to Juliet Capulet, written 50 years previously. On a whim, she replies to it and finds the now grey-haired author, Claire Smith-Wyman, turning up to search for her lost Romeo. With Vanessa Redgrave playing Claire, this Mills & Boon romance is elevated several notches, particularly as Franco Nero, by whom Ms Redgrave had a child in 1969, plays the focus of Claire's search. The rest is cack-handed and laughably predictable – although the gorgeous scenery takes up the slack. JC-W

In fair Verona: Vanessa Redgrave in Gary Winick's cack-handed *Letters to Juliet.*

▶ Amanda Seyfried, Chris Egan, Gael García Bernal, Vanessa Redgrave, Franco Nero.
▶ *Dir* Gary Winick, *Pro* Ellen Barkin, Mark Canton, Caroline Kaplan, Patrick Wachsberger and Eric Feig, *Screenplay* Jose Rivera and Tim Sullivan, *Ph* Marco Pontecorvo, *Pro Des* Stuart Wurtzel, *Ed* Bill Pankow, *M* Andrea Guerra, *Cos* Nicoletta Ercole.

**Summit Entertainment/Applehead Pictures-E1
Entertainment.**

105 mins. USA. 2010. Rel: 9 June 2010. Cert. PG.

Life As We Know It ★★

Holly Berenson (Katherine Heigl) and Eric Messer (Josh Duhamel) hate each other's guts after a disastrous first date arranged by their best friends. But when their friends die in a car accident they are forced to share the responsibility of bringing up their orphaned goddaughter Sophie. Heigl and Duhamel work well together but the repetitive and predictable script prevents them from exploring their underwritten characters. GS

▶ Katherine Heigl, Josh Duhamel, Josh Lucas, Hayes McArthur, Christina Hendricks.
▶ *Dir* Greg Berlanti, *Pro* Paul Brooks and Barry Josephson, *Screenplay* Ian Deitchman and Kristina Rusk Robinson, *Ph* Andrew Dunn, *Pro Des* Maher Ahmad, *Ed* Jim Page, *M* Blake Neely, *Cos* Debra McGuire.

**Josephson Entertainment/Gold Circle Films/Village
Roadshow Pictures-Warner Bros.**

114 mins. USA. 2010. Rel: 8 Oct 2010. Cert. 12A.

Life During Wartime ★★★½

Knowledge of the original is not necessary but in this sequel to *Happiness* (1998) Todd Solondz takes up the story of the characters he introduced then, albeit with a totally different cast. The title misleads since, if there is a battlefield, it would appear to be that of personal relationships. The brief appearance of a ghost figure jars, but this is nevertheless prime Solondz. Nobody is more adept at creating scenes which make you want to laugh and cry almost simultaneously. MS

▶ Shirley Henderson, Ciarán Hinds, Allison Janney, Dylan Riley Snyder, Ally Sheedy, Charlotte Rampling, Paul Reubens, Michael Lerner, Michael Kenneth Williams, Rich Pecci.
▶ *Dir* and *Screenplay* Todd Solondz, *Pro* Christine Kunewa Walker, Derrick Tseng and others, *Ph* Ed Lachman, *Pro Des* Roshelle Berliner, *Ed* Kevin Messman, *Cos* Catherine George.

Werc Werk Works-Artificial Eye.

98 mins. USA. 2009. Rel: 23 April 2010. Cert. 15.

The Limits of Control ★★★½

Bizarre even by Jim Jarmusch's standards, this is a thriller set in a world of paranoia and conspiracy but with the thrills cut out. Something of a Spanish road movie, it follows a man on a mysterious mission in that country and makes play with star actors in small roles. It has a kinship both with Rivette's *Paris Belongs To Us* (1961) and with Welles' *Confidential Report* (1955). Visually it's great cinema and an auteur's film, but it's too odd to satisfy fully and some will reject it outright. MS

▶ Isaach de Bankolé, John Hurt, Tilda Swinton, Bill Murray, Gael García Bernal, Hiam Abbass, Jean-François Stévenin, Luis Tosar, Paz de la Huerta. Alex Descas.

▶ *Dir* and *Screenplay* Jim Jarmusch, *Pro* Stacey Smith and Gretchen McGowan, *Ph* Christopher Doyle, *Pro Des* Eugenio Caballero, *Ed* Jay Rabinowitz, *M* Boris, *Cos* Bina Daigeler.

Focus Features/Entertainment Farm/PointBlank etc-Revolver Entertainment.

116 mins. USA/Japan. 2008. Rel: 11 Dec 2009. Cert. 15.

Mystery kill: Tilda Swinton in Jim Jarmusch's road thriller *The Limits of Control.*

Lion's Den ★★★

Shot authentically inside a maximum security jail in Argentina, Pablo Trapero's drama exposes the stern regimes there, especially the plight of women prisoners with young children. Martina Gusman impresses as one such woman suspected of murder, but her story invites unanswered questions. That leads to some disappointment with the film, but its best scenes are very powerful. (Original title: *Leonera*) MS

▶ Martina Gusman, Elli Medeiros, Rodrigo Santoro, Laura Garcia, Tomás Plotinsky.
▶ *Dir* Pablo Trapero, *Pro* Trapero and Suh Young-joo, *Screenplay* Alejandro Fadel, Martín Mauregui, Santiago Mitre and Trapero, from an idea by Trapero, *Ph* Guillermo Nieto, *Art Dir* Coca Oderigo, *Ed* Ezequiel Borovinsky and Trapero, *Cos* Marisa Urruti.

Matanza Cine/Cineclick Asia (Fantom)/Patagonik Film Group/Videofilmes etc-Axiom Films.

113 mins. Argentina/Republic of Korea/Brazil. 2008. Rel: 26 Mar 2010. Cert. 15.

Little Big Soldier ★★★★

In ancient China thousands of warriors perish after a brutal battle between rival kingdoms. One peasant soldier (Jackie Chan) survives and rescues a wounded prince whom he wants to deliver for a large reward. But their journey is plagued by endless attacks from numerous forces who want the prince for themselves. The exciting action sequences are imaginatively choreographed by Chan, whose mischievous sense of fun is highly infectious. The cinematography is simply magnificent and the plot, although set in ancient China, has got 'Western' written all over it. (Original title: *Da bing xiao jiang*) GS

▶ Jackie Chan, Ken Lo, Steve Yoo, Wang Leehom, Rongguang Yu, Peng Lin.
▶ *Dir* Sheng Ding, *Pro* Chan and Solon So, *Screenplay* Chan, *Ph* Zhao Xiaoding, *Art Dir* Sun Li, *Ed* Ding Sheng, *M* Xiao Ke.

Beijing Dragon Garden Culture & Art Co Ltd/Jackie & JJ Productions/Talent International Film Cultural Company/Bona Entertainment/JCE Movies-Showbox Media Group.

96 mins. China/Hong Kong. 2010. Rel: 1 Oct 2010. Cert. 15.

Martial heart: Jackie Chan in Sheng Ding's exciting *Little Big Soldier.*

The Godfockers: Robert De Niro and Ben Stiller fail to see eye-to-eye in Paul Weitz' *Little Fockers*.

Little Fockers ★★★½

Just as an ailing Jack Byrnes (Robert De Niro) decides to elect his son-in-law Greg as his official successor ('the Godfocker'), he suspects Greg of conducting an extramarital affair… Third acts are always hard to pull off yet *Little Fockers* – following on from *Meet the Parents* and *Meet the Fockers* – is actually very funny. This is largely because a powerhouse cast plays its lines very straight and the lines are very good. Only De Niro mugs to camera, leaving Ben Stiller to sharpen his comic timing to a very fine point. (Also known as *Meet the Parents: Little Fockers*) JC-W

▶ Robert de Niro, Ben Stiller, Owen Wilson, Dustin Hoffman, Barbra Streisand, Blythe Danner, Laura Dern, Harvey Keitel.
▶ *Dir* Paul Weitz, *Pro* De Niro, Jane Rosenthal, Jay Roach and John Hamburg, *Screenplay* Hamburg and Larry Stuckey, based on characters created by Greg Glienna and Mary Ruth Clarke, *Ph* Remi Adefarasin, *Pro Des* William Arnold, *Ed* Greg Hayden and Leslie Jones, *M* Stephen Trask, *Cos* Molly Maginnis.
Universal Pictures/Paramount Pictures/Relativity Media/ Tribeca/Everyman Pictures/DW Studios-Paramount Pictures. 98 mins. USA. 2010. Rel: 22 Dec 2010. Cert. 12A.

London Boulevard ★★½

Fresh out of prison, Mitchell (Colin Farrell) is determined to go straight. However, his connections in the underworld keep on dragging him to the brink of criminal activity – until he lands a job as bodyguard to a film star-cum-supermodel. With its powerhouse cast and cracking script, this refit of *Sunset Blvd* behaves like a first-rate British gangster movie. Yet, in spite of a few welcome distractions, this is actually a fairly standard romantic thriller. Still, it's always a joy to see Ray Winstone behaving diabolically, while the dialogue contains a number of memorable gems. JC-W

▶ Colin Farrell, Keira Knightley, Ray Winstone, David Thewlis, Anna Friel, Ben Chaplin, Eddie Marsan, Sanjeev Bhaskar.
▶ *Dir* and *Screenplay* William Monahan, based on the novel by Ken Bruen, *Pro* Monahan, Quentin Curtis, Tim Headington and Graham King, *Ph* Chris Menges, *Pro Des* Martin Childs, *Ed* Dody Dorn and Robb Sullivan, *M* Sergio Pizzorno, *Cos* Odile Dicks-Mireaux.
G K Films/Henceforth Pictures/London Boulevard/ Projection Pictures-Entertainment Film Distributors. 103 mins. USA/UK. 2010. Rel: 26 Nov 2010. Cert. 18.

London River ★★★½

Rachid Bouchareb's new film follows *Days of Glory* and again exhibits a deep human concern reminiscent of the cinema of Satyajit Ray. Here, on a more intimate scale, he tells the story of two people, a white woman (Brenda Blethyn) and a Muslim (the marvellously dignified Sotigui Kouyaté), whose paths cross as they seek news of their missing children after the London terrorist bombing of 7 July 2005. Not all of it rings true but Bouchareb's heart is emphatically in the right place. MS

▶ Brenda Blethyn, Sotigui Kouyaté, Sami Bouajila, Roschdy Zem, Bernard Blancan.
▶ *Dir* Rachid Bouchareb, *Pro* Jean Bréhat, *Screenplay* Bouchareb with Olivier Lorelle and Zoé Galeron, *Ph* Jérôme Alméras, *Art Dir* Jean-Marc Tran Tan Ba, *Ed*

Yannick Kergoat, *M* Armand Amar, *Cos* Karine Serrano.

ARTE France/3B Productions/The Bureau/Tassili Films etc-Trinity Filmed Entertainment.
88 mins. France/UK/Algeria. 2009. Rel: 9 July 2010. Cert. 12A.

Loose Cannons ★★★

That talented Turkish film-maker Ferzan Özpetek again uses an Italian setting for this family tale centred on a younger son and his thwarted attempt to come out as gay. The tone is light, more comic than one expects from Özpetek. That's fine until the piece broadens into exaggerated comedy while also moving uncomfortably close to melodrama. Consequently the first half of the film is far more enjoyable than the second. (Original title: *Mine vaganti*) MS

▶ Riccardo Scamarcio, Nicole Grimaudo, Alessandro Preziosi, Ennio Fantastichini.
▶ *Dir* Ferzan Özpetek, *Pro* Domenico Procacci, *Screenplay* Ivan Cotroneo and Özpetek, *Ph* Maurizio Calvesi, *Art Dir* Andrea Crisanti, *Ed* Patrizio Marone, *M* Pasquale Catalano, *Cos* Alessandro Lai.

Domenico Procacci/Fandango/Rai Cinema/Apulia Film Commission etc-Peccadillo Pictures.
113 mins. Italy. 2010. Rel: 17 Dec 2010. Cert. 12A.

The Losers ★★

Joel Silver-produced adaptation of DC/Vertigo comic book series about an elite Special Forces unit who, following a disastrous mission to Bolivia, are double-crossed by the mysterious Max and have to clear their name. A kickboxing Zoe Saldana provides feminine interest and intrigue, but otherwise this is pretty standard US action fare with little to raise it above the ordinary. JC

▶ Idris Elba, Zoe Saldana, Jason Patric, Jeffrey Dean Morgan, Chris Evans.
▶ *Dir* Sylvain White, *Pro* Joel Silver, Akiva Goldsman and Kerry Foster, *Screenplay* Peter Berg and James Vanderbilt, *Ph* Scott Kevan, *Pro Des* Aaron Osborne, *Ed* David Checel, *M* John Ottman, *Cos* Magali Guidasci.

DC Entertainment/Dark Castle Entertainment/Weed Road Pictures-Optimum Releasing.
97 mins. USA. 2010. Rel: 28 May 2010. Cert. 12A.

Lourdes ★★★

The undervalued Sylvie Testud gives a great performance as a visitor to Lourdes who experiences what could be a temporary remission from multiple sclerosis, but might also be a cure and therefore a miracle. Stylishly directed by the atheist Jessica Hausner, this film on the surface is open in its attitude. But I never felt that Hausner, who gives her characters no depth, was other than wholly sceptical. This for me robs the film of drama but many admire it. MS

▶ Sylvie Testud, Léa Seydoux, Bruno Todeschini, Elina Löwensohn, Gilette Barbier.
▶ *Dir* and *Screenplay* Jessica Hausner, *Pro* Martin Gschlacht, Susanne Marian and Philippe Bober, *Ph* Martin Gschlacht, *Art Dir* Katharina Woppermann, *Ed* Karina Ressler, *Cos* Tanja Hausner.

coop99 filmproduktion/Essential Filmproduktion/Parisienne de Production/Thermidor Filmproduktion etc-Artificial Eye.
99 mins. Austria/Germany/France. 2009. Rel: 26 Mar 2010. Cert. 15.

Love and Other Drugs ★★★★

Jamie Randall is a self-centred pharmaceutical salesman with too much charm for his own good. Then he gets to flog a new drug called Viagra and meets the fragile, volatile Maggie Murdock. Ed Zwick (*Glory, Blood Diamond*) returns to the genre of his very first film, *About Last Night…*, and shows that he has considerably sharpened his skills since, eliciting career-high performances from both Jake Gyllenhaal and Anne Hathaway. Indeed, this is a funny, engaging and ultimately touching movie about lust, commitment and pharmaceuticals – and is probably the smartest tearjerker-cum-date movie of its year. JC-W

In the wake of war: Brenda Blethyn and Sotigui Kouyaté in Rachid Bouchareb's heartfelt *London River*.

Amorous miscellany: Director Sono Sion on the set of his *Love Exposure*.

▶ Jake Gyllenhaal, Anne Hathaway, Oliver Platt, Hank Azaria, George Segal, Jill Clayburgh.
▶ *Dir* Edward Zwick, *Pro* Zwick, Pieter Jan Brugge, Marshall Herskovitz, Scott Stuber and Charles Randolph, *Screenplay* Zwick, Randolph and Herskovitz, based on Jamie Reidy's book *Hard Sell: The Evolution of a Viagra Salesman*, *Ph* Steven Fierberg, *Pro Des* Patti Podesta, *Ed* Steven Rosenblum, *M* James Newton Howard, *Cos* Deborah L Scott.

Fox 2000 Pictures/Regency Enterprises/New Regency/ Bedford Falls/Stuber Productions-20th Century Fox. 112 mins. USA. 2010. Rel: 29 Dec 2010. Cert. 15.

Love Exposure ★★★½

This Japanese film by Sono Sion is a real oddity and one that calls for stamina since it lasts for close on four hours. The plot cannot be described succinctly but it's more important to know that this is a blend of rom-com, sex comedy, religious meditation and horror film. There's a distracting use of music (Ravel's *Bolero* is heard at length) but Sono is an adept film-maker and encourages one to ponder the film's sub-text where lurk such issues as cult religions vs Christianity, sexual repression and the need to find your true self even if society would damn you as a pervert. Not a run of the mill movie! (Original title: *Ai no mukidashi*) MS

▶ Nishijima Takahiro, Mitsushima Hikari, Ando Sakura, Watanabe Makiko, Watabe Atsuro.
▶ *Dir* and *Screenplay* Sono Sion, *Pro* Umekawa Haruo, *Ph* Tanikawa Sohei, *Pro Des* Matsuzka Takashi, *Ed* Ito Junichi, *M* Harada Tomohide and Teikoku YuraYura, *Cos* Matsumoto Chieko and Karasawa Isao.

Omega Project/Entertainment Inc./Studio 3-Third Window Films. 236 mins. Japan. 2008. Rel: 30 Oct 2009. No Cert.

Love Happens ★★★

Aaron Eckhart becomes a grief guru to help others mourn and move on after his wife dies in a car crash – but he doesn't dealt with his own heartache until he meets florist Jennifer Aniston, who could be the key to helping him move forward. This serious-minded romantic story about overcoming grief is a tricky subject, but it soon proves worthwhile. Eckhart is just right as a model of handsome goodness whose only flaw is that something terrible has happened to him. In a modest support role, Aniston is excellent too, proving she doesn't need funny lines to be appealing and affecting. DW

▶ Aaron Eckhart, Jennifer Aniston, Dan Fogler, John Carroll Lynch, Judy Greer, Martin Sheen.
▶ *Dir* Brandon Camp, *Pro* Mary Parent, Scott Stuber and Mike Thompson, *Screenplay* Camp and Thompson, *Ph* Eric Edwards, *Pro Des* Sharon Seymour, *Ed* Dana E Glauberman, *M* Christopher Young, *Cos* Trish Keating.

Universal Pictures/Relativity Media/Stuber Productions/ Camp-Thompson Pictures/Scion Films-Contender Entertainment Group. 109 mins. USA/Canada/UK. 2009. Rel: 9 Oct 2009. Cert. 12A.

Love the Beast ★★½

This documentary is a labour of love for actor/ director Eric Bana, who picks up a camera and goes back to his Melbourne roots in order to highlight his passion for cars. Bana and three of his friends decide to fulfil their childhood dream and enter the dangerous Targa Tasmania Rally with Bana's beloved first car, a Ford GT Falcon Coupe. The film is interesting, with some fascinating contributions from Bana's parents, but it never actually fulfils its potential. GS

▶ Eric Bana, Jeremy Clarkson, Steve Coad, Grant Denyer, Todd Kelly, Jay Leno, Phil McGraw.
▶ Dir Eric Bana, Pro Bana, Matt Hill and Peter Hill, Ph Rod Pollard and David Rose, Ed Conor O'Neill, M Yuri Worontschak.

Pick Up Truck Pictures/White House Productions-Metrodome Distribution.
92 mins. Australia. 2009. Rel: 13 Nov 2009. Cert. 15.

The Lovely Bones ★★

Alice Sebold's best-selling 2002 novel was an original and chilling contemplation on death, grief and paedophilia. Peter Jackson's adaptation is a corny, overblown travesty, a film that, instead of downplaying the novel's faults, has embraced them with an embarrassing bravado. There are good turns from Susan Sarandon and Stanley Tucci (the latter Oscar-nominated for his efforts), but even they are encouraged to over-act. Dying has to be simpler than this… JC-W

▶ Mark Wahlberg, Rachel Weisz, Susan Sarandon, Stanley Tucci, Saoirse Ronan.
▶ Dir Peter Jackson, Pro Jackson, Fran Walsh, Carolynne Cunningham, and Aimée Peyronnet, Screenplay Jackson, Walsh and Philippa Boyens, from the novel by Alice Sebold, Ph Andrew Lesnie, Pro Des Naomi Shohan, Ed Jabez Olssen, M Leo Abrahams and Brian Eno, Cos Nancy Steiner.

DreamWorks Pictures/Film 4/Wingnut Films/Key Creatives-Paramount Pictures UK.
136 mins. USA/UK/New Zealand. 2009. Rel: 19 Feb 2010. Cert. 12A.

Lymelife ★★½

With some good actors involved and the name of Martin Scorsese attached as executive producer, this film sounded promising. However, as a dissection of American life which aims at both comedy and drama, it reveals itself as a pale echo of such works as *American Beauty* and *The Ice Age*. That's because the humour is too knowing and the drama too manipulative. But what really cooks the film's goose is an ending at once patently calculated and utterly phoney. MS

▶ Alec Baldwin, Kieran Culkin, Rory Culkin, Jill Hennessy, Timothy Hutton.
▶ Dir Derick Martini, Pro Steven Martini, Barbara DeFina, Alec Baldwin etc, Screenplay Derick and Steven Martini, Ph Frank Godwin, Pro Des Kelly

McGehee, Ed Steven and Derick Martini and Mark Yoshikawa, Cos Erika Munro.

CinemaVault/El Dorado Pictures/Cappa/DeFina Productions etc-Network Releasing.
94 mins. USA. 2008. Rel: 2 July 2010. Cert. 15.

MacGruber ★★½

Beware the film extracted from a recurring comedy sketch. And beware the film with a character called Dieter Von Cunth. *MacGruber* started life as a skit on *Saturday Night Live*, in which Will Forte spoofed the TV series *MacGyver*. Here, Forte essays the mullet-sporting former Green Beret/Navy SEAL who's on the tail of Val Kilmer's ruthless Von Cunth. Of course, it's all very silly and *very* scatological, but with Kristen Wiig and a straight-faced Ryan Phillippe in the mix, it's often quite funny. CB

▶ Will Forte, Kristen Wiig, Ryan Phillippe, Val Kilmer, Powers Boothe.
▶ Dir Jorma Taccone, Pro John Godwin and Lorne Michaels, Screenplay Taccone and Forte, Ph Brandon Trost, Pro Des Robb Wilson-King, Ed Jamie Gross, M Matthew Compton, Cos Susanna Puisto.

Michaels-Goldwyn/Relativity Media-Universal Pictures International.
99 mins. USA. 2010. Rel: 18 June 2010. Cert. 15.

Machan ★★★

Uberto Pasolini, who produced *The Full Monty*, thinks he has the know-how to replicate that film's feel-good appeal. He takes a story drawn from real life about youngsters from Sri Lanka

Paradise lost out: Susan Sarandon in Peter Jackson's misconceived The Lovely Bones.

Sex matters: Andrea Riseborough, Jaime Winstone (in hot pants) and Sally Hawkins defend their gender in Nigel Cole's *Made in Dagenham*.

getting to Germany by pretending to be a handball team able to represent their country in a tournament. The first half with its convincing background is promising, but once the scene switches to Europe credibility flies out the window. Good intentions are not really enough. MS

▶ Dharmapriya Dias, Gihan de Chickera, Dharshan Dharmaraj, Mahendra Perera.
▶ *Dir* Uberto Pasolini, *Pro* Prasanna Vithanage, Conchita Airoldi and Pasolini, *Screenplay* Ruwanthie de Chickera and Pasolini, *Ph* Stefano Falivene, *Pro Des* Errol Kelly, *Ed* Masahiro Hirakubo, *M* Stephen Warbeck with Lakshman Joseph de Saram, *Cos* Sandhiya Jayasuriya and Rob Navis.

Rai Cinema/StudioUrania/Babelsberg Film/Shakthi Films/Redwave Films etc-Yume Pictures.
108 mins. Italy/Germany/Sri Lanka/UK. 2008. Rel: 20 Nov 2009. Cert. 15.

Machete ★★

As a faux trailer that preceded the 'double-feature' *Grindhouse*, *Machete* was sort-of fun. Now it's been blown up into a movie in its own right, with Robert Rodriguez casting his old friend Danny Trejo in the title role as a Mexican superhero, a taciturn hunk who dispenses his own brand of justice with a very big knife. Amid the animatronic pile-up of the headless, limbless and bleeding obvious, the film strives for a sort of fast-food gore factor with a wink to the B-movies of yore.

But, depending on how you like your misogyny, this is overworked by anybody's standards. JC-W

▶ Danny Trejo, Robert De Niro, Jessica Alba, Steven Seagal, Michelle Rodriguez, Jeff Fahey, Cheech Marin, Don Johnson, Lindsay Lohan.
▶ *Dir* Ethan Maniquis and Robert Rodriguez, *Pro* Robert Rodriguez, Rick Schwartz and Elizabeth Avellan, *Screenplay* Robert Rodriguez and Álvaro Rodriguez, *Ph* Jimmy Lindsey, *Pro Des* Christopher Stull, *Ed* Robert Rodriguez and Rebecca Rodriguez, *M* John Debney and Carl Thiel, *Cos* Nina Proctor.

Overnight Films/Troublemaker Studios/Dune Entertainment etc-Sony Pictures Releasing.
105 mins. USA. 2010. Rel: 26 Nov 2010. Cert. 18.

Mad, Sad & Bad ★½

After a considerable leg-up from *Slumdog Millionaire*, English-speaking Indian culture suffers a major setback with this bittersweet sitcom. Flat and deadly unfunny, the film features three grown-up siblings stuck with a dipsomaniac mum. All the old stereotypes are trotted out, with only Andrea Riseborough registering strongly as a Caucasian sculptor entangled with two of the brothers. The film itself is not so much mad as sad and very, very bad. JC-W

▶ Meera Syal, Nitin Ganatra, Zubin Varla, Andrea Riseborough.
▶ *Dir* and *Screenplay* Avie Luthra, *Pro* Bex Hopkins

and Christine Alderson, *Ph* Stuart Biddlecombe, *Pro Des* Katie MacGregor, *Ed* Liz Roe, *M* Mat Davidson, *Cos* Cecile Dauby.

Ipso Facto Films/a Roister Doister and Moxie Makers production, etc-Soda Pictures
98 mins. UK. 2009. Rel: 31 July 2009. Cert. 15.

Made in Dagenham ★★★★

Far superior to Nigel Cole's earlier hit *Calendar Girls*, this neatly constructed piece is at once comic and serious. Without ever becoming heavy-handed it tells a story centred on the 1968 strike by female machinists in Ford's Dagenham factory. This entertaining movie celebrates the achievements of these women whose actions eventually contributed to the passing of the Equal Pay Act in 1970. Furthermore, it gives Sally Hawkins her best role yet as the working class heroine and, in a good supporting cast, Bob Hoskins is spot-on. MS

▶ Sally Hawkins, Bob Hoskins, Miranda Richardson, Rosamund Pike, Geraldine James, Andrea Riseborough, Jaime Winstone, Daniel Mays, Rupert Graves, John Sessions.
▶ *Dir* Nigel Cole, *Pro* Stephen Woolley and Elizabeth Karlsen, *Screenplay* William Ivory, *Ph* John de Borman, *Pro Des* Andrew McAlpine, *Ed* Michael Parker, *M* David Arnold, *Cos* Louise Stjernsward.

BBC Films/UK Film Council/HanWay Films/Number 9 Films-Paramount Pictures UK.
113 mins. UK/Ireland. 2010. Rel: 1 Oct 2010. Cert. 15.

Made in Jamaica ★★★★

Jérome Laperrousaz's entertaining documentary creates a fascinating picture of the history and development of reggae and the Dancehall Music movement, which gave a voice to the people in the ghettos. It also celebrates Jamaican music,

featuring diverse talent from Gregory Isaacs and Lady Saw to Bunny Wailer and Beres Hammond. This illuminating film is highly enjoyable and by the end you will be dancing along to these exciting sounds. GS

▶ Lady Saw, Toots Hibbert, Bounty Killer, Bunny Wailer, Elephant Man, Capleton.
▶ *Dir* and *Screenplay* Jérome Laperrousaz, *Pro* Pascal Hérold, *Ph* Jean-Marie Dreujou, *Ed* Delphine Desfons.

Hérold and Family/Lawrence Pictures-Network Releasing.
120 mins. France/USA. 2006. Rel: 23 Oct 2009. Cert. 15.

The Magic Hour ★★★★

Few films manage to be as unusual or as thought-provoking as this portmanteau piece, a quintet of short films united by one factor – each one is the product of a disabled creator. Combining science fiction, animation, autobiography, war drama and even ribald satire, this is a daring, touching, entertaining and wholly novel undertaking. It not only puts our own lives – and concerns – into perspective, but highlights the humanitarian potential of the cinema. JC-W

▶ Elijah Muhammad, Andy Biddle, Matt Kirby, Nicola Stapleton, Claire Louise Amias, Jenna Harrison.
▶ *Dir* John Williams, William Mager, Andrew Gibbs, Katharine Araniello, *Pro* Scott Bassett, Justin Edgar, *Ph* Stuart Bentley, Zac Nicholson, Alex Ryle, *Ed* Philip Arkinstall, Nigel Bunyan, Mark Burgess, Andrew Jadavji, *M* Phil Mountford.

104 Films/UK Film Council/Studio of the North-104 Films.
70 mins. UK. 2009. Rel: 13 Nov 2009. Cert. 15.

The Maid ★★★★

In his second feature (a prize-winner at Sundance), Sebastián Silva draws on his

Going Dutch in Jérome Laperrousaz's documentary *Made in Jamaica*.

A world apart:
Gael García
Bernal in Lukas
Moodysson's
all too topical
Mammoth.

childhood memories to depict a well-off family living in Chile. They have had the same maid for over 20 years but she becomes antagonistic when other staff are taken on to help out. It's a film about class but one which splendidly avoids being over-simplistic in its characterisations. Indeed, quite unexpectedly it becomes the story of how a friendship enables someone to grow and develop. In the title role Catalina Saavedra is ideal. (Original title: *La nana*) MS

▶ Catalina Saavedra, Claudia Celedón, Mariana Loyola, Andrea García-Huidobro.
▶ *Dir* Sebastián Silva, *Pro* Gregorio González, *Screenplay* Silva and Pedro Peirano, *Ph* Sergio Armstrong, *Art Dir* Pablo González, *Ed* Danielle Fillios, *Cos* Francisca Román.

Forastero and Diroriro/Tiburón Films/Punto Guionpunto Producciones-Artificial Eye.
96 mins. Chile/Mexico. 2009. Rel: 27 Aug 2010. Cert. 15.

Malice in Wonderland ★★★

There's action, romance and fantasy drama in this likeable modern take on Lewis Carroll, starring Maggie Grace (from *Lost*) as an American law student called Alice who wakes up in the back of a London cab with amnesia after being knocked down. Danny Dyer gives his usual lovable Londoner turn another lively workout as Whitey, who drives her around a weird underworld of eccentric prostitutes, gangsters and thieves. The script is sparky and inventive, the direction slick and the stars form an effective odd-couple double act, making for an amusing and entertaining little movie. DW

▶ Maggie Grace, Danny Dyer, Matt King, Bronagh Gallagher, Anthony Higgins, Nathaniel Parker, Dave Lynn.
▶ *Dir* Simon Fellows, *Pro* Alberto Martinez Martin and Mark Williams, *Screenplay* Jayson Rothwell, *Ph* Christopher Ross, *Pro Des* Lisa Hall, *Ed* Lisa Clifford-Owen, *M* Christian Henson and Joe Henson, *Cos* Alice Wolfbauer.

Mark Williams Films/Future Films/2B Pictures/Zero Gravity Management-Sony Pictures Releasing.
87 mins. UK. 2009. Rel: 4 Feb 2010. Cert. 15.

Mammoth ★★★½

This is not Lukas Moodysson's finest hour but, even so, his first English language film has been undervalued. Michelle Williams plays a surgeon living in New York whose husband (Gael García Bernal) has work which takes him abroad. Even if over-extended, *Mammoth* develops a valid theme: it shows us a world more connected than ever before through technology yet one in which ironically it is all too easy for people to become disconnected. (Original title: *Mammut*) MS

▶ Gael García Bernal, Michelle Williams, Marife Necesito, Tom McCarthy, Sophie Nyweide.
▶ *Dir* and *Screenplay* Lucas Moodysson, *Pro* Lars Jönsson, *Ph* Marcel Zyskind, *Pro Des* Josefin Åsberg, *Ed* Michal Leszczylowski, *M* Jesper Kurandsky, Erik Holmquist and Linus Gierta, *Cos* Denise Östholm.

Memfis Film Rights 6 AB/Zentropa Entertainments etc-Soda Pictures.
125 mins. Sweden/Denmark/Germany/Norway. 2009. Rel: 5 Nov 2010. Cert. 15.

Management ★★

Jennifer Aniston may be a name but she can't sell a film as misjudged as this. It offers an off-beat romance between Aniston as a travelling salewoman and Steve Zahn as an oddball who pursues her after encountering her at a motel run by his parents. A weak screenplay is further hindered by miscasting since there is absolutely no chemistry between the two leads. MS

➤ Jennifer Aniston, Steve Zahn, Woody Harrelson, Fred Ward, Margo Martindale.
➤ *Dir* and *Screenplay* Stephen Belber, *Pro* Sidney Kimmel, Wyck Godfrey and Marty Bowen, *Ph* Eric Edwards, *Pro Des* Judy Becker, *Ed* Kate Sanford, *M* Mychael Danna and Rob Simonsen, *Cos* Christopher Lawrence.

Sidney Kimmel Entertainment/Temple Hill-Metrodome Distribution.
93 mins. USA. 2008. Rel: 25 Sep 2009. Cert. 15.

The Market: A Tale of Trade ★★★★

It is 1994 in Eastern Turkey; Mihram (Tayanç Ayaydin), a small-time trader, dreams of hitting the big time. He is in desperate need of capital in order to go legit and jumps at the opportunity to find medicine on the black market when a hospital supply truck is robbed. But first he has to gamble... Ben Hopkins' engrossing film wisely takes its time in building up character as the plot gradually unfolds and is blessed with a mesmerising performance from Ayaydin. (Original title: *Pazar – Bir ticaret masali*) GS

➤ Genco Erkal, Tayanç Ayaydin, Senay Aydin, Hakan Sahin, Rojîn Ulker.

➤ *Dir* and *Screenplay* Ben Hopkins, *Pro* Roshanak Behesht Nedjad, *Ph* Konstantin Kröning, *Pro Des* Atilla Yilmaz, *Ed* Alan Levy, *M* Cihan Sezer, *Cos* Zeynep Firlikaya.

Flying Moon Film Produktion/Eurasia Film/Tigerlily Films/Pi Film etc-The Works UK Distribution.
93 mins. Germany/UK/Turkey/Kazakhstan. 2008. Rel: 16 Apr 2010. No Cert.

Marmaduke ★★½

Owen Wilson is perfectly cast as the voice of the mischievous Great Dane, Marmaduke, in this uneven family entertainment. Marmaduke and his family move to California for new opportunities. But Marmaduke is desperate to impress his new friends in the canine community and unsurprisingly he soon gets into trouble... The opening and climactic sequences are engaging but the repetitive bit in the middle where the action loses momentum is boring. GS

➤ Voices of Owen Wilson, Steve Coogan, Kiefer Sutherland, Damon Wayans Jr, Marlon Wayans, Sam Elliott plus David Walliams, Lee Pace, Judy Greer.
➤ *Dir* Tom Dey, *Pro* Dey and John Davis, *Screenplay* Tim Rasmussen and Vince Di Meglio, based on the comic by Brad Anderson and Phil Leeming, *Ph* Greg Gardiner, *Pro Des* Sandy Cochrane, *Ed* Don Zimmerman, *M* Christopher Lennertz, *Cos* Karen L Matthews.

Twentieth Century Fox/Regency Enterprises/Davis Entertainment Company/Dune Entertainment/Intrigue-20th Century Fox.
87 mins. USA. 2010. Rel: 20 Aug 2010. Cert. U.

Mary and Max ★★★★

Australian animator Adam Elliot, who made the Oscar-winning short *Harvie Krumpet*, comes up with an equally literate full-length feature that is both highly amusing and deeply touching. It's

Below left: Steve Zahn hasn't a sporting chance of saving Stephen Belber's weak *Management*.

Below: Adam Elliot's amusing and deeply touching *Mary and Max*.

the story of eight-year-old Mary, who, unhappy at home in Australia, starts to correspond with a stranger, Max, a solitary New Yorker. Since their letters go on for over 20 years, there's an echo here of *84 Charing Cross Road*. Like *Chico & Rita* [qv], this feature successfully takes on material that's unexpected in an animated film. The voicing, not least by Philip Seymour Hoffman as Max and Barry Humphries as the narrator, is simply superb. MS

▶ With the voices of Philip Seymour Hoffman, Bethany Whitmore, Toni Collette, Barry Humphries, Eric Bana.
▶ *Dir*, *Screenplay* and *Design* Adam Elliot, *Pro* Melanie Coombs, *Ph* Gerald Thompson, *Ed* Bill Murphy, *M* Dale Cornelius.

Screen Australia/Melodrama Pictures etc-Soda Pictures. 92 mins. Australia. 2008. Rel: 22 Oct 2010. Cert. 12A.

Mascarades ★★★★

Comedian turned director Lyès Salem also plays Mounir Mekbek, a proud family man in a small Algerian village determined to find a suitable husband for his beautiful but narcoleptic sister Rym. He soon begins to regret the rumour that he innocently starts by boasting that his sister is engaged to a rich European. This is a charming film and a fine directorial debut by Salem, whose sharp and satirical script highlights the hypocrisy of a small community. GS

▶ Lyès Salem, Sarah Reguieg, Mohamed Bouchaib, Rym Takoucht, Merouane Zmirli, Mourad Khen.
▶ *Dir* Lyès Salem, *Pro* Yacine Laloui and Isabelle Madelaine, *Screenplay* Salem and Nathalie Saugeon, *Ph* Pierre Cottereau, *Pro Des* Jaoudet Gassouma, *Ed* Florence Ricard, *M* Mathias Duplessy, *Cos* Hamida Hamzal.

Dharamsala/Laith Média/arte France Cinéma/Canal + etc-Ciné Lumière. 94 mins. France/Algeria. 2008. Rel: 11 Dec 2009. No Cert.

Me and Orson Welles ★★★★★

Christian McKay's brilliant performance as Orson Welles, the finest on-screen impersonation yet, dominates this tale of the 1937 New York staging by Welles of Shakespeare's *Julius Caesar*. We enter this world with a hopeful young actor (persuasively played by Zac Efron) who is taken on as a member of the company. What follows is not just a delight for fans of Welles but also a wonderfully engaging evocation of life on stage, when rehearsals leave you uncertain whether you are headed for triumph or disaster. MS

▶ Christian McKay, Claire Danes, Zac Efron, Zoe Kazan, Eddie Marsan, Ben Chaplin.
▶ *Dir* Richard Linklater, *Pro* Linklater, Marc Samuelson and Ann Carli, *Screenplay* Holly Gent Palmo and Vince Palmo, from the novel by Robert Kaplow, *Ph* Dick Pope, *Pro Des* Laurence Dorman, *Ed* Sandra Adair, *M* Michael J. McEvoy, *Cos* Nic Ede.

CinemaNX/Isle of Man Films/Framestore Features/ Detour Filmproduction-Warner Bros. 114 mins. UK/USA. 2009. Rel: 4 Dec 2009. Cert. 12A.

The Meerkats ★★★★

The Kalahari Desert, South Africa. With its remarkable posture and vigilante stare, the meerkat is fast approaching the stature of the dolphin and penguin in the public's affection. This engaging 83 minutes was born from the desire of the BBC Natural History Unit and BBC Films to work together, and they've done their subject proud. With Paul Newman supplying an Uncle Remus voice-over for his last film project, this is a high-calibre production. The versatile photography, filming the meerkats from every possible viewpoint – as well as the creatures they interact with – is simply miraculous. JC-W

▶ Narrator Paul Newman.
▶ *Dir* James Honeyborne, *Pro* Trevor Ingman and Joe Oppenheimer, *Screenplay* story by Honeyborne, narration by Alexander McCall Smith, *Ph* Barrie Britton, Mark Payne-Gill and Tony Miller, *Ed* Justin Krish, *M* Sarah Class.

BBC Films/BBC Natural History/The Weinstein Company/Yaffle Films-The Weinstein Company. 83 mins. UK. 2008. Rel: 7 Aug 2009. Cert. PG.

Mega Piranha ★

This appalling *Piranha*-style sea-creature feature may be good for a few desperate laughs at its expense, but nothing disguises the fact that it's totally pathetic. Paul Logan stars as a Special Forces agent and Tiffany as a scientist who take on a shoal of mutant, super-sized, flesh-eating piranha that go on the rampage in Venezuela before they swim off to eat up Florida. Low budget and low imagination from The Global Asylum, who brought you *Mega Shark vs Giant Octopus*, it's more risible than funny. Though the acting's ropey, it's the effects that deserve special mention in the hall of shame. DW

Compare the meerkats: Two of the stars of James Honeyborne's miraculous documentary, *The Meerkats*.

▶ Paul Logan, Tiffany, Barry Williams, Jesse Daly, William Morse, Cooper Harris, Jude Gerard Prest.
▶ *Dir* and Screenplay Eric Forsberg, *Pro* David Michael Latt, *Ph* Bryan Olinger, *Pro Des* Marissa Leguizamon, *Ed* Bill Parker, *M* Chris Ridenhour, *Cos* Gregory Paul Smith.

The Global Asylum-Metrodome Distribution.
92 mins. USA. 2010. Rel: 16 July 2010. Cert. 15.

Mega Shark vs Giant Octopus ★

This low budget B-movie was originally an internet trailer sensation and despite the fun title it turns out to be really bad – not funny bad, just bad and boring, with wooden acting to match. Debbie Gibson plays a marine biologist who puts her life on the line in order to save the world from the title's prehistoric beasts. The special effects are as unreal as those of 1950s television. GS

▶ Deborah Gibson, Lorenzo Lamas, Vic Chao, Jonathan Nation, Mark Hengst, Michael The.
▶ *Dir* and *Screenplay* Jack Perez, *Pro* David Michael Latt, *Ph* Alexander Yellen, *Pro Des* Nino Zagaroli, *Ed* Marq Morrison, *M* Chris Ridenour, *Cos* Michelle Hodnett.

The Asylum/Giant Seafood-Metrodome Distribution.
85 mins. USA. 2009. Rel: 7 Aug 2009. Cert. 15.

Megamind ★★★★

Megamind (Will Ferrell) is the number one super villain of Metro City who thrives on evil. But when he exterminates his nemesis – the city's protector superhero, Metro Man (Brad Pitt) – he becomes the City's leader and finds that there is no one to challenge his evil plans. The script is fun and boasts a terrific energy that makes this

look quite fresh and original despite similarities to *The Incredibles* and *Despicable Me*. GS

▶ Voices of Will Ferrell, Jonah Hill, Tina Fey, Brad Pitt, David Cross, Ben Stiller.
▶ *Dir* Tom McGrath, *Pro* Lara Bream and Denise Nolan Cascino, *Screenplay* Alan Schoolcraft and Brent Simons, *Pro Des* David James, *Ed* Michael Andrews, *M* Lorna Balfe and Hans Zimmer.

DreamWorld Animation/Pacific Data Images/Red Hour Films-Paramount Pictures.
95 mins. USA. 2010. Rel: 3 Dec 2010. Cert. PG.

The Men Who Stare at Goats ★★

You'd think a film with Clooney, McGregor, Bridges, Spacey, Stephen Lang, Robert Patrick and the BBC on board would have something going for it, but it doesn't. It's based on an allegedly true story by journalist Jon Ronson about US soldiers who claim to have psychic powers in their defeat of the enemy. Ewan McGregor plays a reporter in Iraq with veteran George Clooney explaining such powers as making clouds disappear and killing goats at a glance. The film can't decide whether it's a serious study or a wacky comedy so fails on both counts, ending up a puzzling mess. MHD

▶ George Clooney, Ewan McGregor, Jeff Bridges, Kevin Spacey, Stephen Lang, Robert Patrick.
▶ *Dir* Grant Heslov, *Pro* Heslov and Paul Lister, *Screenplay* Peter Straughan, from the book by Jon Ronson, *Ph* Robert Elswit, *Pro Des* Sharon Seymour, *Ed* Tatiana S Riegel, *M* Rolfe Kent, *Cos* Louise Frogley.

BBC Films/Smoke House/Westgate Film Services/ Winchester Capital Partners-Momentum Pictures.
94 mins. USA/UK. 2009. Rel: 6 Nov 2009. Cert. 15.

Staring mad: George Clooney takes a dive in Grant Heslov's *The Men Who Stare at Goats.*

Director Jean-François Richet discusses a scene with his star, Vincent Cassel, on the set of *Mesrine: Killer Instinct.*

The Merry Gentleman ★★★

Described in publicity as a truly original Christmas story about the meeting of two lonely souls, this film quickly turns expectations on their head. It reveals itself as a romantic triangle drama involving a fleeing wife abused by her husband, a fat policeman who is attracted to her, and the man who appeals to her but proves to be a murderer. This bizarre piece is well played, especially by Kelly Macdonald, but Michael Keaton as star and director never finds the tone that could make it work. But it's so odd one is never bored. MS

▶ Michael Keaton, Kelly Macdonald, Tom Bastounes, Bobby Cannavale, Darlene Hunt.
▶ *Dir* Michael Keaton, *Pro* Ron Lazzeretti, Steven A Jones, Tom Bastounes and Paul J Duggan, *Screenplay* Lazzeretti, *Ph* Chris Seager, *Pro Des* Jennifer Dehghan, *Ed* Howard E Smith and Grant Myers, *M* Jon Sadoff and Ed Shearmur, *Cos* Susan Kaufmann.

Southwater Pictures-The Works UK Distribution. 97 mins. USA. 2009. Rel: 4 Dec 2009. Cert. 15.

Mesrine: Killer Instinct ★★★
Mesrine: Public Enemy No. 1 ★★★

Released in two parts rather than as a single four-hour movie, this French thriller traces the career of real-life criminal Jacques Mesrine, played by Vincent Cassel. It's staged with assurance but despite being taken from life the film lacks the subtleties and insights of a biographical portrait, opting instead for a larger than life style that on occasion reminds one of the James Bond franchise. MS

Mesrine: Killer Instinct

▶ Vincent Cassel, Cécile de France, Gérard Depardieu, Ludivine Sagnier, Roy Dupuis.
▶ *Dir* Jean-François Richet, *Pro* Thomas Langmann, *Screenplay* Abdel Raouf Dafri and Richet, based on Jacques Mesrine's book *L'instinct de mort*, *Ph* Robert Gantz, *Art Dir* Émile Ghigo, *Ed* Hervé Schneid, *M* Eloi Painchaud, *Cos* Virginie Montel and Gina Aller.

Natixis Coficiné/La Petite Reine/Remstar/Novo RPI/M6 Films etc-Momentum Pictures. 113 mins. France/Canada/Italy. 2008. Rel: 7 Aug 2009. Cert. 15.

Mesrine: Public Enemy No.1

▶ Vincent Cassel, Ludivine Sagnier. Mathieu Amalric, Olivier Gourmet, Gérard Lanvin.
▶ as per *Mesrine: Killer Instinct* except *Ed* Bill Pankow, *M* Marco Beltrami, Marcus Trumpp.

La Petite Reine/M6 Films/Remstar etc-Momentum Pictures. 133 mins. France/Canada. 2008. Rel: 28 Aug 2009. Cert. 15.

Metropolis [restored version] ★★★★★

Fritz Lang's timeless 1927 masterpiece can now be fully enjoyed as he originally envisaged with an extra 25 minutes of footage recently discovered in Buenos Aires and previously thought lost. In the year 2026 the workers of Metropolis live underground while the rich enjoy a life of luxury above. Meanwhile, a mad scientist is preparing to turn his robot into a woman and crush those revolutionaries underground. Lang's impeccable visionary epic has been copied endlessly throughout the years but never matched. See it and marvel! GS

▶ Brigitte Helm, Alfred Abel, Gustav Fröhlich, Fritz Alberti, Fritz Rasp, Heinrich George.
▶ *Dir* and *Ed* Fritz Lang, *Pro* Erich Pommer, *Screenplay* Lang and Thea von Harbou based on von Harbou's novel, *Ph* Karl Freund, Günther Rittau and Walter Ruttman, *Art Dir* Otto Hunte, Erich Kettelhut and Karl Vollbrecht *M* Gottfried Huppertz and Bernd Schultheis, *Cos* Aenne Willkomm.

Universum Film (UFA)-UFA and other distributors.
153 mins. Germany. 1927. Re-Release: 10 Sep 2010. Cert. PG.

Michael Jackson: This Is It ★★★★

When this documentary was rushed into cinemas after Michael Jackson's untimely death everybody assumed that it was just trying to cash in. But, surprisingly, this compilation of rehearsals as Jackson prepares for his highly anticipated London shows is sharply directed by Kenny Ortega and was exactly what his plethora of fans needed at the time. It begins with interviews and the dance auditions but it soon focuses on Jackson's professionalism and sheer perfectionism as he rehearses. GS

▶ Michael Jackson, Alex Al, Alexandra Apjarova, Nick Bass, Kenny Ortega.
▶ *Dir* Kenny Ortega, *Pro* Ortega, Paul Gongaware, Randy Phillips and John Meglen, *Ph* Sandrine Orabona and Tim Patterson, *Pro Des* Bernt Amadeus Capra and Michael Cotten, *Ed* Patterson, Don Brochu, Brandon Key and Kevin Stitt, *M* Michael Bearden, *Cos* Michael Bush, Topaz Erin Lareau, Dennis Tompkins.

Columbia Pictures/Michael Jackson Company/AEG Live-Sony Pictures Entertainment.
111 mins. USA. 2009. Rel: 28 Oct 2009. Cert. PG.

Micmacs ★★★

Jean-Pierre Jeunet's visual imagination is as acute as that of Terry Gilliam and his prints are all over this bizarre comedy, just as they were in *Delicatessen*. Serious themes can be tackled through comedy but here a genuine hatred for arms dealers produces a work that never finds a successful tone. There's black comedy and off-beat comedy but also shots of real amputees. The clash makes for a very messy film but one that is technically adroit and lovingly photographed. (Original title: *Mic Macs à tire-larigot*) MS

▶ Dany Boon, André Dussolier, Yolande Moreau, Dominique Pinon, Omar Sy.
▶ *Dir* Jean-Pierre Jeunet, *Pro* Frédéric Brillion, Gilles Legrand and Jeunet, *Screenplay* Jeunet and Guillaume Laurant, *Ph* Tetsuo Nagata, *Pro Des* Aline Bonnetto, *Ed* Hervé Schneid, *M* Raphael Beau, *Cos* Madeline Fontaine, *Animated Scenes* Romain Segaud.

Epithète Films/Tapioca Films/Warner Bros. Entertainment France etc-E1 Films.
104 mins. France. 2009. Rel: 26 Feb 2010. Cert. 12A.

Mid-August Lunch ★★★

One would like to be able to praise this gentle Italian movie because it touchingly looks at old age and features a group of women who are looked after by the son of one of them during the

À la cartoon: Dany Boon and Julie Ferrier in Jean-Pierre Jeunet's wildly inventive *Micmacs*.

Then in Rome: Gianni Di Gregorio in his own Mid-August Lunch.

two August days recognised as holidays in Italy. The bachelor son is played by writer/director Gianni Di Gregorio; his film has humour and humanity but it lacks a plot. Short as it is, the situation set up needs to be developed if one is not to feel that sadly the film has nowhere to go. (Original title: *Pranzo di Ferragosto*) MS

▶ Gianni Di Gregorio, Valeria De Franciscis, Marina Cacciotti, Maria Calì.
▶ *Dir* and *Screenplay* Gianni Di Gregorio, from a story by him and Simone Riccardini, *Ph* Gian Enrico Bianchi, *Art Dir* Susanna Cascella, *Ed* Marco Spoletini, *M* Ratchev & Caratello, *Cos* Silvia Polidori.

Archimede/Rai Cinema etc-Artificial Eye.
76 mins. Italy. 2008. Rel: 14 Aug 2009. Cert. U.

The Milk of Sorrow ★★

A surprise winner of the Golden Bear at Berlin, this comes across less as minimal drama than as metaphor. It features a heroine who has stuffed her vagina with a potato to protect herself from being raped like her late mother. All this may reflect the problem that Peru has in getting over its tragic history while also touching on issues of class. But, possessing neither visual poetry nor a gripping narrative, the film fails to engage. (Original title: *La teta asustada*) MS

▶ Magaly Solier, Susi Sánchez, Efrain Solis, Marino Ballón, Bárbara Lazón.
▶ *Dir* and *Screenplay* Claudia Llosa, *Pro* Antonio Chavarrias, José María Morales and Llosa, *Ph* Natasha Braier, *Art Dir* Patricia Bueno and Susanna Torres, *Ed*

Frank Gutiérrez, *M* Selma Mutal, *Cos* Ana Villanueva.

Oberon Cinematogràfica/Wanda Visión/Vela Producciones etc-Dogwoof Pictures.
98 mins. Spain/Peru/Switzerland/Germany. 2008. Rel: 30 Apr 2010. Cert. 12A.

Miral ★★½

On paper this new film from Julian Schnabel sounds interesting. Miral is an orphan looked after at the real-life establishment set up by Hind Husseini in Jerusalem in 1948. However, in trying to tell Miral's story, her mother's story and that of the late Hind Husseini, the film becomes bitty. Furthermore, characterisations are often too simplistic and it is difficult to assess what stance is being taken on violent action for political ends. MS

▶ Freida Pinto, Hiam Abbass, Yasmine Al Massri, Ruba Blal, Stella Schnabel, Willem Dafoe, Vanessa Redgrave.
▶ *Dir* Julian Schnabel, *Pro* Jon Kilik, *Screenplay* Rula Jebreal, from her novel, *Ph* Éric Gautier, *Pro Des* Yoel Herzberg, *Ed* Juliette Welfling, *Cos* Walid Mawed.

Jérôme Seydoux/Pathé/ER Productions/Eagle Pictures/India Take One Productions etc-Pathé Distribution.
112 mins. France/Israel/Italy/India. 2010. Rel: 3 Dec 2010. Cert. 12A.

Miss March: Generation Penetration ★

Directed, written by and starring the comedy duo Zach Cregger and Trevor Moore, *Miss March* fancies itself as a gross-out comedy in the *Road Trip* mould. The problem is that Moore – who channels

Matthew Lillard by way of Jim Carrey – is just not funny. Silly faces, lots of screaming and double-takes that would bore a sloth are not funny. In fact, it's hard to imagine how a film as worthless and irrational as this was ever bankrolled, let alone released. It's simply insulting. JC-W

▶ Zach Cregger, Trevor Moore, Raquel Alessi, Molly Stanton, Craig Robinson, Hugh M Hefner.
▶ *Dir* and *Screenplay* Zach Cregger and Trevor Moore, from a story by Ryan Homchick, *Pro* Dennis Hagerty and Thomas Mimms, *Pro* Tobie Haggerty, Tom Jacobson, Vincent Cirricione and Steven J Wolfe, *Ph* Anthony B Richmond, *Pro Des* Cabot McMullen, *Ed* Tim Mirkovich, *M* Jeff Cardoni, *Cos* Sarah de Sa Rego and Alexis Scott.
Fox Atomic/Sneak Preview Entertainment/The Jacobson Company-20th Century Fox.
89 mins. USA. 2009. Rel: 11 Sep 2009. Cert. 15.

Monsters ★★★★

Gareth Edwards' cheaply made feature has been rightly acclaimed. It may concern a photographer and the daughter of his boss attempting to escape from alien creatures that have landed in Mexico but the film is more of a love story than a horror movie. Scoot McNairy and Whitney Able, a real-life couple, share chemistry and acting talent, and if the last section is more conventional the special effects are nevertheless remarkable for a low-budget film. MS

▶ Scoot McNairy, Whitney Able, Mario Zuñiga Benavides.
▶ *Dir*, *Screenplay*, *Ph*, *Pro Des* and *Visual Effects* Gareth Edwards, *Pro* Allan Niblo and James Richardson, *Ed* Colin Goudie, *M* Jon Hopkins.
Vertigo Films-Vertigo Films.
94 mins. UK. 2010. Rel: 3 Dec 2010. Cert. 12A.

Moon ★★★★½

Duncan Jones (son of David Bowie) impresses mightily with this fascinating debut feature film based on his own story. Sam Rockwell plays astronaut Sam Bell, who is injured while out fixing a machine. Waking up he discovers he has been cloned – or has he? Nearer to *Dark Star*, *Silent Running* or better yet *2001: A Space Odyssey* (with GERTY, the onboard computer, voiced by Kevin Spacey) – together with a nod to Dad's *Space Oddity*? – Jones' vision is more acute than all the technological wizardry of *Avatar* and at a fraction of the cost. Yet it never looks like a budget production. MHD

▶ Sam Rockwell, Kevin Spacey, Dominique McElligott, Rosie Shaw, Adrienne Shaw, Benedict Wong.
▶ *Dir* Duncan Jones, *Pro* Stuart Fenegan and Trudie Styler, *Screenplay* Nathan Parker, from a story by Jones, *Ph* Gary Shaw, *Pro Des* Tony Noble, *Ed* Nicolas Gaster, *M* Clint Mansell, *Cos* Jane Petrie.

Liberty Films UK/Xingu Films/Limelight/Lunar Industries-Sony Pictures Releasing.
97 mins. UK. 2009. Rel: 17 July 2010. Cert. 15.

Morning Light ★★½

Morning Light is the name of a TP52 class yacht, so don't expect *Titanic*. In fact, this is a documentary that focuses on the training for and competing in the 44th Transpacific Yacht Race from Long Beach, California, to Honolulu. That's 2,560 miles of unpredictable water to negotiate and director Monroe (who scripted the Oscar-winning *The Cove*) dishes up some impressive action photography. For fans of tacking and gybing this is, literally, a wet dream, although there's precious little human interest. CB

▶ Chris Branning, Graham Brant-Zawadski, Chris Clark, Charlie Enright, Jesse Fielding.
▶ *Dir* Mark Monroe, *Pro* Morgan Sackett, *Ph* Josef Nalevansky, *Ed* Monroe and Paul Crowder , *Music Supervisor* Liz Gallacher.
Walt Disney Pictures-Buena Vista International (UK).
100 mins. USA. 2008. Rel: 11 Sep 2009. Cert. PG.

Morris: A Life With Bells On ★★

Another mockumentary purporting to tell the story of Morris dancing and how one man tried

Earth dreams: Sam Rockwell recalls less lonely days in Duncan Jones' atmospheric and disturbing *Moon*, with Dominique McElligott.

to make it more modern and popular for today's tastes. It's given an air of pseudo-intellectualism with appearances by so-called academics but, with a cast of easily recognisable stars such as Derek Jacobi, Ian Hart, Harriet Walter, Clive Mantle, Sophie Thompson and even Dominique Pinon, the documentary element goes for nought. Men dancing while banging sticks and waving hankies is, anyway, not the most exciting subject to satirise and the film may well lose some of its audience well before the end credits start rolling. MHD

❧ Charles Thomas Oldham, Lucy Akhurst, Brodie Bass, Andy Black, Ben Bela Böhm, Jasper Britton, Greg Wise.
❧ *Dir* Lucy Akhurst, *Pro* Akhurst, Oldham and Roger Chapman, *Screenplay* Oldham, *Ph* Chapman, *Pro Des* Caroline Story, *Ed* Nick Carew, *M* Richard Lumsden, *Cos* Alexandra Mann.

Twist Films-Twist Films Morris Ltd.
100 mins. UK. 2009. Rel: 27 Sep 2009. Cert. 12A.

Mother ★★★½

A thriller but also something more, this Korean film was conceived by Bong Joon-ho as a vehicle for the actress Kim Hye-ja. She seizes the chance to portray a mother unlike the paragons of virtue she has played on television. Here she is the mother of a retarded son accused of murder and just how far she will go to protect him is central to the tale. *Mother* may be over-long and it does not wholly satisfy, but it's certainly interesting. (Original title: *Madeo*) MS

❧ Kim Hye-ja, Won Bin, Jin Goo, Yoon Jae-moon, Lee Young-suck.
❧ *Dir* Bong Joon-ho, *Pro* Moon Yang-kwon etc, *Screenplay* Park Eun-kyo and Bong, from the latter's story, *Ph* Hong Kyung-pyo, *Pro Des* Ryo Seong-hee, *Ed* Moon Sae-kyoung, *M* Lee Byeong-woo, *Cos* Choi Se-yeon.

Barunson/CJ Entertainment etc-Optimum Releasing.
129 mins. Republic of Korea. 2009. Rel: 20 Aug 2010. Cert. 15.

Motherhood ★½

Eliza Welch (Uma Thurman), a former fiction writer, puts her career on hold in order to raise her two children in Greenwich Village. She hardly has a moment to herself but is determined to win a magazine competition where she has to write on the theme of 'What Does Motherhood Mean to Me?' Katherine Dieckmann's interesting idea is let down by her underdeveloped script, which is neither very funny nor touching. Thurman is a strong presence as ever but sadly her performance is wrongly pitched. GS

❧ Uma Thurman, Anthony Edwards, Minnie Driver, David Schallipp, Matthew Schallipp, Daisy Tahan, Alice Drummond.

❧ *Dir* and *Screenplay* Katherine Dieckmann, *Pro* Rachel Cohen, John Wells, Christine Vachon, Pamela Koffler and Jana Edelbaum, *Ph* Nancy Schreiber, *Pro Des* Debbie DeVilla, *Ed* Michael R Miller, *M* Joe Henry, *Cos* Susan Lyall.

Killer Films/John Wells Productions/iDeal Partners Film Fund-Metrodome Distribution.
90 mins. USA. 2009. Rel: 5 Mar 2010. Cert. 15.

Mr Nice ★★★

Rhys Ifans dominates this film in a star part: subtly played, it is his best role to date. Unfortunately, the film itself is decidedly less winning. Based on the best-selling memoir by Howard Marks, it stresses his life as a drug baron at the expense of the rest and glamorises that aspect by presenting him as an anti-establishment hero. If you buy that view, you'll like the film more than I did. MS

❧ Rhys Ifans, Chloë Sevigny. David Thewlis, Luis Tosár, Crispin Glover, Christian McKay.
❧ *Dir* and *Ph* Bernard Rose, *Pro* Luc Roeg, *Screenplay* Rose, from the book by Howard Marks, *Pro Des* Max Gottlieb, *Ed* Rose and Teresa Font, *M* Philip Glass, *Cos* Caroline Harris.

Independent/Prescience Pictures/KanZaman Productions etc-E1 Entertainment.
121 mins. UK/Spain. 2009. Rel: 8 Oct 2010. Cert. 18.

Mr Right ★

It is impossible to find anything positive to say about this dull gay rom-com that takes place in contemporary Soho. Louise (Georgia Harris) begins to regret deeply her decision to introduce her current lover Paul (Jeremy Edwards) to her gay friends. The idea is not bad but the dodgy acting and lazy script fail to convince and the one-dimensional characters are better put back into the closet. GS

❧ Luke De Woolfson, James Lance, Benjamin Hart, Georgia Zaris, David Morris, Leon Ockendon, Rocky Marshall, Jan Waters, Jeremy Edwards.
❧ *Dir* David and Jacqui Morris, *Pro* Jacqui Morris, *Screenplay* David Morris, *Ph* Michael Wood, *Pro Des* Malin Lindholm, *Ed* Warren Meneely, *M* Jacqueline Croft, *Cos* Clare Harries.

Mugshots-Verve Pictures.
95 mins. UK. 2009. Rel: 27 Nov 2009. Cert. 15.

Mugabe and the White African ★★★★★

An over-insistent music score is the only weakness in what is otherwise a superlative documentary. It's a work of great power which invites us to follow day by day what happens to a farmer in Zimbabwe, a model white South African, who is confronted by the violent hostility of Mugabe's regime and goes to court to defend his interests. Watching it is a deeply emotional experience. MS

▶ With Mike Campbell, Ben Freeth, Angela Campbell, Jeremy Gauntlett.
▶ *Dir* Lucy Bailey and Andrew Thompson, *Pro* David Pearson and Elizabeth Morgan Hemlock, *Ph* Thompson, *Ed* Tim Lovell, *M* Jonny Pilcher.
Arturi Films/Explore Films etc-Dogwoof Pictures.
94 mins. UK. 2009. Rel: 8 Jan 2010. Cert. 12A.

My Afternoons with Margueritte ★★★★

This feel-good movie concerns an over-weight ageing illiterate who becomes captivated by literature on meeting a nonagenarian ex-teacher named Margueritte. This quintessentially French piece (the reading matter touched on includes *The Plague* by Camus!) is so unlikely that it has to be taken with several pinches of salt. Yet it delights, and that's because 95-year- old Gisèle Casadesus is wonderful while Gérard Depardieu, in the other lead role, unexpectedly gives one of his best performances ever. (Original title: *La Tête en friche*) MS

▶ Gérard Depardieu, Gisèle Casadesus, Maurane, Jean-François Stévenin, Claire Maurier.
▶ *Dir* Jean Becker, *Pro* Louis Becker, *Screenplay* Jean-Louis Dabadie and Becker, from the novel *La Tête en friche* by Marie-Sabine Roger, *Ph* Arthur

Cloquet, *Art Dir* Thérèse Ripaud, *Ed* Jacques Witta, *M* Laurent Voulzy, *Cos* Annie Périer-Bertaux.
ICE 3/KJB Production/Studio Canal/France 3 Cinéma etc-Picturehouse Entertainment.
82 mins. France. 2010. Rel: 12 Nov 2010. Cert. 15.

My Father My Lord ★★★

This short feature with spot-on casting is about a Jewish family in Jerusalem. The mother looks on while the world of her young child is entirely coloured by the fact that her husband is a rabbi. The flashback narrative makes us suspect that the story is leading to the boy's death and, except for those especially drawn to a portrayal of Jewish life, the film would be far more interesting if it started at the point where it ends. (Original title: *Hofshat kaits*) MS

▶ Assi Dayan, Sharon Hacochen Bar. Ilan Grif, Yehuda Grovais.
▶ *Dir* and *Screenplay* David Volach, *Pro* Eyal Shiray, *Ph* Boaz Yackov, *Art Dir* Yoav Sinai, *Ed* Haim Tabeckman, *Cos* Neli Horovitz.
Golden Cinema/The New Israeli Foundation for Cinema & TV-Artificial Eye.
77 mins. Israel. 2007. Rel: 26 Dec 2009. Cert. PG.

My Last Five Girlfriends ★★★

Here's an oddity: a British rom-com that aims at the same sophistication you find in an American movie like *(500) Days of Summer* [qv]. That may

Brought to book: Gérard Depardieu and Gisèle Casadesus in Jean Becker's unlikely My Afternoons with Margueritte.

A nanny state of mind: Emma Thompson casts her spell in Susanna White's box-office hit, *Nanny McPhee and the Big Bang*.

be explained by its roots in a book by Alain de Botton. But the lead actor, playing a youth required to recall his bad luck with girls, is Brendan Patricks, when what is required instead is someone with the charisma of the young Hugh Grant. It's good that the film is ambitious but sadly it falls short. MS

▶ Brendan Patricks, Naomie Harris, Cécile Cassel, Kelly Adams, Jane March.
▶ *Dir*, *Ed* and *Screenplay* (from Alain de Botton's novel *Essays in Love*) Julian Kemp, *Pro* Marion Pilowsky, David Willing and Michael Kel, *Ph* Dave Miller, *Pro Des* Kit Line, *M* Marten Joustra and Andy Blythe, *Cos* Lyn Noiram.

Willing + Pilowsky Productions/Wire Films-Paramount Pictures.
87 mins. 2009. Rel: 19 Mar 2010. Cert. 12A.

My Son, My Son, What Have Ye Done ★★½

Even Werner Herzog has rarely been more quirky than in this piece about a would-be actor in San Diego who killed his mother with a sword. What might have played as a strong thriller is made semi-comic from the start, and it's bizarre rather than insightful or effective. The opening shots are quite beautifully composed, but for better or worse this movie exists in a world of total eccentricity. MS

▶ Michael Shannon, Willem Dafoe, Chloë Savigny, Udo Kier, Michael Peña, Brad Dourif, Irma Hall, Grace Zabriskie.
▶ *Dir* Werner Herzog, *Pro* Eric Bassett, *Screenplay* Herbert Golder and Herzog, *Ph* Peter Zeitlinger,

Pro Des Danny Caldwell, *Ed* Joe Bini and Omar Daher, *M* Ernst Reijseger, *Cos* Mikel Padilla.

Industrial Entertainment/Absurda/Paper Street Films etc-Scanbox Entertainment UK.
91 mins. USA/Germany. 2009. Rel: 10 Sep 2010. No Cert.

Nanny McPhee and the Big Bang ★★★½

Emma Thompson is as delightful as before in this second adventure of the ugly nanny with magical powers that bring mischievous children to heel. This time the setting is the Second World War period but the film suffers from passages of exaggerated broad comedy that are less appealing than the rest. However, as with the original, what you remember are the engaging bits presented with such warmth and sincerity. MS

▶ Emma Thompson, Maggie Gyllenhaal, Rhys Ifans, Asa Butterfield, Eros Vlahos, Maggie Smith, Bill Bailey, Ralph Fiennes, Ewan McGregor.
▶ *Dir* Susanna White, *Pro* Lindsay Doran, Tim Bevan and Eric Fellner, *Screenplay* Emma Thompson, based on the character 'Nurse Matilda' created by Christanna Brand, *Ph* Mike Eley, *Pro Des* Simon Elliott, *Ed* Sim Evan-Jones, *M* James Newton Howard, *Cos* Jacqueline Durran.

Universal Pictures/Studio Canal/Relativity Media/Working Title etc-Universal Pictures.
109 mins. USA/UK/Japan/France. 2010. Rel: 26 March 2010. Cert. U.

Nativity! ★★

This is feel-good comedy gone bonkers as Debbie Isitt defies even the slightest touch of plausibility to ensure that her rather timid teacher hero (Martin Freeman) triumphs in Coventry with his Christmas nativity play by winning support from Hollywood! If you long to see gap-toothed kids, this is the film for you. But one has to admire the way in which Isitt goes the whole hog with a musical finale featuring songs by her and her partner, the film's editor Nicky Ager. MS

▶ Martin Freeman, Marc Wootton, Jason Watkins, Alan Carr, Ricky Tomlinson, Pam Ferris.
▶ *Dir* and *Screenplay* Debbie Isitt, *Pro* Nick Jones, *Ph* Sean Van Hales, *Pro Des* Chris Roope, *Ed* Nicky Ager, *M* Ager and Isitt, *Cos* Stephanie Collie.

BBC Films/Screen WM/Limelight/Mirrorball Films etc-E1 Films.
106 mins. UK. 2009. Rel: 27 Nov 2009. Cert. U.

Night of the Demons ★½

This pointless remake of the 1988 horror film revisits the notorious Broussard Mansion in New Orleans on Halloween night, where a group of youngsters are eager to party all night long. But the demons are waiting to be reborn... The acting is bad and the unlikeable teenagers deserve what they get. It is sad to see the formerly promising Edward Furlong appearing in this drivel. GS

▶ Edward Furlong, Monica Keena, Shannon Elizabeth, Jamie Harris, Diora Baird, John F Beach.
▶ *Dir* Adam Gierasch, *Pro* Michael Arata, Greg McKay, Raymond J Markovich, Jerry Daigle and Kevin Tenney, *Screenplay* Gierasch and Jace Anderson, *Ph* Yaron Levy, *Pro Des* Raymond Pumilia, *Ed* Andrew Cohen, *M* Joseph Bishara, *Cos* Oakley Stevenson.
Seven Arts Pictures/Cold Fusion Media Group/Parallel Media/Voodoo Production Services-Kaleidoscope Home Entertainment.
93 mins. USA. 2010. Rel: 17 Sep 2010. Cert. 18.

A Nightmare on Elm Street ★½

The bastard son of a hundred maniacs returns in stripy-suited, bloodily rebooted form, still slashing teens in their dreams as charred, scarred molester Freddy Krueger (Jackie Earle Haley). Only this time the sleep-deprived Elm Street kids can't help but lapse into inconveniently timed micro-sleeps, so you never really know when Freddy's going to strike next. Largely, though, this is a carbon copy of the first, only with mobile phones, and much as we love freaky little Jackie Earle, he doesn't quite cut it as Freddy. We miss Robert Englund: a shameless ham, and we loved him for it. This just isn't any fun. MJ

▶ Jackie Earle Haley, Kyle Gallner, Rooney Mara, Katie Cassidy, Thomas Dekker, Kellan Lutz.
▶ *Dir* Samuel Bayer, *Pro* Michael Bay, *Screenplay* Wesley Strick and Eric Heisserer, from a story by Strick, based on characters by Wes Craven, *Ph* Jeff Cutler, *Pro Des* Patrick Lumb, *Ed* Glen Scantlebury, *M* Steve Jablonsky, *Cos* Mari-An Ceo.
New Line Cinema/Platinum Dunes-Warner Bros.
95 mins. USA. 2010. Rel: 7 May 2010. Cert. 18.

Nightwatching ★★★★

Released belatedly (it was made in 2006), this film finds Peter Greenaway exploring in his characteristic way the possibility that Rembrandt's famous painting 'The Night Watch' contains hidden statements: coded denunciations, in fact. Superb in its Scope visuals, this film also looks at Rembrandt's life and does so, in typically Greenaway mode, with much stylisation and nudity. But for his admirers this will come across as a return to form. MS

▶ Martin Freeman, Emily Holmes, Jodhi May, Eva Birthistle, Toby Jones, Natalie Press.
▶ *Dir* and *Screenplay* Peter Greenaway, *Pro* Kees Kasander, *Ph* Reinier van Brummelen, *Pro Des* Maarten Piersma, *Ed* Karen Porter, *M* Wlodek Pawlik, *Cos* Jagna Janicka and Marrit van der Burgt.
ContentFilm International/Nightwatching Productions Inc/UK Film Council etc-Axiom Films.
141 mins. The Netherlands/Canada/UK/Poland. 2007. Rel: 26 Mar 2010. Cert. 18.

9 ★★★

Director Shane Acker's animated feature-length expansion of his 2004 Oscar-nominated short of the same name sets up a compelling future dystopian wasteland where humans have been wiped out, but irritatingly cute, small, puppet-like creatures survive named after the numerals 1 through 9. The producers include directors Tim Burton and Timur Bekmambetov. JC

▶ Voices of Christopher Plummer, Martin Landau, John C Reilly, Crispin Glover, Jennifer Connelly, Elijah Wood.
▶ *Dir* Shane Acker, *Pro* Tim Burton, Timur Bekmambetov, Dana Ginsburg, Jim Lemley, *Screenplay* Pamela Pettler, from a story by Shane

Elijah Wood, as the eponymous rag doll, finds himself in a fantastical universe (again) in Shane Acker's 9.

Nine

Acker, *Pro Des* Robert St Pierre and Fred Warter, Ed Nick Kenway, M Deborah Lurie.

Focus Features/Relativity Media/Starz Animation/Tim Burton Productions-Universal Pictures International. 79 mins. USA. 2009. Rel: 28 Oct 2009. Cert. 12A.

Nine ★★★★½

It may not earn a ten since the songs are not quite of the top rank, but Rob Marshall here follows up *Chicago* with a well-judged and cinematically conceived take on the 1982 stage musical based on Fellini's film *8½*. Daniel Day-Lewis is on form as the Italian film-maker faced by a creative block and chaos in his private life, and a great cast, not least Marion Cotillard as the wife, portray the women around him. Fellini's admirers will be interested, but to enjoy this film you need to love not so much art-house cinema as Broadway pizzazz. If you do, it gets even better with each viewing. MS

▶ Daniel Day-Lewis, Marion Cotillard, Penélope Cruz, Judi Dench, Nicole Kidman, Fergie, Kate Hudson, Sophia Loren.
▶ *Dir* Rob Marshall, *Pro* Marc Platt, Harvey Weinstein, John DeLuca and Marshall, *Screenplay* Michael Tolkin and Anthony Minghella, based on the Broadway musical with book by Arthur Kopit from the Italian by Mario Fratti, *Ph* Dion Beebe, *Pro Des* John Myhre, *Ed* Claire Simpson and Wyatt Smith, *M* Maury Yeston and Andrea Guerra, *Cos* Colleen Atwood.

The Weinstein Company/Relativity Media/Marc Platt Productions/Lucamar etc-Entertainment Film Distrubutors. 119 mins. USA. 2009. Rel: 18 Dec 2009. Cert. 12A.

Ninja Assassin ★★

Blending old-school action sensibilities with ridiculously over-enhanced visuals, *Ninja Assassin* stars Korean pop superstar Rain as a well-meaning lethal weapon with an unparalleled talent for separating bad guys from their limbs, for splashing their blood about like water from a garden sprinkler, and for healing supernaturally from appalling, mortal wounds. Tearing through a virtually inexhaustible supply of murderous Ninjas, often in slow motion and with a thousand computer-generated stars whizzing all around him, Rain's quite pretty, and pretty capable, but bland, much like the supporting cast and the movie itself. MJ

▶ Rain, Naomi Harris, Ben Miles, Rick Yune, Sho Kosugi, Lee Joon.
▶ *Dir* James McTeigue, *Pro* Joel Silver, Grant Hill and Andy and Lana Wachowski, *Screenplay* Matthew Sand and J Michael Straczynski, from a story by Sand, *Ph* Karl Walter Lindenlaub, *Pro Des* Graham Walker, *Ed* Gian Ganziano, *M* Ilan Eshken, *Cos* Carlo Poggioli.

Warner Bros Pictures/Silver Pictures/Legendary Pictures/Dark Castle Entertainment/Anarchos Productions/Studio Babelsberg etc-Warner Bros. 99 mins. USA/Germany. 2009. Rel: 22 Jan 2010. Cert. 18.

No Impact Man ★★½

Eco-themed documentaries are becoming so abundant that they are going to need their own landfill. This one was timed to coincide with the publication of Colin Beavan's memoir in which he chronicles his year on the breadline. Or, to be fair, this was the year that Colin (and his reluctant wife and daughter) attempted to do without taxis, electricity and non-seasonal produce – in, of all places, Manhattan. Another problem is that these sorts of documentaries are already littering the small screen, although this one is reasonably entertaining. CB

▶ Colin Beavan, Michelle Conlin.
▶ *Dir* Laura Gabbert and Justin Schein, *Pro* Gabbert and Eden Wurmfeld, *Ph* Justin Schein, *Ed* Matthew Martin and William Haugse, *M* Bobby Johnston.

Eden Wurmfeld Films/Shadowbox Films Inc-Dogwoof Pictures. 93 mins. USA. 2009. Rel: 3 Sep 2010. No Cert.

No One Knows About Persian Cats ★★★½

This brave film from Bahman Ghobadi illustrates the extent to which pop musicians in Iran can find themselves in trouble when using music to express views disapproved of by the existing regime. For some the featured music will be welcome, while for others it could be the least appealing aspect. Nevertheless, the film-maker's insistence on telling the truth has to be admired even if his film is less than perfect. MS

▶ Negar Shaghaghi, Ashikan Koshanejad, Hamed Behdad, Babak Mirzakhani.
▶ *Dir, Pro* and *Set Designer* Bahman Ghobadi,

Mama's boy: Aaron Johnson as John Lennon in Sam Taylor-Wood's Nowhere Boy.

Of monks and Muslims: Olivier Rabourdin and Lambert Wilson in Xavier Beauvois' highly acclaimed *Of Gods and Men.*

Screenplay Ghobadi, Hossein M Abkenar and Roxana Saberi, *Ph* Touraj Aslani, *Ed* Hayedeh Safiyari.

Mij Film Company/Mitosfilm-Network Releasing. 107 mins. Iran. 2009. Rel: 26 Mar 2010. Cert. 12A.

Nowhere Boy ★★★★

Screenwriter Matt Greenhalgh has an aptitude for stories about British pop singers and now moves on from *Control* (about Joy Division's Ian Curtis) to this appealing look at John Lennon's teenage years in Liverpool. Music is inevitably part of the story, but the central focus is on the aunt (Kristin Scott Thomas at her best) who brought up the boy, and on his mother (Anne-Marie Duff, impressive) who reappeared in his life. There are minor misjudgments in Sam Taylor-Wood's direction but this is a film to relish, not least for the acting. MS

▶ Aaron Johnson, Anne-Marie Duff, Kristin Scott Thomas, David Threlfall, David Morrissey, Thomas Brodie Sangster.
▶ *Dir* Sam Taylor-Wood, *Pro* Robert Bernstein, Douglas Rae and Kevin Loader, *Screenplay* Matt Greenhalgh, *Ph* Seamus McGarvey, *Pro Des* Alice Normington, *Ed* Lisa Gunning, *M* Will Gregory and Alison Goldfrap, *Cos* Julian Day.

Film4/UK Film Council/Ecosse Films etc-Icon Film Distribution. 86 mins. UK. 2009. Rel: 26 Dec 2009. Cert. 15.

Of Gods and Men ★★★★½

One of the best French films of recent years, Xavier Beauvois' drama concerns Cistercian monks residing in Algeria in the 1990s who are threatened as a result of local violence. Should they leave as is suggested or should they put their trust in God, thus continuing to support the people of the region and to uphold what they themselves stand for? I find one scene in this tale taken from life too calculated for my taste, but otherwise this impeccably acted film is perfectly judged and the finest religious film to come out of France since the death of Robert Bresson. (Original title: *Des hommes et des dieux*) MS

▶ Lambert Wilson, Michael Lonsdale, Olivier Rabourdin, Farid Larbi, Jacques Herlin.
▶ *Dir* Xavier Beauvois, *Screenplay* Etienne Comar with Beauvois, *Ph* Caroline Champetier, *Art Dir* Michel Barthelémy, *Ed* Marie-Julie Maille, *Cos* Marielle Robaut.

Armada Films/Why Not Productions/France 3 Cinéma etc-Artificial Eye. 122 mins. France. 2010. Rel: 30 Dec 2010. Cert. 15.

Oil City Confidential ★★★★

Julien Temple's intriguing rock documentary follows the lives of four men, their friends and family as they reminisce about life on Thames Delta's Canvey Island and how the legendary band of Dr Feelgood was created. The four childhood friends grew up in this bleak wasteland somewhere off the edge of Essex at a time when the island was recovering from a Biblical flood, before they emerged as one of the most extraordinary rock groups of the 1970s. It is fascinating and entertaining. GS

▶ Lee Brilleaux, Wilko Johnson, John Martin, John B Sparkes, Christopher Fenwick, Jools Holland, Glen

Matlock, Suggs, Alison Moyet, Joe Strummer.
‣ *Dir* Julien Temple, *Pro* Stephen Malit, *Ph* Stephen Organ, *Pro Des* Max Reeve, *Ed* Caroline Richards, *M* J C Carroll and Dr Feelgood.

A Product of Malitsky/Cadiz Music Ltd-Arts Alliance Media.
104 mins. UK. 2009. Rel: 2 Feb 2010. Cert. 15.

Old Dogs ★

This is one of the worst films of the year. Best friends and business partners Charlie (John Travolta) and Dan (Robin Williams) lead a carefree life until Dan finds out that he is the father of seven-year-old twins. The two friends attempt to bond with the children while trying to finalise the biggest business deal of their lives. The utterly unfunny dialogue, atrocious acting and ridiculous set-pieces are almost guaranteed to put you off going to the cinema ever again. GS

‣ John Travolta, Robin Williams, Kelly Preston, Seth Green, Matt Dillon, Ann-Margret.
‣ *Dir* Walt Becker, *Pro* Peter Abrams, Andrew Panay and Robert L Levy, *Screenplay* David Diamond and David Weissman, *Ph* Jeffrey L Kimball, *Pro Des* David Gropman, *Ed* Ryan Folsey and Tom Lewis, *M* John Debney, *Cos* Joseph G Aulisi.

Walt Disney Pictures/Tapestry Films-Walt Disney Studios Motion Pictures.
88 mins. USA. 2009. Rel: 19 Mar 2010. Cert. PG.

On Tour ★

Mathieu Amalric, both star and director here, provides us with an atmospheric view of a burlesque show featuring Americans touring in France. Some people appear to like the film, but nothing seen in the stage show strikes me as being of the slightest interest and the characters remain unengaging throughout. Only a brief scene with Aurélia Petit sparks into life. (Original title: *Tournée*) MS

‣ Mathieu Amalric, Miranda Colclasure, Suzanne Ramsey, Linda Marracini, Julie Ann Muz.

Fisherman's friend: Colin Farrell befriends a mermaid in Neil Jordan's poetic and bewitching *Ondine*.

‣ *Dir* Mathieu Amalric, *Pro* Laetitia Gonzalez and Yaël Fogiel, *Screenplay* Amalric, Philippe Di Folco, Marcelo Novais Teles and Raphaëlle Valbrune, *Ph* Christophe Beaucarne, *Art Dir* Stéphane Taillasson, *Ed* Annette Dutertre, *Cos* Alexia Crisp-Jones.

Les Films du Poisson/ARTE France Cinéma/WDR/Arte etc-Artificial Eye.
111 mins. France/Germany. 2010. Rel: 10 Dec 2010. Cert. 15.

Ondine ★★★

Neil Jordan brings a strong poetic flavour to this bewitching tale set on Ireland's rugged south-west coast. Like John Sayles' *The Secret of Roan Inish*, it is enshrouded in myth, centring on the emergence of a beautiful young woman caught in the net of a local fisherman called Syracuse (Colin Farrell). Jordan artfully juggles the mystical with grimy reality and his film only loses its grip when its more mundane realities undermine the magic. The acting, though, and Christopher Doyle's cinematography, are exceptional. JC-W

‣ Colin Farrell, Alicja Bacaleda, Tony Curran, Stephen Rea, Dervla Kirwan.
‣ *Dir* and *Screenplay* Neil Jordan, *Pro* Jordan, James Flynn and Ben Browning, *Ph* Christopher Doyle, *Pro Des* Anna Rackard, *Ed* Tony Lawson, *M* Kjartan Sveinsson, *Cos* Eimer Ni Mhaoldomhnaigh.

Octagon Films/Little Wave Productions/Irish Film Board/Wayfarer Entertainment/RTE-Paramount Pictures.
111 mins. Ireland/USA. 2009. Rel: 5 Mar 2010. Cert. 12A.

1 Day ★★★★

Penny Woolcock's highly energetic hip hop drama takes place among the Afro-Caribbean community in the West Midlands. Flash (Dylan Duffus) is in deep trouble – he is not only being pursued by two rival gangs after he has been summoned to deliver £500k but also by three women claiming he's the father of their babies. It bravely portrays a true picture of the gun culture among the black community and is done with great flair and a good sense of humour, particularly in the rap set-pieces involving the mothers. GS

‣ Dylan Duffus, Ohran Whyte, Duncan Tobias, Yohance Watkins, Chris Wilson.
‣ *Dir* and *Screenplay* Penny Woolcock, *Pro* Woolcock, Claire Bosworth and Amy Flanagan, *Ph* Graham Smith, *Pro Des* Sophy Millington, *Ed* John Dinwoodie, *M* Urban Monk, *Cos* Nathania Atkinson.

Blast! Films/Screen West Midlands-Vertigo Films.
102 mins. UK. 2009. Rel: 6 Nov 2009. Cert. 15.

One Night in Turin ★★★

This stirring, nostalgic documentary of the England football team's bid to win the World

The band plays on: The eponymous *1234* rehearse their stuff.

Cup in 1990 makes the most of its surging emotional highlights: David Platt's winner against Belgium, Lineker's equaliser against West Germany, Waddle's penalty miss and Gazza's tears as England lost on penalties in the semi-finals. Around 26 million of us watched the semi in Turin; many fans with longer memories will want to re-live the thrills as director James Erskine sifts among the copious archive clips. Proving the right choice, Gary Oldman narrates in style. Bizarrely, it enjoyed a nationwide cinema release for one night only. DW

▶ Elliot Francis and Gary Oldman (narrator).
▶ *Dir* and *Screenplay* James Erskine, *Pro* Erskine and Victoria Gregory, *Pro Des* Rebecca Henry, *Ed* Robin Peters, *M* Stuart Hancock.

New Black Films-Kaleidoscope Home Entertainment. 97 mins. UK. 2010. Rel: 7 May 2010. Cert. 15.

1234 ★★½

Guitarist Stevie (Ian Bonar) works in a call centre but dreams of hitting the big time in the music business. His colleague Neil (Mathew Baynton) is the first to join his group, playing the drums, while the cool and much more experienced Billy (Kieran Bew) agrees to join as long as his friend Emily (Lyndsey Marshal) plays the bass. Giles Borg's little independent feature debut has a certain charm, but ultimately it is rather unmemorable and adds nothing new to the genre, despite a strong leading performance from Bonar. GS

▶ Ian Bonar, Lyndsey Marshal, Kieran Bew, Mathew Baynton, Giles Maythan, Luke Rutherford, Matthew Sim.

▶ *Dir* and *Screenplay* Giles Borg, *Pro* Simon Kearney, *Ph* Mike Eley, *Pro Des* Richard Campling, *Ed* Kevin Austin, *M* Remy Felix Vas, Nick Burton etc, *Cos* Alice Wolfbauer.

Carson Films/Lypsync Productions-Soda Pictures. 76 mins. UK. 2008. Rel: 5 Mar 2010. Cert. 15.

Ong Bak: The Beginning ★★★★

Thai action legend Tony Jaa returns for the second *Ong Bak* instalment which, unlike the first, he also wrote and directed. Far from the vanity project one might expect, this is just as good as the first one. Less a sequel than a reboot, it takes place around 600 years before the first film. Gripping stuff with amazing action set-pieces: among other things, the best crocodile pit ever seen in the movies. (Original title: *Ong Bak 2*) JC

▶ Tony Jaa, Sorapong Chattlee, Sarunyu Wong Krachang, Nirut Sirichinya.
▶ *Dir* Tony Jaa and Panni Rittikrai, *Pro* and *Screenplay* Rittikrai, *Ph* Natawut Kittikhun, *Pro Des* Suprasit Putakarm, *Ed* Murat Seelacharoen and Saravut Nakachul, *M* Terdsak Janpan, *Cos* Chatchav Chaiyon.

Sahamongkol Film International/Iyara Films-Revolver Entertainment. 98 mins. Thailand. 2008. Rel: 16 Oct 2009. Cert. 15.

Only When I Dance ★★★★

This attractive and engaging documentary is about two aspiring ballet dancers. The fact that they come from Rio de Janeiro is highly significant because their art offers both of these teenagers, Irlan and Isabela, a chance to escape from poverty and a criminal milieu. Film-maker Beadie Finzi, aided by her editors, uses locations

atmospherically and creates a fluid drama
without losing a sense of authenticity. MS

❧ With Santos Da Silva, Isabela Coracy Alves, Mariza
Estrella, Irlan Santos Da Silva.
❧ *Dir* Beadie Finzi, *Pro* Giorgia Lo Savio and Nikki
Parrott, *Based on an idea by* Lo Savio and Christina
Daniels, *Ph* Finzi and others, *Ed* Alan Levy and Felipe
Lacerda, *M* Stephen Hilton.

**Channel 4/ARTE France/NPS/Tigerlily Films etc-Revolver
Entertainment.**
**81 mins. UK/France/Netherlands. 2008. Rel: 4 Dec 2009.
Cert. PG.**

An Ordinary Execution ★★★★

The suffering of the Russian people under Stalin
is not a new theme but here we have a very
individual approach to it. We see how a couple's
lives were almost destroyed. This occurred when
Stalin (André Dussollier) secretly took on as
his personal consultant a married doctor noted
for her healing powers (Marina Hinds) while
ordering her to say nothing about it, not even
to her husband. It's admirably acted (albeit with
French-speaking players as Russians) and a telling
small film, even if one is left pondering whether
or not it is all fiction. MS

❧ André Dussollier, Marina Hinds, Édouard Baer,
Denis Podalydès, Tom Novembre.
❧ *Dir* Marc Dugain, *Pro* Jean-Louis Livi, *Screenplay*
Dugain, from his novel *Une Exécution ordinaire*,
Ph Yves Angelo, *Art Dir* Yves Fournier, *Ed* Fabrice
Rouaud, *Cos* Jackie Budin.

**F Comme Film/Studio Canal/France 3 Cinéma/Canal +
etc-Verve Pictures.**
105 mins. France. 2009. Rel: 26 Nov 2010. Cert. 12A.

Orphan ★★★★

A couple bereaved of a child decide to adopt a
Russian orphan to rebuild their family. However,
little Esther is not what she seems and a body
count starts to build in her wake. This horror
thriller is cleverly constructed around an
unguessable twist of a premise, not revealed until
well into the final reel. JC

❧ Vera Farmiga, Peter Sarsgaard, Isabelle Fuhrman,
C C H Pounder, Jimmy Bennett.
❧ *Dir* Jaume Collet-Serra, *Pro* Leonardo Di Caprio,
Susan Downey, Jennifer Davisson, Joel Silver
Screenplay David Johnson, from a story by Alex
Mace, *Ph* Jeff Cutter, *Pro Des* Tom Meyer, *Ed* Tim
Alverson, *M* John Ottman, *Cos* Antoinette Messam.

**Warner Bros Pictures/Dark Castle Entertainment/Appian
Way/Studio Babelsberg Motion Pictures/Studio Canal
etc-Optimum Releasing.**
**123 mins. USA/Canada/Germany/France. 2009.
Rel: 7 Aug 2009. Cert. 15.**

OSS 117: Lost in Rio ★★★

Another in the French spy spoof series mocking
everything from Bond to 'B' movies, this is as
hit and miss as its predecessor, *Cairo Nest of
Spies*. It's hardly subtle and sometimes silly but
it incorporates lots of jokes to engage film buffs,
Hitchcock being a particular point of reference
here. (Original title: *OSS 117 Rio ne répond plus*) MS

❧ Jean Dujardin, Louise Monot, Rüdiger Vogler,
Alex Lutz, Reem Kherici, Ken Samuels.
❧ *Dir* Michel Hazanavicius, *Pro* Éric Altmayer and
Nicolas Altmayer, *Screenplay* Jean-François Halin and
Hazanavicius, based on the *OSS 117* novels by Jean

Bruce, *Ph* Guillaume Schiffman, *Art Dir* Maamar Ech-Cheikh, *Ed* Reynald Bertrand, *M* Ludovic Bource, *Cos* Charlotte David.

Mandarin Cinéma/Gaumont/M6 Films etc-ICA Films. 101 mins. France. 2009. Rel: 15 Jan 2010. Cert. 15.

The Other Guys ★★★

Will Ferrell and Mark Wahlberg play hopelessly mismatched loser cops who seize a slim chance of glory and pursue it with all guns blazing in this flawed but sporadically hilarious movie. Funny though Ferrell is as a straight-faced, by-the-book wallflower-type, it's Wahlberg's endless annoyance and frustration with his partner that really steal the show. The most relevant nugget of info on this one is that it was directed by Adam McKay, best known previously for most of Ferrell's funniest movies, namely *Anchorman, Talladega Nights* and *Step Brothers*. Though this doesn't reach their comedic heights, and falls apart during the final act, it remains an enjoyable time-waster. MJ

▶ Will Ferrell, Mark Wahlberg, Samuel L Jackson, Eva Mendes, Damon Wayans Jr, Michael Keaton, Steve Coogan, Dwayne Johnson, Derek Jeter, Brooke Shields.
▶ *Dir* Adam McKay, *Pro* Jimmy Miller and Patrick Crowley, *Screenplay* McKay and Chris Henchy, *Ph* Oliver Wood, *Pro Des* Clayton Hartley, *Ed* Brent White, *M* Jon Brion, *Cos* Carol Ramsey.

Columbia Pictures/Gary Sanchez Productions/Mosaic/ Wintergreen Productions-Columbia Pictures. 107 mins. USA. 2010. Rel: 17 Sep 2010. Cert. 12A.

Our Beloved Month of August ★★★

Miguel Gomes likes to play with narrative. Here he turns the concept of the film-within-a-film on its head. The first half of his docudrama-cum-mockumentary chronicles the cultural pastimes of his native Portugal while he – Gomes, playing himself – auditions natives to play variations on themselves. Then, halfway through, the film slips into the story that Gomes has been trying to tell all along. Or maybe not. It's an intriguing conceit, with some striking imagery, and is a rewarding one if you're willing to glide along with the director's vision. (Original title: *Aquele Querido Mês de Agosto*) CB

▶ Sónia Bandeira, Fábio Oliveira, Joaquin Carvalho, Manuel Soares.
▶ *Dir* Miguel Gomes, *Pro* Sandro Aguilar, Luis Urbano and Thomas Ordonneau, *Screenplay* Gomes, Mariana Ricardo and Telmo Churro, *Ph* Rui Poças, *Pro Des* Bruno Duarte, *Ed* Gomes and Churro, *Music Mixer* António Lopes, *Cos* Bruno Duarte.

Shellac Films/O Som e a Fúria-Ciné Lumière 147 mins. Portugal/France. 2008. Rel: 29 Jan 2010. Cert. 12A.

Out of the Ashes ★★★★

A documentary about the Afghan cricket team may not sound the most exciting prospect but Lucy Martens, Leslie Knott and Timothy Albone's admirable film defies all expectations. The team is followed from their humble beginnings determined to succeed against all odds and qualify for the World Cup. Their first trip abroad takes them to Jersey, which starts their meteoric rise into the international arena. It is a captivating and joyous journey to success. GS

▶ *Dir* Tim Albone, Leslie Knott and Lucy Martens, *Pro* Knott and Rachel Wexler, *Ph* Albone and Martens, *Ed* Gregor Lyon, *M* Andrew Philips.

Bungalow Town Productions/Shabash Productions-British Broadcasting Corporation. 86 mins. UK. 2010. Rel: 29 Oct 2010. No Cert.

Outcast ★★★★

Another British horror film set on a council estate, this one scores points for transferring a Sídhe witch and her teenage son to a convincingly bleak Edinburgh backwater, where they're tracked down by a psychotic Irish avenger who might be the boy's father. The storyline mistakes blatant obfuscation for tantalising ambiguity, but the details of Celtic magic are intriguing and the estate's marauding monster

It's all an allusion: Jean Dujardin in Michel Hazanavicius's *OSS 117: Lost in Rio.*

Shower scene: James Nesbitt stalks his lupine prey in the impressive *Outcast.*

is a suitably grotesque manifestation of the son's sexual panic. The whole thing is carried, however, by Kate Dickie and James Nesbitt, who qualify as genuinely awesome antagonists despite being kept apart until the final reel. JR

▶ Ciarán McMenamin, James Nesbitt, Kate Dickie, Niall Bruton, Clare Catterson.
▶ *Dir* Colm McCarthy, *Pro* Brendan McCarthy, John McDonnell and Eddie Dick, *Screenplay* Colm McCarthy and Tom K McCarthy, *Ph* Darran Tiernan, *Pro Des* Tom Sayer, *Ed* Helen Chapman, *M* Giles Packham, *Cos* Rhona Russell.
Fantastic Films/Head Gear Films/Makar Productions-Vertigo Films.
98 mins. UK/Ireland. 2010. Rel: 10 Dec 2010. Cert. 18.

Over Your Cities Grass Will Grow ★★★

There's real visual distinction in this documentary about the German artist Anselm Kiefer. Those familiar with his work may be fascinated by Sophie Fiennes' film with its adroit use of music. But those like myself who lack knowledge of Kiefer will find the film frustrating. The interview footage with the artist is singularly unrevealing about his work, including the on-site structures that he creates. MS

▶ With Anselm Kiefer.
▶ *Dir* Sophie Fiennes, *Pro* Fiennes, Kees Kasander and Emilie Blézat, *Ph* Remko Schnorr etc, *Ed* Ethel Shepherd.
Amoeba Film/Kasander/Sciapode/ARTE France etc-Artificial Eye.

105 mins UK/France/The Netherlands. 2010. Rel: 15 Oct 2010. Cert. U.

Paa ★★★★

13-year-old Auro (Bollywood star Amitabh Bachchan) suffers from progeria, a rare disorder that causes accelerated ageing. His protected life with his single mother Vidya (Vidya Balan) changes when politician Amol (Abhishek Bachchan) visits Auro's school. But, unbeknown to both of them, Amol is Auro's real father. This touching story about a father/son relationship is interestingly played by a real father and son, but here the roles are reversed and the son is played by the father. This stylish film boasts superb production values and equally strong performances. GS

▶ Amitabh Bachchan, Abhishek Bachchan, Vidya Balan, Paresh Rawal, Arundathi Nag.
▶ *Dir* and *Screenplay* R Balki and Ricky Sandhu, *Pro* Rajesh Sawhney, *Ph* P C Sreeram, *Ed M* Anil Haidu, *M* Ilayaraja.
Amitabh Bachchan Corporation/Mad Entertainment-Reliance Big Pictures.
133 mins. India. 2009. Rel: 4 Dec 2009. Cert. 12A.

Pandorum ★★½

2174; outer space. Pandorum is a dysfunction that affects anybody isolated in space for exceptional lengths of time, leading to nosebleeds, hallucinations and the shakes. When both Lt Payton (Dennis Quaid) and Corporal Bower (Ben

Foster) awake from an enforced hyper-sleep, they realise that they have been out for the count for eight years. Director Christian Alvart certainly knows how to lay on the claustrophobia and crank up the suspense. However, *Pandorum* suffers from a certain familiarity – aliens in space, anyone? – and the editing is so frenzied that it's hard to grasp what's going on. JC-W

➤ Dennis Quaid, Ben Foster, Cam Gigandet, Antje Traue, Cung Le.
➤ *Dir* Christian Alvart, *Pro* Paul W S Anderson, Jeremy Bolt, Martin Moszkowicz, *Screenplay* Travis Malloy, from a story by Malloy and Alvart, *Ph* Wedigo von Schultzendorff, *Pro Des* Richard Bridgland, *Ed* Philipp Stahl and Yvonne Valdez, *M* Michi Britsch, *Cos* Ivana Milos.

Constantin Film Produktion/Impact Pictures-Icon Film Distribution.
108 mins. USA/Germany. 2009. Rel: 2 Oct 2009. Cert. 15.

Paper Heart ★★

The multi-talented comic Charlyne Yi is an engaging, offbeat presence. However, her personality can only take her screenwriting debut so far. This mockumentary about love is a slender novelty that outstays its welcome by a good hour. 'Chuck' (as her on-screen director calls her) travels across the US looking for love, interviewing happy old couples, homosexuals and children about the meaning of the elusive emotion. Chuck doesn't believe in love but we know she does really, while her blossoming romance with the actor Michael Cera (playing himself) is at first sweet and then just nauseating. JC-W

➤ Charlyne Yi, Michael Cera, Jae M Johnson, Gill Summers, Martin Starr, Seth Rogen.
➤ *Dir* Nicholas Jasenovec, *Pro* Sandra Murillo and Elise Salomon, *Screenplay* Jasenovec and Yi, *Ph* Jay Hunter, *Ed* Ryan Brown, *M* Cera and Yi.

Paper Heart Productions/Anchor Bay Entertainment-Overture Films.
88 mins. USA. 2009. Rel: 6 Nov 2009. Cert. PG.

Paranormal Activity ★★½

When a spectral presence follows Katie to her new home, her boyfriend decides to set up a video camera in the bedroom. Working on the premise that in terms of horror less is more, first-time director Oren Peli has scared up a neat little frightener. Grossing over $142m worldwide on a budget of $15,000, the film is one of the most profitable of all time, helped by the best buzz on the internet since *The Blair Witch Project*. However, expectations somewhat blighted the film's impact and too often it comes off more dull than truly unnerving. JC-W

➤ Katie Featherstone, Micah Sleat, Mark Fredrichs, Amber Armstrong, Ashley Palmer.
➤ *Dir, Screenplay, Ph, Ed* Oren Peli, *Pro* Peli and Jason Blum.

Blumhouse Productions-Icon Film Distribution.
86 mins. USA. 2007. Rel: 25 Nov 2009. Cert. 15.

Paranormal Activity 2 ★★★★

This atmospheric sequel to last year's surprise horror hit boasts more scary set-pieces than the original. When a family moves to a new home, they set up security cameras around the house following a break-in when, mysteriously, nothing was taken. Meanwhile, the baby boy's Mexican nanny suspects that something spooky is going on but nobody believes her... The whole film is seen from the point of view of the security cameras and the result is genuinely creepy, with many hair-raising moments. GS

➤ Brian Boland, Molly Ephraim, Sprague Grayden, William Juan Pieto, Micah Sloat, Seth Ginsberg.

Morning sickness: A scene from Tod Williams' spookily successful *Paranormal Activity 2*.

War torn: Paul Gross stars in his own take on the historical bloodbath, in *Passchendaele*.

▶ *Dir* Tod Williams, *Pro* Jason Blum, *Screenplay* Michael R Perry, Tom Pabst and Christopher Landon, based on a story by Perry, *Ph* Michael Simmonds, *Pro Des* Jennifer Spence, *Ed* Gregory Plotkin, *Cos* Kristin M Burke.

Paramount Pictures/Blumhouse/Room 101 Inc.-Paramount Pictures.
91 mins. USA. 2010. Rel: 22 Oct 2010. Cert. 15.

Passchendaele ★★★

For those unfamiliar with Canada's role in the 1917 bloodbath, this is a revelatory history lesson. Produced, directed and written by and starring Paul Gross (who played Benton Fraser in TV's *Due South*), it's an earnest, somewhat old-fashioned war movie with dialogue that doesn't entirely convince. Even so, it's an involving piece of war memorabilia and the battle scenes are suitably harrowing. CB

▶ Paul Gross, Caroline Dhavernas, Joe Dinicol, Meredith Bailey, Jim Mezon, Michael Greyeyes.
▶ *Dir* and *Screenplay* Paul Gross, *Pro* Gross and Niv Fichman, *Ph* Gregory Middleton, *Pro Des* Carol Spier, *Ed* David Wharnsby, *M* Jan A P Kaczmarek, *Cos* Wendy Partridge.

Damberger Film 7 Cattle Company/Rhombus Media/ Whizzbang Films Inc-High Fliers Distribution.
114 mins. Canada. 2008. Rel: 4 Sep 2009. Cert. 15.

Peepli Live ★★★½

In a small Central Indian village a poor farmer called Natha is unable to repay a loan and is convinced by his brother to take advantage of a government programme which offers compensation to the families of any farmers who commit suicide. Anusha Rizvi creates a believable world in this likeable satire about the increase of suicides among the farming community. It is a strong central idea cleverly combined with humour and pathos. GS

▶ Nasee Ruddin Shah, Omkar Das Manikpuri, Raghuvir Yadav, Shalini Vatsa.
▶ *Dir* Anusha Rizvi and Mahmood Farooqui, *Pro* Kiran Rao and Aamir Khan, *Screenplay* Rizvi, *Ph* Shanker Raman, *Pro Des* Suman Roy Mahapatra, *Ed* Hemanti Sarkar, *M* Indian Ocean, *Cos* Maxima Basu.

Aamir Khan Productions-Artificial Eye.
95 mins. India. 2010. Rel: 24 Sep 2010. Cert. 15.

Percy Jackson and the Lightning Thief ★★★

American high school teenager Percy (Logan Lerman) is shocked to learn that he is the son of Greek God Poseidon (Kevin McKidd). And then Zeus (Sean Bean) accuses Percy of stealing his lightning bolt... Chris Columbus' entertaining modern adventure is a clever but rather bland way of bringing Greek mythology to younger audiences. It is evident that the producers want the same success as *Harry Potter* but this lacks that series' sophistication. However, Uma Thurman and Pierce Brosnan have a ball: "I have a horse's ass," boasts Brosnan as Chiron the centaur. (Original title: *Percy Jackson and the Olympians: The Lightning Thief*). GS

▶ Logan Lerman, Brandon T Jackson, Alexandra Daddario, Kevin McKidd, Jake Abel, Sean Bean, Pierce Brosnan, Uma Thurman, Steve Coogan.
▶ *Dir* Chris Columbus, *Pro* Michael Barnathan, Marc Radcliffe, Guy Oseary, Mark Morgan, Karen Rosenfelt, *Screenplay* Craig Titley, based on the novel by Rick Riordan, *Ph* Stephen Goldblatt, *Pro Des* Howard Cummings, *Ed* Peter Honess, *M* Christophe Beck, *Cos* Renée April.

Fox 2000 Pictures/1492 Pictures/Imprint Entertainment/ Sunswept Entertainment/TCF Vancouver Productions- 20th Century Fox.
118 mins. Canada/USA. 20110. Rel: 12 Feb 2010. Cert. PG.

Perestroika ★★

Sarah Turner's experimental but overlong film is a love poem to her dear friend who died 20 years earlier. Turner takes her camera and revisits her friend's last journey on the Trans-Siberian train in order to investigate how ghostly images of the past invade the present. It is a mesmerising trip but it verges on the pretentious, and ultimately the experience of watching these endlessly repetitive images becomes an endurance test. GS

▶ *Dir, Pro, Screenplay, Ed* Sarah Turner, *Ph* Turner and Matthew Walter.

Institute of Contemporary Arts.
115 mins. USA/UK/Russia. 2009. Rel: 1 Sep 2010. No Cert.

A Perfect Getaway ★★½

There's a killer or two on the loose on a remote Hawaiian island in this twisty, turny thriller which would love to be described as Hitchcockian. While it doesn't quite reach those lofty heights, it's certainly not short of surprises or suspenseful moments. Co-starring Steve Zahn, Timothy Olyphant and Milla Jovovich, it's a tale of (mostly) beautiful people doing increasingly desperate things against a beautiful, tropical setting. And there's blood. Quite a bit of blood. The word is watchable. MJ

▶ Steve Zahn, Timothy Olyphant, Milla Jovovich, Kiele Sanchez, Marley Shelton, Chris Hemsworth.
▶ *Dir* and *Screenplay* David Twohey, *Pro* Robbie Brenner, Mark Canton, Tucker Tooley and Ryan Kavanaugh, *Ph* Mark Plummer, *Pro Des* Joseph C Nemec III, *Ed* Tracy Adams, *M* Boris Elkis, *Cos* Laura Goldsmith.

Rogue/Relativity Media/QED International/Davis Entertainment/Tooley Productions-Momentum Pictures.
98 mins. USA. 2009. Rel: 14 Aug 2009. Cert. 15.

Perrier's Bounty ★★★★★

This is the Irish equivalent of a road movie with Cillian Murphy's Michael on the run from the villain of the title (the superb Brendan Gleeson), to whom he owes some loot. Jim Broadbent as Murphy's dad is afraid to fall asleep in case he

never wakes up again. Along with Murphy's neighbour Brenda (Jodie Whittaker), the trio hightail it around Dublin trying to avoid Perrier's hit men. It's a spirited journey, both hilarious and tragic, and in just 88 minutes director Ian Fitzgibbon brings Mark O'Rowe's marvellously brutal screenplay to perfect violent fruition in this, the best thriller of its year. MHD

▶ Cillian Murphy, Jim Broadbent, Jodie Whittaker, Brendan Gleeson, Conleth Hill, Gabriel Byrne, Domhnall Gleeson.
▶ *Dir* Ian Fitzgibbon, *Pro* Elizabeth Karlsen, Alan Moloney and Stephen Woolley, *Screenplay* Mark O'Rowe, *Ph* Seamus Deasy, *Pro Des* Amanda McArthur, *Ed* Tony Cranstoun, *M* David Holmes, *Cos* Keith Madden.

Parallel Film Productions/Number 9 Films/Premiere Picture-Optimum Releasing.
88 mins. Ireland/UK. 2009. Rel: 26 Mar 2010. Cert. 15.

Petropolis Aerial Perspectives on the Alberta Tar Sands ★★★★

The notion that actions speak louder than words is confirmed here. Commissioned by Greenpeace, this extraordinary work finds director Peter Mettler minimising words as he uses stunning helicopter shots to show the devastation of the area in Northern Canada that has been transformed by man's quest for the oil in the sand. The novel approach and a sensibly short length (43 minutes) ensure that this film stands out from others with comparable aims. MS

▶ *Dir* and *Screenplay* Peter Mettler, *Pro* Sandy Hunter and Laura Severinac, *Ph* Ron Chapple, *Ed* Roland Schlimme, *M* Gabriel Scotti and Vincent Hänni.

Greenpeace Canada etc-Dogwoof Pictures.
43 mins. Canada/UK/USA. 2009. Rel: 14 May 2010. Cert. U.

Better late than vapour: A scene from Peter Mettler's Petropolis Aerial Perspectives on the Alberta Tar Sands.

Little jaws: Ving Rhames up to his knees in *Piranha*.

Philip Pullman's The Butterfly Tattoo ★★

It's not a good sign when a film's genesis turns out to be more interesting than what's left on screen. A Dutch production financed by selling shares to the public, this is actually a frightfully English romantic drama adapted from Philip Pullman's novel. As a love story – between two 17-year-old Oxford students – it works rather well. However, the flashbacks auguring something nasty in the woodshed upend the whole thing. CB

❯ Duncan Stuart, Jessica Blake, Aidan Macgrath, Christopher Dane, Dan Morgan.
❯ *Dir* and *Ed* Phil Hawkins, *Pro* Wesley Kloppenburg, Jolies Van Emburg and Rik Visser, *Screenplay* Stephen Potts, from the book by Philip Pullman, *Ph* Michael Costelloe, *Pro Des* Gareth Thomas , *M* Richard Bodgers, *Cos* Geri Spencer.

Dynamic Entertainment DEH-Cinema Epoch.
101 mins. Netherlands. 2009. Rel: 30 Oct 2009. Cert. 12A.

Pianomania ★★★½

An engaging film about a piano tuner? Well, yes, this fascinating documentary follows Vienna's master tuner Stefan Knüpfer as he prepares for major concerts and recordings. Knüpfer's immense patience and expertise enable remarkable concert pianists such as Lang Lang, Pierre-Laurent Aimard and Alfred Brendel to fulfil their vision and achieve perfection. It is a clever portrait of an unsung hero with illuminating footage of rehearsals and music recordings. GS

❯ Stefan Knüpfer, Lang Lang, Ian Bostridge, Julius Drake, Pierre-Laurent Aimard, Till Fellner, Alfred Brendel.
❯ *Dir* and *Pro* Robert Cibis and Lilian Franck, *Ph* Cibis and Jeremy Palacz, *Ed* Michèle Barbin, *M* Matthias Petsche.

Oval Filmemacher/Wild Art-More2 Screen.
93 mins. Austria/Germany. 2009. Rel: 30 Aug 2010. No Cert.

Pimp ★★

Writer-director Robert Cavanah casts himself as a Soho pimp called Woody in this guilty little pleasure, an iffy, stereotypical London drama seen through the lens of a pretend documentary film crew that's supposedly recording a chaotic week in his life. Like it or not, Danny Dyer's familiar act gets another workout as sinister club boss Stanley, who's giving Woody a hard time. There's a load of sex, violence and strong language, as you'd expect, but some laughs along the way too, as well as a busy if predictable plot and some good actors (Billy Boyd, Martin Compston) doing their things. DW

❯ Robert Cavanah, Danny Dyer, Billy Boyd, Gemma Chan, Martin Compston.
❯ *Dir* Robert Cavanah, *Pro* Paul de Vos, Matthew Stradling, Boyd Tolkien and Crispin Manson, *Screenplay* Cavanah and Jon Kirby, from a story by Kirby, *Ph* Steven Annis, *Pro Des* Simon Pickup, *Ed* Rob Redford, *M* Tom Hodge, *Cos* Georgina Napier.

Cinematic Productions/Coppola Productions/Jubilee Pictures/Triple S Films etc-Stealth Media Group and Revolver Entertainment.
91 mins. UK. 2010. Rel: 21 May 2010. Cert. 18.

Piranha 3D ★★★

With his focus on flesh – both unclothed and torn – director Alexandre Aja is like the Lucien Freud of celluloid. Appropriating Joe Dante's 1978 *Jaws* rip-off, Aja completes the circle by casting Richard Dreyfuss as the first victim of a multitude of hungry prehistoric piranha. *Piranha* is also the only mainstream Hollywood film of 2010 to show a penis being gobbled – by a fish. In short, this is pulp cinema with the pips left in. NB: The last remake appeared in 1995. JC-W

▶ Elisabeth Shue, Adam Scott, Jerry O'Connell, Ving Rhames, Christopher Lloyd, Richard Dreyfuss, Kelly Brook.
▶ *Dir* Alexandre Aja, *Pro* Aja, Gregory Levasseur, Marc Toberoff and Mark Canton, *Screenplay* Peter Goldfinger and Josh Stolberg, *Ph* John R Leonetti, *Pro Des* Clark Hunter, *Ed* Baxter, *M* Michael Wandmacher, *Cos* Sanja Milkovic Hays.

The Weinstein Company/Chako Film Company/Dimension Films/Aja-Levasseur Productions/IPW/Atmosphere Entertainment MM-Entertainment Film Distributors. 88 mins. USA. 2010. Rel: 20 Aug 2010. Cert. 18.

Planet 51 ★★½

An amusing tale of alien invasion with a simple but effective twist, this likeable family film follows the exploits of a clean-cut, all-American astronaut who lands on a 1950s-style planet with a green, antennaed population. So *he's* the alien and *they're* freaked out. Get it? It's not exactly rocket science, and ten minutes after it's done you'd be hard pressed to remember much about it, but as a sci-fi primer for younger viewers designed to introduce them to the genre, it works pretty well, and for grown-ups there's a stack of moderately diverting movie references and in-jokes. MJ

▶ Voices of Dwayne Johnson, Jessica Biel, Justin Long, Gary Oldman, Seann William Scott, John Cleese, Matthew Horne, James Corden.
▶ *Dir* Jorge Blanco, Javier Abad and Marcos Martinez, *Pro* Guy Collins and Ignacio Pérez Dolset, *Screenplay* Joe Stillman, *Pro Des* Julian Muñoz Romero, *Ed* Alex Rodriguez, *M* James Seymour Brett.

Ilion Animation/HandMade Films/Antenna 3 Films-Entertainment Film Distributors. 91 mins. Spain/UK/USA. 2009. Rel: 4 Dec 2009. Cert. U.

Please Give ★★★★½

Although set in New York, this film from Nicole Holofcener, her best to date, is closer to the work of Mike Leigh than that of Woody Allen. Comic but also touching, it lacks any big climax but its everyday study of two families gains from our growing sense that we really believe in these people. There's great work from Catherine Keener and Rebecca Hall in particular, but everybody's good. MS

▶ Catherine Keener, Rebecca Hall, Oliver Platt, Amanda Peet, Ann Guilbert, Lois Smith.
▶ *Dir* and *Screenplay* Nicole Holofcener, *Pro* Anthony Bregman, *Ph* Yaron Orbach, *Pro Des* Mark White with Kris Moran, *Ed* Robert Frazen, *M* Marcelo Zarvos, *Cos* Ane Crabtree.

Sony Pictures Classics/Likely Story-Sony Pictures Releasing. 90 mins. USA. 2009. Rel: 18 June 2010. Cert. 15.

Police, Adjective ★★½

Corneliu Porumboiu's second feature, once again set in Romania, refashions the police thriller to comment on serious issues – its very title would appear to refer to a police state. But, where *12.08 East of Bucharest* utilised comedy to comment tellingly on significant matters, this snail-paced second feature succeeds only in its climactic confrontation scene, which makes play with linguistics. Until then the lethargic pacing renders the film boring. Those who gave it awards obviously disagree. MS

▶ Dragos Bucur, Vlad Ivanov, Ion Stoica, Irina Saulescu, Radu Costin, Alexandru Sabadac.
▶ *Dir* and *Screenplay* Corneliu Porumboiu, *Ph* Marius Panduru, *Art Dir* Mihaela Poenaru, *Ed* Roxana Szel, *Cos* Giorgiana Bostan.

42 Km film/HBO Romania etc-Artificial Eye. 115 mins. Romania. 2009. Rel: 1 Oct 2010. Cert. 12A.

Sweet charity: Rebecca Hall in a world of give-and-take in Nicole Holofcener's *Please Give.*

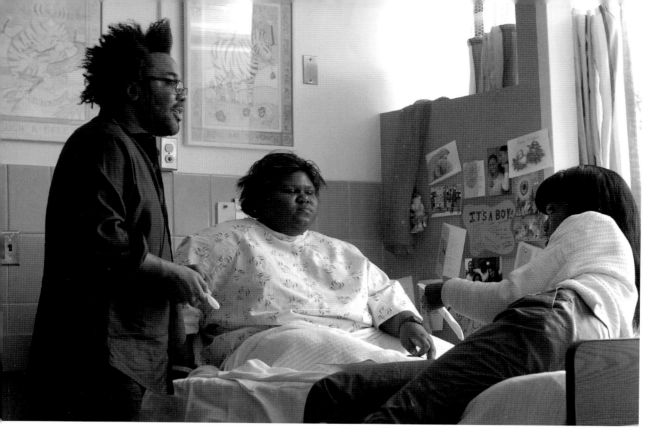

Pontypool ★★½

Charismatic shock-jock Grant Mazzy has been
demoted to the morning slot of a small-town
Ontario radio station and is determined to shake
things up a bit. However, nothing he can say
can equal the unsettling bulletins that talk of a
crazed mob taking the law into their own hands.
Dubbed a cross between *Talk Radio* and *The Fog*,
Pontypool knits together several genre favourites
and then gives the whole thing an unexpected
tug. The acting standard of the three principals
keeps the premise afloat for a while and the
claustrophobia mounts nicely. But all this would
have been better suited as a play. JC-W

▶ Stephen McHattie, Lisa Houle, Georgina Reilly,
Hrant Alianak, Tony Burgess.
▶ *Dir* Bruce McDonald, *Pro* Jeffrey Coghlan and
Ambrose Roche, *Screenplay* Tony Burgess,
Ph Miroslaw Baszak, *Pro Des* Lea Carlson, *Ed* Jeremiah
L Munce, *M* Claude Foisy, *Cos* Sarah Armstrong.

**Ponty Up Pictures/Shadow Shows-Kaleidoscope.
93 mins. Canada. 2008. Rel: 16 Oct 2009. Cert. 15.**

Ponyo ★★★★

Less quintessentially Japanese than *Spirited Away*,
this stylish animated work, hand-drawn and
imaginative, from Hayao Miyazaki draws loosely
on Hans Christian Andersen's *The Little Mermaid*.
In its depiction of a five-year-old boy's love for a
goldfish washed ashore, it evokes the universality
of childhood affection but then becomes more
of a fantasy adventure, linked to the goldfish
being the child of a once human sorcerer and a

creature of the sea. There's a subtitled version but
the more widely available dubbed presentation
is ably handled and it looks great. (Original title:
Gake no ue no Ponyo) MS

▶ With the voices in the dubbed version of Noah
Cyrus, Liam Neeson, Tina Fey, Matt Damon,
Cate Blanchett, Frankie Jonas, Lily Tomlin, Cloris
Leachman, Betty White.
▶ *Dir* and *Screenplay by* Hayao Miyazaki (English
language version written by Melissa Mathison), *M*
Joe Hisaishi, *Animation* Katsuya Kondo, *US production
dir* John Lasseter, Brad Lewis and Peter Sohn.

**Studio Ghibli/Nihon Telebi/Walt Disney Studios Home
Entertainment/Mitsubishi/Toho etc-Optimum Releasing.
103 mins. Japan/USA. 2008. Rel: 12 Feb 2010. Cert. U.**

Post Grad ★★½

Recent college graduate Ryden (Alexis Bledel) is
over-confident that a job in a top Los Angeles
publishing firm is hers. But when she fails to
get the job, or any other for that matter, she
is forced to move back in with her parents.
There are no surprises in Vicky Jenson's likeable
film, which benefits from Bledel's charming
performance. She is well supported by Michael
Keaton, Jane Lynch and Carol Burnett as her
eccentric family. GS

▶ Alexis Bledel, Zach Gilford, Michael Keaton, Carol
Burnett, Jane Lynch, Bobby Coleman.
▶ *Dir* Vicky Jenson, *Pro* Jeffrey Clifford, Ivan Reitman
and Joe Medjuck, *Screenplay* Kelly Fremon,
Ph Charles Minsky, *Pro Des* Mark Hutman, *Ed* Dana
Congdon, *M* Christophe Beck, *Cos* Alexandra Welker.

Fox Atomic/Cold Spring Pictures/The Montecito Picture Company-20th Century Fox.
88 mins. USA. 2009. Rel: 1 Jan 2010. Cert. 12A.

Precious ★★★★

As a film about Afro-Americans gaining from education, this movie is not far removed from 2007's Hilary Swank vehicle *Freedom Writers*. Like that film, it's an unsophisticated but sympathetic work. Here the centre is the titular figure, the terrifyingly put-upon obese black heroine incarnated by Gabourey Sidibe, with Oscar-winner Mo'Nique as her mother. On its own terms it successfully balances grim reality with elements of hope and fantasy. MS

▶ Gabourey Sidibe, Mo'Nique, Paula Patton, Mariah Carey, Lenny Kravitz.
▶ *Dir* Lee Daniels, *Pro* Daniels, Sarah Siegel-Magness and Gary Magness, *Screenplay* Geoffrey Fletcher, based on the book *Push* by Sapphire, *Ph* Andrew Dunn, *Pro Des* Roshelle Berliner, *Ed* Joe Klotz, *M* Mario Grigorov, *Cos* Marina Draghici.

Lionsgate/Oprah Winfrey/Tyler Perry/Lee Daniels Entertainment/Smokewood Entertainment Group-Icon Film Distribution.
110 mins. USA. 2008. Rel: 29 Jan 2010. Cert. 15.

Predators ★★★

The third in the series takes place in a remote jungle after a group of mercenaries have parachuted from the sky. They have nothing in common but their desire to survive against all odds the menace of an unseen enemy... Nimrod Antal keeps the action flowing and doesn't give you a second to question the script's flaws. Adrien Brody makes an impressive action hero as does Alice Braga, who proves that she can kick ass as well as any thug stranded in the jungle. GS

▶ Adrien Brody, Laurence Fishburne, Topher Grace, Alice Braga, Walton Goggins.
▶ *Dir* Nimrod Antal, *Pro* Robert Rodriguez, John Davis and Elizabeth Avellan, *Screenplay* Alex Litvak and Michael Finch, *Ph* Gyula Pados, *Pro Des* Caylah Eddleblute and Steve Joyner, *Ed* Dan Zimmerman, *M* John Debney, *Cos* Nina Proctor.

Twentieth Century Fox Film Corporation/Davis Entertainment/Troublemaker Studios-20th Century Fox.
107 mins. USA. 2010. Rel: 9 July 2010. Cert. 15.

Prince of Persia: The Sands of Time ★★½

Pumped-up scoundrel prince Jake Gyllenhaal, slightly miscast, and beautiful, spirited princess Gemma Arterton, not the greatest actress in the world, unite in a moderately exotic, not entirely horrible, but also utterly corny and commonplace adventure from the King of Homogenised

Entertainment, producer Jerry Bruckheimer. Based on the best-selling videogame series, which is hardly a phrase that inspires confidence, it sees Jake and Gem unite against a sneeringly evil Ben Kingsley, dastardly as ever as a power-mad rotter bent on bending time. Easily watchable, adequately entertaining, yet completely forgettable. MJ

▶ Jake Gyllenhaal, Gemma Arterton, Ben Kingsley, Alfred Molina, Richard Coyle, Ronald Pickup.
▶ *Dir* Mike Newell, *Pro* Jerry Bruckheimer, *Screenplay* Boaz Yakin, Doug Miro and Carlo Bernard, *Ph* John Seale, *Pro Des* Wolf Kroeger, *Ed* Martin Walsh, Michael Kahn and Mick Audsley, *M* Harry Gregson-Williams, *Cos* Penny Rose.

Walt Disney Pictures/Jerry Bruckheimer Films-Walt Disney Studios Motion Pictures.
116 mins. USA. 2010. Rel: 21 May 2010. Cert. 12A.

The Princess and the Frog ★★★★

Harking back to its golden era of the 1990s and maybe even further back to *Snow White*, *Bambi* and *Dumbo*, Disney's neat spin on the classic Frog Prince story is a delightfully old-fashioned

The time of his life: Jake Gyllenhaal lords it over Mike Newell's forgettable *Prince of Persia: The Sands of Time.*

'The adaptable enigma': Robin Wright with her much older husband Alan Arkin in Rebecca Miller's deeply moving *The Private Lives of Pippa Lee*.

cartoon, appealingly created in the traditional way, that is to say hand-drawn with no CGI. Anika Noni Rose is the sweet voice of Disney's first black princess, Tiana, and the New Orleans-set story follows what happens after she kisses the frog prince Naveen (Bruno Campos), who doesn't like being a tiny green thing. The nifty story-telling, good humour and old-style animation is slightly let down by Randy Newman's rather run-of-the-mill songs. DW

▶ Voices of Anika Noni Rose, Bruno Campos, John Goodman, Keith David, Jennifer Cody, Michael-Leon Wooley, Oprah Winfrey.
▶ *Dir* Ron Clements and John Musker, *Pro* Peter Del Vecho, *Screenplay* Clements, Musker and Rob Edwards etc, from a story by E D Baker, *Pro Des* James Aaron Finch, *Ed* Jeff Draheim, *M* Randy Newman.
Walt Disney Animation Studios/Walt Disney Pictures-Walt Disney Studios Motion Pictures. 97 mins. USA. 2009. Rel: 5 Feb 2010. Cert. U.

The Private Lives of Pippa Lee
★★★★

Here's a film that looks at life from a woman's perspective. Since this is an adaptation of her own novel by Rebecca Miller, that applies to the psychology of the characters, to the way they talk and to where the emphasis falls in this tale. It tells of a woman, Pippa Lee, married to an older man and rethinking her life in middle age. The title role is played by Robin Wright Penn in a career-best performance, and if the tale sometimes brings to mind the marriage of Miller's father, Arthur, to Marilyn Monroe that only adds to the interest. MS

▶ Robin Wright Penn, Alan Arkin, Maria Bello, Monica Bellucci, Blake Lively, Julianne Moore, Keanu Reeves, Winona Ryder.
▶ *Dir* and *Screenplay* Rebecca Miller, *Pro* Dede Gardner and Lemore Syvan, *Ph* Declan Quinn, *Pro Des* Michael Shaw, *Ed* Sabine Hoffman, *M* Michael Rohatyn, *Cos* Jennifer von Mayrhauser.
Winchester Capital Management/Plan B Entertainment/ Inspired Actions etc-Icon Film Distribution. 98 mins. USA. 2008. Rel: 10 July 2009. Cert. 15.

A Prophet ★★★★★

Jacques Audiard's truly great prison drama tells of Malik (Tamar Rahim), a French Arab in a jail where Muslims and Arabs live separately from the Corsicans. When Corsican leader Luciani (Niels Arestrup) gets Malik to kill an Arab, Malik becomes Luciani's sidekick, although remaining an outsider to both Arabs and Corsicans. On leave from the prison Malik begins trading in hashish, a move that leads to further violence. *A Prophet* is all too believable, with a documentary feel to it and a superb performance by Tamar Rahim as Malik, hell-bent on improving his lot, albeit through crime. (Original title: *Un prophète*) MHD

▶ Tamar Rahim, Niels Arestrup, Adel Bencherif, Hichem Yacoubi, Reda Kateb.
▶ *Dir* Jacques Audiard, *Pro* Lauranne Bourrachot, Martine Cassinelli and Marco Cherqui, *Screenplay* Audiard and Thomas Bidegain, from an original screenplay by Abdel Raouf Dafri and Nicolas Peufaillit, *Ph* Stéphane Fontaine, *Pro Des* Michel Barthélémy, *Ed* Juliette Welfling, *M* Alexandre Desplat, *Cos* Virginie Montel.

Why Not Productions/Chic Films/Page 114/France 2
Cinéma/Canal + etc-Optimum Releasing.
155 mins. France/Italy. 2009. Rel: 21 Jan 2010. Cert. 18.

The Proposal ★★★

When New York book editor Margaret (Sandra
Bullock) faces deportation back to Canada she
offers promotion to her poor assistant Andrew
(Ryan Reynolds) in exchange for a marriage of
convenience. The plot is fun and frothy and
the two protagonists bounce off each other
effectively, but don't expect any real immigration
issues to be explored here. It loses its momentum
half way through but the strong supporting cast,
which includes Betty White as Grandma Annie
and Mary Steenburgen as Andrew's mother,
make up for it. GS

▶ Sandra Bullock, Ryan Reynolds, Mary
Steenburgen, Craig T Nelson, Betty White.
▶ *Dir* Anne Fletcher, *Pro* David Hoberman and
Todd Lieberman, *Screenplay* Pete Chiarelli, *Ph* Oliver
Stapleton, *Pro Des* Nelson Coates, *Ed* Priscilla
Nedd-Friendly, *M* Aaron Zigman, *Cos* Catherine
Marie Thomas.

Touchstone Pictures/Kurtzman-Orci/Mandeville
Films-Buena Vista International.
108 mins. USA. 2009. Rel: 22 July 2009. Cert. 12A.

Psych 9 ★★

Roslyn (Sara Foster), a young woman with a
troubled past, begins a job as a collator of the
patients' files in a recently abandoned hospital.
It is a dangerous job as she only works at night
in a remote setting where a number of women
are being murdered not far away. The story
is not bad but Andrew Shortell's slow-paced
psychological thriller gives his audience plenty
of opportunities to put the pieces together in this
rather flawed script. GS

▶ Sara Foster, Cary Elwes, Michael Biehn, Gabriel
Mann, Colleen Camp, Susie Amy.
▶ *Dir* Andrew Shortell, *Pro* Shortell, Philip Waley and
Daniel S Frisch, *Screenplay* Lawrence Robinson, *Ph*
Shane Daly, *Pro Des* David Baxa, *Ed* Nick McCahearty,
M James Edward Barker, *Cos* Marielle Shortell.

Green Card Pictures/International Production
Company-Galaxy Pictures.
98 mins. USA/UK/Czech Republic. 2010. Rel: 7 May
2010. Cert. 18.

Public Enemies ★★★

Although it's superbly photographed by Dante
Spinotti, this fresh take on the life of John
Dillinger, that famous American gangster of the
1930s, is not Michael Mann's finest hour. Christian
Bale is rather wooden as Dillinger's nemesis while
Dillinger himself is hardly a rewarding role for

Johnny Depp; Marion Cotillard's girlfriend is the
performance that stands out. Sharper and more
interesting in its characterisations, Ridley Scott
reworked the terrain to much greater effect in his
2007 film *American Gangster*. MS

▶ Johnny Depp, Christian Bale, Marion Cotillard,
Billy Crudup, Stephen Dorff.
▶ *Dir* Michael Mann, *Pro* Kevin Misher and
Mann, *Screenplay* Ronan Bennett, Mann and Ann
Biderman, based on Bryan Burrough's book,
Ph Dante Spinotti, *Pro Des* Nathan Crowley,
Ed Paul Rubell and Jeffrey Ford, *M* Elliot Goldenthal,
Cos Colleen Atwood.

Universal Pictures/Relativity Media/Forward Pass/
Misher Films etc-Universal Pictures.
140 mins. USA/Japan. 2009. Rel: 1 July 2009. Cert. 15.

Rage ★★★½

Much more interesting than some dismissive
reviews from Berlin suggested, Sally Potter's *Rage*
bypassed cinemas for immediate availability
on the internet, on mobile phones and on
DVD. This reflects its own emphasis on modern
technology, since it tells its story indirectly
through taped interviews at a New York fashion
show where deaths occur off screen. As in
Antonioni's classic *L'Avventura*, the mystery

Prophet margin:
Tahar Rahim in
Jacques Audiard's
accomplished
A Prophet, voted
best film of the year
by the London Film
Critics' Circle.

Naughty forty: Catherine Zeta-Jones plays the field in spite of nudging middle age in Bart Freundlich's sweet and formulaic *The Rebound*.

element is not the point. Its comments on the fashion world are too predictable, but it's well acted, it looks great and its observations on today's obsession with talentless celebrities are potent. MS

▶ Simon Abkarian, Lily Cole, Judi Dench, Jude Law, Bob Balaban, Riz Ahmed, Eddie Izzard, Steve Buscemi, John Leguizamo, Dianne Wiest, David Oyelowo, Patrick J Adams.
▶ *Dir* and *Screenplay* Sally Potter, *Pro* Christopher Sheppard and Andrew Fierberg, *Ph* Steven Fierberg and Mia Barker, *Ed* Daniel Goddard, *M* Potter and Fred Frith, *Cos* Marina Draghici and Es Devlin.
UK Film Council/Adventure Pictures etc-Adventure Pictures. 98 mins. UK/USA. 2009. Rel: 24 Sep 2009. Cert. 15.

Ramchand Pakistani ★★★½

Fact-based but somewhat fictionalised, this is the story of young Ramchand, first encountered at the age of eight. He lives with his parents in a village on the border between Pakistan and India and imprisonment follows when the child accidentally crosses over into India. In trying to bring him back, father suffers the same fate. Colourful costumes contrast with the bleak setting as the prisoners accused of spying hope for release. It's worth seeing, but it's not the first Indian film to suffer from the realisation that the late Satyajit Ray would have made it more moving. MS

▶ Shaood Alvi, Adarsh Ayaz, Atif Badar, Karim Bux Baloch, Nandita Das.
▶ *Dir* Mahreen Jabbar, *Pro* Javed Jabbar and Mariam Mukaty, *Screenplay* Mohammad Ahmad and Javed Jabbar, *Ph* Sofian Khan, *Ed* Mahreen Jabbar and Aseem Sinha, *M* Debajyoti Michra.
Project One/J J Mena/Namak Films-ICA
103 mins. Pakistan. 2008. Rel: 17 July 2009. No Cert.

Ramona and Beezus ★★

Mischievous young Ramona (Joey King) and her big sister Beezus (Selena Gomez) try hard to save their home after their father (John Corbett) loses his job in this adaptation of Beverly Cleary's book. The central idea is fine but the actors work too hard in their attempt to make this work under Elizabeth Allen's laboured direction, which unnecessarily prolongs the action of this over-extended comedy. GS

▶ Joey King, Selena Gomez, John Corbett, Bridget Moynahan, Josh Duhamel.
▶ *Dir* Elizabeth Allen, *Pro* Denise Di Novi and Alison Greenspan, *Screenplay* Laurie Craig and Nick Pustay, based on the novels by Beverly Cleary, *Ph* John Bailey, *Pro Des* Brent Thomas, *Ed* Jane Moran, *M* Mark Mothersbaugh, *Cos* Patricia Hargreaves.
Fox 2000 Pictures/Walden Media/DiNovi Pictures-20th Century Fox.
103 mins. USA. 2010. Rel: 22 Oct 2010. Cert. U.

Rapt ★★★★

This little-seen but highly adept thriller from Lucas Belvaux deals with the kidnapping of a French industrialist (Yvan Attal) and plays tellingly on the conflict between our dislike of what he stands for and our concern for him as a victim. The film also comments on the media and on their relish for keeping past bad behaviour in the headlines. It's far superior to the much better-known *The Secret in their Eyes* [qv]. MS

▶ Yvan Attal, Anne Consigny, André Marcon, Françoise Fabian, Alex Descas.
▶ *Dir* and *Screenplay* Lucas Belvaux, *Pro* Patrick Sobelman, Diana Elbaum and Sébastien Delloye, *Ph* Pierre Milon, *Art Dir* Frédéric Belvaux, *Ed* Danielle Anezin, *M* Riccardo Del Fra, *Cos* Nathalie Raoul.

AGAT Films & Cie/Entre Chien & Loup/France 3 Cinéma etc-Artificial Eye.
126 mins.France/Belgium. 2009. Rel: 16 July 2010. Cert. 15.

Rare Exports: A Christmas Tale ★★★½

This weirdly fresh and original film from Finland tells the story of a young boy in the depths of Lapland's Korvanturi Mountains as he uncovers the truth about Santa Claus one week before Christmas. Jalmari Helander's impressive feature debut is very atmospheric and enjoyable in an eccentric sort of way. It is also very violent and it is clearly aimed at adults, not children. (Original title: *Rare Exports*) GS

▶ Per Christian Ellefsen, Peeter Jakobi, Onni Tommila, Jorma Tommila, Tommi Korpela.
▶ *Dir* and *Pro Des* Jalmari Helander, *Pro* Agnès B, Anna Björk, Knut Skoglund etc, *Screenplay* Helander, Sami Parkkinen and Petri Jokiranta, from an original idea by Jalmari and Juuso Helander, *Ph* Mika Orasmaa, *Ed* Kimo Taavila, *M* Juri Seppa and Miska Seppa, *Cos* Saija Siekkinen.

Agnès B Productions/Cinet/Davaj Film/FilmCamp/Filmpool Nord/Love Streams Productions-Icon Film Distribution.
84 mins. Finland/Norway/France/Sweden. 2010. Rel: 3 Dec 2010. Cert. 15.

The Rebound ★★½

When a housewife and mother catches her husband cheating (on webcam!), she moves to New York City to start a new life… Considering how generic and polished *The Rebound* is, it's hard to believe now that Bart Freundlich began life in the indie sector. Yet beneath the conventions of this high-concept rom-com runs a very sweet thread that holds the whole thing together. Bolstered by pleasing performances from Justin Bartha and Catherine Zeta-Jones, the film develops nicely once it has kicked away the formulaic rungs leading to its central premise. The kids are a pain, but the conclusion is refreshingly non-committal. JC-W

▶ Catherine Zeta-Jones, Justin Bartha, Gabrielle Aimee, Megan Byrne, Eliza Callahan, Art Garfunkel.
▶ *Dir* and *Screenplay* Bart Freundlich, *Pro* Freundlich, Mark Gill, Tim Perell and Robert Katz, *Ph* Jonathan Freeman, *Pro Des* Ford Wheeler, *Ed* Christopher Tellefsen, *M* Clint Mansell, *Cos* Melissa Toth.

Blue Sky Films/The Film Department/Process/A & F Productions-Paramount Pictures.
95 mins. USA. 2009. Rel: 23 July 2010. Cert. 15.

[Rec]² ★½

An apartment block in Barcelona is sealed off and a SWAT team is sent in to find out what *really* happened… Viral infection mutates into demonic possession in a desperate attempt to inject fresh blood into the video diary genre. But

it's an oeuvre based on a gimmick that didn't even make sense in the first place. It should have stopped way before *Cloverfield*, *Diary of the Dead* and the original *[Rec]*. JC-W

▶ Jonathan Mellor, Oscar Zafra, Ariel Casas, Alejandro Casaseca
▶ *Dir* Jaume Balagueró and Paco Plaza, *Pro* Julio Fernández, *Scr* Balagueró, Plaza and Manu Diez, *Ph* Pablo Rosso, *Art Dir* Gemma Fauria, *Ed* David Galliart, *Cos* Gloria Viguer Zabala.

Castelao Producciones/Filmax etc-Magnet Releasing.
85 mins. Spain. 2009. Rel: 28 May 2010. Cert: 18.

RED ★★★½

Feeling bored and lonely in his retirement, former black-ops CIA agent Frank Moses (Bruce Willis) strikes up a long-distance relationship with a telephone operator (Mary-Louise Parker) at his pension office. But when he visits her in Kansas City, she becomes the unwitting target of a ruthless team of assassins. RED stands for 'Retired, Extremely Dangerous' and the retirees here are played by some top-drawer actors who

Retired and emotional: John Malkovich in Robert Schwentke's deliciously witty *RED*.

know how to hone a one-liner to a sharper point than John Rambo's survival knife. *The Expendables* with wit (and minus the gratuitous violence), this is a guilty pleasure. JC-W

▶ Bruce Willis, Helen Mirren, Mary-Louise Parker, Karl Urban, Richard Dreyfuss, Morgan Freeman, Rebecca Pidgeon, Ernest Borgnine, Brian Cox, John Malkovich.
▶ *Dir* Robert Schwentke, *Pro* Lorenzo di Bonaventura, *Screenplay* Jon Hoeber and Erich Hoeber, from the graphic novel by Warren Ellis and Cully Hamner, *Ph* Florian Ballhaus, *Pro Des* Alec Hammond, *Ed* Thom Noble, *M* Christophe Beck, *Cos* Susan Lyall.

Di Bonaventura Pictures/DC Entertainment/Summit Entertainment-E1 Entertainment.
111 mins. USA. 2010. Rel: 22 Oct 2010. Cert 12A.

Red & White ★★★

The novelty here is that this is a film from Indonesia. It's a war movie set in 1947 (the title refers to the colours of the Indonesian flag) and is technically able. However, the screenplay is weak. The events depicted may be real but the characters are clichéd and the tone is reminiscent of patriotic Hollywood product that supported the war effort in the 1940s. (Original title: *Merah putih*) MS

▶ Lukman Sardi, Donny Alamsyah, Darius Sinathrya, T. Rifnu Wikana, Astri Nurdin.
▶ *Dir* Yadi Sugandi, *Pro* Conor Allyn and Gary Hayes, *Screenplay* Conor and Rob Allyn, *Ph* Padri Nadeak, *Pro Des* Iri Supit, *Ed* Sastha Sunu, *M* Thoersi Argeswara.

PT Media Desa/Margate House-Kaleidoscope Home Entertainment.
113 mins. Australia/Indonesia. 2009. Rel: 5 Nov 2010. Cert. 15.

The Red Baron ★★★½

This German movie follows Roger Corman's 1971 film in telling the story of the celebrated First World War pilot Manfred von Richthofen, whose nickname provides the title. It's a decent, unexceptional film bringing the 1914-18 conflict to a young audience without glamorising it, even though von Richthofen (the well-cast Matthias Schweighöfer) is its hero. The shortened release print shown here may or may not be helpful but the dubbing of the German actors is unfortunate. (Original title: *Der rote Baron*) MS

▶ Matthias Schweighöfer, Lena Headey, Til Schweiger, Volker Bruch, Joseph Fiennes.
▶ *Dir* and *Screenplay* Nikolai Muellerschoen, *Pro* Don Maag, Thomas Reisser and Muellerschoen, *Ph* Klaus Merkel, *Pro Des* Yvonne von Wallenberg, *Ed* Olivia Retzer, Emmelie Mansee and Adam P Scott, *M* Dirk Reichardt and Stefan Hansen, *Cos* Gudrun Schretzmeier.

Niama-Film-Showbox Media Group.
101 mins. Germany. 2008. Rel: 4 Sep 2009. Cert. 12A.

Red Mist ★★★

A troubled hospital janitor (Andrew Lee Potts) falls into a coma after being bullied and forced into an orgy of drugs by a group of medical students, after which the students one by one meet gruesome deaths... The story is not dissimilar to *Tormented* but the acting and set-pieces are superior. As in his earlier *Shrooms*, Paddy Breathnach demonstrates how capable he is in building the right atmosphere, despite a familiar premise and predictable ending. (Original title: *Freakdog*) GS

Flying high: Throttle jockey Til Schweiger in Nikolai Muellerschoen's unexceptional *The Red Baron*.

▶ Arielle Kebbel, Sarah Carter, Stephen Dillane, Andrew Lee Potts, Michael Jibson.
▶ *Dir* Paddy Breathnach, *Pro* Simon Bosanquet, Mark Huffam and Michael Kelly, *Screenplay* Spence Wright, *Ph* Ruari OBrien, *Pro Des* David Craig, *Ed* Dermot Diskin, *M* Stephen Warbeck, *Cos* Hazel Webb-Crozier.

Geronimo Films/Generator Entertainment/Framestore CFC/Northern Ireland Screen-Revolver Entertainment. 82 mins. UK. 2008. Rel: 3 July 2009. Cert. 18.

Le Refuge ★★★★

François Ozon is on his best form here, although his story comes to an abrupt end which does not fully satisfy. Nevertheless, it's effective in portraying the bond between a basically gay man (Louis-Ronan Choisy) and the pregnant woman (the very able Isabelle Carré, herself pregnant during the filming) whom he supports after her lover has died of a drug overdose. Imperfect, perhaps, but impressive all the same. MS

▶ Isabelle Carré, Louis-Ronan Choisy, Melvil Poupaud, Pierre Louis-Calixte.
▶ *Dir* François Ozon, *Pro* Claudie Ossard and Chris Bolzli, *Screenplay* Ozon and Mathieu Hippeau, *Ph* Mathias Raaflaub, *Art Dir* Katia Wyszkop, *Ed* Muriel Breton, *M* Louis-Ronan Choisy, *Cos* Pascaline Chavanne.

Eurowide Film Production/FOZ/France 2 Cinéma/Sofica Coficup/Backup Films etc-Artificial Eye. 88 mins.France/Italy. 2009. Rel: 13 Aug 2010. Cert. 15.

Release ★★½

Ironically, *Release* got anything but in Britain. Still, for those who managed to catch this self-consciously poetic drama, they will have been rewarded by an unusual love story and a compelling performance from Daniel Brocklebank. The latter plays a priest who happens to be behind bars and is carrying on a homosexual affair with his guard. A little on the sentimental side and, at times, rather perplexing, the film boasts an eloquence and originality that sets it apart. CB

▶ Daniel Brocklebank, Garry Summers, Bernie Hodges, Wayne Virgo, Simon Pearce.
▶ *Dir* and *Pro Des* Darren Flaxstone and Christian Martin, *Pro* and *Cos* Martin, *Screenplay* Flaxstone and Martin, *Ph* Simon Pearce, *Ed* Flaxstone, *M* Thom Petty.

F A Q S/Parasol Pictures Releasing. 87 mins. UK. 2010. Rel: 17 Sep 2010. No Cert.

Remember Me ★★★★½

The surprise is not that Robert Pattinson can act but that he can hold his own against such an outstanding cast. A tapestry of well etched characters emerges from the fabric of pre-9/11 New York in which a young man is looking for a way to heal some major wounds. A tale of flawed family members trying to connect makes for a deeply moving, credible and smouldering drama,

The undead again: Milla Jovovich returns in Paul W S Anderson's mindless *Resident Evil: Afterlife 3D.*

magnificent fight sequence in slow mo' with a buffed-up Jude Law and a hacksaw. JC-W

▶ Jude Law, Forest Whitaker, Alice Braga, Chandler Canterbury, Liev Schreiber, Carice Van Houten.
▶ *Dir* Miguel Sapochnik, *Pro* Scott Stuber, *Screenplay* Eric Garcia and Garrett Lerner, from the novel *The Repossession Mambo* by Garcia, *Ph* Enrique Chediak, *Pro Des* David Sandefur, *Ed* Richard Francis-Bruce, *M* Marco Beltrami, *Cos* Caroline Harris.
Universal Pictures/Relativity Media/Stuber Productions/ Mambo Film Productions-Universal Studios.
111 mins. USA. 2010. Rel: 16 Apr 2010. Cert. 18.

Resident Evil: Afterlife 3D ★★★½

This is the fourth instalment of the popular video game series. The deadly virus, which turns its victims into murderous zombies, has now spread all over the world. Alice (Milla Jovovich) is still searching for more survivors but is running out of time... There are some terrific set-pieces that look amazing in 3D, especially the sequence where Alice is surrounded by thousands of zombies on a roof in a burnt-out Los Angeles. Mindless but fun. GS

▶ Milla Jovovich, Ali Larter, Sienna Guillory, Kim Coates, Wentworth Miller.
▶ *Dir* and *Screenplay* Paul W S Anderson, *Pro* Anderson, Jeremy Bolt, Don Carmody, Bernd Eichinger, Samuel Hadida and Robert Kulzer, *Ph* Glen MacPherson, *Pro Des* Arvinder Grewal, *Ed* Niven Howie, *M* tomandandy, *Cos* Denise Cronenberg and Azalia Snail.
Constantin Film/David Films/Impact Pictures-Sony Pictures Releasing.
97 mins. Germany/France/UK. 2010. Rel: 10 Sep 2010. Cert. 15.

its time-frame adding an agonising tension and poignancy. JC-W

▶ Robert Pattinson, Emile De Ravin, Chris Cooper, Lena Olin, Pierce Brosnan.
▶ *Dir* Allen Coulter, *Pro* Trevor Engelson and Nick Osborne, *Screenplay* William Fetters, *Ph* Jonathan Freeman, *Pro Des* Scott P Murphy, *Ed* Andrew Mondshein, *M* Marcelo Zarvos, *Cos* Susan Lyall.
Underground Films/Summit Entertainment-Summit Entertainments.
113 mins. USA. 2010. Rel: 2 Apr 2010. Cert. 12A.

Repo Men ★★★★

Dystopian futures are the fashionable currency of science fiction but the science here is more interesting than in most of this ilk. Lifelong friends Jude Law and Forest Whitaker have grown up to be corporate repossession agents of mechanical organs. Half the US population seem to have a mortgage on one part of their viscera and Heaven help them in an economic crisis. Debutant director Miguel Sapochnik exhibits enormous stylistic flourish, cramming his film with delicious visual throwaways and offering a

Restrepo ★★★★

Brilliantly assembled as a 93-minute documentary feature taken from 150 hours of footage, this absorbing view of American soldiers in Afghanistan was filmed in 2007 and 2008. Refusing to be didactic, it simply introduces us to a group of young soldiers, shows us their contact with local villagers and then their first experience of war. We come to see how all this marks them for life and the film conveys the reality of war as effectively as did the re-enactment of a real-life drama in *Lebanon* [qv]. MS

▶ With the men of Battle Company 2nd of the 503rd Infantry Regiment, 173rd Airborne Brigade Combat Team.
▶ *Dir*, *Pro* and *Ph* Tim Hetherington and Sebastian Junger, *Ed* Michael Levine.
Outpost Films in association with National Geographic Channel-Dogwoof Pictures.
94 mins. USA. 2010. Rel: 8 Oct 2010. Cert. 15.

Revanche ★★★½

The work of the Austrian Götz Spielmann is new to me and, even if this film is far less telling towards the end, it nevertheless bears a singular stamp of film-making authority. The drama, with religious elements implied, brings a village policeman and his wife into contact with another couple. The latter comprise a prostitute and a man who had worked for her boss: he has fallen in love with her and turns to robbery to finance their joint escape. Even if the initial brilliance leads to a less persuasive second half, Spielmann is a talent to note. MS

▶ Johannes Krisch, Ursula Strauss, Irina Potapenko, Andreas Lust, Hannes Thanheiser.
▶ *Dir* and *Screenplay* Götz Spielmann, *Pro* Mathias Forberg, Heinz Stussak, Sandra Bohle and Spielmann, *Ph* Martin Gschlacht, *Art Dir* Maria Gruber, *Ed* Karina Ressler, *Cos* Monika Buttinger.

Prisma Film/Spielmannfilm-Artificial Eye.
122 mins. Austria. 2008. Rel: 30 Apr 2010. Cert. 15.

The Road ★★★

Admirers of Cormac McCarthy's post-apocalyptic novel may wish to see this technically adroit film version. The story episodically follows two survivors, a father and son, on their journey across a devastated America to the sea. Viggo Mortensen and young Kodi Smit-McPhee are excellent, but the tale is so unrelentingly grim (any positive element in its conclusion is the one part that is unpersuasive) that I can't see the point of it. MS

▶ Viggo Mortensen, Kodi Smit-McPhee, Robert Duvall, Charlize Theron, Guy Pearce.
▶ *Dir* John Hillcoat, *Pro* Nick Wechsler, Paula Mae Schwartz and Steve Schwartz, *Screenplay* Joe Penhall, from the novel by Cormac McCarthy, *Ph* Javier Aguirresarobe, *Pro Des* Chris Kennedy, *Ed* Jon Gregory, *M* Nick Cave and Warren Ellis, *Cos* Margot Wilson.

Dimension Films/2929 Productions/Nick Wechsler/ Chockstone Pictures etc-Icon Film Distribution. 112 mins. USA. 2009. Rel: 8 Jan 2010. Cert. 15.

Road to Las Vegas ★★★★

Filmed between 2005 and 2008, this honest and engrossing documentary follows an African-American couple, believers in God's word, who set out with their young children to follow his behest and start a new life in Las Vegas. The problems that they encounter there (difficulties in getting work, the husband's cocaine habit) enable us to see the relationship of this couple in all its revealing complexity. There are insights into human behaviour here equal to anything you might hope for in a distinguished work of fiction. MS

▶ With Maurice Melton, Vanessa Melton, Marcel Melton, Maurice Melton Jr, Isis Melton.
▶ *Dir* and *Ph* Jason Massot, *Pro* Teddy Leifer and

Road to ruin: Viggo Mortensen in John Hillcoat's post-apocalyptic *The Road.*

Robbin' the rich: Russell Crowe takes instruction from his director, Ridley Scott, in a spectacular and politically pertinent *Robin Hood*.

Massot, *Ed* Alan Mackay, *M* Glenn Jones.

More 4/RISE Films/Borderland Films-ICA Cinema. 90 mins. UK. 2010. Rel: 1 Dec 2010. No Cert.

Robin Hood ★★★

Considering the money lavished on the visuals of this historical epic, one can't help wondering how much more a voice coach would have cost for Russell Crowe. As it is, Eileen Atkins steals the acting honours from the Americans and the Swedish, while, to be fair, Ridley Scott does make the Middle Ages seem fresh (and politically pertinent). The action scenes are sensational, although Robin Hood himself is a dull, unintelligible figure and the film that bears his name feels more like a prequel to something better. JC-W

▶ Russell Crowe, Cate Blanchett, Matthew McFadyen, Max von Sydow, William Hurt, Mark Strong, Oscar Isaac, Danny Huston, Eileen Atkins, Douglas Hodge.
▶ *Dir* Ridley Scott, *Pro* Crowe, Scott and Brian Grazer, *Screenplay* Brian Helgeland from a story by Helgeland, Ethan Reiff and Cyrus Voris, *Ph* John Mathieson, *Pro Des* Arthur Max, *Ed* Pietro Scala, *M* Marc Streitenfeld, *Cos* Janty Yates.

Universal Pictures/Scott Free Productions/Imagine Entertainment/Relativity Media-Universal Pictures. 140 mins. USA/UK. 2010. Rel: 12 May 2010. Cert. 12A.

Robinson in Ruins ★★★★

Patrick Keiller's experimental sequel to *Robinson in Space* is again a clever mix of fiction with documentary. Vanessa Redgrave takes over from Paul Scofield as narrator and her dry delivery adds much enjoyment to this oddly eccentric exercise. The mischievous filmmaker's alter ego, the mysterious Robinson, revisits the English landscape and comments on almost everything relating to current environmental and economic affairs. A unique film from a unique film-maker! GS

▶ Narrator Vanessa Redgrave.
▶ *Dir, Written by, Ph* and *Ed* Patrick Keiller, *Exec Pro* Keith Griffiths.

Realised with the support of the British Film Institute/ Calouste Gulbenkian Foundation etc-British Film Institute. 101 mins. UK. 2010. Rel: 19 Nov 2010. Cert. U.

A Room and a Half ★★★★½

Where Terence Davies' *Of Time and the City* was an essay, this Russian take on the life of the poet Joseph Brodsky – exiled from his particular city, St Petersburg, in 1972 – is best described as a poetic meditation. It imagines Brodsky returning as a much older man and moves effectively beyond naturalism, although I'm not sure that occasional animated scenes fully fit in. Essentially it's all about what anybody with truly loving parents owes to them and veteran director Andrey Khrzhanovsky can be proud of what he has achieved. MS

▶ Alisa Freindilkh, Sergei Yursky, Grigoriy Dityatkovsky, Artem Smola, Evgeniy Ogadzhanyan.
▶ *Dir* Andrey Khrzhanovsky, *Pro* Khrzhanovsky and Artern Vassilev, *Screenplay* Yuri Arabov and Khrzhanovsky, *Ph* Vladimir Brylyakov, *Art Dir* Marina Azizian, *Ed* Vladimir Grigorenko and Igor Malachov, *Cos* Natalya Baranova and Marina Nikolaeva.

School Studio SHAR-Yume Pictures.
130 mins. Russia (Republic). 2009. Rel: 7 May 2010.
Cert. 12A.

Rough Aunties ★★★★

This is another powerful documentary from the acclaimed Kim Longinotto – the director of *Divorce Iranian Style* and *The Day I Will Never Forget*. She now moves to Durban, South Africa, and follows the compelling lives of several women from the 'Bobbi Bear' group. Their purpose is to rescue abused children and make sure that the perpetrators are brought to justice. It is an honest and deeply moving film about a poverty-stricken rural community where AIDS and sexual abuse of children are sadly on the increase. GS

▶ Jackie Branfield, Eureka, Thuli, Ladyfair, Mildrid, Studla.
▶ *Dir* and *Pho* Kim Longinotto, *Pro* Teddy Leifer and Paul Taylor, *Ed* Ollie Huddleston.

Rise Films/Vixen Films-Channel 4 TV Corporation.
103 mins. UK/South Africa. 2008. Rel: 16 July 2010. Cert. 15

Rumba ★★★½

This deadpan French comedy sometimes evokes Buster Keaton but is even more under the influence of Jacques Tati. Featuring a loving couple who adore dance, it starts engagingly but arguably misses its step when the woman loses a leg and the man suffers from periodic memory loss. This is by now black comedy, but that's a genre that needs to be heartless to work and we don't want to laugh at the couple's tragic situation. *Rumba* is a rare mix of terrific moments and elements that seem wholly misjudged, but it's short and interesting. MS

▶ Fiona Gordon, Dominique Abel. Philippe Martz, Clément Morel, Bruno Romy.
▶ *Dir* and *Screenplay* Dominique Abel, Fiona Gordon and Bruno Romy *Pro* Marin Karmitz and Nathanaël Charles Gilbert, Abel and Gordon, *Ph* Claire Childéric, *Art Dir* Nicolas Girault, *Ed* Sandrine Deegen, *Cos* Claire Dubien.

MK2 Productions/Courage Mon Amour/RTBF (Télévision belge) etc-Network Releasing.
77 mins. France/Belgium. 2008. Rel: 31 July 2009. Cert. PG.

The Runaways ★★★★

Hollywood 1975. This is the real-life story of an all-girl rock band, but it's their manager (Michael Shannon) who calls the shots. The audience can sympathise with Joan Jett (Kristen Stewart), who sticks with it regardless, or with Cherie Currie (Dakota Fanning), who rejects the compromises and gives up. This is a tough, realistic film, very well made and boasting several great performances. MS

▶ Kristen Stewart, Dakota Fanning, Michael Shannon, Alia Shawkat, Tatum O'Neal.
▶ *Dir* Floria Sigismondi, *Pro* John Linson, Art Linson and Bill Pohlad, *Screenplay* Sigismondi, from the book *Neon Angel* by Cherie Currie, *Ph* Benoît Debie, *Pro Des* Eugenio Caballero, *Ed* Richard Chew, *M* Lillian Berlin, *Cos* Carol Beadle.

River Road Entertainment/Linson Entertainment-E1 Entertainment UK.
106 mins. USA. 2010. Rel: 10 Sep 2010. Cert. 15.

Rock solid: Dakota Fanning and Kristen Stewart in Floria Sigismondi's tough, realistic *The Runaways*.

Bourne again: Angelina Jolie flexes her physical versatility in Philip Noyce's fast-paced *Salt*.

Salt ★★★½

Two years after CIA agent Evelyn Salt is released from North Korea, she becomes directly involved in an acceleration of the Cold War. Sandwiched between its clunky opening and ludicrous closing sequence, *Salt* is a slick slab of escapism that keeps its 'is she or isn't she?' premise spinning nicely. And here we have the full Angelina: in her underwear (albeit briefly), sporting blond hair and later a dark short-back-and-sides – and even in drag. She certainly earns her action-heroine stripes, this being a sort of *Bourne* with boobs and a memory. JC-W

▷ Angelina Jolie, Liev Schreiber, Chiwetel Ejiofor, Daniel Olbrychski, August Deal.
▷ *Dir* Philip Noyce, *Pro* Lorenzo di Bonaventura and Sunil Perkash, *Screenplay* Kurt Wimmer, *Ph* Robert Elswit, *Pro Des* Scott Chambliss, *Ed* Stuart Baird and John Gilroy, *M* James Newton Howard, *Cos* Sarah Edwards.
Columbia Pictures/Di Bonaventura Pictures/Relativity Media/Wintergreen Productions-Sony Pictures Releasing.
100 mins. USA. 2010. Rel: 18 Aug 2010. Cert. 12A.

Salvage ★½

It is Christmas and Beth's (Neve McIntosh) estranged daughter Jodie (Linzey Cocker) comes to visit. But when she finds her mother in bed with a stranger she runs away to a neighbour's house. In the meantime heavily armed military personnel storm the area and order the residents to retreat to their homes. There is something mysterious lurking in the neighbourhood... The central idea is passable enough but the hysterical acting and unconvincing dialogue in Laurence Gough's muddled film prevent us from caring. GS

▷ Neve McIntosh, Linzey Cocker, Shahid Ahmed, Dean Andrews, Sufian Ashraf, Ben Batt, Shaun Dooley.
▷ *Dir* Laurence Gough, *Pro* Julie Lau, *Screenplay* Colin O'Donnell, from a story by O'Donnell, Gough and Alan Pattison, *Ph* Simon Tindall, *Pro Des* Mally Smith and Colin Taylor, *Ed* Anthony Ham, *M* Stephen Hilton, *Cos* Nicky Baron.
Hoax Films-Revolver Entertainment.
79 mins. UK. 2009. Rel: 19 Mar 2010. Cert. 18.

Samson & Delilah ★★½

In visual terms this is a delight, reminding one of the idea that photography is painting with light. Nevertheless, given the minimal dialogue and lack of background detail, I can't share the enthusiasm of some for this largely downbeat Aboriginal romance. Subsidiary figures conveniently appear only when the drama requires it and I remained a distant observer. You may feel differently. MS

▷ Rowan McNamara, Marissa Gibson, Mitjili Gibson, Scott Thornton.
▷ *Dir*, *Screenplay* (with Beck Cole), *Ph* and *M* Warwick Thornton, *Pro* Kath Shelper, *Pro Des* Daran Fulham, *Ed* Roland Gallois, *Cos* Heather Wallace.
Screen Australia/New South Wales Film and Television Office etc-Trinity Filmed Entertainment.
101 mins. Australia. 2009. Rel: 2 April 2010. Cert. 15.

Saw VI ★

First of all, unless you've seen the previous five *Saw* movies, and not just watched them but absorbed every single detail, this sixth instalment isn't going to make one shred of sense. Secondly, even if you know the first five films back to front, and get what it's going on about – come on guys, this is just more of the same, only not as good. By which I mean, even worse that the last four. The first was amazing, no question. But this is just nasty, empty-headed, tedious trash. MJ

▷ Tobin Bell, Costas Mandylor, Mark Rolston, Betsy Russell, Shawnee Smith.
▷ *Dir* Kevin Greutert, *Pro* Mark Burg and Oren Koules, *Screenplay* Marcus Dunstan and Patrick Melton, *Ph* David A Armstrong, *Pro Des* Anthony A Ianni, *Ed* Andrew Coutts, *M* Charlie Clouser, *Cos* Alex Kavanagh.
Twisted Pictures/A Bigger Boat-Lionsgate.
90 mins. Canada/USA/UK/Australia. 2009. Rel: 23 Oct 2009. Cert. 18.

Saw 3D: The Final Chapter ★★½

This is the seventh of the never-ending and highly successful saga. The repetitive formula has become tiresome, but at least this time you have 3D to keep you entertained. Jigsaw has long been dead but his legacy is very much alive and a group of new victims are about to enter his cruel world of death and torture. This is the tightest since the original and mildly enjoyable despite its sick and brutal premise. GS

‣ Tobin Bell, Cary Elwes, Costas Mandylor, Betsy Russell, Sean Patrick Flanery.
‣ *Dir* Kevin Greutert, *Pro* Mark Burg and Oren Koules, *Screenplay* Patrick Melton and Marcus Dunstan, *Ph* Brian Gedge, *Pro Des* Anthony A Ianni, *Ed* Andrew Coutts, *M* Charlie Clouser, *Cos* Alex Kavanagh.

Twisted Pictures/A Bigger Boat/Serendipity Productions-Lionsgate.
90 mins. Canada/USA. 2010. Rel: 29 Oct 2010. Cert. 18.

The Scar Crow ★

Anyone cherishing the (perfectly reasonable) notion that no film featuring a homicidal scarecrow can be all bad will be sadly disillusioned by this Am-Dram effort. It seeks to unite British horror traditions both old (the witchy hi-jinks of *Blood on Satan's Claw*) and new (the team-building outward bound course of *Severance* and several other recent titles), but eventually falls back on blood-soaked eviscerations to eke out viewer interest. Worst of all, the laddish protagonists are the kind of supposed 'identification' figures who say things like "Let's do ourselves a bit of raping and pillaging." JR

‣ Marysia Kay, Gabriella Douglas, Anna Tolputt, Michael Walker, Anya Lahiri, Kevyn Connett, Tim Major.
‣ *Dir* and *Screenplay* Peter Benson and Andy Thompson, *Pro* Thompson, *Ph* Trevor Speed, *Pro Des* Melanie Light, *Ed* Jake Proctor, *M* Jon Samsworth, *Cos* Nell Knudsen.

Gaia Media-Metrodome Distribution.
84 mins. UK. 2009. Rel: 26 Nov 2010. Cert. 18.

Scott Pilgrim vs the World ★★

Toronto; today. For those immersed in the worlds of the graphic novel and video game, this cartoon ride may make some sense. However, for the moderately intelligent cinemagoer the film's initial invention and freshness quickly become wearisome as the whiz-bang graphics take over. As the nerdy hero fighting off the ex-boyfriends of his new squeeze, Michael Cera exhibits as little personality as the girl of his dreams, whose only mark of variety is the changing colour of her hair. There are a few good lines and some novel uses of the CGI swipe but the rest is depressingly juvenile. JC-W

‣ Michael Cera, Alison Pill, Mary Elizabeth Winstead, Kieran Culkin, Mark Webber.
‣ *Dir* Edgar Wright, *Pro* Wright, Eric Gitter, Marc Platt and Nira Park, *Screenplay* Wright and Michael Bacall, from the Oni Press graphic novels by Bryan Lee O'Malley, *Ph* Bill Pope, *Pro Des* Marcus Rowland, *Ed* Jonathan Amos and Paul Machliss, *M* Nigel Godrich, *Cos* Laura Jean Shannon.

Comic schtick: Michael Cera and Mary Elizabeth Winstead in Edgar Wright's depressingly juvenile *Scott Pilgrim vs The World*.

Pacifique overtures: Astrid Bergès-Friseby in Rithy Panh's *The Sea Wall*.

Universal Pictures/Marc Platt/Dentsu Inc/Big Talk Films/ Closed on Mondays etc-Universal Pictures International. 112 mins. USA/UK/Canada. 2010. Rel: 25 Aug 2010. Cert. 12A.

The Scouting Book for Boys
★★★

This oddly titled film set in Norfolk is a study of youth and of a young teenager's bond with a girl, growing from brotherly affection into a kind of obsessive love. Thomas Turgoose and Holliday Grainger play it for all it's worth, but the later stages are as melodramatic as *Misery* and the tragic finale is way over the top. MS

❧ Thomas Turgoose, Holliday Grainger, Susan Lynch, Rafe Spall, Steven Mackintosh.
❧ *Dir* Tom Harper, *Pro* Christian Colson and Ivana MacKinnon, *Screenplay* Jack Thorne, *Ph* Robbie Ryan, *Pro Des* Paul Cripps, *Ed* Mark Eckersley, *M* Jack Arnold, *Cos* Julian Day.

Celador Films/Screen East Content Investment Fund/ Film4 etc-Pathé Distribution.
93 mins. UK. 2009. Rel: 19 Mar 2010. Cert. 15.

The Sea Wall ★★★

Back in 1958 René Clément made a not-too-satisfactory film taken from Marguerite Duras' novel that evoked her childhood in Indo-China in the 1930s. Now comes this new version, subtitled, from Rithy Panh. But it too, sketching in the social background rather loosely, fails to make us feel real concern for this family story centred on rebellion against a matriarch. As the mother, Isabelle Huppert replaces Jo Van Fleet. (Original title: *Un Barrage contre le Pacifique*) MS

❧ Isabelle Huppert, Astrid Bergès-Friseby, Gaspard Ulliel, Randal Douc.
❧ *Dir* Rithy Panh, *Pro* Catherine Dussart, *Screenplay* Michel Fessler and Panh, from the novel by Marguerite Duras, *Ph* Pierre Milon, *Art Dir* Yan Arlaud, *Ed* Marie-Christine Rougerie, *M* Marc Marder, *Cos* Édith Vespérini.

Catherine Dussart Productions/Studio 37/France 2 Cinéma/Scope Pictures/Canal+ etc-Axiom Films.
116 mins. France/Belgium/Cambodia. 2008. Rel: 20 Nov 2009. Cert. 12A.

The Secret in Their Eyes ★★★

Despite its Oscar as Best Foreign Language Film, this ably acted Argentinian offering is an unconvincing mix of investigative thriller, love story and psychological drama. Its main narrative is set in 1974 and the high praise bestowed may be down to the tale's political background and to its implied need to challenge false histories about what was happening then in Argentina. To carry any real weight the film needs to be more believable than this watchable but often over-the-top piece. (Original title: *El secreto de sus ojos*) MS

❧ Ricardo Darin, Soledad Villamil, Pablo Rago, Javier Godino. Guillermo Francella.
❧ *Dir* and *Ed* Juan José Campanella, *Pro* Mariela Besuievsky and Campanella, *Screenplay* Eduardo Sacheri and Campanella, from the novel *La pregunta de sus ojos* by Sacheri, *Ph* Félix Monti, *Art Dir* Marcelo Pont, *M* Federico Jusid, *Cos* Cecilia Monti.

Alta Classics/Tornasol Films/Haddock Films/100 Bares Producciones etc-Metrodome Distribution.
129 mins. Spain/Argentina. 2009. Rel: 13 Aug 2010. Cert. 18.

The Secret of Kells ★★★½

This animated feature from Ireland is traditional enough to focus on a 12-year-old boy and his adventures but in other respects it is novel. The year is 813, the setting Iona and the boy is a youth capable of helping in the completion of the gospel illustrations required to make up the Book of Kells. The tests that the boy undergoes provide action, as do threats from the Vikings. In trying to engage a modern audience, the tone lacks the purity of the films of Michel Ocelot, but this is certainly an interesting endeavour. MS

▶ With the voices of Evan McGuire, Mick Lally, Christen Mooney, Brendan Gleeson.
▶ *Dir* Tomm Moore with Nora Twomey, *Pro* Didier Brunner, Viviane Vanfleteren and Paul Young, *Screenplay* Fabrice Ziolkowski, from Moore's story, *Ed* Fabienne Alvarez-Giro , *M* Bruno Coulais.

Les Armateurs/Vivi Film/Cartoon Saloon/France 2 Cinéma etc-Optimum Releasing.
79 mins. France/Belgium/Ireland. 2008. Rel: 1 Oct 2010. Cert. PG.

Secretariat ★★

Secretariat was the Big Red horse that became a horse-racing legend in the 1970s, so this is a true story. The stellar cast includes Diane Lane as the Denver housewife who, with the help of her eccentric trainer (John Malkovich), made history in the world of racing. It is a good story let down by the less than average script and by Randall Wallace's mediocre direction. A sad waste of acting talent. GS

▶ Diane Lane, James Cromwell, John Malkovich, Scott Glenn, Margo Martindale, Roger D Smith, Dylan Walsh.
▶ *Dir* Randall Wallace, *Pro* Mark Ciardi, Pete De Stefano and Gordon Gray, *Screenplay* Mike Rich, based on the book by William Nack, *Ph* Dean Semler, *Pro Des* Thomas E Sanders, *Ed* John Wright, *M* Nick Glennie-Smith, *Cos* Michael T Boyd and Julie Weiss.

Walt Disney Pictures/Fast Track Productions/Mayhem Pictures-Walt Disney Studios Motion Pictures.
123 mins. USA. 2010. Rel: 3 Dec 2010. Cert. PG.

Separado! ★★★★

This wonderfully eccentric Western musical follows Welsh pop artist Gruff Rhys on a trip to Patagonia in search of his long-lost uncle, the poncho-wearing guitarist René Griffiths. He visits theatres, nightclubs, desert teahouses and radio stations, and gets to know many members of the Welsh community which flourishes deep in the heart of the Andes. It is a fun road movie and an enlightening journey with many delightful characters, especially the singing brothers Alejandro and Leonardo Jones. GS

Kell surprise: A scene from Tomm Moore and Nora Twomey's *The Secret of Kells.*

A sight for sore eyes: Soledad Villamil in Juan José Campanella's *The Secret in Their Eyes* (which is already being adapted for a Hollywood remake).

➤ Gruff Rhys, Alejandro and Leonardo Jones etc.
➤ *Dir* Dylan Goch and Gruff Rhys, *Pro* Catryn Ramasut, *Written* and *Performed by* Gruff Rhys, *Ph* and *Ed* Dylan Gooch, *M* Gruff Rhys.

le le Productions-Soda Pictures.
84 mins. UK/Argentina/Brazil. 2010. Rel: 30 July 2010. Cert. PG.

The September Issue ★★★

After Meryl Streep's hilarious turn in *The Devil Wears Prada*, a performance allegedly based on Anna Wintour, legend-in-her-own-lunchtime editor of *Vogue* magazine, one expected more from *The September Issue*, R J Cutler's documentary on how the Big Issue (ie, the September 2007 number of *Vogue*, the largest ever, weighing nearly five pounds) came into being. Apart from amusing asides from Wintour's assistant Grace Coddington and daughter Bee, matters are far too low-key for their own good – no big fights, no coat-throwing, no walking out, no slamming doors, just odd glimpses of fashionistas Gaulthier, Lagerfeld, Galliano et al to sustain interest. MHD

➤ Anna Wintour, Oscar De La Renta, Patrick DeMarchelier, John Galliano, Jean-Paul Gaultier, Karl Lagerfeld, Mario Testino.
➤ *Dir* R J Cutler, *Pro* Cutler, Sadia Shepherd and Eliza

Hindmarch, *Ph* Robert Richman, *Ed* Azin Samari and Jessica Schilling, *M* Craig Richey.

A & E Indie Films/Actual Reality Pictures-Momentum Pictures.
90 mins. USA. 2009. Rel: 11 Sep 2009. Cert. 12A.

Séraphine ★★★★

Yolande Moreau gives a fine performance in this biopic about the untutored naïve painter Séraphine Louis. Starting in 1912, the film shows how she was discovered by a German art critic and goes through to 1927 and beyond, when this religiously inclined woman became insane. On a first viewing I missed the depth that Robert Bresson would have found in it, but as a portrait of an artist it has strong appeal on its own terms. MS

➤ Yolande Moreau, Ulrich Tukur, Anne Bennent, Nico Rogner, Françoise Lebrun.
➤ *Dir* Martin Provost, *Pro* Miléna Poylo and Gilles Sacuto, *Screenplay* Provost and Marc Abdelnour, *Ph* Laurent Brunet, *Art Dir* Thierry François, *Ed* Ludo Troch, *M* Michael Galasso, *Cos* Madeline Fontaine.

TS Productions/France 3 Cinéma/Climax Films etc-Metrodome Distribution.
126 mins. France/Belgium. 2008. Rel: 27 Nov 2009. Cert. PG.

A Serbian Film ★★★½

Milos (Srdjan Todorovic), a retired porn star, accepts one last job in order to make ends meet. He is encouraged by his wife to take the job and Milos unwillingly enters a world of seedy perversion and brutality worse than he could possibly imagine... This controversial film is very violent and highly explicit and purposely leaves a bad taste in the mouth. But, as director Srdjan Spasojevic claims, this is an allegory on his country's molestation by the Serbian government. (Original title: *Srpski film*) GS

➤ Srdjan Todorovic, Sergej Trifunovic, Jelena Gavrilovic, Katarina Zutic, Anna Sakic.
➤ *Dir* and *Pro* Srdjan Spasojevic, *Screenplay* Spasojevic and Aleksandar Radivojevic, *Ph* Nemanja Jovanov, *Pro Des* Nemanja Petrovic, *Ed* Darko Simic, *M* Sky Wikluh, *Cos* Jasmina Sanader.

Contra Films-Revolver Entertainment.
104 mins. Serbia. 2010. Rel: 10 Dec 2010. Cert. 18.

A Serious Man ★★½

This film has its admirers but I am not one of them, despite the good cast and its technical accomplishment. An invented Yiddish folk-tale provides an effective prologue, but thereafter sympathy is invited for an underdog whose reactions to personal misfortune are so passive that you want to shake him. With the Coen Brothers going back to their Jewish roots it should have

Au naturel: Yolande Moreau as Séraphine Louis in Martin Provost's ambitious *Séraphine*.

been revealing, but the film's send-up of rabbis left me bored and quite unclear regarding the faith, or lack of it, on the part of the film-makers. MS

▶ Michael Stuhlbarg, Richard Kind, Fred Melamed, Sari Lennick, Aaron Wolff.
▶ *Dir*, *Pro* and *Screenplay* Joel Coen and Ethan Coen, *Ph* Roger Deakins, *Pro Des* Jess Gonchor, *Ed* Roderick Jaynes (ie, Joel and Ethan Coen), *M* Carter Burwell, *Cos* Mary Zophres.

Focus Features/Studio Canal/Relativity Media/Working Title Films etc-Universal Pictures.
105 mins. USA/UK/France. 2009. Rel: 20 Nov 2009. Cert. 15.

The Seventh Dimension ★

Zoe (Lucy Evans) persuades her friend Sarah (Kelly Adams) to accompany her to the council flat of her tutor, with whom she is in love. But he is not alone – he is part of a trio of computer hackers determined to enter the Vatican's top secret archives... Brad Watson's dull project mixes science and religion in the form of a supernatural thriller and it is certainly not *The Da Vinci Code*. Even the classy presence of Kelly Adams can't rescue this from mediocrity. GS

▶ Kelly Adams, Jonathan Rhodes, Lucy Evans, Calita Rainfors, David Horton.
▶ *Dir* and *Ed* Brad Watson, *Pro* Janice De La Mare, *Screenplay* Watson and Debbie Moon, based on a story by Watson, *Ph* Tim Wooster, *Pro Des* Kay Brown, *M* Mark Teitler, *Cos* Rebecca Gore.

Revolt Films-Kaleidoscope Home Entertainment.
95 mins. UK. 2009. Rel: 8 July 2010. Cert. 15.

Sex & Drugs & Rock & Roll ★★★

This picture about the highly idiosyncratic entertainer Ian Dury is a stylised work, lively but sometimes exhausting as it veers, somewhat erratically, between enthusiastic tribute and a critical view of his troubled life and character. What is certain is that Andy Serkis, doing his own singing, is sensationally good in every way. How much you enjoy the film as a whole, however, is probably down to a matter of taste. MS

▶ Andy Serkis, Bill Milner, Naomie Harris, Olivia Williams, Toby Jones, Tom Hughes.
▶ *Dir* Mat Whitecross, *Pro* Damian Jones, *Screenplay* Paul Viragh, *Ph* Christopher Ross and Brian Tufano, *Pro Des* Richard Bullock, *Ed* Peter Christelis, *M* Chaz Jankel, *Cos* Joanna Eatwell.

UK Film Council/Aegis Film Fund/DJ Films/New Boots & Panties etc-Entertainment Film Distributors.
115 mins. UK. 2009. Rel: 8 Jan 2010. Cert. 15.

Sex and the City 2 ★★★

It's always a pleasure to see the old girls – old being the operative word, as the foursome are now showing their age – but it's sad to see them scraping the barrel on a trip to Abu Dhabi. Here Carrie and co are out of their NY comfort zone with too many iffy references to foreigners' funny ways to make this sequel as witty as the first movie or even the TV series, which still holds up well. If there is a third film, get the girls back to the Big Apple, their natural habitat where they can either flourish or fail with fun. MHD

Group mentality: Andy Serkis heads the Blockheads as Ian Dury in Mat Whitecross' *Sex & Drugs & Rock & Roll.*

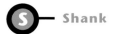

➤ Sarah Jessica Parker, Kim Cattrall, Cynthia Nixon, Kristin Davis, Willie Garson, Mario Cantone, Art Malik, Lynn Cohen, Liza Minnelli.
➤ *Dir* and *Screenplay* Michael Patrick King, based on characters created in the book by Candace Bushnell and in the television series by Darren Star, *Pro* King, Star, John P Melfi and Sarah Jessica Parker, *Ph* John Thomas, *Pro Des* Jeremy Conway, *Ed* Michael Berenbaum, *M* Aaron Zigman, *Cos* Pat Field, Molly Rogers, Jacqueline Oknaian and Jessica Replansky.

New Line Cinema/Home Box Office/HBO Films/Village Roadshow Pictures-New Line Cinema.
146 mins. USA. 2010. Rel: 28 May 2010. Cert. 15.

Shank ★★½

You wait years for a film called *Shank*… And then both *Shank*s feature first-time directors, deal with gangs and arrive on pretty meagre budgets. This one tells the story of Cal, an 18-year-old gang member who's into coke, sex and violence and is the sort of hoodie you wouldn't want to meet on a dark alley in Bristol. But Cal harbours a surprising secret, as does this rough-and-ready romance with a rather sweet – if gritty – heart. And while the film is mired in a few too many platitudes, it's blessed with a strong central presence in Wayne Virgo. CB

➤ Wayne Virgo, Marc Laurent, Alice Payne, Tom Bott, Garry Summers, Bernie Hodges.
➤ *Dir* Simon Pearce, Darren Flaxstone and Christian Martin, *Pro* Martin and Robert Shulevitz, *Screenplay* Flaxstone and Martin, *Ph* Pearce, *Pro Des* Jez Hunziker, *Ed* Flaxstone, *M* Barnaby Taylor, *Cos* Stewart Meachem.

FAQs-Parasol Pictures Releasing.
89 mins. UK. 2009. Rel: 11 Sep 2009. Cert. 15.

Shank ★★½

There are some interesting ideas bouncing around Mo Ali's directorial debut. Set in a dystopian London of 2015, the film focuses on a gang who trade in the scarce commodity of food, which has replaced drugs as a black market need. Ali adopts a jerky, music-video style to give his film a pop-cultural immediacy. There's also an adrenaline-fuelled parkour-style chase that opens the film, although there's not enough plot or characterisation to make this anything but a quick cinematic fix. CB

➤ Kedar Williams-Stirling, Adam Deacon, Ashley Bashy Thomas, Michael Socha, Jan Uddin.
➤ *Dir* Mo Ali, *Pro* Peter Van Carter, Daniel Toland, Nick Taussig and Terry Stone, *Screenplay* Van Carter, *Ph* Adam Frisch, *Pro Des* Rob Nicholls, *Ed* Julian Tranquille, *M* Chad Hobson, *Cos* Avigail Claire and Damian Collins.

Gunslinger/Gateway Films/Cinematic Productions-Revolver Entertainment.
90 mins. UK. 2010. Rel: 23 Mar 2010. Cert. 15.

She, A Chinese ★★★

The title refers to a Chinese woman who leaves her village and ends up in London. The first half gains from the relatively unfamiliar setting, but the focus shrinks and the London sequences slip inconsequentially into a drama about her relationships with men. The film then concludes with a sequence that resolves nothing. MS

➤ Huang Lu, Wei Yi Bo, Geoffrey Hutchings, Chris Ryman, Wu Leiming.

Food for fighting: Kedar Williams-Stirling in Mo Ali's *Shank*.

▶ *Dir* and *Screenplay* by Xiaolu Guo, *Pro* Natasha Dack, *Ph* Zillah Bowes, *Pro Des* Tine Mette Jespersen, *Ed* Andrew Bird, *M* John Parish, *Cos* Sam Perry.

Tigerlily Films/Warp X/UK Film Council/Film4 etc-Optimum Releasing.

103 mins. UK/Germany/France. 2009. Rel: 26 Feb 2010. Cert. 18.

Shed Your Tears and Walk Away ★★★★½

Set in Hebden Bridge, Yorkshire, this remarkable documentary by Jez Lewis confronts head on the lives of relatively young people whose lack of purpose is reflected in their obsession with drink and drugs, often leading to suicide. Lewis is here filming people with whom he grew up and, if the material is inevitably downbeat, this portrait of one aspect of our times is suffused with warmth: not just Lewis' regard for his subjects but their willingness to open up in front of the camera. Life itself may sometimes inhibit the shaping of the material but this is a key vision of life today. MS

▶ *Dir* Jez Lewis, *Pro* Rachel Wexler, *Ph* Lewis and others, *Ed* Miranda Watts, *M* Roger McBrien.

Screen East Content Investment Fund/Bungalow Town Productions etc-ICO (Independent Cinema Office) 90 mins. UK. 2009. Rel: 11 June 2010. No Cert.

Shelter ★★★

Forensic shrink Julianne Moore finds her patient Jonathan Rhys Meyers suffering from multiple personality disorder. When he snaps back his head and moans, he becomes a different person – one of many murder victims. Intense, imaginative direction and increasingly eerie sequences create a big buzz in this moody and creepy chiller. The weird backwoods folk are assets, the striking filming style produces some eye-catching visuals and Moore is perfect in this kind of role. Meyers seems like an odd choice but is fine, Frances Conroy adds class as a bereaved mother and Jeffrey DeMunn is pretty ripe as Moore's shrink dad. DW

▶ Julianne Moore, Jonathan Rhys Meyers, Jeffrey DeMunn, Frances Conroy, Brooklyn Proulx.
▶ *Dir* Måns Mårlind and Björn Stein, *Pro* Darlene Caamano Loquet, Neal Edelstein, Mike Macari and Emilio Diez Barroso, *Screenplay* Michael Cooney, *Ph* Linus Sandgren, *Pro Des* Tim Galvin, *Ed* Steve Mirkovich, *M* John Frizzell, *Cos* Luca Mosca.

NALA Films/Macari-Edelstein/Shelter Productions etc-Icon Film Distribution.

112 mins. USA. 2010. Rel: 9 Apr 2010. Cert. 15.

Sherlock Holmes ★★

Guy Ritchie's latest is not as bad as some of his recent stinkers. Robert Downey's Holmes

Shrink rapt: Julianne Moore in Måns Mårlind and Björn Stein's moody and creepy *Shelter.*

is a strong presence but his rapid delivery is almost incomprehensible, whereas Jude Law's Dr Watson is far too stagey and perhaps more suited to Drury Lane. Rachel McAdams provides solid support as the mysterious American who makes Sherlock tremble with desire while Mark Strong makes a suitably evil villain. Overall this is a mixture of styles, with some impressive set-pieces, but it is loud, hollow and ultimately devoid of any thrills. GS

▶ Robert Downey Jr, Jude Law, Rachel McAdams, Mark Strong, Eddie Marsan, Geraldine James, Kelly Reilly, James Fox.
▶ *Dir* Guy Ritchie, *Pro* Susan Downey, Dan Lin, Joel Silver and Lionel Wigram, *Screenplay* Michael Robert Johnson, Anthony Peckham and Simon Kinberg from a story by Johnson and Wigram, based on characters created by Sir Arthur Conan Doyle, *Ph* Philippe Rousselot, *Pro Des* Sarah Greenwood, *Ed* James Herbert, *M* Hans Zimmer *Cos* Jenny Beavan.

Warner Bros Pictures/Village Roadshow Pictures/Wigram Productions/Silver Pictures/Lin Pictures etc-Warner Bros. 128 mins. USA/Germany. 2009. Rel: 26 Dec 2009. Cert. 12A.

She's Out of My League ★★★

Goofy underachiever Jay Baruchel meets the perfect woman in cute, capable Alice Eve. She likes him too, but soon he thinks She's Out of His League. This is a consistently funny, charming film with good, sometimes big, laughs throughout. The two stars are spot-on – amusing, attractive and appealing – and T J Miller, Mike Vogel, Nate Torrance and Kyle Bornheimer raise plenty of chuckles as Baruchel's buddies. There are a few *Something About Mary* moments, but this is mostly sweet, feel-good stuff. Eve's parents are played by her real-life ones, Trevor Eve and Sharon Maughan, who could have had more to do. DW

Shorts

Fantasy life: Shrek with Rumpelstiltskin in Mike Mitchell's mildly engaging *Shrek Forever After*.

▶ Jay Baruchel, Alice Eve, T J Miller, Mike Vogel, Natie Torrence, Kyle Bornheimer, Trevor Eve, Sharon Maughan.

▶ *Dir* Jim Field Smith, *Pro* Jimmy Miller, Eric Gold and David B Householter, *Screenplay* John Morris and Sean Anders, *Ph* Jim Denault, *Pro Des* Clayton Hartley, *Ed* Dan Schalk, *M* Michael Andrews, *Cos* Molly Maginnis.

DreamWorld Pictures/Mosaic Media-Paramount Pictures. 104 mins. USA. 2010. Rel: 4 June 2010. Cert. 15.

Shorts ★★

Robert Rodriguez's disappointing film tells the story of 11-year-old Toe Thompson (Jimmy Bennett), whose life takes an unexpected turn when he finds a mysterious Rainbow Rock which grants wishes to anyone who holds it. Toe's endless bullying is now over but everyone at Black Falls, including the adults, wants to possess the magical Rock. The amiable story is similar to Stephen Chow's superior *CJ7* but Rodriguez's chopped-up narrative fails to disguise a repetitive script. GS

▶ Jimmy Bennett, Jake Short, Kat Dennings, Trevor Gagnon, James Spader, William H Macy, Devon Gearhart, Rebel Rodriguez.

▶ *Dir* and *Ph* Robert Rodriguez, *Pro* Elizabeth Avellan and Rodriguez, *Screenplay* Robert and Álvaro Rodriguez, *Pro Des* Steve Joyner, *Ed* Ethan Maniquis, *M* Robert Rodriguez, George Oldziey and Carl Thiel, *Cos* Nina Proctor.

Warner Bros Pictures/Lin Pictures/Imagenation Abu Dhabi/Media Rights Capital/Troublemaker Studios-Warner Bros. 89 mins. USA/United Arab Emirates. 2009. Rel: 21 Aug 2009. Cert. PG.

The Shouting Men ★★

This good-natured Britcom starts with wheelchair-user Terry (Matt Daniel-Baker) telling a group of Gillingham footie fans he can get them a free minibus and fuel if they take him along up north to their 'game of a lifetime' against Newcastle United in the FA Cup quarter finals. A lot of obvious and vulgar jokes ensue in this low-budget movie of Carry On-style comic trials and tribulations. But still, with a nice cast that includes Craig Fairbrass, Dudley Sutton and Malcolm Freeman, it remains warm, likeable and often quite funny. Sutton's straight-talking granddad proves the outstanding turn. DW

▶ Craig Fairbrass, Warren Llambias, Matt Daniel-Baker, Dudley Sutton, Malcolm Freeman, Tony Denham.

▶ *Dir* Steve Kelly, *Pro* Matt Daniel-Baker, Warren Llambias, Joanne Podmore and Rhian Williams, *Screenplay* Daniel-Baker and Llambias, *Pro Des* Pal Burns, *Ed* Gary Dollner, *Cos* Alice Wolf Bauer.

Purple Rogue Films-Kaleidoscope Home Entertainment. 92 mins. USA. 2010. Rel: 5 Mar 2010. Cert. 15.

Shrek Forever After ★★★

The first two *Shrek* films were a hard act to follow and *Shrek the Third* was inevitably disappointing. This is no better and the freshness of the original has long been replaced by a certain laziness in the detail. Even so, its premise – brazenly embezzled from *It's a Wonderful Life* – is a strong one. Growing blind to the intrinsic joys of domesticity, Shrek goes looking for his inner ogre and is suckered into a Faustian, metaphysical pact with a jealous little creep called Rumpelstiltskin. There's plenty to engage the kids but this won't be one to purchase for the home library. JC-W

➤ Voices of Mike Myers, Eddie Murphy, Cameron Diaz, Antonio Banderas, Julie Andrews, John Cleese, Jane Lynch, Larry King.
➤ *Dir* Mike Mitchell, *Pro* Gina Shay and Teresa Cheng, *Screenplay* Darren Lemke and Josh Klausner, *Ph* Yong Duk Jhun, *Pro Des* Peter Zaslav, *Ed* Nick Fletcher, *M* Harry Gregson-Williams.

DreamWorks Animation/Pacific Data Images-Paramount Pictures.
93 mins. USA. 2010. Rel: 2 July 2010. Cert. U.

Shrink ★★

Contemporary Hollywood is the setting for a multi-threaded tale in the manner of *Short Cuts*, *Magnolia* and Paul Haggis' *Crash*. Kevin Spacey, on good form, is the eponymous doctor whose own problems are hardly less than those of the patients on his couch. However, Thomas Moffett's screenplay opts for unearned happy resolutions and the main impression is of a talented cast playing it for more than it's worth. MS

➤ Kevin Spacey, Keke Palmer, Mark Webber, Saffron Burrows, Robin Williams, Pell James, Dallas Roberts, Robert Loggia, Jack Huston, Gore Vidal.
➤ *Dir* Jonas Pate, *Pro* Michael Burns, Braxton Pope, Kevin Spacey and Dana Brunetti, *Screenplay* Thomas Moffett, from a story by Henry Reardon, *Ph* Lukas Ettlin, *Pro Des* Mark Hutman, *Ed* Luis Carballar, *M* Brian Reitzell and Ken Andrews, *Cos* Johanna Argan.

Roadside Attractions/Ignite Entertainment/Ithaka Films/Trigger Street Productions-Lionsgate UK.
104 mins. USA. 2009. Rel: 4 June 2010. Cert. 15.

Shutter Island ★★★

Martin Scorsese pays homage to movies of the 1960s such as Samuel Fuller's *Shock Corridor*. It's technically accomplished but bloated and hardly worthy of a film-maker of Scorsese's standing. Leonardo DiCaprio arrives at the titular island off Boston intent on investigating the disappearance of an institutionalised inmate, but the big plot twist is easy to guess and to incorporate references to Dachau is a lapse of taste. Patricia Clarkson's cameo helps to renew interest in the second half of this over-extended yarn. MS

➤ Leonardo DiCaprio, Ben Kingsley, Mark Ruffalo, Michelle Williams, Emily Mortimer, Patricia Clarkson, Jackie Earle Haley, Max von Sydow, Elias Koteas, Ted Levine.
➤ *Dir* Martin Scorsese, *Pro* Mike Medavoy, Arnold W Messer, Bradley J Fischer and Scorsese, *Screenplay* Laeta Kalogridis, from the novel by Dennis Lehane, *Ph* Robert Richardson, *Pro Des* Dante Ferretti, *Ed* Thelma Schoonmaker, *Cos* Sandy Powell.

Paramount Pictures/Phoenix Pictures etc-Paramount Pictures UK.
138 mins. USA. 2009. Rel: 12 Mar 2010. Cert. 15.

Institute for the criminally inane: Leonardo DiCaprio and Mark Ruffalo strut their stuff in Martin Scorsese's bloated, old-fashioned *Shutter Island*.

Road to ruin: Paulina Gaitan in Cary Fukunaga's heartbreaking and uncompromising *Sin Nombre.*

Sin Nombre ★★★½

This award-winning drama about illegal immigrants seeking to cross the Mexican border into America is a great calling card for its debutant director, Cary Joji Fukunaga, and the colour photography by Adriano Goldman is superb. The weakness lies in storylines that become increasingly unlikely, leading to a climax that feels set up. Social comment thus rather loses out to the other elements present, those of the love story and the thriller, but some may find in that a welcome sweetening of the pill. MS

▶ Paulina Gaitán. Edgar Flores, Kristyan Ferrer, Tenoch Huerta Mejía, Diana Garcia.
▶ *Dir* and *Screenplay* Cary Joji Fukunaga, *Pro* Amy Kaufman, *Ph* Adriano Goldman, *Pro Des* Claudio 'Pache' Contreras, *Ed* Luis Carballar and Craig McKay, *M* Marcelo Zarvos, *Cos* Leticia Palacios.
Focus Features/Primary Productions/Canana etc-Revolver Entertainment.
95 mins. USA/Mexico/UK. 2008. Rel: 14 Aug 2009. Cert. 15.

A Single Man ★★★½

Designer Tom Ford's film of Christopher Isherwood's brilliant 1964 novel is less than completely satisfying, although for a first feature it's admirable. Knowing the novel, the reader already has a mental picture of George, a gay, uptight English LA college professor. He has lost his lover Jim and decides to kill himself. Even fleshed out in Colin Firth's subtle performance, George appears almost absent, as if his own personality had died with Jim. He visits friends and has a drink with a student (Nicholas Hoult) who's coming to terms with his own sexuality. It's good, cool too, but still coldly dispassionate and oddly uninvolving. MHD

Living in the past: Colin Firth and Julianne Moore cut up in Tom Ford's meticulously crafted *A Single Man.*

▶ Colin Firth, Julianne Moore, Nicholas Hoult, Matthew Goode, Jon Kortajarena.

▶ *Dir* Tom Ford, *Pro* Ford, Andrew Miano, Chris Weitz and Robert Salerno, *Screenplay* Ford and David Scearce, based on the novel by Christopher Isherwood, *Ph* Eduard Grau, *Pro Des* Dan Bishop, *Ed* Joan Sobel, *M* Abel Korzeniowski, *Cos* Arianne Phillips.
Artina Films/Depth of Field/Fade to Black Productions-Icon Film Distribution.
101 mins. USA. 2009. Rel: 12 Feb 2010. Cert. 12A.

Skeletons ★★★

Nick Whitfield's impressive feature debut was a surprise Michael Powell Award winner for Best New Feature Film at the Edinburgh Film Festival. This surreal comedy tells the story of two travelling salesmen who are able to enter into other people's lives and bring the skeletons out of their closets. It is highly original and works well in the first half, but later feels over-extended and cannot disguise the fact that it was originally a short film. GS

▶ Jason Isaacs, Tuppence Middleton, Andrew Buckley, Paul Dallison, Paprika Steen, Will Adamsdale.
▶ *Dir* and *Screenplay* Nick Whitfield, *Pro* Tracy Brimm, Paul Welsh and Kate Myers, *Ph* Zac Nicholson, *Pro Des* James Lapsley, *Ed* Rachel Tunnard, *M* Simon Whitfield, *Cos* Alison McLaughlin.
Forward Films/Edge City Films-Soda Pictures.
94 mins. UK. 2010. Rel: 2 July 2010. Cert. 15

Skin ★★★½

Skin is a laudable endeavour by Anthony Fabian to bring to the screen a drama that tells the real-life tale of Sandra Laing, whose life was shaped by the colour of her skin. Born in South Africa to a white couple but with a dark skin caused by a throwback to some black blood in their ancestry, changing racial laws became central to her existence. This is the story of a survivor, but the film's sincerity doesn't prevent it from playing as a weepie. A less commercial tone would have made it more potent. MS

▶ Sophie Okonedo, Sam Neill, Alice Krige, Tony Kgoroge, Ella Ramangwane.
▶ *Dir* Anthony Fabian, *Pro* Fabian, Genevieve Hofmeyr and Margaret Matheson, *Screenplay* Helen

Crawley, Jessie Keyt and Helena Kriel, from Fabian's story, *Ph* Dewald Aukema and Jonathan Partridge, *Pro Des* Billy Keam, *Ed* St. John O'Rourke, *M* Hélène Muddiman, *Cos* Fotini Dimou.

Elysian Films/Bard Entertainment/Moonlighting Films etc-ICA Films.
107 mins. UK/South Africa/Cayman Islands. 2008. Rel: 24 July 2009. Cert. 12A.

The Sky Crawlers ★★★

Acclaimed animation director Mamoru Oshii (*Ghost in the Shell*, *Avalon*, *Ghost in the Shell 2: Innocence*) brings considerable heart and intelligence to bear on his lovingly crafted Japanese anime sci-fi adventure. Adapted by Chihiro Ito from Hiroshi Mori's story, the film is set in a world where youngsters called Kildren, who don't age or die of natural causes, fight a continuous aerial war. The teenagers include warrior Yuichi (Ryo Kase), expert in flying the sky crawler plane, funny wingman Tokino (Shosuke Tanihara) and woman commander Kusanagi (Rinko Kikuchi). With a script packed with provocative ideas there's plenty to think about and enjoy. (Original title: *Sukai Kurora*) DW

▶ Voices of Rinko Kikuchi, Chiaki Kuriyama, Shosuke Tanihara, Ryo Kase, Bryce Hitchcock.
▶ *Dir* Mamoru Oshii, *Pro* Tomohiko Ishii, *Screenplay* Hiroshi Mori and Chihiro Ito, *Ph* Hisashi Ezura, *Pro Des* Kazuo Nagai, *Ed* Junichi Uematsu, *M* Kenji Kawai.

Nippon Television Network Corporation/Production IG-Sony Pictures Classics.
122 mins. Japan. 2008. Rel: 27 Feb 2010. Cert. 12A.

Skyline ★★★

Jarrod (Eric Balfour) and his pregnant girlfriend Elaine (Scottie Thompson) travel to LA to see their friends Terry (Donald Faison) and Candice (Brittany Daniel), but their visit turns into a nightmare when thousands of alien ships begin to fill the skyline... This is basically a B-movie but with big production values and impressive special effects. The acting is not bad but it is the dark nature of the story which makes this different from the average sci-fi blockbuster. GS

▶ Eric Balfour, Scottie Thompson, Brittany Daniel, Donald Faison, Neil Hopkins, Tanya Newbould, David Zayas.
▶ *Dir* Colin Strause and Greg Strause, *Pro* Colin and Greg Strause, Kristian James Andresen and Liam O'Donnell, *Screenplay* O'Donnell and Joshua Cordes, *Ph* Michael Watson, *Pro Des* Drew Dalton, *Ed* Nicholas Wayman-Harris, *M* Matthew Mareson, *Cos* Bobbie Mannix.

Black Monday Film Services/Relativity Media/ Rogue/Hydraulx Entertainment/Transmission/Rat Entertainment-Momentum Pictures.
94 mins. USA. 2010. Rel: 12 Nov 2010. Cert. 15.

Slackistan ★

A Pakistani take on *Slackers* and its ilk, this is an aimless and self-indulgent wallow in what it means to be bored and privileged in Islamabad. Based on the director's own experiences – along with those of his Westernised intimates – the film fails to engage, due largely to its technical and thespian ineptitude. It was banned in Pakistan for, apparently, entirely spurious reasons. CB

▶ Aisha Linnea Akthar, Rafey Alam, Osman Khalid Butt, Uzair Taswal, Adil Omar.
▶ *Dir*, *Ph* and *Ed* Hammad Khan, *Pro* and *Screenplay* Khan and Shandana Ayub.

Big Upstairs Films/Stealth Films-Mara Pictures.
85 mins. Pakistan. 2010. Rel: 28 Nov 2010. Cert. 15.

Illegal aliens: Scottie Thompson and Eric Balfour encounter a bit of extraterrestrial inconvenience in *Skyline*.

About Face:
Eduardo Saverin
(Andrew Garfield)
contemplates his
future in David
Fincher's sexy,
exciting *The Social
Network*.

The Social Network ★★★★½

In 2003, 19-year-old Harvard student Mark Zuckerberg dreams up Facebook... If the movers and shakers of the 1970s were the president's men, these days they are undergraduates or the denizens of suburban bedrooms. The subject of Facebook alone is fascinating enough, yet the obsessive, double-dealing and friendless engine of the social revolution gives the story its own hero and villain rolled into one. Add the cinematic energy of David Fincher, the verbal smarts of Aaron Sorkin's Oscar-winning screenplay and a sexy up-and-coming cast and you have an entertainment made in cyber-heaven. JC-W

▶ Jesse Eisenberg, Andrew Garfield, Justin Timberlake, Armie Hammer, Max Minghella, Rooney Mara, Brenda Song, Joseph Mazzello, John Getz, David Selby.
▶ *Dir* David Fincher, *Pro* Fincher, Scott Rudin, Dana Brunetti, Michael De Luca, Ceán Chaffin and Kevin Spacey, *Screenplay* Aaron Sorkin, *Ph* Jeff Cronenweth, *Pro Des* Donald Graham Burt, *Ed* Kirk Baxter and Angus Wall, *M* Trent Reznor and Atticus Ross, *Cos* Jacqueline West.

Columbia/Relativity Media/Scott Rudin Prods-Sony Pictures.
120 mins. USA. 2010. Rel: 15 October 2010. Cert 12A.

The Soloist ★★½

A journalist in Los Angeles rescues a cellist from Skid Row and finds that this man, despite being a down-and-out and a schizophrenic, has much to teach him about life. It's a true story presented with a fictional gloss and the film veers between maladroit schmaltz and an honesty that makes the cellist tiresome company. It's well intentioned and Robert Downey Jr (journalist) and Jamie Foxx (musician) give it their best shot, but the film's approach is seriously misjudged. MS

▶ Jamie Foxx, Robert Downey Jr, Catherine Keener, Tom Hollander, Lisagay Hamilton.
▶ *Dir* Joe Wright, *Pro* Gary Foster and Russ Krasnoff, *Screenplay* Susannah Grant, from the book by Steve Lopez, *Ph* Seamus McGarvey, *Pro Des* Sarah Greenwood, *Ed* Paul Tothill, *M* Dario Marianelli, *Cos* Jacqueline Durran.

Universal Pictures/DreamWorks Pictures/Studio Canal/
Working Title Films etc-Universal.
117 mins. USA/UK. 2008. Rel: 25 Sep 2009. Cert. 12A.

Solomon Kane ★★½

A period actioner from the mind of *Conan* creator Robert E Howard, this is one of those movies that you'd hesitate to label good, but without question it's a good laugh. James Purefoy takes the lead in grand style, fighting to save his soul by slaying all manner of turn-of-the-17th-century baddies and beasties. Atmospheric and unrestrained, this mid-budget hack-and-slasher offers gorily violent, ridiculous, frenetic fun for all those in search of such things, the icing on the cake being a solid supporting cast including Pete Postlethwaite and Max von Sydow. MJ

▶ James Purefoy, Geoff Bell, Pete Postlethwaite, Max von Sydow, John Comer, Jason Flemyng, Mackenzie Crook, Alice Krige.
▶ *Dir* Michael J Bassett, *Pro* Paul Berrow and Samuel Hadida, *Screenplay* Bassett, based on a character created by Robert E Howard, *Ph* Dan Laustsen, *Pro Des* Ricky Eyres, *Ed* Andrew MacRitchie, *M* Klaus Badelt, *Cos* John Bloomfield.

Davis-Films/Czech Anglo Productions/Wandering Star-Entertainment Film Distributors.
104 mins. France/Czechoslovakian Republic/UK. 2009. Rel: 19 Feb 2010. Cert. 15.

Somewhere ★★★½

Sofia Coppola goes minimalist with this portrait of a Hollywood star on the skids. It's an art-house movie with little commercial appeal but much honesty in its representation of a world that Coppola, writer as well as director, knows intimately. Stephen Dorff eschews sentimentality in this central role and is superbly partnered by Elle Fanning as his daughter. Possibly it is too slow and it won't please everybody, but this film comes across as exactly what the film-maker wanted to say. MS

▶ Stephen Dorff, Elle Fanning, Chris Pontius, Michelle Monaghan.
▶ *Dir* and *Screenplay* Sofia Coppola, *Pro* G Mac Brown, Roman Coppola and Sofia Coppola, *Ph* Harris Savides, *Pro Des* Anne Ross, *Ed* Sarah Flack, *M* Phoenix, *Cos* Stacey Battat.

Focus Features/Pathé Distribution/American Zoetrope etc-Universal.
98 mins. USA/UK/Italy/Japan. 2010. Rel: 10 Dec 2010. Cert. 15.

Sons of Cuba ★★★★

Andrew Lang's much-celebrated documentary follows the stories of three young boys as they prepare for Cuba's national boxing championship for under-12s and their eventual dream of representing their country in the 2012 Olympics. Lang's eloquent and honest work presents a clear picture of the boys' hard training as well as the immense sacrifices they have to endure in order to achieve their goal. It is a moving and exhilarating experience. GS

▶ Ysvani Bonachea, Cristian Martinez, Santos Urguelles.
▶ *Dir* Andrew Lang, *Pro* Laura Giles, Francine Heywood and Andrew Lang, *Ph* Lang and Domingo Triana, *Ed* Simon Rose, *M* Jack Ketch and Mark Russell.

Windfall Films/Trinamite Productions-Sons of Cuba Ltd.
88 mins. UK. 2009. Rel: 19 Mar 2010. No Cert.

The Sorcerer's Apprentice ★★

Medieval sorcerer Balthazar Blake (Nicolas Cage) arrives in modern-day Manhattan still fighting his nemesis Maxim Horvath (Alfred Molina). He must save the city but first he needs assistance from the young Dave Stutler (Jay Baruchel), whom he trains in the science of magic... The action is repetitive and loud and, despite the delightful reference to the *Fantasia* Mickey Mouse sequence, Jon Turteltaub's direction falls into every cliché. GS

▶ Nicolas Cage, Monica Bellucci, Alice Krige, Jay Baruchel, Alfred Molina, Teresa Palmer.
▶ *Dir* Jon Turteltaub, *Pro* Jerry Bruckheimer, *Screenplay* Matt Lopez, Doug Miro and Carl Bernard, based on a screen story by Lopez, Mark Rosenthal and Lawrence Konner, *Ph* Bojan Bazelli, *Pro Des* Naomi Shohan, *Ed* William Goldenberg, *M* Trevor Rabin, *Cos* Michael Kaplan.

Walt Disney Pictures/Jerry Bruckheimer Films/Saturn Films/Broken Road Productions/Junction Entertainment-Walt Disney Studios Motion Pictures.
109 mins. USA. 2010. Rel: 11 Aug 2010. Cert. PG.

Sorority Row ★½

Megan (Audrina Partridge) dies when a prank at a Sorority party goes disastrously wrong. The sisters panic and throw their friend's body in an old mineshaft and try to erase the incident from their minds. But they soon start receiving mysterious text messages while an armed masked psycho is lurking in the dark... A good premise but Stewart Hendler's muddled film fails to give

Hollywood sigh: Elle Fanning in Sofia Coppola's *Somewhere*, a study of the downside of stardom.

his characters a proper introduction and things are made worse as the attractive cast are almost indistinguishable from one another. GS

▶ Briana Evignon, Leah Pipes, Audrina Partridge, Rumer Willis, Jamie Chung, Margo Harshman, Julian Morris.
▶ *Dir* Stewart Hendler, *Pro* Darren Holender and Mike Karz, *Screenplay* Josh Solberg and Peter Goldfinger, based on the 1983 screenplay *Seven Sisters* by Mark Rosman, *Ph* Ken Seng, *Pro Des* Philp Toolin, *Ed* Elliot Greenberg, *M* Lucian Piane, *Cos* Marian Toy.

Karz Entertainment/Summit Entertainment-Summit Distribution.
101 mins. USA. 2009. Rel: 9 2009. Cert. 18.

Soul Power ★★★★

During the time of the celebrated Rumble in the Jungle fight between Muhammad Ali and George Foreman, musician Hugh Masekela and producer Stewart Levine invited the world's most famous R&B acts to perform. James Brown, Miriam Makeba, The Spinners and B B King among others played to an ecstatic audience in this unequalled historical event. Jeffrey Levy-Hinte's remarkable documentary has been crafted from masses of unused footage from *When We Were Kings* and focuses on this three-day concert that in 1974 made Zaire the centre of the world. GS

▶ Archive footage of Muhammad Ali, James Brown, Celia Cruz, B B King, Miriam Makeba, Hugh Masekela, Bill Withers, The Spinners etc.
▶ *Dir* Jeffrey Levy-Hinte, *Pro* Levy-Hinte, Leon Gast and David Sonnenberg, *Ph* Paul Goldsmith, Albert Maysles, Kevin Keating and Roderick Young, *Ed* David A Smith.

Antidote Films-Eureka Entertainment.
93 mins. USA. 2008. Rel: 10 July 2009. Cert. 12A.

SoulBoy ★★

Joe McCain (Martin Compston) is a delivery van worker in Stoke-on-Trent in 1974. He is bored with his job until his life takes an unexpected turn

Rumble to the rhythm: James Brown gives his all in Jeffrey Levy-Hinte's Soul Power.

when he discovers night dancing at the Wigan Casino. He wants to become a 'soul boy' but first he has to learn all the important dance moves. Shimmy Marcus' likeable but one-dimensional film wants to be a British *Saturday Night Fever* but unfortunately it lacks depth and tension. GS

▶ Martin Compston, Felicity Jones, Craig Parkinson, Alfie Allen, Nichola Burley, Pat Short, Huey Morgan.
▶ *Dir* Shimmy Marcus, *Pro* Christine Alderson, *Screenplay* Jeff Williams, *Ph* Vladimir Trivic, *Pro Des* Rachel Payne, *Ed* Andrew Hulme, *M* Len Arran, *Cos* Elvis Davis.

Ipso Facto Films/Dreamfinder Productions/Screen West Midlands-Soda Pictures.
82 mins. UK. 2010. Rel: 3 Sep 2010. Cert. 15.

South of the Border ★★★★

Oliver Stone's intelligent documentary examines the rise of left wing South American presidents following years of CIA-backed coups and elections. It begins with an in-depth interview with Venezuela's controversial President Hugo Chávez before Stone moves on to his next six subjects around the continent. Ironically, the Americans declare that these leaders are dictators, ignoring the fact that at the same time their president, George W Bush, was causing havoc around the globe. It is informative and always fascinating. GS

▶ Tariq Ali, Raúl Castro, Hugo Chávez, Rafael Correa, Evo Morales, Cristina and Néstor Kirchner.
▶ *Dir* Oliver Stone, *Pro* Robert S Wilson, Fernando Sulichin and José Ibáñez, *Screenplay* Mark Weisbrot and Tariq Ali, *Ph* Albert Maysles, Lucas Fuica and Carlos Marcovich, *Ed* Elisa Bonora and Alexis Chavel, *M* Adam Peters.

Pentagrama Films/Good Apple Productions/New Element Productions/Muse Productions/Ixtlan-Dogwoof Pictures.
78 mins. USA. 2009. Rel: 30 July 2010. Cert. 15.

Southern Softies ★

This extremely low-budget effort proves that almost anyone can make a film these days. In this spoof documentary, director Graham Fellows also plays popular Sheffield comedian John Shuttleworth who, along with his incompetent agent Ken Worthington on camera, visits the Channel Islands in order to prove that southerners are softer than the tough northerners. The shaky black and white photography has more than a whiff of amateurism about it and the result is a rather pointless affair. GS

▶ John Shuttleworth (i.e. Graham Fellows).
▶ *Dir, Pro* and *Screenplay* Graham Fellows, *Ed* Mervyn Cloud.

Northern Pictures/Chicken Productions-Voiceprint.
80 mins. UK. 2009. Rel: 20 Nov 2009. Cert. U.

Space Chimps 2: Zartog Strikes Back ★

Considering the leaps and bounds that cartoons are taking, it's extraordinary that this meaningless sequel saw the light of day, let alone found a theatrical release. Here, we have a ruthless alien called Zartog and it's up to the simian Comet to find his inner hero. The flimsy, unimaginative plot is hardly aided by the third-rate 3D animation. Bonzo will be spinning in his grave. CB

▶ Voices of Patricia Warburton, Cheryl Hines, Laura Bailey, John Di Maggio, Patrick Breen, Jane Lynch.
▶ *Dir* John H Williams, *Pro* Williams and Jeremy Ross, *Screenplay* Robert Moreland, *Storyboard Artist* Sterling Sheehy, *Ed* Eric Lake, *M* Samuel Stewart, *Animation* Rupert Sequeira.

Prana Studios/Wonderworld Studios/Vanguard Animation-Entertainment Film Distributors.
76 mins. USA. 2010. Rel: 28 May 2010. Cert. U.

The Spell ★

This laughable low-budget British film claims that it is based on a true story about a young girl's horrific experiences when her boyfriend puts a spell on her. She (Rebecca Pitkin) then begins a long struggle in order to exorcise the demons. Owen Carey Jones' unconvincing dialogue and pedestrian direction is matched by dreadful performances. Avoid this at all costs. GS

▶ Rebecca Pitkin, Pietro Herrera, Amber Hodgkiss,

Julia Curle, Laura O'Donoughue.
▶ *Dir, Pro, Screenplay, Ed* Owen Carey Jones, *Ph* Stephen J Nelson, *Pro Des* Eileen Aldous, *M* Alan Moore.

Carey Films-Carey Films.
88 mins. UK. 2009. Rel: 2 Oct 2009. Cert. 15.

Spiderhole ★★½

Daniel Simpson's low-budget British horror takes place in a squat where four art students expect to pay no rent while partying all night long, but end up fighting for their lives instead. The story is simple but Simpson injects enough energy to make this a suitably claustrophobic experience, while the actors deliver committed performances despite their obvious lack of experience. GS

▶ Amy Noble, Emma Griffiths Malin, George Maguire, John Regan, Reuben-Henry Biggs, Moya Farrelly.
▶ *Dir* and *Screenplay* Daniel Simpson, *Pro* Patrick O'Neill, *Ph* Vinit Borrison, *Pro Des* Daithi Magner, *Ed* Johnny Megalos and Jeremy Munce, *M* Jason Cooper and Oliver Kraus.

Spiderhole Productions-Soda Pictures.
82 mins. Ireland. 2010 Rel: 29 Oct 2010. Cert. 18.

Splice ★★★★

This is an intelligent horror film in the tradition of such titles as *The Fly* where scientific experiments go wrong. Genetic engineers Clive (Adrien Brody) and Elsa (Sarah Polley) begin to regret deeply their decision to create a new hybrid with human DNA. The result is Dren

Looking-glass whore: Ashton Kutcher sleeps his way into the Hollywood Hills in David Mackenzie's *Spread*.

(Delphine Chaneac), an exotic and strangely beautiful creature of rare intelligence... The acting is excellent in this sensual and deeply atmospheric tale. GS

‣ Adrien Brody, Sarah Polley, Delphine Chaneac, David Hewlett, Brandon McGibbon, Abigail Chu, Simona Maicanesca.
‣ *Dir* Vincenzo Natali, *Pro* Steven Hoban, *Screenplay* Natali, Doug Taylor and Antoinette Terry Bryant, *Ph* Tetsuo Nagata, *Pro Des* Todd Cherniawsky, *Ed* Michele Conroy, *M* Cyrille Aufort, *Cos* Alex Kavanagh.
Gaumont/Copperheart Entertainment/Dark Castle Entertainment/Senator Entertainment Company-Optimum Releasing.
104 mins. Canada/France/USA. 2009. Rel: 23 July 2010. Cert. 15.

Splintered ★

Sophie, a virginal supermodel, has managed to coax four friends to go on a camping trip to North Wales. Of course, she has a hidden agenda – to photograph a supernatural beast – but keeps on falling asleep at inopportune moments... Few films have been so unlucky as to be cursed with such risible dialogue, illogical plotting, dire acting, poor sound and ham-fisted editing. In fact, if it weren't for the appearance of a werewolf (and an oft-sighted full moon), one would be hard-pressed to guess the genre of this amateur production. A new low for horror, then. JC-W

‣ Holly Weston, Stephen Martin Walters, Sacha Dhawan, Sadie Pickering, Jonathan Readwin, Sol Heras.
‣ *Dir* Simeon Halligan, *Pro* Rachel Richardson Jones, *Screenplay* Steve Trimingham and Matt Archer,

Ph Michael Costelloe, *Pro Des* Paul Kondras, *Ed* Tom Grimshaw and Celia Haining, *M* Richard Bodgers, *Cos* Scott Langridge.
Not a Number/Splintered Films-Kaleidoscope Home Entertainment.
85 mins. UK. 2010. Rel: 3 Sep 2010. Cert. 18.

Spread ★★★★

Nikki (Ashton Kutcher) is an attractive predator in an unfriendly, ruthless environment and his latest conquest is the attractive attorney Samantha (Anne Heche) who, in exchange for sex, invites him to share her luxurious mansion in the Hollywood Hills... Kutcher relishes a role that fits him like a glove and gives an incredible performance as the utterly egotistical and self-obsessed sex object under David Mackenzie's stylish and confident direction, turning the American Dream inside out. GS

‣ Ashton Kutcher, Anne Heche, Margarita Levieva, Sebastian Stan, Ashley Johnson, Sonia Rockwell.
‣ *Dir* David Mackenzie, *Pro* Kutcher, Jason Goldberg and Peter Morgan, *Screenplay* Jason Hall, from a story by Hall and Paul Kolsby, *Ph* Steven Poster, *Pro Des* Cabot McMullen, *Ed* Nicholas Erasmus, *M* John Swihart, *Cos* Ruth E Carter.
Barbarian Films/Katalyst Films/Oceana Media Finance-Optimum Releasing.
97 mins. USA. 2009. Rel: 1 Jan 2010. Cert. 18.

The Spy Next Door ★★

Jackie Chan has seemingly effortless charm to carry off this daft family action comedy, in which he's China's ex-CIA spy Bob Ho, who's not thrilled to be left by his single mom girlfriend (Amber Valletta) to look after her obstreperous kids (Madeline Carroll, Will Shadley, Alina Foley). While ma visits her sick father, Russian mobsters plot to control the world's oil supply. Chan and the children get involved and have to go on the run, with the initially hostile kids warming to old Jackie. It's also easy to warm to such good-natured slapstick, which will appeal to young kids. DW

▶ Jackie Chan, Amber Valletta, Madeline Carroll, Will Shadley, Alina Foley, Billy Ray Cyrus, George Lopez.
▶ *Dir* Brian Levant *Pro* Robert Simonds, *Screenplay* Jonathan Bernstein, James Greer and Gregory Poirier, based on a story by Greer and Poirier, *Ph* Dean Cundey, *Pro Des* Stephen Lineweaver, *Ed* Lawrence Jordan, *M* David Newman, *Cos* Lisa Jensen.

Relativity Media/Robert Simonds Company-Momentum Film Distributors.
94 mins. USA. 2010. Rel: 19 Mar 2010. Cert. PG.

St Trinian's 2: The Legend of Fritton's Gold ★½

The recent remake was silly but fun whereas this lazy and shambolic sequel is just plain silly. It begins like a *Pirates of the Caribbean* pastiche when the notorious swashbuckler Fritton (Rupert Everett) steals Pomfrey's (David Tennant) treasure. Now, 500 years later, Pomfrey's descendant (Tennant) believes that the gold is hidden at St Trinian's while headmistress Camilla Fritton (Everett) is determined to find it first – with her schoolgirls' help of course. The idea is not bad but the thinly scripted plot is utterly unbelievable, with a preposterous climax at the Globe Theatre. GS

▶ Rupert Everett, Colin Firth, David Tennant, Gemma Arterton, Tallulah Riley, Jodie Whittaker, Ella Smith, Celia Imrie.
▶ *Dir* and *Pro* Oliver Parker and Barnaby Thompson, *Screenplay* Piers Ashworth and Nick Moorcroft, additional material by Jamie Minoprio and Jonathan M Stern, *Ph* David Higgs, *Pro Des* Amanda McArthur, *Ed* Emma E Hickox, *M* Charlie Mole, *Cos* Rebecca Hale.

Ealing Studios/Fragile Films-Entertainment Film Distributors.
106 mins. UK. 2009. Rel: 18 Dec 2009. Cert. PG.

Starsuckers ★★★★

In his 2007 documentary *Taking Liberties* Chris Atkins adopted a tone that was far too jokey for my taste, but for this new documentary he has somewhat toned down his style. In any case, the subject matter – the appeal of so-called celebrities as fostered by the media – is more suited to his approach. Offering five segments, each a lesson about this phenomenon, the film is wide-ranging, includes a memorable interview with

publicist Max Clifford, and is biting to a degree on the subject of Live Aid. MS

▶ With Max Clifford, Robert Russell, Charlotte de Backer, Jake Halpern, Alex Simon.
▶ *Dir* and *Screenplay* Chris Atkins, *Pro* Christina Slater and Felicity Leabeater, *Ph* Chris Smith, *Ed* Nick Fenton, *M* Vince Watts.

S2S Productions/MET Film/Halidom Productions-S2S Distribution.
103 mins. UK. 2009. Rel: 30 Oct 2009. Cert. 12A.

Staten Island ★★★

There's strong language and violence in this entertaining and darkly comic thriller about residents of New York's Staten Island who try to change their lives. Ethan Hawke is a septic-tank cleaner who steals money from small-time mob boss Vincent D'Onofrio to pay for a new IVF procedure that could make his unborn child smarter. Seymour Cassel co-stars as a deaf-mute deli worker who secretly cuts up corpses for D'Onofrio but comes into some money. Hawke convinces in a very impressive turn, but he's out-acted by D'Onofrio, though it's canny old Cassel's expressive mute acting that is the making of the movie. (Original title: *Little New York*) DW

▶ Ethan Hawke, Vincent D'Onofrio, Seymour Cassel, Ian Brennan, Lynn Cohen, Michael Hogan.
▶ *Dir* and *Screenplay* James DeMonaco, *Pro* Sebastien LeMercier, *Ph* Chris Norr, *Pro Des* Stephen Beatrice, *Ed* Hervé de Luze and Christel Dewynter, *M* Frédéric Verrières, *Cos* Rebecca Hoffherr.

Europa Corporation/Open City Films/Why Not Productions-EuropaCorp.
96 mins. France/USA. 2009. Rel: 19 Mar 2010. Cert. 15.

Bob Ho, Ho, Ho: Jackie Chan gets into the PG-rated swing of things with co-star Alina Foley in *The Spy Next Door.*

Step Up 3D ★½

The third in the series, although it is filmed in 3D, is the weakest of them all. The first was fun with a star-making performance from Channing Tatum, the second was OK, but this one is simply dull and charmless. A group of New York street dancers join forces for a competition against the city's best hip hop dancers... The choreography is not bad but there is no suspense and no thrills – and it pales by comparison with the UK's *Streetdance 3D*. GS

❧ Sharni Vinson, Rick Malambri, Adam G Sevani, Alyson Stoner, Keith Stallworth.
❧ *Dir* Jon Chu, *Pro* Erik Feig, Jennifer Gibgot, Patrick Wachsberger and Adam Shankman, *Screenplay* Amy Adelson and Emily Meyer, based on characters created by Duane Adler, *Ph* Ken Seng, *Pro Des* Devorah Herbert, *Ed* Andrew Marcus, *M* Bear McCreary, *Cos* Kurt and Bart.
Touchstone Pictures/Summit Entertainment/Offspring Entertainment-Universal Pictures International.
107 mins. USA. 2010. Rel: 6 Aug 2010. Cert. 12A.

The Stepfather ★★½

In this rather pointless remake, David (Dylan Walsh), who has just brutally murdered his previous family, moves to a new town with a new identity and charms his way into divorced Susan's (Sela Ward) home. Only her elder son Michael (Penn Badgley) begins to suspect that there is something not quite right with his new stepfather... Nelson McCormick's thriller may be predictable and implausible towards the end but it is efficiently delivered. GS

❧ Dylan Walsh, Sela Ward, Penn Badgley, Amber Heard, Shirley Stringfield.
❧ *Dir* Nelson McCormick, *Pro* Greg Mooradian and Mark Morgan, *Screenplay* J S Cardone, based on an earlier screenplay by Donald Westlake, story by Westlake, Carolyn Starin and Brian Garfield, *Ph* Patrick Cady, *Pro Des* Steven J Jordan, *Ed* Eric L Beason, *M* Charlie Clouser, *Cos* Lyn Elizabeth Paolo.
Screen Gems/Maverick Films/Imprint Entertainment/Granada-Sony Pictures Entertainment.
101 mins. USA. 2009. Rel: 11 Dec 2009. Cert. 15.

Still Walking ★★★★½

Japan's Kore-Eda Hirokazu is a director who varies his approach from film to film. Here he offers a family drama self-evidently derived from Ozu's style in which everyday realism is key. A family gathering provides the setting – one undertaken each year to mark the anniversary of the death by drowning of the eldest son. It reveals generational tensions and the power of the past to influence attitudes in the present. Less moving than the best of Ozu, it is nevertheless a highly accomplished work and well worth seeking out. (Original title: *Aruitemo, Aruitemo*) MS

❧ Abe Hiroshi, Kiki Kirin, Natsukawa Yui, You, Takahashi Kazuya, Harada Yoshiro.
❧ *Dir*, *Screenplay* and *Ed* Kore-eda Hirokazu, *Pro* Kato Yoshihiro and Taguchi Hijiri, *Ph* Yamazaki Yutaka, *Pro Des* Isomi Toshihiro and Mitsumatsu Keiko, *Cos* Kurosawa Kazuko.
Engine Network, Inc./Bandai Visual Company/TCV Man Union/Cinequanon etc-New Wave Films.
114 mins. Japan. 2008. Rel: 15 Jan 2010. Cert. U.

A stroll down memory lane: a scene from Hirokazu Koreeda's warmly received *Still Walking*.

The Stoning of Soraya M. ★★★

The material here derives from the real-life Soraya being stoned to death in an Iranian village in 1986. It shows how a trumped-up charge of adultery brought this about and comparable yet more recent events underline the relevance of this film. But not all of the acting is top class and sadly the film chooses not to suggest the horror but to wallow in it. It does so in a way that will distress the very audience likely to be drawn to the film. MS

▶ Shohreh Aghdashloo, Mozhan Marnò, Jim Caviezel, Navid Negahban, Parviz Sayyad.
▶ *Dir* Cyrus Nowrasteh, *Pro* Stephen McEveety and John Shepherd, *Screenplay* Betsy Giffen Nowrasteh and Cyrus Nowrasteh, from the book by Freidoune Sahebjam, *Ph* Joel Ransom, *Pro Des* Judy Rhee, *Ed* Geoffrey Rowland and David Handman, *M* John Debney, *Cos* Jane Anderson.

Roadside Attractions/Mpower Distribution/Mpower Pictures etc-High Fliers Distribution.
114 mins. USA. 2008. Rel: 22 Oct 2010. No Cert.

Storm ★★★½

Following his impressive *Requiem* of 2006, Hans-Christian Schmid is again engaged with his subject matter here. It focuses on the difficulty of getting justice when witnesses of wartime atrocities may be endangered by speaking out. In effect it's a court drama centred on the International Criminal Tribunal at The Hague and dealing with a prosecution concerning the Serbian War in the 1990s. Some scenes are in English and are inclined to be stilted, but the film's heart is in the right place and Anamaria Marinca is quite splendid as the woman who takes the risk of agreeing to testify. MS

▶ Anamaria Marinca, Kerry Fox, Stephen Dillane, Rolf Lassgård, Drazen Kühn.
▶ *Dir* Hans-Christian Schmid, *Pro* Britta Knöller and Schmid, *Screenplay* Bernd Lange and Schmid, *Ph* Bogumil Godfrejów, *Pro Des* Christian M Goldbeck, *Ed* Hansjörg Weißbrich, *M* The Notwist, *Cos* Steffi Bruhn.

Piffl Medien/Zoo Pictures/23/5 Filmproduktion GmbH/ Zentropa etc-Soda Pictures.
103 mins. Germany/Denmark/The Netherlands/ Sweden. 2009. Rel: 26 Mar 2010. Cert. 15.

StreetDance 3D ★★★

A London dance crew aiming to win a Street Dance Championship decides to work with ballet dancers for their rehearsal space. Nichola Burley is Carly, who takes over the crew when her boyfriend walks out. She meets the ballet director (Charlotte Rampling), who offers her the space in return for mixing her passion-free students in with

War crimes: Kerry Fox and Anamaria Marinca in Hans-Christian Schmid's *Storm*.

her crew. If you like George Sampson, Diversity and Flawless, this movie showcases their awesome acts. Rampling and Eleanor Bron (camping it up as the ballet mistress) make their marks. Both Burley and Richard Winsor, the sexy ballet boy, look a shade too old but are expert and appealing. DW

▶ Charlotte Rampling, Nichola Burley, Eleanor Bron, George Sampson, Patrick Baladi, Jeremy Sheffield.
▶ *Dir* Max Giwa and Dania Pasquini, *Pro* Allan Niblo and James Richardson *Screenplay* Jane English, *Ph* Sam McCurdy, *Pro Des* Richard Bullock, *Ed* Tim Murrell, *Music Editor* Dominik Schleier, *Cos* Andre Cox.

BBC Films/Little Gaddesden Productions-Vertigo Films.
98 mins. UK. 2010. Rel: 21 May 2010. Cert. PG.

Surrogates ★★½

A moderately cerebral science fiction thriller, *Surrogates* is a not-too-distant-futuristic tale that sees pale and flabby folks living their lives remotely from the safety of their homes via hot, robotic avatars. It's like *The Sims* only for real, but when murder rears its ugly head, detective Bruce Willis is forced by events to hit the streets in his regrettably genuine body. Fairly well made and played with occasional bursts of decent action, it's an earnest throwback to the brainier sci-fi of the 1970s and, though it doesn't fire on all cylinders, it remains a worthy ride. MJ

▶ Bruce Willis, Radha Mitchell, Rosamund Pike, Boris Kodjoe, James Frances Ginty, James Cromwell, Ving Rhames.

Dir Jonathan Mostow, *Pro* Max Handelman, David Hoberman and Todd Lieberman, *Screenplay* Michael Ferris and John D Brancato, based on the graphic novel by Robert Venditti and Brett Weldele, *Ph* Oliver Wood, *Pro Des* Jeff Mann, *Ed* Kevin Stitt, *M* Richard Marvin, *Cos* April Ferry.

Touchstone Pictures/Mandeville Films/Road Rebel/Top Shelf Productions/Wintergreen Productions-Walt Disney Studios Motion Pictures.
89 mins. USA. 2009. Rel: 25 Sep 2009. Cert. 12A.

Surviving Evil ★★

This one must have given Natalie Mendoza an acute case of déjà vu; having battled subterranean 'crawlers' in *The Descent*, here she battles tree-dwelling Aswang on a Filippino island. (In a defensive touch, we're told that the one thing these hideous critters *cannot* do is go below ground!) All comparisons with *The Descent* end there, however, for *Surviving Evil* (terrible title) is just standard-issue horror fare – good-looking, efficiently made, forgettable. Playing the host of the 183rd edition of TV's *Surviving the Wilderness*, Billy Zane clearly isn't going to make it to the 184th but still gives an agreeably laid-back performance. JR

▶ Billy Zane, Christina Cole, Natalie Jackson Mendoza, Joel Torre, Louise Barnes, Colin Moss.
▶ *Dir* and *Screenplay* Terence Daw, *Pro* Anton Ernst, David Pupkewitz and Maximilian Kohll, *Ph* Mike Downie, *Pro Des* Mich Gordon, *Ed* Adam Recht, *M* Colin Baldry and Tom Kane, *Cos* Mariano Gomez.

Focus Films/Anton Ernst Entertainment/Entertainment Motion Pictures/Motion Investment Group-Kaleidoscope.
90 mins. USA/South Africa. 2009. Rel: 2 Oct 2009. Cert. 15.

SUS ★★★★

Robert Heath's urgent cinematic treatment of Barrie Keeffe's powerful play is based on a true story and takes place in a London Police Interrogation room during the Election night of 1979. Delroy (Clint Dyer), an articulate black man, is arrested yet again on SUS but this time the racist policemen claim that he has killed his pregnant wife. DS Karn (Ralph Brown) and his equally sadistic partner DC Wilby (Rafe Spall) begin a night of torture and humiliation... The acting is superb and Dyer deserves awards for his deeply moving performance. GS

▶ Ralph Brown, Clint Dyer, Anjela Lauren Smith, Rafe Spall.
▶ *Dir* Robert Heath, *Pro* Dyer, Heath, Jono Smith, Robin Mahoney and Oliver James Ledwith, *Screenplay* Barrie Keeffe, based on his own play, *Ph* Jono Smith, *Pro Des* Mark Sutherland, *Ed* Mahoney, *M* Sally Herbert, *Cos* Linda Haysman.

Mensch Films/3rd Eye Films/Thin Films Productions-Independent.
91 mins. UK. 2010. Rel: 7 May 2010. Cert. 15.

The Switch ★★★★

Kassie (Jennifer Aniston) is a single woman determined to have a baby despite her best friend Wally's (Jason Bateman) objections. She finally finds the perfect specimen – the highly intelligent and strikingly handsome Roland (Patrick Wilson)... Bateman is excellent as the neurotic man who accidentally makes a last-minute switch of the sperm, but the success of the film lies in the ingenious casting of Thomas

Able semen: Patrick Wilson (with the horny hat) is the man with the DNA. Juliette Lewis looks on, admiringly, in Josh Gordon and Will Speck's *The Switch*.

Subterranean villainy: John Travolta in murderous mood in Tony Scott's dynamic and entertaining remake of *The Taking of Pelham 123*.

Robinson as Kassie's seven-year-old son; he steals the film effortlessly. GS

▶ Jason Bateman, Jennifer Aniston, Jeff Goldblum, Patrick Wilson, Juliette Lewis, Thomas Robinson.
▶ *Dir* Josh Gordon and Will Speck, *Pro* Albert Berger and Ron Yerxa, *Screenplay* Allan Loeb, from the story *Baster* by Jeffrey Eugenides, *Ph* Jess Hall, *Pro Des* Adam Stockhausen, *Ed* John Axelrad, *M* Alex Wurman, *Cos* Kasia Walicka-Maimone.
Echo Films/Bona Fide Productions/Mandate Pictures-Lionsgate.
101 mins. USA. 2010. Rel: 1 Sep 2010. Cert. 12A.

Takers ★★½

A group of young criminals continue to enjoy the good life after a series of carefully planned bank robberies, although a dedicated police officer (Matt Dillon) is determined to nail them. This flashy heist thriller looks impressive, has a lot of energy and style, but feels hollow as the characters are so one-dimensional. Only Dillon makes an impression as the blinkered LA detective. GS

▶ Chris Brown, Idris Elba, Hayden Christensen, Matt Dillon, Michael Ealy, Jay Hernandez, Tip 'TI' Harris.
▶ *Dir* John Luessenhop, *Pro* Harris, Jason Geter and William Packer, *Screenplay* Luessenhop, Avery Duff, Peter Allen and Gabriel Casseus, *Ph* Michael Barnett, *Pro Des* Jon Gary Steele, *Ed* Armen Minasian, *M* Paul Haslinger, *Cos* Maya Lieberman.
Screen Gems/Rain Forest Films/Grand Hustle Films/Overbrook Entertainment-Sony Pictures Releasing.
107 mins. USA. 2010. Rel: 1 Oct 2010. Cert. 12A.

Takeshis' ★★

That this film – first shown at the Venice and Toronto film festivals in September 2005 – is not a total bore is evidence of Kitano Takeshi's flair for cinematic visuals. But unfortunately what in theory could have been an intriguing look at variations on a single personality (Kitano's on-screen persona, his manner off screen and the contrasted life of a lookalike with acting ambitions) gets lost in a sea of self-indulgence. MS

▶ Beat Takeshi, Kyono Kotomi, Kishimoto Kayoko, Ohsugi Ren, Terajima Susumu.
▶ *Dir* and *Screenplay* Kitano Takeshi, *Pro* Mori Masayuki and Yoshida Takio, *Ph* Yanagijima Katsumi, *Pro Des* Isoda Norihiro, *Ed* Kitano and Ota Yoshinori, *M* Nagi, *Cos* Yamamoto Yohji.
Bandai Visual/Tokyo FM/Dentsu/TV Asahi/Office Kitano-Artificial Eye.
107 mins. Japan. 2005. Rel: 12 Feb 2010. Cert. 15.

The Taking of Pelham 123
★★★★

New York; today. The Pelham is a subway train and it's 'taken' by a gang of faceless, brilliant killers who demand $10 million in return for 17 hostages. Negotiations fall to subway dispatcher Walter Garber, a man already embroiled in his own professional problems. Smart, colourful characters, the New York subway system and an audacious plan are giddy components for any thriller. Tony Scott, like an aspiring rapper with something to prove, pumps up the energy to entertaining effect, sometimes to the detriment of the plot. But this is Scott at his most cinematic,

Hardy heroine (in both senses of the word): Gemma Arterton in Stephen Frears' rude and rustic *Tamara Drewe*.

taking the brightest colours of his palette and splashing them across a spectacular canvas. JC-W

▶ Denzel Washington, John Travolta, John Turturro, Luis Guzman, Michael Rispoli, James Gandolfini.
▶ *Dir* Tony Scott, *Pro* Scott, Steve Tisch, Todd Black and Jason Blumenthal, *Screenplay* Brian Helgeland, from the novel by John Godey, *Ph* Tobias Schliesser, *Pro Des* Chris Siegers, *Ed* Chris Lebenzon, *M* Harry Gregson-Williams, *Cos* Renée Ehrlich Kalfuss.

Columbia Pictures/Metro-Goldwyn-Mayer Pictures/ Relativity Media/Scott Free (Productions)/Escape Artists-Sony Pictures Releasing.
106 mins. USA/UK. 2009. Rel: 31 July 2009. Cert. 15.

Taking Woodstock ★★★

Ang Lee's film looks back to the Woodstock music festival of 1969 through a memoir-based story about a youth from that area and his relationship with his parents. As the mother Imelda Staunton is a comic joy, and the film gains from Lee's unshowy yet flowing directorial style. Sadly, the film becomes increasingly uncertain of its aim and ends up as an overly nostalgic tribute to the age of the hippies. MS

▶ Demetri Martin, Dan Fogler, Henry Goodman, Imelda Staunton, Jonathan Groff, Eugene Levy, Emile Hirsch, Jeffrey Dean Morgan, Liev Schreiber.
▶ *Dir* Ang Lee, *Pro* James Schamus, Lee and Celia Costas, *Screenplay* Schamus, from the book by Eliot Tiber with Tom Monte, *Ph* Éric Gautier, *Pro Des* David Gropman, *Ed* Tim Squyres,

M Danny Elfman, *Cos* Joseph G Aulisi.

Focus Features/Twins Financing LLC-Universal Pictures International.
120 mins. USA. 2009. Rel: 13 Nov 2009. Cert. 15.

Tales from the Golden Age ★★★½

Romania's Cristian Mungiu, famed for his harsh drama *4 Months, 3 Weeks, 2 Days*, now offers a lighter portmanteau piece by himself and others which looks humorously but by no means uncritically at life in his country when Ceausescu was in charge. The first two of the five tales (none ascribed to a specific director) work well, but the rest of this long film, which also includes a black farce reminiscent of Alan Bennett's *A Private Function* (1984), is much less sure-footed. Interesting but uneven. (Original title: *Amintiri din epoca de aur*) MS

▶ Alexandru Potocean, Avram Birau, Ion Sapdaru, Radu Iacoban, Diana Cavaliotti.
▶ *Dir* Cristian Mungiu, Ioana Uricaru, Hanno Höfer, Razvan Marculescu and Constantin Popescu, *Pro* Oleg Mutu and Mungiu, *Screenplay* Mungiu, *Ph* Mutu, Alex Sterian and Liviu Marghidan, *Art Dir* Cezara Armasu, Mihaela Poenaru, Dana Istrate and Simona Paduretu, *Ed* Dana Bunescu, Theodora Penciu and Uricaru, *M* Höfer and Laco Jimi, *Cos* Istarte, Brandusa Ioan, Luminita Mihai and Ana Ioneci.

Mobra Films/Centrului National al Cinematografiei etc-Trinity Filmed Entertainment.
131 mins. Romania. 2009. Rel: 30 Oct 2009. Cert. 12A.

Tamara Drewe ★★★½

Posy Simmonds' graphic book is the basis of this comedy which, parodically echoing the works of Thomas Hardy, makes fun of a modern-day writers' community in Dorset. There's lovely playing by Tamsin Greig and Bill Camp in particular, but the tone fluctuates uneasily in the second half and perhaps too many of the characters are dislikeable. It is, however, a highly original work not without high spots. MS

▶ Gemma Arterton, Roger Allam, Bill Camp, Dominic Cooper, Luke Evans, Tamsin Greig.
▶ *Dir* Stephen Frears, *Pro* Alison Owen, Paul Trijbits and Tracey Seaward, *Screenplay* Moira Buffini, based on the graphic novel by Posy Simmonds, *Ph* Ben Davis, *Pro Des* Alan MacDonald, *Ed* Mick Audsley, *M* Alexandre Desplat, *Cos* Consolata Boyle.
WestEnd Films/BBC Films/UK Film Council/Ruby Films/ Notting Hill Films etc-Momentum Pictures.
111 mins. UK. 2010. Rel: 10 Sep 2010. Cert. 15.

Tetro ★★★

Set in Buenos Aires and presented as a family drama about two brothers, sons of a famous father, and about the possibility of these two becoming reconciled, this finds Francis Ford Coppola partially recovering from the disaster of *Youth Without Youth*. But while the first half grips strongly the second becomes increasingly pretentious and the finale is ludicrous. With most of the film shot in black and white 'Scope it's visually very striking. MS

▶ Vincent Gallo, Alden Ehrenreich, Maribel Verdú, Carmen Maura, Klaus Maria Brandauer.
▶ *Dir*, *Pro* and *Screenplay* Francis Ford Coppola, *Ph* Mihai Malaimare Jr, *Pro Des* Sebastian Orgambide, *Ed* Walter Murch, *M* Osvaldo Golijov, *Cos* Cecilia Monti.
American Zoetrope etc-Soda Pictures.
127 mins. Argentina/Italy/Spain/USA. 2009. Rel: 25 June 2010. Cert. 15.

Thirst ★★½

This horror movie from the stylish Korean film-maker Park Chan-wook shared the Jury Prize at the 2009 Cannes Film Festival and it does promise novelty by featuring a priest who, infected by bad blood, finds that he has become a vampire. Where *Let The Right One In* won me over, this film seems so completely over the top that it suggests a parody of itself. Horror fans may, of course, think differently. (Original title: *Bakjwi*) MS

▶ Song Kang-ho, Kim Ok-bin, Kim Hae-sook, Shin Ha-kyun, Park In-hwan.
▶ *Dir* Park Chan-wook, *Pro* Park and Ahn So-hyun,

Screenplay Park and Chung Seo-kyung, inspired by Émile Zola's *Thérèse Raquin*, *Ph* Chung Chung-hoon, *Art Dir* Ryu Sung-hee, *Ed* Kim Sang-beom and Kim Jae-beom, *M* Jo Yeong-uk, *Cos* Jo Sang-gyeong.
CJ Entertainment/Universal Pictures/Moho Films etc-Metrodome Distribution.
134 mins. Republic of Korea/USA. 2009. Rel: 16 Oct 2009. Cert. 18.

31 North 62 East ★

In this low-budget British conspiracy thriller, which uses every cliché of the genre, a female SAS Captain (Heather Peace) is the only survivor after an attack on her unit in Afghanistan. She is believed to be dead but returns to the UK two months later looking for those responsible for sacrificing her unit for political reasons. The dialogue never rings true and the acting is variable. John Rhys-Davies' OTT performance as the Prime Minister belongs to a different film altogether. GS

▶ Heather Peace, Marina Sirtis, John Rhys-Davies, Craig Fairbrass, Nathalia Ramos, Ian Lavender.
▶ *Dir*, *Pro* and *Ed* Tristan Loraine, *Screenplay* Tristan Loraine and Leofwine Loraine , *Ph* Sue Gibson, *Pro Des* Eileen Kelly, *M* Paul Garbutt, David Leo Kemp and Moritz Schmittat, *Cos* Kate Mottershead etc.
31 N 62 E/Fact Not Fiction Films-DFT Enterprises.
99 mins. UK. 2009. Rel: 18 Sep 2009. Cert. 15.

35 Shots of Rum ★★★½

Paris today in all its ethnic variety is the setting for this interesting but arguably over-praised feature from Claire Denis. She doesn't always identify the characters and their relationships as well as one would wish but there's a clear central focus on a father and daughter, underlining the film's Ozu-like intentions. Lack of clarity and

Thirst degree murder: Kang-ho Song as the priest-turned-vampire in Park Chan-wook's *Thirst*.

explanation may sometimes irritate but at its best this film is very fine. MS

▶ Alex Descas, Mati Diop, Nicole Dogué, Grégoire Colin, Ingrid Caven.
▶ *Dir* Claire Denis, *Pro* Bruno Pesery, Karl Baumgartner, Christoph Friedel and Claudia Steffen, *Screenplay* Denis and Jean-Pol Fargeau, *Ph* Agnès Godard, *Art Dir* Arnaud de Moléron, *Ed* Guy Lecorne, *M* Tindersticks, *Cos* Judy Shrewsbury.

Soudaine Compagnie/ARTE France Cinéma/Pandora Film Produktion etc-New Wave Films.
101 mins. France/Germany. 2008. Rel: 10 July 2009. Cert. 12A.

This Prison Where I Live ★★★★

Underrated by some, this documentary sees film-maker Rex Bloomstein accompanying German comic Michael Mittermeier to Burma, making contacts that will help to make this a revealing film about the fate of imprisoned Burmese anti-authoritarian comedian Zarganar. It's true that the plan was thwarted through people's fears of reprisals preventing them from speaking, but even so this film fully conveys the state of things in Burma and Zarganar emerges as an admirably brave figure. MS

▶ With Maung Thura aka 'Zarganar', Michael Mittermeier, Rex Bloomstein.
▶ *Dir* Rex Bloomstein, *Pro* Bloomstein and Astrid Eckstein, *Ph* Alexander Boboschewski, *Ed* Paul Binns.

Rex Entertainment/Yo Man Media/Cinema for Peace etc-Dogwoof Pictures.
90 mins. UK/Germany. 2010. Rel: 29 Oct 2010. No Cert.

The Thorn in the Heart ★★★½

This is less a film to appeal to the public than a home movie from Michel Gondry. He uses documentary techniques to look at members of his family living in France. In particular there's his aunt Suzette, a retired teacher, and

Temporal shift: Elia Suleiman in his episodic and often confusing The Time That Remains.

her gay son Jean-Yves. There's warmth here but it's also unsettling when it comes to some of its disclosures. It is though a genuine oddity. (Original title *L'épine dans le coeur*) MS

▶ With Michel Gondry, Suzette Gondry, Jean-Yves Gondry.
▶ *Dir* and *Screenplay* Michel Gondry, *Pro* Georges Bermann, *Ph* Jean-Louis Bompoint, *Ed* Marie-Charlotte Moreau.

Partizan Films-Soda Pictures.
86 mins. France. 2009. Rel: 10 Dec 2010. Cert. PG.

Three Miles North of Molkom ★★★

The location in question is in Scandinavia and this documentary was filmed at the No Minds Festival in Ängsbacka in 2007. This is a tree-hugging venue where visitors go in order to get in touch with their inner selves. Despite some initial scepticism, the film seems to fall for the mumbo jumbo. It's certainly different and those who can't wait to pack their bags for Ängsbacka may positively love it. MS

▶ With Siddharta, Peter, Nick, Marit, Mervi, Arjuna Ardagh, Regina Lund.
▶ *Dir*, *Pro* and *Ed* Robert Cannan and Corinna Villari-McFarlane, *Ph* Joseph Russell.

Third Eye Film Productions/Goalpost Film etc-Metrodome Distribution.
107 mins. UK. 2009. Rel: 18 Sep 2009. Cert. 15.

The Time That Remains ★★½

Central to the vision here of writer/director Elia Suleiman from Nazareth is his own family's history from 1948 onwards. Certain passages in the film are masterly but, since the family were 'Israeli Arabs' (those Palestinians living as a minority in their own homeland), politics play a vital role. Those without detailed knowledge of the wider scene may well query Suleiman's assertion that his film is one you don't need to understand but just 'feel'. Episodic, often confusing and featuring contrived humorous scenes that clash with the harsher reality, the film, despite some great moments, is frustrating. (Original title: *Le Temps qu'il reste*) MS

▶ Saleh Bakri, Samar Qudha Tanus, Shafika Bajjali, Elia Suleiman.
▶ *Dir* and *Screenplay* Elia Suleiman, *Pro* Michaël Gentile and Suleiman, *Ph* Marc-André Batigne, *Pro Des* Sharif Waked, *Ed* Véronique Lange, *Cos* Judy Shrewsbury.

The Film/Nazira Films/Artémis Films/BIM Distribuzione/France 3 Cinéma/RTBF (Télévision Belge) etc-New Wave Films.
110 mins. France/Belgium/Italy/United Arab Emirates/UK. 2009. Rel: 28 May 2010. Cert. 15.

The Time Traveler's Wife ★★½

A librarian with a rare genetic disorder finds himself slipping back and forth through time as he attempts to pin down a meaningful relationship… So eager is this adaptation of Audrey Niffenegger's literary phenomenon to cut to the chase that the audience is left gasping in its slipstream. Just minutes in, the time traveller – Henry DeTamble – explains his predicament, depriving us of much of the fun of the premise. Even so, it's hard to follow the temporal shifts, while the episodic nature of the film works against the romantic interest. JC-W

‣ Rachel McAdams, Eric Bana, Arliss Howard, Ron Livingston, Jane McLean, Stephen Tobolowsky.
‣ *Dir* Robert Schwentke, *Pro* Dede Gardner and Nick Wechsler, *Screenplay* Bruce Joel Rubin, from the novel by Audrey Niffenegger, *Ph* Florian Ballhaus, *Pro Des* Jon Hutman, *Ed* Thom Noble, *M* Mychael Danna, *Cos* Julie Weiss.

New Line Cinema/Nick Wechsler/Plan B Entertainment-Entertainment Film Distributors.
107 mins. USA. 2009. Rel: 14 Aug 2009. Cert. 12A.

Tinker Bell and the Great Fairy Rescue ★★★½

This is a sweet animation from Disney about Tinker Bell long before she encountered Peter Pan. She is very curious and wants to explore pastures new and, despite warnings from her fellow fairies, she befriends a little girl. In the meantime her friends believe that her life is in danger and prepare a daring mission to rescue her. The story is fun and the sparkling animation is imaginative and colourful. GS

‣ Voices of Michael Sheen, Mae Whitman, Lucy Liu, Pamela Adlon, Kristin Chenoweth, Faith Prince.
‣ *Dir* Bradley Raymond, *Pro* Helen Kalafatic and Margot Pipkin, *Screenplay* Bob Hilgenberg, Paul German, Joe Ansolabehere and Rob Muir, based on a story by Jeffrey M Howard and Bradley Raymond, *Pro Des* Fred Warter, *Ed* Mark W Rosenbaum, Tony Mizgalski, Kevin Locarro and Lisa Linder, *Music Orchestrator* David Slonaker.

DisneyToon Studios-Walt Disney Studios Motion Pictures.
76 mins. USA. 2010. Rel: 13 Aug 2010. Cert. U.

Tony ★★★

With its scary portrait of everyday, mundane evil, you'll find this broodingly wicked serial killer flick haunting your nightmares and footsteps. Peter Ferdinando does eerily well as one of those creepy loner types in the best British chiller traditions. A man with a dodgy moustache and mad keen on action movies, he welcomes all manner of strangers into his seedy East London council flat, an offer that's a mixed blessing for his guests. Despite its obvious low budget, first-time feature director Gerard Johnson's horror thriller is remarkably polished, often terrifying and a gripping watch at just an hour and a quarter. DW

Quantum leap: Rachel McAdams swats up on quantum physics in Robert Schwentke's episodic *The Time Traveler's Wife*.

Mission in Venice: Angelina Jolie in Florian Henckel von Donnersmarck's preposterous *The Tourist*.

▶ Peter Ferdinando, Frank Boyce, Lorenzo Camporese, Cyrus Desir, Lucy Flack.
▶ *Dir* and *Screenplay* Gerard Johnson, *Pro* Dan McCulloch, *Ph* David Higgs, *Pro Des* Naomi Reed, *Ed* Ian Davies, *M* Matt Johnson and The The, *Cos* Suzie Harman.

Abbott Vision/Chump Films/Dan McCulloch Productions-Revolver Entertainment. 76 mins. UK. 2009. Rel: 5 Feb 2010. Cert. 18.

Tooth Fairy ★

Don't you hate it when beefy action stars play against type in family films to get cheap laughs? They seem to be saying, "Look at me! I'm in a dress! Isn't this hilarious?" Well, no. It isn't. We don't want to laugh at them. We want to laugh with them as they kill bad guys. Sadly, this is not a violent film. Years ago Arnold Schwarzenegger announced he was going to play the Tooth Fairy in a family film. But here we have Dwayne 'The Rock' Johnson. The horror. MJ

▶ Dwayne 'The Rock' Johnson, Ashley Judd, Julie Andrews, Stephen Merchant, Brandon T Jackson.
▶ *Dir* Michael Lembello, *Pro* Jason Blum, Mark Ciardi and Gordon Gray, *Screenplay* Lowell Ganz, Babaloo Mandel, Randy Mayem Singer, Jeffrey Ventimilia and Joshua Sternin, from a story by Jim Piddock, *Ph* David Tattersall, *Pro Des* Marcia Hinds, *Ed* David Finfer, *M* George S Clinton, *Cos* Angus Strathie.

Twentieth Century Fox/Walden Media/Mayhem Pictures/ Blumhouse/Foxvan Productions-20th Century Fox. 101 mins. USA. 2010. Rel: 28 May 2010. Cert. PG.

The Tourist ★★★

This Hitchcockian thriller is an unexpected movie to come from the director of that serious award winner *The Lives of Others*. Absolutely derided by some critics, it strikes me as at least passable entertainment for a wet evening and there's certainly good location shooting in Paris and Venice. It's preposterous but fun, even if it does suffer from Johnny Depp and Angelina Jolie floundering as they vainly seek to find the right style in which to play it. MS

▶ Angelina Jolie, Johnny Depp, Paul Bettany, Timothy Dalton, Steven Berkoff, Rufus Sewell.
▶ *Dir* Florian Henckel von Donnersmarck, *Pro* Graham King, Tim Headington, Roger Birnbaum, Gary Barber and Jonathan Glickman, *Screenplay* Donnersmarck, Christopher McQuarrie and Julian Fellowes, based on the motion picture *Anthony Zimmer* by Jérôme Salle, *Ph* John Seale, *Pro Des* Jon Hutman, *Ed* Joe Hutshing and Patricia Rommel, *M* James Newton Howard, *Cos* Colleen Atwood.

GK Films/Columbia Pictures/Spyglass Entertainment/ Birnbaum/Barber etc-Optimum Releasing. 103 mins. USA/France. 2010. Rel: 10 Dec 2010. Cert. 12A.

The Town ★★★½

Ben Affleck is director and star of this Boston-set tale of two friends, one of whom (Affleck) tries to put his criminal past behind him when he falls for a bank manager (Rebecca Hall) taken hostage during a robbery. There's strong support from the late Pete Postlethwaite and as a blend of thriller and love story *The Town* works. Even so, it's less memorable than Affleck's directorial debut *Gone Baby Gone*, which had the same setting. MS

▶ Blake Lively, Ben Affleck, Rebecca Hall, Jon Hamm, Jeremy Renner, Pete Postlethwaite, Chris Cooper.
▶ *Dir* Ben Affleck, *Pro* Graham King and Basil Iwanyk, *Screenplay* Peter Craig, Affleck and Aaron Stockard, from the novel *Prince of Thieves* by Chuck Hogan, *Ph* Robert Elswit, *Pro Des* Sharon Seymour, *Ed* Dylan Tichenor, *M* Harry Gregson-Williams and David Buckley, *Cos* Susan Matheson.

Warner Bros. Pictures/Legendary Pictures/GK Films/ Thunder Road Film-Warner Bros.
125 mins. USA. 2010. Rel: 24 Sep 2010. Cert. 15.

A Town Called Panic ★★★½

This affectionate animated feature about the adventures of such characters as Cowboy, Indian and Horse (the latter by far the most intelligent) reminds one of the love that Nick Park displays for Wallace and Gromit. Belgian animators Stéphane Aubier and Vincent Patar previously featured these characters in a TV series and one feels that the attempt to provide a feature-length plot for them is less than wholly successful. But while the first half is much more amusing than the second, the film when at its best is a delight. (Original title: *Panique au village*) MS

▶ With the voices of Stéphane Aubier, Jeanne Balibar, Vincent Patar, Bruce Ellison.
▶ *Dir* and *Screenplay* Stéphane Aubier and Vincent Patar, *Pro* Philippe Kauffmann and Vincent Tavier, *Ph* Jan Vandenbussche, *Ed* Anne-Laure Guégan, *Animation* Steven De Beul etc.

La Parti Production/Melusine Productions/Les Films du Grognon/Beast Productions etc-Optimum Releasing.
77 mins Belgium/France/Luxembourg. 2009.
Rel: 8 Oct 2010. Cert. PG.

Toy Story 3 ★★★★½

The original concept of *Toy Story* was so ingenious that it easily supported a worthy sequel. Here, Pixar have managed to close the book with a third film so good that you'd be perfectly happy for the company to risk another. The joy of the latest instalment is that the animation is even better, the story as strong, the wisecracks as funny and the new characters – an avuncular and unscrupulous bear, a menacing baby doll and a spectacularly vain Ken – as rich as any of our old friends. JC-W

▶ Voices of Tom Hanks, Tim Allen, Joan Cusack, Ned Beatty, Michael Keaton, Whoopi Goldberg, Timothy Dalton, Wallace Shawn, John Ratzenberger, Don Rickles, Bonnie Hunt.
▶ *Dir* Lee Unkrich, *Pro* Darla K Anderson, *Screenplay*

Civic liberties: Ben Affleck in his own gripping, heart-stopping *The Town*.

Michael Arndt, from a story by Unkrich, John Lasseter and Andrew Stanton, *Pro Des* Bob Pauley, *Ed* Unkrich and Ken Schretzmann, *M* Randy Newman.

Pixar Animation Studios/Walt Disney Pictures-Walt Disney Studios.
103 mins. USA. 2010. Rel: 19 July 2010. Cert. U

Treeless Mountain ★★★

The Korean film-maker So Yong Kim turns to her own childhood to tell a story seen through the eyes of a six-year-old child and her even younger sister. While their mother seeks their absconding father, they live with an aunt and are young enough to believe the tale that their father will return when their piggy bank is full. The child players are admirably natural but the style – much hand-held camera and big close-ups – is unhelpful. Comparisons with Ozu are evoked but do not help this film, despite its patent sincerity. (Original title: *Min-dung-san*) MS

▶ Kim Hee-yeon, Kim Song-hee, Kim Mi-hyang, Lee Soo-ah, Park Boon-tak.
▶ *Dir* and *Screenplay* So Yong Kim, *Pro* Bradley Rust

Kids play?: Ken and Barbie click in *Toy Story 3*, the highest-grossing cartoon of all time.

Gray, Kim, Ben Howe and others, *Ph* Anne Misawa, *Art Dir* Kim Se-hee, *Ed* Kim and Gray.

Soandbrad/Parts and Labor/Strange Loop
Entertainment-Soda Pictures.
89 mins. USA/Republic of Korea. 2008. Rel: 8 Jan 2010.
Cert. PG.

Triangle ★★★★

Christopher Smith's stylish thriller boasts a strong premise, with some clever Greek mythology touches, and benefits from Melissa George's committed performance. She plays Jess, a distraught young woman who joins a group of friends for a voyage on a yacht, but whose nightmares become reality when they are hit by a storm and forced to board a passing ocean liner named Aeolus. The ship seems abandoned but suddenly events take an unexpected turn... Smith's intriguing film is strong on atmosphere and curiously its repetitiveness works in its favour. GS

❧ Melissa George, Joshua McIvor, Jack Taylor, Michael Dorman, Henry Nixon.
❧ *Dir* and *Screenplay* Christopher Smith, *Pro* Julie Baines, Chris Brown and Jason Newmark, *Ph* Robert Humphreys, *Pro Des* Melinda Doring, *Ed* Stuart Gazzaro, *M* Christian Henson, *Cos* Steven Noble.

Icon Entertainment International/Framestore/UK Film
Council/Pacific Film & TV Commission/Dan Films/
Pictures in Paradise/Triangle Films-Icon Film Distributors.
99 mins. UK/Australia. 2009. Rel: 16 Oct 2009. Cert. 15.

Tricks ★★

On paper this Polish film sounds promising: a young boy living with his mother and older sister seeks to connect with a man seen at the local railway station who is his absentee father. Unfortunately, there's simply too little detail and background to spark the appropriate sense of involvement. While the ending is rather obscure and dream-like, most of the film is naturalistic but dull. (Original title: *Sztuczki*) MS

❧ Damian Ul, Ewelina Walendziak, Tomasz

Sapryk, Joanna Liszowska, Iwona Fornalczyk.
❧ *Dir*, *Pro* and *Screenplay* Andrzej Jakimowski, *Ph* Adam Bajerski, *Art Dir* Ewa Jakimowska, *Ed* Cezary Grzesiuk, *M* Tomasz Gassowski, *Cos* Aleksandra Staszko.

Telewizja Polska S.A./Canal+/Opus Film etc-New
Wave Films.
96 mins. Poland. 2007. Rel: 4 Sep 2009. Cert. 12A.

Triomf ★½

It is 1994 in South Africa, five days before the first general democratic election. The action takes place in Triomf, the poor white suburb of Johannesburg. The Benades are not your average white trash family; Lambert, the slow-witted and epileptic son, will soon be 21 and his uncle is arranging a woman for him as a gift. In the meantime Lambert has sex with his mother while re-enacting scenes from *Star Wars*... Michael Raeburn's deeply unpleasant and clichéd film tries hard to shock. But his unimaginative direction lacks the necessary pace to make it work while his actors never truly convince. GS

❧ Pam Andrews, Obed Baloi, Vanessa Cooke, Paul Lückhoff, Lionel Newton.
❧ *Dir* Michael Raeburn, *Pro* Raeburn, Lyndon Plant and Natalie Stange, *Screenplay* Raeburn and Malcolm Kohll, *Ph* Jamie Ramsay, *Pro Des* Tiaan van Tonder, *Ed* Marie Quinton, *M* Philip Miller.

Focus Films/GH Films/Giraffe Creations/Red Pill
Productions-Contemporary.
118 mins. South Africa/France/UK. 2008. Rel: 14 May
2010. No Cert.

TRON: Legacy ★★

When *TRON* was released in 1982, it threw open the doors to a whole new cinematic technology. Twenty-eight years later the sequel arrives in the wake of *Avatar* and feels like a step backwards. Its one ace card – the transformation of a 60-year-old Jeff Bridges into a younger version of himself – uses a technique deployed with greater finesse in *The Curious Case of Benjamin Button*. There is an engagingly camp cameo from Michael Sheen (channelling everybody from Bowie and Chaplin to Tony Blair) and a terrific score, but little else to qualify this as the event movie it aspires to be. JC-W

❧ Jeff Bridges, Garrett Hedlund, Olivia Wilde, Bruce Boxleitner, James Frain, Michael Sheen, Cillian Murphy.
❧ *Dir* Joseph Kosinski, *Pro* Sean Bailey, Jeffrey Silver and Steven Lisberger, *Screenplay* Edward Kitsis and Adam Horowitz, *Ph* Claudio Miranda, *Pro Des* Darren Gilford, *Ed* James Haygood, *M* Daft Punk, *Cos* Michael Wilkinson.

Walt Disney/LivePlanet/Sean Bailey Productions-Walt
Disney Pictures.
125 mins. USA. 2010. Rel: 17 Dec 2010. Cert PG.

Garrett Hedlund and Olivia Wilde show off their cyber threads in Joseph Kosinski's disappointing *TRON: Legacy*.

A steppe in time: Askhat Kuchencherekov in Sergei Dvortsevoy's Kazakh masterpiece *Tulpan*.

True Legend 3D ★★★★

Yuen Woo Ping's superb adventure tells the true story of Su Can, whose ambition was to create a martial arts school and live happily ever after with his wife and son. But things take an unexpected turn when his evil brother-in-law seeks revenge for his father's death... This is a striking film with some terrifically well choreographed sequences. The 3D is used only in a couple of sequences; they look great, but finally this excellent film works perfectly well without the 3D. (Original title: *Su qi-er*) GS

▶ Vincent Zhao, Michelle Yeoh, Guoh Xiaodong, Zhou Xun, Andy On, Jay Chou, David Carradine.
▶ *Dir* Yuen Woo Ping, *Pro* William Kong and Zhenyan Zhang, *Screenplay* Chi Long To, *Ph* Zhao Xiaoding, *Pro Des* Huo Tingxiao, *Ed* Wenders Li, *M* Shigeru Umebayashi, *Cos* Chung Man Yee.
EDKO Film/Focus Features/Shanghai Film Group etc-EDKO Films.
115 mins. China. 2010. Rel: 24 Sep 2010. Cert. 15.

Tulpan ★★★★

Despite humorous aspects this is not really a comedy, as some critics have suggested, but a look at what could be a dying lifestyle. Set in the Steppes of Kazakhstan, it tells of a youngster wooing the reluctant girl of the title, since only as a married man can he expect to be given land for himself. Sheep feature prominently and a detailed scene of a lamb giving birth is one of the most remarkable and haunting scenes in recent cinema. The drama lies in whether or not the sincere youth will stay or opt for life in the city

instead. Audiences who loved *The Story of the Weeping Camel* should certainly seek this out. MS

▶ Askhat Kuchinchirekov, Samal Yeslyamova, Ondasyn Besikbasov, Bereke Turganbayev.
▶ *Dir* Sergey Dvortsevoy, *Pro* Karl Baumgartner, Valerie Fischer, Gulnara Sarsenova and others, *Screenplay* Dvortsevoy and Gennady Ostrovski, *Ph* Jola Dylewska, *Pro Des* Roger Martin, *Ed* Isabel Meier, Petar Markovic and Dvortsevoy, *Cos* Gaziza Korshiyeva.
Pandora Films/Cobra Film AG/Eurasia Film/Slovo Studios etc-New Wave Films.
103 mins. Germany/Kazakhstan/Russia (Republic)/ Poland/Italy/Switzerland. 2008. Rel: 13 Nov 2009. Cert. 12A.

2012 ★★★½

Roland Emmerich has inflicted all sorts of carnage on our planet, from alien to ecological sources. Now it's the turn of the sun to threaten the world as freak solar eruptions turn the globe into a microwave oven, destabilising its very crust. As various caricatures jump through more and more ludicrous hoops, the audience can but sigh, sit back and marvel at the CGI wizardry. It's quite a show, especially if one relishes the detailed destruction of our earth and yet another variation on the demise of the White House. JC-W

▶ John Cusack, Amanda Peet, Chiwetel Ejiofor, Oliver Platt, Thandie Newton, Woody Harrelson, Danny Glover.
▶ *Dir* Roland Emmerich, *Pro* Emmerich, Larry J Franco and Harald Kloser, *Screenplay* Emmerich

New flats for old: a scene from Zhang Ke Jia's *24 City*.

and Kloser, *Ph* Dean Semler, *Pro Des* Barry Chusid, *Ed* David Brenner and Peter S Elliot, *M* Kloser and Thomas Wander, *Cos* Shay Cunliffe.

Columbia Pictures/Centropolis/The Bridge Studios/ Farewell Productions/The Mark Gordon Company-Sony Pictures Releasing.
158 mins. USA/Canada. 2009. Rel: 13 Nov 2009. Cert. 12A.

22 Bullets ★★★

This drama of the Marseilles underworld draws on a real-life figure, a man left for dead in a parking lot in 1977 who survived wounds from 22 bullets. Around this a fictional tale has been built, showing how this man seeks to escape from his former criminal identity to take on a new life. The director is the actor Richard Berry but he misses out on subtlety and goes instead for an emphasis on violence and unpersuasive sentimentality. On that level it's competent, but potentially the story offered so much more. (Original title: *L'Immortel*) MS

➤ Jean Réno, Kad Merad, Jean-Pierre Darroussin, Marina Foïs, Richard Berry.
➤ *Dir* Richard Berry, *Pro* Pierre-Ange le Pogam, *Screenplay* Berry, Matthieu Delaporte and Alexandre de la Patellière, from the novel *L'Immortel* by Franz-Olivier Giesbert, *Ph* Thomas Hardmeier, *Art Dir* Philippe Chiffre, *Ed* Camille Delamarre, *M* Klaus Badelt, *Cos* Carine Sarfati.

Europacorp/TF1 Films etc-Anchor Bay Entertainment UK.
117 mins. France. 2010. Rel: 3 Sep 2010. Cert. 18.

24 City ★★★

Superb photography and a great cinematic eye make this film by Jia Zhangke memorable. However, his aim would seem to be to create an authentic picture of Chengdu, a Chinese city dominated by its state-owned factory, now undergoing changes. Consequently, the use of four actors in what appears to be a documentary undermines our confidence in a film which in any case is overlong. (Original title: *Ershisi cheng ji*) MS

➤ Joan Chen, Lü Liping, Zhao Tao, Chen Jianbin.
➤ *Dir* Jia Zhangke, *Pro* Jia, Ichiyama Shozo and Wang Hong, *Screenplay* Jia and Zhai Yongming, *Ph* Yu Likwai and Wang Yu, *Art Dir* Liu Qiang, *Ed* Li Haiyang, *M* Yoshhiro Hanno and Lim Giong, *Cos* Zhao Tong.

Xstream Pictures/Shanghai Film Group Corporation etc-New Wave Films.
112 mins. Hong Kong/People's Republic of China/Japan. 2008. Rel: 22 Apr 2010. Cert. U.

The Twilight Saga: Eclipse ★½

The best thing that can be said about the *Twilight* films is that each new one comes with a different director. Even so, this faithful bridge from *New Moon* to *Breaking Dawn* is as machine-tooled, anodyne and plodding as any teenage pap on daytime TV – and this from the British wunderkind who brought us the daring and provocative *Hard Candy*. Kristen Stewart reduces teenage angst to emotional anaemia, while RPattz himself has little to do but polish his American accent. So the most exciting bit must be when Taylor Lautner takes his shirt off, girls. JC-W

▶ Kristen Stewart, Robert Pattinson, Taylor Lautner, Billy Burke, Peter Facinelli, Michael Sheen, Dakota Fanning, Anna Kendrick, Jamie Campbell Bower.
▶ *Dir* David Slade, *Pro* Wyck Godfrey and Karen Rosenfelt, *Screenplay* Melissa Rosenberg, *Ph* Javier Aguirresarobe, *Pro Des* Paul D Austerberry, *Ed* Art Jones, Nancy Richardson, *M* Howard Shore, *Cos* Tish Monaghan.

Summit Entertainment/Temple Hill Entertainment/ Maverick Films-E1 Films.
123 mins. USA. 2010. Rel: 9 July 2010. Cert 12A.

The Twilight Saga: New Moon ★★½

No longer content to play second fiddle to pale British actor Robert Pattinson, a.k.a. tortured blood-sucker Edward Cullen, tanned, toned boy toy Taylor Lautner seizes his share of the limelight in this slow second chapter of *The Twilight Saga*, basically a bridge between events we don't care much about and their long-overdue conclusion. With Edward largely absent from the movie in a bid to ensure the safety of his beloved Bella (as played by the utterly miserable Kristen Stewart), shirtless werewolf Jacob comes sniffing around in search of romance. And that's basically it, spread impossibly thin over two mind-numbing hours. MJ

▶ Kristen Stewart, Taylor Lautner, Robert Pattinson , Billy Burke, Ashley Greene, Anna Kendrick, Jamie Campbell Bower, Michael Sheen.
▶ *Dir* Chris Weitz, *Pro* Wyck Godfrey, *Screenplay* Melissa Rosenberg, from the novel *New Moon* by Stephenie Meyer, *Ph* Javier Aguirresarobe, *Pro Des* David Brisbin, *Ed* Peter Lambert, *M* Alexandre Desplat, *Cos* Tish Monaghan.

Imprint Entertainment/Summit Entertainment/ Sunswept Entertainment/Temple Hill Entertainment-E1 Entertainment.
130 mins. USA. 2009. Rel: 20 Nov 2009. Cert. 12A.

The Ugly Truth ★½

The Ugly Truth is a public access TV programme presented by the ultimate alpha male chauvinist pig (Gerard Butler). When the latter is hired to spice up a magazine show run by the righteous Abby Richter (Katherine Heigl), all sorts of ordure hits the fan… This witless farce would like to think it's *When Harry Met Sally* re-imagined by Judd Apatow. The hideous reality, though, is that it's a below-par sitcom with a tragic sense of its own prurience. JC-W

▶ Katherine Heigl, Gerard Butler, Bree Turner, Eric Winter, Nick Searcy.

▶ *Dir* Robert Luketic, *Pro* Kimberley di Bonaventura, Gary Lucchesi, Kirsten Smith, Deborah Jelin Newmyer, Steven Reuther and Tom Rosenberg, *Screenplay* Nicole Eastman, Karen McCullah Lutz and Kirsten Smith, from a story by Eastman, *Ph* Russell Carpenter, *Pro Des* Missy Stewart, *Ed* Lisa Zeno Churgin, *M* Aaron Zigman, *Cos* Betsy Heimann.

Lakeshore Entertainment/Relativity Media-Sony Pictures Releasing.
96 mins. USA. 2009. Rel: 5 Aug 2009. Cert. 15.

Uncle Boonmee Who Can Recall His Past Lives ★★½

Praised mightily by some and winner of the Palme d'Or at Cannes, this Thai film is very atmospheric but its impenetrable narrative and dreamlike style offer no explanations. It may well endorse the director's comment that he believes in the transmigration of souls between humans, plants, animals and ghosts, all of which feature here. But with no insight given I suspect that many people will ultimately find this film, despite its integrity, as boring as I did. (Original title: *Lung Boonmee Raluek Chat*) MS

▶ Thanapat Saisaymar, Jenjira Pongpas, Sakda Kaewbuadee, Natthakam Aphaiwonk.
▶ *Dir* Apichatpong Weerasethakul, *Pro* Simon Field,

New moon, same old, same old: Kristen Stewart as Bella Swan in Chris Weitz' *The Twilight Saga: New Moon.*

Keith Griffiths, Charles de Meaux, Weerasethakul etc, *Screenplay* Weerasethakul, inspired by the book *A Man Who Can Recall Past Lives* by Phra Sripariyattiweti, *Ph* Sayombhu Mukdeeprom, *Pro Des* Akekarat Homlaor, *Ed* Lee Chatametikool, *Cos* Chatchai Chaiyon and Buangoen Ngamcharoenputtasri.

Illuminations Films/Kick the Machine/Match Factory etc-New Wave Films.
113 mins. Thailand/UK/France/Germany/Spain/The Netherlands/USA. 2010. Rel: 19 Nov 2010. Cert. 12A.

Under Great White Northern Lights ★★★★

Emmett Malloy follows the White Stripes – Detroit siblings Jack and Meg – as they embark on an ambitious tour of every province of Canada in the summer of 2007. His discreet camera allows the audience to gradually get to know the eloquent Jack and the mostly silent Meg, whose sporadic comments are generally incomprehensible and therefore subtitled. The black and white photography works well, with a terrific climax celebrating their tenth anniversary at the famous Savoy Theatre in Nova Scotia. (Original title: *The White Stripes Under Great White Northern Lights*) GS

➤ Jack White, Meg White.
➤ *Dir* Emmett Malloy, *Pro* Ian Montone and Mike Sarkissian, *Ph* Giles Dunning, *Ed* Tim Wheeler, *M* Jack White and Meg White.

Three Foot Giant/Woodshed Films Inc.-More2 Screen.
93 mins. USA. 2009. Rel: 12 Mar 2010. Cert. PG.

Undertow ★★★½

In some ways this sympathetic first feature is a companion piece to the Israeli film *Eyes Wide Open* [qv] in that it deals with a gay relationship in an environment where discovery of it leads to hostility. The setting here is a Peruvian fishing village and there's much local colour and no trace of melodrama. However, the switch from naturalism to ghost story is a disturbing gear-change. Even so, it's promising, well acted and has its heart in the right place. (Original title: *Contracorriente*) MS

➤ Cristian Mercado, Tatiana Astengo, Manolo Cardona, Atilia Boschetti.
➤ *Dir* and *Screenplay* Javier Fuentes-León, *Pro* Rodrigo Guerrero and Fuentes-León, *Ph* Mauricio Vidal, *Art Dir* Diana Trujillo, *Ed* Roberto Benavides and Fuentes-León, *M* Selma Mutal, *Cos* Leslie Hinojosa.

Elcalvo Films/Dynamo Contracorriente Producciones/La Cinefacture/Memento Films, Neuecameo Films etc-Axiom Films.
101 mins. Peru/Colombia/France/Germnay. 2009. Rel: 6 Aug 2010. Cert. 15.

The Unloved ★★★

Samanthà Morton turns director for this heartfelt drama about an 11-year-old girl and what happens to her in a Midlands care home. The young lead actors are fine and Morton's work recalls that of Lynne Ramsay and Carine Adler. Even so, the concern demonstrated fails to propel the drama and the detail that might have involved us more fully is lacking. It certainly means well but it is not dramatically invigorating. MS

➤ Molly Windsor, Lauren Socha, Craig Parkinson, Robert Carlyle, Susan Lynch.

Dirty linen: Michiel Huisman and Déborah François in Alexis Dos Santos' occasionally endearing *Unmade Beds*.

▶ *Dir* Samantha Morton, *Pro* Kate Ogborn,
Screenplay Tony Grisoni, from material by Morton,
Ph Tom Townend, *Pro Des* Jane Levick, *Ed* Colin
Monie, *M* Colleen, *Cos* Sarah Blenkinsop.

**Film4/EM Media/Revolution Films etc-ICA Films.
106 mins. UK. 2009. Rel: 2009. No Cert.**

Unmade Beds ★★½

Alexis Dos Santos comes from Argentina and in
this second feature reflects his own experience of
London by setting it amongst foreigners sharing
accommodation in the East End. His lead actor,
Fernando Tielve, is an appealing presence and
there's youthful energy in the direction. But
the interlinked plot lines become increasingly
improbable (especially the one about Tielve
seeking his English father). By the close one feels
disappointed, despite some endearing elements. MS

▶ Déborah François, Fernando Tielve, Michiel
Huisman, Richard Lintern, Iddo Goldberg.
▶ *Dir* Alexis Dos Santos, *Pro* Soledad Gatti-Pascual
and Peter Ettedgui, *Screenplay* Dos Santos with
Marianela Maldonado, *Ph* Jakob Ihre, *Pro Des* Kristian
Milsted, *Ed* Olivier Bugge Coutté, *Cos* Kate Forbes.

**Film4/UK Film Council/EM Media/The Bureau etc-Soda
Pictures.
97 mins. UK/France. 2009. Rel: 11 Dec 2009. Cert. 15.**

Unstoppable ★★★★½

The suit on the other end of the phone begs one
more question: "How do you mean to stop it?"

The unstoppable 'it' – thanks to a chain of worst-
case scenarios – happens to be an unmanned,
half-mile freight train jammed on full throttle…
In the arena of the action-thriller this has to be
one of the most exciting of the year and one of
the best in Tony Scott's career. For once, Scott
keeps his camera flourishes to a minimum and
punches all the other buttons with aplomb.
Above all, though, it's a terrific story – and a
beautiful piece of emotional engineering. JC-W

▶ Denzel Washington, Chris Pine, Rosario Dawson,
Ethan Suplee, Kevin Dunn, Kevin Corrigan, Jeff Wincott.
▶ *Dir* Tony Scott, *Pro* Tony Scott, Ridley Scott, Julie
Yorn, Mimi Rogers, Eric McLeod and Alex Young,
Screenplay Mark Bomback, *Ph* Ben Seresin, *Pro Des*
Chris Seagers, *Ed* Robert Duffy and Chris Lebenzon,
M Harry Gregson-Williams, *Cos* Penny Rose.

**Twentieth Century Fox/Scott Free Productions/Prospect
Park/Firm Films/Millbrook Farm Productions-20th
Century Fox.
98 mins. USA. 2010. Rel: 24 Nov 2010. Cert. 12A.**

Up ★★★½

Imagination, daring and originality are all to
the fore in this acclaimed animated feature
from Disney/Pixar. It's not often that a crusty
septuagenarian is the central figure in such a work,
even if his abode does sail up into the air with a
boy on board. But perhaps this has been oversold
because the second half sidelines the central
relationship for less effective chases and pursuits,
while the famed opening section summarising

Mobile home:
the widowed
Carl Fredricksen
makes a big
move in Pixar/
Disney's hugely
entertaining *Up*.

the widower's past life engages less than expected. There's perfect voicing of the two leading figures and, of course, *Up* is worth seeing. But personally I got more satisfaction from *Fantastic Mr Fox* [qv], while Michel Ocelot's 2006 feature *Azur & Asmar: The Princes' Quest* outshines both. MS

▶ With the voices of Ed Asner, Christopher Plummer, Jordan Nagai, Bob Peterson.
▶ *Dir* Pete Doctor with Bob Peterson, *Pro* Jonas Rivera, *Screenplay* Peterson and Doctor, from a story by them and Tom McCarthy, *Ph* Patrick Lin and Jean-Claude Kalache, *Pro Des* Ricky Nierva, *Ed* Kevin Nolting, *M* Michael Giacchino, *Supervising Animator* Scott Clark.

Walt Disney Pictures/Pixar Animation Studios-Buena Vista. 96 mins. USA. 2009. Rel: 9 Oct 2009. Cert. U.

Up in the Air ★★★★

George Clooney plays a smooth firer of redundant employees. For him it's a job, flying in and out to give people their cards. When it's suggested that he could work by videolink, to save on airfares, he baulks at the thought. His life is on the move, aboard a plane or settling into a hotel. He even has an airborne girlfriend

Air miles high: George Clooney in Jason Reitman's smart, sparkling *Up in the Air.*

(Vera Farmiga) who checks in between flights. It would have been Cary Grant years ago and here Clooney does a perfect impression of same. Farmiga, Anna Kendrick as Ryan's colleague and Amy Morton as his disillusioned sister all shine in this fine light comedy. MHD

▶ George Clooney, Vera Farmiga, Anna Kendrick, Jason Bateman, Amy Morton, Sam Elliott.
▶ *Dir* Jason Reitman, *Pro* Jason and Ivan Reitman, Jeffrey Clifford and Daniel Dubiecki, *Screenplay* Jason Reitman and Sheldon Turner, based on the novel by Walter Kirn, *Ph* Eric Steelberg, *Pro Des* Steve Saklad, *Ed* Dana E Glauberman, *M* Rolfe Kent, *Cos* Danny Glicker.

Paramount Pictures/Coldspring Pictures/DW Studios/Monecito Picture Company etc-Paramount Pictures. 108 mins. USA. 2009. Rel: 15 Jan 2010. Cert. 15.

Valentine's Day ★★★

Various good-looking individuals fall in and out of love on Valentine's Day in the City of Angels... A cynically retooled *Love Actually* for an American audience, *Valentine's Day* is slick, often predictable and ruthlessly likeable. With a cast like this and a director of Garry Marshall's experience, the film was bound to sound a number of high notes. It is also unforgivably corny and owes an immeasurable debt to Richard Curtis, loosely acknowledged in a copyright credit for the *Love Actually* poster. JC-W

▶ Jessica Alba, Kathy Bates, Jessica Biel, Bradley Cooper, Patrick Dempsey, Hector Elizondo, Jamie Foxx, Jennifer Garner, Anne Hathaway, Ashton Kutcher, Queen Latifah, Taylor Lautner, Shirley MacLaine, Emma Roberts, Julia Roberts, Taylor Swift.
▶ *Dir* Garry Marshall, *Pro* Josie Rosen, Mike Karz and Wayne Allan Rice, *Screenplay* Katherine Fugate, *Ph* Charles Minsky, *Pro Des* Albert Brenner, *Ed* Bruce Green, *M* John Debney, *Cos* Gary Jones.

New Line Cinema/Rice Films/Karz Entertainment-Warner Bros. 125 mins. USA. 2010. Rel:12 Feb 2010. Cert. 12A.

Valhalla Rising ★★★

Nicolas Winding Refn's Viking epic is an interesting cultural brew, a Norse saga filmed in Scotland with Tibetan extras playing Native Americans. Anyway, the Copenhagen-born Mads Mikkelsen gives his central, one-eyed savage a noble dignity, as if Clint Eastwood had stumbled into a Werner Herzog movie. At times self-indulgently portentous and at others just plain daft, it's a gory, stirring and brave attempt at being something completely different. CB

▶ Mads Mikkelsen, Jamie Sives, Gary Lewis, Douglas Russell, Ewan Stewart.
▶ *Dir* Nicolas Winding Refn, *Pro* Johnny Andersen,

Henrik Danstrup and Bo Ehrhardt, *Screenplay* Refn and Roy Jacobsen, *Ph* Molten Søborg, *Pro Des* Laurel Wear, *Ed* Matthew Newman, *M* Peter Kyed and Peterpeter, *Cos* Gill Horn.

BBC Films/La Belle Allee Productions/NWR Film Productions/Nimbus Film Productions/One Eye Productions etc-Momentum Pictures.
93 mins. Denmark/UK. 2009. Rel: 30 Apr 2010. Cert. 15.

Vampires Suck ★

Jason Friedberg and Aaron Seltzer's dull parody of the *Twilight* saga is utterly laugh-free. The story is identical to the first of the trilogy and is as slow as the third one. The miserably unhappy Becca (Jenn Proske) is torn between two men – the bloodsucking Edward (Matt Lanter) and Jacob (Christopher N Riggi), who begins experiencing his own strange transformation... It is directed by remote control with a script which simply lacks any bite! GS

▶ Jenn Proske, Matt Lanter, Diedrich Bader, Christopher N Riggi, Anneliese van der Pol, Kelsey Ford.
▶ *Dir* and *Screenplay* Jason Friedberg and Aaron Seltzer, *Pro* Friedberg, Seltzer and Peter Saffran, *Ph* Shawn Maurer, *Pro Des* William A Elliott, *Ed* Peck Prior, *M* Christopher Lennertz, *Cos* Alix Hester.

Regency Enterprises/Road Rebel-20th Century Fox.
82 mins. USA. 2010. Rel: 15 Oct 2010. Cert. 12A.

Vanishing of the Bees ★★★½

The faults in this film should not be ignored entirely – it's over-long, suffers from banal writing in its narration and suggests a work structured for advertising breaks during a TV transmission. Nevertheless, it tackles clearly important environmental issues as it unravels the mystery of 'Colony Collapse Disorder', involving increasingly large-scale disappearances of bees. It's a welcome film that would be ideal for viewing in schools. MS

▶ With Simon Buxton, Tom Theobald, Dr Jeffrey Pettis. Narrated by Emilia Fox.
▶ *Dir* and *Pro* George Langworthy and Maryam Henein, *Screenplay* Henein, Langworthy and James Erskine, *Ph* Langworthy, *Ed* William Gazecki, *M* Brian Standefer, Bukka Allen and Brian McBride, *Animation* Jeremy Angier and Machine Graphics.

Hive Mentality Films/New Black Films/Hipfuel etc-Dogwoof Pictures.
97 mins. USA/UK. 2009. Rel: 9 Oct 2009. Cert. U.

Videocracy ★★

This attempt to expose Silvio Berlusconi's manipulation of the Italian people through his control of the media finds scant material for its purpose. A few incidental passages are telling

Norse and South: Mads Mikkelsen's tattoos are a cause for concern in Nicolas Winding Refn's brave and gory *Valhalla Rising*.

Giovanna Mezzogiorno gives a heartfelt performance in Marco Bellocchio's *Vincere*.

but I've rarely seen a film in which scenes are so drawn out to little effect. Italian TV looks dire, but the film never gets far enough beyond that to prove its case and this is one of the few recent documentaries that is a dud. MS

‣ With Ricky Canevali, Fabrizio Corona, Lele Mora, Fabio Calvi, Silvio Berlusconi. Narrated by Erik Gandini.
‣ *Dir* Erik Gandini, *Pro* Mikael Olsen, *Ph* Manuel Alberto Claro, Lukas Eisenhauer and others, *Art Dir* Martin Hultman, *Ed* Johan Söderberg.

Atmo/Zentropa/Sveriges Television SVT etc-Dogwoof Pictures.
84 mins. Sweden/Denmark/UK/Finland/Norway. 2009. Rel: 4 June 2010. Cert. 15.

Villa Amalia ★★★★

Some will find this too slow, too lacking in action and too indeterminate, but Isabelle Huppert is at her best as a married pianist who makes a discovery that stops her in her tracks. Is her subsequent attempt at a new life a sign of wisdom or of folly, even madness? We are drawn into her story and ponder its subtle emotional moments as well as the key issue of withdrawal from society as a gesture of rejection versus the need for human attachment. Recommended. MS

‣ Isabelle Huppert, Jean-Hugues Anglade, Xavier Beauvois, Clara Bindi.

‣ *Dir* Benoît Jacquot, *Pro* Edouard Weil, *Screenplay* Jacquot with Julien Boivent, from Pascal Quignard's novel, *Ph* Caroline Champetier, *Art Dir* Katia Wyszkop, *Ed* Luc Barnier, *M* Bruno Coulais, *Cos* Nathalie LeCoultre.

Rectangle Productions/Europa Corp/Point Prod/ France 2 Cinéma/La Télévision Suisse Romande etc-Peccadillo Pictures.
94 mins. France/Switzerland. 2008. Rel: 25 June 2010. Cert. PG.

Vincere ★★★½

Still best known for his first feature, *Fists in the Pocket* of 1965, Marco Bellocchio here tells the story of Mussolini's ill-treated mistress Ida Dalser and their son. The bravura operatic style fascinates yet also limits our emotional involvement, the balance being far less astute than in Paolo Sorrentino's recent *Il Divo*, which overshadows this film. The later sections have structural problems too, but even so this is striking and intriguing film-making. MS

‣ Giovanna Mezzogiorno, Filippo Timi, Fausto Russo Alesi, Micaela Cescon.
‣ *Dir* Marco Bellocchio, *Pro* Mario Gianani, *Screenplay* Bellocchio and Daniela Ceselli from Bellocchio's story, *Ph* Daniele Ciprì, *Art Dir* Marco Dentici, *Ed* Francesca Calvelli, *M* Carlo Crivelli, *Cos* Sergio Ballo.

Rai Cinema/Offside/Celluloid Dreams etc-Artificial Eye.
125 mins. Italy/France. 2009. Rel: 14 May 2010. Cert. 15.

Vinyan ★★★½

Naïve and sophisticated by turns, this drama from Fabrice du Welz, shot in English, has a novel location. It is the story of a mother's desperate search for the son who, probably a victim of the 2005 tsunami, might instead have been seized by child traffickers. With a doubting father in tow, mother pays locals to take them into the jungles of the Thai/Burma border where the child might be located. Ultimately, *Vinyan* recalls *Lord of the Flies* and is midway between exploitation cinema and an imaginative art-house film. MS

▶ Emmanuelle Béart, Rufus Sewell, Petch Osathanugrah, Julie Dreyfus.
▶ *Dir* and *Screenplay* Fabrice du Welz, *Pro* Michaël Gentile, *Ph* Benoît Debie, *Pro Des* Arin Pinijvararak, *Ed* Colin Monie, *M* François-Eudes Chanfrault.

Michael Gentile/Film4/The Film/Pilchard Productions/ One Eyed/K2 SA/RTBF/BeTV etc-Revolver Entertainment. 96 mins. France/UK/Australia/Belgium. 2008. Rel: 2 Oct 2009. Cert. 18.

Vote Afghanistan! ★★★★

From the makers of the excellent *Afghan Star* comes another strong documentary, this time about Afghanistan's doomed Presidential election of 2009. The film is seen through the eyes of the political candidates and of their supporters as they risk their lives to challenge President Karzai in order to make it a fair election. It is an enlightening piece of filmmaking but very bleak in its outcome. GS

▶ *Dir* and *Pro* Havana Marking and Martin Herring.
Channel 4 Television. 78 mins. UK. 2010. Rel: 23 Apr 2010. No Cert.

Waiting for 'Superman' ★★½

Davis Guggenheim's *An Inconvenient Truth* was billed as "by far the most terrifying film you will ever see," won the Oscar for best documentary and grossed $50 million. It's hard to engender as much enthusiasm for Guggenheim's follow-up (about the failings of public education in the US), particularly for an audience without a child in the American education system. It's a workmanlike, articulate documentary that follows the template of Jeffrey Blitz's *Spellbound* but without the emotional connection or freak-show attraction. For all that, it does throw up some intriguing statistics and is certainly food for thought. JC-W

▶ *Dir* Davis Guggenheim, *Pro* Lesley Chilcott, *Screenplay* Guggenheim and Billy Kimball, *Ph* Bob Richman and Erich Roland, *Ed* Jay Cassidy, Greg Finton and Kim Roberts, *M* Christophe Beck.

Electric Kinney Films/Participant Media/Walden Media-Paramount Pictures. 111 mins. USA. 2010. Rel: 26 Nov 2010. Cert PG.

Wall Street: Money Never Sleeps ★★★

While no longer working from his own screenplay, Oliver Stone offers a sequel to his *Wall Street* (1987) which is a mix of family drama and chicanery in the business world. Michael Douglas retains his charisma as ex-financier Gordon Gekko and Carey Mulligan is fine as his daughter. But Shia LaBeouf as the daughter's boyfriend is bland and uninvolving. The film is much too long and capped by a final scene that is totally banal. MS

▶ Michael Douglas, Shia LaBeouf, Josh Brolin, Carey Mulligan, Eli Wallach, Susan Sarandon, Frank Langella, Sylvia Miles.
▶ *Dir* Oliver Stone, *Pro* Edward R Pressman and Eric Kopeloff, *Screenplay* Allan Loeb and Stephen Schiff, based on characters created by Stanley Weiser and Stone, *Ph* Rodrigo Prieto, *Pro Des* Kristi Zea, *Ed* David Brenner and Julie Monroe, *M* Craig Armstrong, *Cos* Ellen Mirojnick.

Gekko gets even: Michael Douglas reprising his Oscar-winning role in *Wall Street: Money Never Sleeps*.

The great escape: Ed Harris in Peter Weir's controversial and extraordinarily ambitious *The Way Back*.

Twentieth Century Fox/Dune Entertainment etc-20th Century Fox.
133 mins. USA. 2010. Rel: 6 Oct 2010. Cert. 12A.

The War You Don't See ★★★★½

An incendiary tract from John Pilger, this is more than just an analysis of the conflicts in Iraq and Afghanistan. It's a testament to the truism that truth is the first casualty of war. The facts are appalling: 90 per cent of the victims killed by our forces are innocent citizens, while the government and media have colluded in a pact to protect us – the British and Americans – from the facts. Pilger offers damning proof of his arguments, along with some shocking, previously unseen footage. This is a film that demands to be seen, digested and discussed. CB

▶ Julian Assange, Tony Blair, Saddam Hussein, Wilfred Burchett, George W Bush, Andrew Marr.
▶ *Dir* John Pilger and Alan Lowery, *Screenplay* John Pilger, *M* Sacha Puttnam.

Independent Television-ITV.
97 mins. UK. 2010. Rel: 12 Dec 2010. No Cert.

The Warrior's Way ★★★

A crazily stylised Eastern-flavoured Western reminiscent of *300* and its green-screened ilk, this tells a familiar tale in an amusing way. Though you're never drawn into the story quite as much as you'd like, because the setting's so artificial, the characters have no depth and the actors play it like panto, it remains a fun, striking oddity with an eccentric cast and cool, if not exciting, comic book-inspired action. As a samurai hiding out in the American badlands, romancing Kate Bosworth and battling boo-able Danny Huston, Korean actor Dong-gun Jang is an inscrutable yet charismatic hero who grows on you, much like the movie itself. MJ

▶ Danny Huston, Kate Bosworth, Dong-gun Jang, Tony Cox, Matt Gillanders, Geoffrey Rush.
▶ *Dir* and *Screenplay* Sngmoo Lee, *Pro* Barrie N Osborne, Michael Peyser and Lee-joo Ick, *Ph* Woo-hyung Kim, *Pro Des* Philip Ivey, *Ed* Jonno Woodford-Robinson, *M* Javier Navarrete, *Cos* James Acheson.

Culture Unplugged Studios/Fuse Media/Sad Flutes-Entertainment Film Distribution.
100 mins. New Zealand. 2010. Rel: 3 Dec 2010. Cert. 15.

The Way Back ★★★★

Absurdly undervalued, this epic film was inspired by a real-life trek to freedom undertaken by prisoners in a Siberian gulag who travelled all the way to Tibet and beyond. It is made with all the mastery that Peter Weir previously brought to *Master and Commander: The Far Side of the World* (2003). The film's integrity is confirmed by the subtitles which appear when characters would not have spoken in English and the screenplay is cleverly structured to bring out all the suspense and tension of the tale. There's a first-class cast too, including Ed Harris, Saoirse Ronan and Colin Farrell, all on top form. Recommended. MS

❧ Jim Sturgess, Ed Harris, Saoirse Ronan, Colin Farrell, Mark Strong, Dragos Bucur.
❧ *Dir* Peter Weir, *Pro* Joni Levin, Weir, Duncan Henderson and Nigel Sinclair, *Screenplay* Weir and Keith Clarke, inspired by the book *The Long Walk* by Slavomir Rawicz, *Ph* Russell Boyd, *Pro Des* John Stoddart, *Ed* Lee Smith, *M* Burkhard Dallwitz, *Cos* Wendy Stites.
Exclusive Films/National Geographic Entertainment/ Imagenation Abu Dhabi/On the Road/Point Blank Productions etc-E1 Films.
133 mins. UK/USA/Poland/United Arab Emirates. 2010. Rel: 26 Dec 2010. Cert. 12A.

We Are What We Are ★★★

Carrying echoes of the much superior *Let the Right One In* (2008), this Mexican tale deals with a family made up not of vampires but of cannibals. The oldest son resists inheriting his late father's role as leader, and this is played very seriously without a hint of black comedy. Any metaphorical comment on social or sexual issues is not strong enough to supply the depth required to make this more than passable but forgettable stuff. (Original title: *Somos lo que hay*) MS

❧ Francisco Barreiro, Alan Chávez, Paulina Galtán, Carmen Beato, Jorge Zárate.
❧ *Dir* Jorge Michel Grau, *Pro* Nicolás Celis, *Screenplay* Grau with Rogelio Guedea, *Ph* Santiago Sánchez,

Art Dir Alejandro García, *Ed* Rodrigo Rios Legaspi, *M* Enrico Chapela, *Cos* Fernanda Vélez Aguilar.
Centro de Capacitación Cinematográfica/Fondo para la producción cinematográfica de Calidad (Mexico) etc-Artificial Eye.
89 mins. Mexico. 2009. Rel: 12 Nov 2010. Cert. 15.

We Live In Public ★★★

This fascinating documentary follows a highly unlikeable individual named Josh Harris, a pioneering figure on the internet. Apart from founding several websites he also created the pretentious project *Quiet*, where 100 people lived together under the eye of a camera in an NYC underground bunker for 30 days. And, even worse, he lived with his girlfriend under 24-hour electronic surveillance. The strength of Ondi Timoner's film is that it makes this loathsome man quite intriguing and watchable. GS

❧ Josh Harris, Tom Harris, Carlos Alvarez, David Amron, Alex Arcadia, Zero Boy.
❧ *Dir* and *Screenplay* Ondi Timoner, *Pro* Timoner and Keirda Bahruth, *Ph* Timoner, Max Heller and Vasco Nunes, *Ed* Joshua Altman, Ondi Timoner and David Timoner, *M* Marco D'Ambrosio and Ben Decter.
Interloper Films/Pawn Shop Creatives-Dogwoof Pictures.
90 mins. USA. 2009. Rel: 13 Nov 2009. Cert. 15.

Welcome ★★★★★

Simon is a French swimming coach who takes pity on Bilal, an Iraqi teenager desperate to flee France to join his girlfriend in England. The authorities pounce from every corner, cracking down on

On the edge of promise: Firat Ayverdi in Philippe Lioret's authentic and topical *Welcome*.

illegal immigration. When all else fails Bilal takes lessons from Simon so that he can swim the Channel to Britain... With affecting performances, especially Firat Ayverdi's seriously doleful Bilal and the superb Vincent Lindon as the bolshie Simon who refuses to give up helping Bilal, Philippe Lioret, co-writer and director, achieves miracles with a humane story that couldn't possibly fail to touch even the hardest of hearts. MHD

▷ Vincent Lindon, Firat Ayverdi, Audrey Dana, Derya Ayverdi, Thierry Godard, Selim Akgul.
▷ *Dir* Philippe Lioret, *Pro* Christophe Rossignon, *Screenplay* Lioret, Olivier Adam and Emmanuel Courcol in collaboration with Serge Frydman, *Ph* Laurent Dailland, *Pro Des* Yves Brover, *Ed* Andrea Sedláčková, *M* Nicola Piovani, *Cos* Magali Cohen.

Nord-Quest Productions/France 3 Cinéma/Mars Distribution/Canal + etc-Cinefile World.
110 mins. France. 2009. Rel: 6 Nov 2009. Cert. 15.

Whatever Works ★★★½

Woody Allen directs but does not appear, leaving Larry David to play with aplomb the central role, an ageing cynic clearly modelled in his attitudes on Allen's established screen persona. There's nothing very fresh in this tale of new loves altering people's lives, but it finds Allen back on home ground in New York and it is agreeable entertainment which should please his fans. This is by far the best of Allen's recent films. MS

▷ Larry David, Evan Rachel Wood, Patricia Clarkson, Ed Begley Jr, Henry Cavill.
▷ *Dir* and *Screenplay* Woody Allen, *Pro* Letty Aronson and Stephen Tenenbaum, *Ph* Harris Savides, *Pro Des* Santo Loquasto, *Ed* Alisa Lepselter, *Cos* Suzy Benzinger.

Sony Pictures Classics/Wild Bunch/Gravier Productions/Perdido Productions-Warner Bros.
92 mins. USA/France. 2009. Rel: 25 June 2010. Cert. 12A.

When in Rome ★★

Museum curator Beth (Kristen Bell) is in the Italian capital for just 48 hours. Still, it's enough time for a magic charm to reap dividends. Back in New York, she is courted by all sorts – including Danny DeVito – and her sister's best man, the perennially suitable Josh Duhamel... There is a dispiriting laziness about all this – the rom-com's conventionality, bumbling slapstick, forced exposition, familiarity – but Bell and Duhamel rise above the material. They even supply a bit of charm. CB

▷ Kristen Bell, Josh Duhamel, Anjelica Huston, Will Arnett, Jon Heder, Danny De Vito.
▷ *Dir* Mark Steven Johnson, *Pro* Johnson, Rikki Lea Bestall, Gary Foster, Ezra Swerdlow and Andrew Panay, *Screenplay* David Diamond and David Weissman, *Ph* John Bailey, *Pro Des* Kirk M Petruccelli, *Ed* Ryan Folsey and Andrew Marcus, *M* Tobias Karlsson and Christopher Young, *Cos* Sarah Edwards.

Kvetch this: Larry David rants and nitpicks with Evan Rachel Wood in Woody Allen's *Whatever Works*.

Rock of all ages: The Doors as they appear in Tom DiCillo's riveting *When You're Strange: A Film About The Doors.*

Touchstone Pictures/Krasnoff Foster Productions-Walt Disney Studios Motion Pictures.
91 mins. USA. 2010. Rel: 25 June 2010. Cert. PG.

When You're Strange: A Film About The Doors ★★★★

In 1991 Oliver Stone wrung The Doors, Jim Morrison and the viewer through his characteristically brutish, self-conscious biographical wringer. Here, the canny and articulate Tom DiCillo (*Johnny Suede*, *Living in Oblivion*) takes a more straightforward approach, allowing authentic (and often rare) film footage (from 1966 to 1971) to speak for itself. It's an intimate, fly-on-the-wall approach, balancing the backstage life, the controversial concerts and contemporary newsreels with a measured, un-histrionic voice-over from Johnny Depp. Part time capsule, part tribute, this is a documentary that is driven by its own subject matter, its music and its visuals, all of which are riveting. JC-W

▶ *Narrator* Johnny Depp.
▶ *Dir* and *Screenplay* Tom DiCillo, *Pro* John Beug, Jeff Jampol and Peter Jankowski, *Ph* Paul Ferrara, *Ed* Micky Blythe and Kevin Krasny, *M* The Doors.

Wolf Films/Strange Pictures-The Works UK.
85 mins. USA. 2009. Rel: 2 July 2010. Cert. 15.

Where the Wild Things Are ★★★★

More a film for adults than for children, Spike Jonze's adaptation of Maurice Sendak's book portrays the world of a nine-year-old boy, Max (the mercifully uncute Max Records), who runs away from home. His fantasy adventures find him on an island with creatures who symbolise at one and the same time the wilder side of himself, the friends with whom he wishes to play games, and the adult world beyond his control of which he is just becoming aware. Short on action, it's essentially a film of psychological insight and is adventurous in its technological approach. MS

▶ Max Records, Catherine Keener, Mark Ruffalo; the voices of Chris Cooper, James Gandolfini, Catherine O'Hara, Forest Whitaker.
▶ *Dir* Spike Jonze, *Pro* Tom Hanks, Gary Goetzman, Maurice Sendak and others, *Screenplay* Jonze and Dave Eggers, from Sendak's book, *Ph* Lance Acord, *Pro Des* K K Barrett, *Ed* Eric Zumbrunnen and James Haygood, *M* Carter Burwell, Karen O and others, *Cos* Casey Storm, *Creature Cos* Jim Henson's Creature Shop, *Animation* Framestore etc.

Warner Bros Pictures/Legendary Pictures/Village Roadshow Pictures etc-Warner Bros.
101 mins. Germany/USA/Australia. 2009. Rel: 11 Dec 2009. Cert. PG.

Whip It ★★★★★

Drew Barrymore's directorial debut (in which she also has a bit part) is a joy. Mother Marcia Gay Harden wants daughter Ellen Page to succeed as a beauty queen. But Page rebels by joining a roller derby team wherein young women race around a track on roller skates at breakneck speed. The track action sequences are terrific, but the characterisation ensures there's a lot more to the proceedings overall.

Heading up an excellent ensemble cast, Page has 'star to watch' written all over her. A gem: seek it out. JC

❧ Ellen Page, Marcia Gay Harden, Kristen Wiig, Drew Barrymore, Juliette Lewis, Jimmy Fallon, Daniel Stern.
❧ *Dir* Drew Barrymore, *Pro* Barry Mendel, *Screenplay* Shauna Cross, based on her novel *Derby Girl*, *Ph* Robert Yeoman, *Pro Des* Kevin Kavanaugh, *Ed* Dylan Tichenor, *M* The Section Quartet, *Cos* Catherine Marie Thomas.

Mandate Pictures/Vincent Pictures/Flower Films/ Rye Road/Babe Ruthless Productions/Barry Mendel Productions-Lionsgate.
111 mins. USA. 2009. Rel: 7 Apr 2010. Cert. 12A.

White Lightnin' ★★★½

This bizarre film takes a real-life living person, Jesco White, who learnt Appalachian Mountain dancing from his father, and then presents him as a criminal type who becomes some kind of a monster and ends up dead! It's as though God and the Devil are fighting for Jesco's soul and it comes to suggest what a horror film might have been like if directed by Robert Bresson. It doesn't always work, yet Edward Hogg's performance as Jesco is remarkable and debutant director Dominic Murphy is a name to note. MS

❧ Edward Hogg, Carrie Fisher, Muse Watson, Owen Campbell, Wallace Merck.
❧ *Dir* Dominic Murphy, *Pro* Mike Downey and Sam Taylor, *Screenplay* Shane Smith and Eddy Moretti,

from a story by Murphy and Smith, *Ph* Tim Maurice-Jones, *Pro Des* Ivo Husnjak, *Ed* Sam Sneade, *M* Nick Zinner, *Cos* Blanka Budak.

UK Film Council/Vice Films/Film & Music Entertainment etc-Momentum Pictures.
88 mins. UK/USA/Croatia. 2008. Rel: 25 Sep 2009. No Cert.

White Material ★★★

This film from the frequently over-rated Claire Denis is set in Africa and begins irritatingly with 'Scope shots featuring a wobbly hand-held camera. Not always easy to follow, the story centres on a coffee planter played by Isabelle Huppert. The piece is strongest as an impressionistic portrayal of tensions in a state where those carrying on colonialist traditions are

at risk, but what Denis really wants to say here is difficult to discern. MS

▶ Isabelle Huppert, Christophe Lambert, Nicolas Duvauchelle, Michel Subor, Isaach De Bankolé, William Nadylam.
▶ *Dir* Claire Denis, *Screenplay* Denis and Marie N'Diaye, *Ph* Yves Cape, *Art Dir* Alain Veissier, *Ed* Guy Lecorne, *M* tindersticks, *Cos* Judy Shrewsbury.

Why Not Productions/Wild Bunch/France 3 Cinéma etc-Artificial Eye.
106 mins. France/Cameroon. 2009. Rel: 2 July 2010. Cert. 15.

The White Ribbon ★★★★

Michael Haneke's drama, set in a German village just before the First World War and photographed in black and white, is film-making of a high calibre. Buffs will be fascinated by the many diverse echoes to be found in it – Ingmar Bergman, *Children of the Damned* and Clouzot's *Le Corbeau* to name but three. Like the Clouzot, it deals with evil events in a community in order to express wider social and political concerns. In this case it's a suggestion that horrors linked with the Nazi era had pre-existing roots in human nature, which always has its darker side even in everyday life. (Original title: *Das weiße Band – eine deutsche Kindergeschichte*) MS

▶ Christian Friedel, Leonie Benesch, Ulrich Tukur, Burghart Klaussner, Leonard Proxauf.
▶ *Dir* and *Screenplay* Michael Haneke, *Pro* Stefan Arndt, Veit Heiduschka, Margaret Ménégoz and Andrea Occhipinti, *Ph* Christian Berger, *Pro Des* Christoph Kanter, *Ed* Monika Willi, *Cos* Moidele Bickel.

X Filme Creative Pool/Wega Film/Les Films du Losange/ Lucky Red etc-Artificial Eye.
144 mins. Germany/Austria/France/Italy. 2009. Rel: 13 Nov 2009. Cert. 15.

Whiteout ★½

At the Amundsen-Scott research base on Antarctica, an unholy set of weather conditions threatens a total whiteout. Meanwhile, US Marshal Carrie Setko is investigating the very first murder on the continent... If you buy into Kate Beckinsale as a US Marshal then you get what you deserve. She does get to perform a classic striptease – from parka to panties – but hardly convinces as a cold-weather law enforcer. The film itself, adapted from a graphic novel, is generic, illogical and all rather pointless. JC-W

▶ Kate Beckinsale, Gabriel Macht, Tom Skerritt, Columbus Short, Shawn Doyle.
▶ *Dir* Dominic Sena, *Pro* Susan Downey and David Gambino, *Screenplay* Jon and Eric Hoeber, Chas and Carey W Hayes, from the graphic novel by Greg Rucka and Steve Lieber, *Ph* Christopher Soos,

Pro Des Graham 'Grace' Walker, *Ed* Martin Hunter, *M* John Frizzell, *Cos* Wendy Partridge.

Warner Bros Pictures/Dark Castle Entertainment/Studio Canal/Stuart Babelsberg Motion Pictures etc-Optimum Releasing.
101 mins. USA/Canada/France. 2009. Rel: 11 Sep 2009. Cert. 15.

Why Did I Get Married Too? ★★

In this sequel to *Why Did I Get Married?* the four couples go to the Bahamas for their annual one-week reunion but their peaceful getaway is disrupted by the arrival of Sheila's (Jill Scott) ex-husband Mike (Richard T Jones). Tyler Perry's ambitious but heavy-handed family drama begins as a light comedy before it develops into a clichéd heavy melodrama. In other words it tries to have it both ways but overstays its welcome long before the final credits. GS

▶ Tyler Perry, Janet Jackson, Jill Scott, Sharon Leal, Richard T Jones, Louis Gossett Jr, Cicely Tyson.
▶ *Dir* and *Screenplay* Tyler Perry, *Pro* Perry and Reuben Cannon, *Ph* Toyomichi Kurita, *Assistant Art Dir* Calvin Ashford, *Ed* Maysie Hoy, *M* Jesse Voccia, *Cos* Keith G Lewis.

Lionsgate/The Tyler Perry Company-Lionsgate.
121 mins. USA. 2010. Rel: 3 Sep 2010. Cert. 12A.

Wild Grass ★★½

The veteran Alain Resnais has lost none of his skill in making the most expressive use of screen space and he has here a most distinguished cast.

Painful speaking: Sabine Azéma and Alain Resnais on the set of *Wild Grass.*

Cold comfort: Martijn Lakemeier in Martin Koolhoven's compassionate *Winter in Wartime.*

Alas, I can't in the least share the pleasure that some have found in this story about people unable to say what they mean. It's a thin concept and the people in question are not so much sympathetic or comic in their weaknesses but downright irritating. (Original title: *Les herbes folles*) MS

▶ Sabine Azéma, André Dussollier, Anne Consigny, Emmanuelle Devos, Mathieu Amalric.
▶ *Dir* Alain Resnais, *Pro* Jean-Louis Livi, *Screenplay* Alex Réval and Laurent Herbiet, based on *L'Incident* by Christian Gailly, *Ph* Éric Gautier, *Art Dir* Jacques Saulnier, *Ed* Hervé de Luze, *M* Mark Snow, *Cos* Jackie Budin.

**F Comme Film/Studio Canal/France 2 Cinéma/BIM Distribuzione etc-New Wave Films.
104 mins. France/Italy. 2008. Rel: 18 June 2010. Cert. 12A.**

Wild Target ★

Considering the talent involved – and the distinction of the French original – this is a crushing disappointment. Bill Nighy replaces Jean Rochefort as the ruthless middle-aged hitman who falls for his mark (Emily Blunt), while Rupert Grint tries to be endearing as his young protégé. Unfortunately, the result is flabby and wildly misconceived, a soufflé with the oven door left open. Even sadder is the thought that the two young leads of the original – Marie Trintignant and Guillaume Depardieu – have since died. CB

▶ Bill Nighy, Emily Blunt, Rupert Grint, Rupert Everett, Eileen Atkins, Martin Freeman, Gregor Fisher, Rory Kinnear.
▶ *Dir* Jonathan Lynn, *Pro* Martin Pope and Michael Rose, *Screenplay* Lucinda Coxon, from the film *Cible*

émouvante by Pierre Salvadori, *Ph* David Johnson, *Pro Des* Caroline Greville-Morris, *Ed* Michael Parker, *M* Michael Price, *Cos* Sheena Napier.

**Isle of Man Film/Magic Light Pictures/CinemaNX/ Matador Pictures/Regent Capital-Vue Entertainment.
98 mins. UK/France. 2010. Rel: 16 June 2010. Cert. 12A.**

The Wildest Dream: Conquest of Everest ★★½

Despite backing from National Geographic, this is a film which freely uses mock-ups and reconstructions to kid the audience that they are seeing the real thing – if, indeed, it *is* real. The contentious issue is the suggestion that the climbers George Mallory and Sandy Irvine, who both died on the mountain, reached the summit of Everest in 1924. The film looks good but its methods may lead the credulous to believe that it proves its case when it does no such thing. MS

▶ With the voices of Liam Neeson, Ralph Fiennes, Natasha Richardson, Hugh Dancy, Alan Rickman.
▶ *Dir* Anthony Geffen, *Pro* Geffen and Claudia Perkins, *Screenplay* Mark Halliley, *Ph* Ken Sauls and Chris Openshaw, *Art Dir* Humphrey Bangham, *Ed* Peter Miller, *M* Joel Douek, *Cos* Jane Wrigley.

**National Geographic Entertainment/Altitude Films/Atlantic Productions-National Geographic Cinema Ventures.
94 mins. UK/USA. 2009. Rel: 24 Sep 2010. Cert. PG.**

Winter in Wartime ★★★½

Like *The Boy in the Striped Pyjamas*, this is a Second World War drama aimed (albeit not exclusively) at young audiences ready to identify with the sometimes harsh experiences of the boy at the centre of the story (the excellent Martijn

Lakemeier). Here we have a tale of the Resistance and of betrayal in occupied Holland. At times the plotting lacks conviction but it's a sympathetic work in spite of occasional melodramatic excesses. (Original title: *Oorlogswinter*) MS

▷ Martijn Lakemeier, Yorick van Wageningen, Jamie Campbell Bower, Melody Klaver.
▷ *Dir* Martin Koolhoven, *Pro* Els Vandervorst and San Fu Maltha, *Screenplay* Paul Jan Nelissen, Mieke de Jong and Koolhaven, from Jan Terlouw's novel, *Ph* Guido van Gennep, *Pro Des* Floris Vos, *Ed* Job ter Burg, *M* Pino Donaggio, *Cos* Alette Kraan.

Isabella Films/Fu Works/Prime Time/Omroep Max etc-Kaleidoscope Home Entertainment.
104 mins. The Netherlands/Belgium. 2008. Rel: 12 Feb 2010. Cert. 12A.

Winter's Bone ★★★½

Reminiscent of the splendid *Frozen River* [qv], this work by director Debra Granik features an outstanding lead performance from Oscar-nominated Jennifer Lawrence, who plays a 17-year-old living in the Ozarks. Because she has an ailing mother, the need to prove that her missing father is dead – and thus to prevent their home being repossessed owing to his arrears – falls upon her. Structurally *Winter's Bone* lacks the cohesion of *Frozen River* but even so it's a fine and atmospheric work of considerable distinction and one that stays in the mind. MS

▷ Jennifer Lawrence, John Hawkes, Dale Dickey, Kevin Breznahan, Garrett Dillahunt.
▷ *Dir* Debra Granik, *Pro* Anne Rosellini and Alix Madigan-Yorkin, *Screenplay* Granik and Rosellini, from the novel by Daniel Woodrell, *Ph* Michael McDonough, *Pro Des* Mark White, *Ed* Alfonso Gonçalves, *M* Dickon Hinchliffe, *Cos* Rebecca Hofherr.

Anonymous Content/Winter's Bone Productions-Artificial Eye.
100 mins. USA. 2010. Rel: 17 Sep 2010. Cert. 15.

The Wolfman ★½

Clearly no expense was spared in making this grand Gothic spectacular – a sweeping tale of mystery and suspense, of men and the wolves they turn into – as lame as humanly possible. Benicio Del Toro steps into the paws of the classic Universal monster, wreaking havoc in Victorian England as a doomed aristocrat whose regrettable inclination to explore his canine side sees him clawing through a selection of bloodied extras and supporting stars, among them Anthony Hopkins, Hugo Weaving and Emily Blunt. If only it had been interesting, credible, involving, exciting or, you know, scary. Let's put this dog down. MJ

▷ Benicio Del Toro, Simon Merrells, Gemma Whelan, Emily Blunt, Hugo Weaving, Art Malik, Anthony Hopkins.
▷ *Dir* Joe Johnston, *Pro* Benicio Del Toro, Sean Daniel, Mick Yorn and Scott Stuber, *Screenplay* Andrew Kevin Walker, based on Curt Siodmak's 1941 screenplay, *Ph* Shelly Johnson, *Pro Des* Rick Heinrichs, *Ed* Walter Murch and Dennis Virkler, *M* Danny Elfman, *Cos* Milena Canonero.

Universal Pictures/Relativity Media/Stuber Pictures-Universal Pictures International.
103 mins. USA/UK. 2010 Rel: 12 Feb 2010. Cert. 15.

Country noir: Jennifer Lawrence in her Oscar-nominated role in Debra Granik's eloquent and arresting *Winter's Bone*.

Hungarian actress Orsi Tóth as Zarin in *Women Without Men*.

Women Without Men ★★½

The American-led coup d'état which in 1953 brought down Iran's Prime Minister Mohammed Mossadegh is here the background to a view of the lives of four contrasted women in Tehran. Initially one welcomes the film, but the political aspects presented realistically clash with non-realistic elements, some symbolic and some ghost-like. Consequently the narrative loses its grip and, given the potential of the piece, one ends up feeling frustrated. MS

▶ Pegah Ferydoni, Arita Shahrzad, Shabnam Tolouei, Orsi Tóth, Bijan Daneshmand.
▶ *Dir* Shirin Neshat with Shoja Azari, *Pro* Susanne Marian, Martin Gschlacht and Philippe Bober, *Screenplay* Neshat and Azari, from the novel by Shahrnush Parsipur, *Ph* Gschlacht, *Pro Des* Katherina Woppermann, *Ed* George Cragg, Jay Rabinowitz and Julia Wiedwald, *M* Ryuchi Sakamoto, *Cos* Thomas Oláh.
Indiepix Films/The Coproduction Office/Coop99 Filmproduktion/Parisienne De Production etc-Artificial Eye.
100 mins. Germany/Austria/France/Italy/Ukraine. 2009. Rel: 11 June 2010. Cert. 15.

World's Greatest Dad ★★½

Robin Williams is not a favourite actor of British film critics these days and his good performance here, taking them by surprise, has led to Bobcat Goldthwait's film being over-praised. This new piece is as provocative as *Sleeping Dogs Lie* (2006) but much less persuasive. It's about a father (Williams) faking an eloquently sensitive diary as that of his disliked dead son (well-cast Daryl Sabara) and thus transforming the deceased youth's reputation. There is potential in this plot but it is undermined by a second half which is increasingly unlikely and ultimately daft. MS

▶ Robin Williams, Alexie Gilmore, Daryl Sabara, Geoff Pierson, Evan Martin.
▶ *Dir* and *Screenplay* Bobcat Goldthwait, *Pro* Tim Perell, Howard Gertler, Sean McKittrick and Richard Kelly, *Ph* Horacio Marquinez, *Pro Des* John Paino, *Ed* Jason Stewart, *M* Gerald Brunskill, *Cos* Sarah De Sa Rego.
Darko Entertainment/Process/Jerkschool Productions etc-The Works.
99 mins. USA. 2009. Rel: 24 Sep 2010. Cert. 15.

The Yes Men Fix the World ★★★★

Political activists Andy Bichlbaum and Mike Bonanno not only direct this powerful satire about world politics but also manage to pull off some amazing pranks that involve multi-million dollar businesses. Before they pose as government officials in New Orleans following Hurricane Katrina, Andy pretends he is a Dow chemical spokesperson and announces on TV that his company will finally pay the overdue compensation to the victims of the 20-year-old Bhopal industrial disaster. It's a brave and powerful film which is also very funny, and it should not be missed! GS

▶ Reggie Watts, Andy Bichlbaum, Mike Bonanno.
▶ *Dir* Bichlbaum, Bonanno and Kurt Engfehr, *Pro* Laura Nix, Juliette Timsit etc, *Screenplay* Bichlbaum and Bonanno, *Ph* Sarah Price and Raul Barcelona, *Ed* April Merl, *M* Neel Murgai and Noisola, *Cos* Salvatore Salamone.
Arte France/Article Z/Renegade Pictures/Channel 4 British Documentary Foundation/Charny-Bachrach Entertainment-Dogwoof Pictures.
87 mins. France/UK/USA. 2009. Rel: 7 Aug 2009. Cert. 12A.

You Again ★★½

Marni (Kristen Bell) is a successful New York PR executive who has managed to put behind her the endless bullying she experienced at school. But her nightmare returns when she hears that her brother is marrying her high school nemesis... This is a strong central idea but sadly the final execution disappoints. Jamie Lee Curtis and Sigourney Weaver add class but the script opts for sentimentality rather than dark humour. A missed opportunity. GS

▶ Kristen Bell, Odette Yustman, Sigourney Weaver, Jamie Lee Curtis, Victor Garber, Betty White, Kristin Chenoweth, Patrick Duffy.
▶ *Dir* Andy Fickman, *Pro* Fickman, Eric Tannenbaum and John J Strauss, *Screenplay* Moe Jelline, *Ph* David Hennings, *Pro Des* Craig Stearns, *Ed* Keith Brachmann and David Rennie, *M* Nathan Wang, *Cos* Genevieve Tyrrell.
Touchstone Pictures/Frontier Pictures/Oops Doughnuts Productions-Walt Disney Studios Motion Pictures.
105 mins. USA. 2010. Rel: 12 Nov 2010. Cert. U.

Youth in Revolt ★★★★

During a trailer holiday with his mother, 16-year-old Nick Twisp (Michael Cera) falls madly for Sheeni Saunders (Portia Doubleday). But she has a boyfriend so Nick has to invent and rely entirely on his alter ego, who encourages him to pursue his dream. No one can plays nerds better than Cera but it is as his alter ego, Francois Dillinger, that he impresses most in Miguel Arteta's likeable film. The central theme is not dissimilar to *Play It Again, Sam*. GS

▶ Michael Cera, Portia Doubleday, Jean Smart, Steve Buscemi, Ray Liotta, M Emmett Walsh, Zack Galifianakis.
▶ *Dir* Miguel Arteta, *Pro* David Permut, *Screenplay* Gustin Nash, based on the novel by C D Payne, *Ph* Chilly Chávez, *Pro Des* Tony Fanning, *Ed* Andy Keir and Pamela Martin, *M* John Swihart, *Cos* Nancy Steiner.

Dimension Films/David Permut/Shangri Entertainment-Momentum Pictures.
90 mins. USA. 2009. Rel: 5 Feb 2010. Cert. 15.

Zombieland ★★½

Columbus (Jesse Eisenberg) is a teenage loner with a big cupboard full of phobias. However, these fears pale in comparison when the world is overrun by zombies and, in order to survive, our hero has to stick to some very scrupulous rules… Up to a point this is one of the slicker, smarter zombie spoofs of recent years. It's also a generic affair, which no amount of in-jokes can hide. The normally exemplary Abigail Breslin is terribly wasted as a fourth wheel, although it's fun to witness the final breath of Bill Murray – as himself. JC-W

▶ Woody Harrelson, Jesse Eisenberg, Emma Stone, Abigail Breslin, Amber Heard, Bill Murray.
▶ *Dir* Ruben Fleischer, *Pro* Gavin Polone, *Screenplay* Rhett Reese and Paul Werrnick, *Ph* Michael Bonvillain, *Pro Des* Maher Ahmad, *Ed* Alan Baumgarten, *M* David Sardy, *Cos* Magali Guidasci.

Columbia Pictures/Relativity Media/Pariah-Columbia Pictures.
88 mins. USA. 2009. Rel: 7 Oct 2009. Cert. 15.

Death by banjo: Woody Harrelson gets medieval on a dead customer in Ruben Fleischer's smart if generic *Zombieland*.

In Memoriam

July 2009 – December 2010

by Jonathan Rigby

Given the hundreds of film personalities who died during the 18-month period under review, the following selection of just 85 must remain a purely personal one. Pressure of space has excluded numerous important people, over a hundred of whom are noted in supplements to the main entries.

DEDE ALLEN

Born: *3 December 1923, Cleveland, Ohio, USA.*
Died: *17 April 2010, Los Angeles, California, USA.*
Among the most innovative editors in post-war US cinema, Dorothea 'Dede' Allen was called upon repeatedly by directors George Roy Hill, Sidney Lumet and (especially) Arthur Penn [qv], together with actor-directors Paul Newman and Warren Beatty. Her first major credit, on Robert Wise's *Odds Against Tomorrow* (1959), was followed by *The Hustler* (1961), *Bonnie and Clyde* (1967, probably her best-known and most influential work), *Rachel, Rachel* (1968), *Little Big Man* (1970), *Slaughterhouse Five* (1972), *Serpico* (1973), *Dog Day Afternoon* (1975, for which she won a BAFTA), *Reds* (1981, on which she was also executive producer), *The Breakfast Club* (1985), *Henry & June* (1990) and *The Addams Family* (1991).

➲ Other noted film editors who died in 2010 included **Adam Alexander Dawson** (*Mister Drake's Duck,*

Dangerous Cargo; in January, aged 96), **Sally Menke** (*Pulp Fiction, Mulholland Falls*; in September, aged 56), **David E Blewitt** (*Butterflies Are Free, Ghostbusters*; in July, aged 81), and **Mauro Alice** (best known outside Brazil for *Kiss of the Spider Woman*; in November, aged 84).

CÉCILE AUBRY

Born: *3 August 1928, Paris, France.*
Died: *19 July 2010, Dourdan, France.*
Cécile Aubry scored for Henri-Georges Clouzot as *Manon* (1949) and Christian-Jacque as the seventh wife of *Barbe-Bleue* (Bluebeard, 1951). In between, her highly exploitable 'sexy French gamine' image transported her to Hollywood for a one-shot flirtation with Twentieth Century-Fox, yielding Henry Hathaway's *The Black Rose* (1950). A handful of further films in Italy, West Germany, Spain and France preceded her reinvention as author of the children's novel *Belle et Sébastien*. The 1965/68 TV series of the same name – which she wrote and co-directed – became a worldwide hit.

ROBERT S BAKER

Born: *17 October 1916, London, England.*
Died: *30 September 2009, Stanmore, Middlesex, England.*
Writer-director-producer-cinematographer Bob Baker was co-head, with Monty Berman, of Tempean Films, a leading light in the lucrative post-war field of

Cécile Aubry

Robert S Baker

Jean Simmons (see page 248)

Ray Barrett

Gene Barry

cheap-to-make second features. Moving beyond noirish crime thrillers, they took a leaf out of Hammer's book with *The Trollenberg Terror* and *Blood of the Vampire* (both 1957), then used a 'true crime' paperback costing 7s 6d as the basis for such money-spinning first features as *Jack the Ripper* (1958), *The Flesh and the Fiends* (1959) and *The Hellfire Club* (1960). Soon afterwards, the pair moved firmly into television with the smash-hit series *The Saint* (1962-68). Splitting with Berman, Baker went into business with Roger Moore, resulting in, among others, the 1969 release *Crossplot*.

ROY WARD BAKER
Born: *19 December 1916, London, England.*
Died: *5 October 2010, London, England.*
One of the most accomplished journeyman directors in British cinema, Roy Baker's career fell into two halves, the split marked in 1967 by his adoption of the middle name 'Ward'. As well as directing Marilyn Monroe in the Hollywood film *Don't Bother to Knock* (1952), Baker's initial phase encompassed *The October Man* (1947), *Tiger in the Smoke* (1956), the classic 'Titanic' drama *A Night to Remember* (1958), *The Singer Not the Song* (1960) and *Flame in the Streets* (1961). After a spell in TV (including *The Saint*), he re-emerged as a horror specialist, directing such Hammer and Amicus titles as *Quatermass and the Pit* (1967), *The Vampire Lovers* (1970), *Dr Jekyll & Sister Hyde* (1971) and *Asylum* (1972).

JILL BALCON
Born: *3 January 1925, London, England.*
Died: *18 July 2009, London, England.*
Though apparently overshadowed by the men in her life – father (Ealing supremo Michael Balcon), husband (poet laureate C Day-Lewis), son (film star Daniel

Day-Lewis) – Jill Balcon maintained a successful career of her own for over 50 years. Her film credits act as bookends to this five-decade span, starting with *Nicholas Nickleby* (1947), *Good-Time Girl* (1948) and *The Lost People* (1949). After much stage, TV and radio work (the latter taking advantage of her famously mellifluous voice), she returned with *Edward II* (1991), *Wittgenstein* (1993) and *An Ideal Husband* (1999).

RAY BARRETT
Born: *2 May 1927, Brisbane, Queensland, Australia.*
Died: *8 September 2009, Goldcoast, Queensland, Australia.*
During an 18-year period in England, Ray Barrett became nationally famous in such TV series as *Emergency – Ward 10* and *The Troubleshooters*, together with films like *Jigsaw* (1962) and *The Reptile* (1965). Returning to Australia for Bruce Beresford's *Don's Party* (1976), he won Australian Film Institute awards for *The Chant of Jimmie Blacksmith* (1978), *Goodbye Paradise* (1983) and *Hotel Sorrento* (1995). He was also instrumental in setting up the Queensland Film Corporation, won an AFI Lifetime Achievement award in 2005, and bowed out in Baz Luhrmann's *Australia* (2008).

GENE BARRY
Born: *14 June 1919, New York City, New York, USA.*
Died: *9 December 2009, Woodland Hills, California, USA.*
Ruggedly handsome Gene Barry enjoyed TV fame in *Bat Masterson* (1958-61) and *Burke's Law* (1963-66). An early incarnation as a star of Broadway musicals was exchanged for a Paramount contract in 1951, with eye-catching roles in *The War of the Worlds* (1953), *Alaska Seas*, *Naked Alibi* (both 1954), opposite Clark Gable in *Soldier of Fortune* (1955), and in the Samuel Fuller films *China Gate* and *Forty Guns* (both 1957). In 1983, he returned to Broadway for a Tony-nominated turn in *La Cage aux folles*.

MARTIN BENSON
Born: *10 August 1918, London, England.*
Died: *28 February 2010, Markyate, Hertfordshire, England.*
The corvine, black-browed features of Martin Benson

made him one of the most recognisable villains in British film and TV. Having played the court chancellor in *The King and I* at Drury Lane in 1953, he repeated the role in the Hollywood film. He was subsequently consigned to a car crusher in *Goldfinger* (1964), played a mad Chinese war lord in *Battle Beneath the Earth*, encountered Morecambe and Wise in *The Magnificent Two* (both 1967), and was the disfigured Father Spiletto in *The Omen* (1976). His last film, in 1999, was *Angela's Ashes*.

❧ Other instantly recognisable British character actors who died during the period under review include **Hugh Millais** (in July 2009, aged 79), **Timothy Bateson** (September 2009, 83), **Iain Cuthbertson** (September 2009, 79), **Donald Pickering** (December 2009, 76), **Geoffrey Hutchings** (July 2010, 71), **Frank Jarvis** (September 2010, 69) and **Graham Crowden** (October 2010, 87). Also familiar from British films, Irish-born **Harry Towb** died in July 2009, aged 83; Polish-born **Guido Lorraine** in December 2009, aged 97; Yorkshire-born Irish

Roy Ward Baker

Grace Bradley

Ian Carmichael

actor **Donal Donnelly** in January 2010, aged 78; and Guyanese-British **Cy Grant** in February 2010, aged 90.

ROBERT F BOYLE

Born: *10 October 1909, Los Angeles, California, USA.*
Died: *1 August 2010, Los Angeles, California, USA.*
Robert Boyle's remarkable career as a production designer stretched across such titles as *The Wolf Man* (1941), *Cape Fear* (1962), *The Shootist* (1976) and *Dragnet* (1987), bringing him four Academy Award nominations; he finally received an Honorary Oscar in 2008. He was particularly valued by directors Alfred Hitchcock and Norman Jewison, working for them on, among others, *North By Northwest*, *The Birds*, *Marnie*, *The Thrill Of It All*, *The Thomas Crown Affair* and *Fiddler on the Roof*. In reference to the first of these, in 2000 he was made the subject of an Oscar-nominated documentary called *The Man on Lincoln's Nose*.

❧ Other distinguished production designers who died in 2009-10 include Kurosawa collaborator **Yoshiro Muraki**, Oscar-nominated for *Yojimbo*, *Tora! Tora! Tora!*, *Kagemusha* and *Ran* (October 2009, aged 85), **Pierre Guffroy**, who won an Oscar for *Tess* (September 2010, aged 84), and **John Graysmark**, Oscar-nominated for *Young Winston* and *Ragtime* (October 2010, aged 75).

GRACE BRADLEY

Born: *21 September 1913, New York City, New York, USA.*
Died: *21 September 2010, Dana Point, California, USA.*
Broadway chorus girl Grace Bradley won a Paramount contract in 1933 and was immediately cast opposite Bing Crosby in *Too Much Harmony*. She soon became a sassy lead in numerous 'B' thrillers and musicals, earning enduring cult status for her leather-clad dance

routine in Henry Hathaway's *Come On Marines*. In the early 1940s, she starred with William Bendix in a trio of Hal Roach comedy featurettes and then retired, aged 29. In 2008 she co-authored *Hopalong Cassidy – An American Legend*, a tribute to her late husband, cowboy star William Boyd.

❧ Other veterans of vintage Hollywood include Fox contract artist **Joan Castle**, who died in December 2009, aged 93, Western stars **Virginia Carroll** (July 2009, 95) and **Pamela Blake** (October 2009, 94), and singer **Lina Romay** (December 2010, 91).

DAVID BROWN

Born: *28 July 1916, New York City, New York, USA.*
Died: *1 February 2010, New York City, New York, USA.*
Having headed the story department at Twentieth Century-Fox and become a major force in New York publishing, David Brown entered into co-production partnership with Richard Zanuck and enjoyed a long line of hits. Among them were *The Sting* (1973), *Jaws* (1975), *The Verdict* (1982), *Cocoon* (1985) and *Driving Miss Daisy* (1989). The pair were duly awarded with Irving Thalberg Memorial and David O Selznick

Lifetime Achievement awards. Not content with that, Brown went it alone for *The Player, A Few Good Men* (both 1992), *Angela's Ashes* (1999) and *Chocolat* (2000).

❧ Other US film producers who died in the period under review include **Robert B Radnitz** (*Sounder, Cross Creek*) and **Steven Reuther** (*Pretty Woman, The Rainmaker*), both of whom died in June 2010, aged 85 and 61 respectively. **Noel Marshall** died the same month, aged 79; as well as being executive producer of *The Harrad Experiment* and *The Exorcist*, he was director-producer of the 'big cats' oddity *Roar*. Though chiefly devoted to documentary, **David L Wolper** (who died in August, aged 82) also produced *Willy Wonka and the Chocolate Factory* and *LA Confidential*. And **Roy Disney**, nephew of Walt, was a vital figure in the 1990s rejuvenation of the studio that bore his name; he died back in December 2009, aged 79.

IAN CARMICHAEL

Born: *18 June 1920, Hull, Yorkshire, England.*
Died: *5 February 2010, Grosmont, Yorkshire, England.*
Ian Carmichael first came to screen prominence in *Simon and Laura* (1955), whereupon the Boulting Brothers set out to make him a film star. Through their satirical comedies he quickly developed an engaging persona as the archetypal well-meaning ass all at sea in post-war Britain, a role exemplified by his playing of Stanley Windrush in both *Private's Progress* (1956) and *I'm All Right, Jack* (1959). His other star vehicles included *Brothers in Law* (1957), *School for Scoundrels* (1960) and *The Amorous Prawn* (1962). He then became Bertie Wooster and Lord Peter Wimsey on TV, with character roles in occasional films such as *Smashing Time* (1967), *The Lady Vanishes* (1978) and *Diamond Skulls* (1989).

❧ Other British leading men of the 1950s included **John Bentley**, who played Paul Temple in a series of 'B' pictures and died in August 2009 aged 92, and Richard Wyler, who had a brief Hollywood career as **Richard Stapley** and died at 86 in March 2010.

SUSO CECCHI D'AMICO

Born: *21 July 1914, Rome, Italy.*
Died: *31 July 2010, Rome, Italy.*
Starting with *Mio figlio professore* in 1946, Suso Cecchi d'Amico was responsible for over 100 screenplays, collaborating in particular with the directors Luigi Comencini, Mario Monicelli [qv] and, pre-eminently, Luchino Visconti. Working in Italian cinema at its neo-realist height, she contributed to Vittorio De Sica's *Ladri di biciclette* (Bicycle Thieves, 1948) and was co-opted by William Wyler to add Italian verisimilitude to his 1953 hit *Roman Holiday*. Her Visconti credits included *Bellissima* (1951), *Senso* (1954), *Rocco e i suio fratelli* (Rocco and His Brothers, 1960), *Il gattopardo* (The Leopard, 1963) and *Ludwig* (1972). Winner of numerous Italian awards, she was Oscar-nominated for Monicelli's *Casanova '70* in 1965.

❧ Sharing Cecchi D'Amico's Oscar nomination for *Casanova '70* – and picking up two further nominations of his own, for *I compagni* (1963) and *Il postino* (1994) – was screenwriter **Furio Scarpelli**. Another close associate of director Mario Monicelli [qv], Scarpelli died in April 2010, aged 90.

CLAUDE CHABROL

Born: *24 June 1930, Paris, France.*
Died: *12 September 2010, Paris, France.*
Starting out as a critic with *Cahiers du cinéma*, Claude Chabrol directed his first film, *Le beau Serge*, in 1958. Yet his speciality – queasy anatomisations of the bourgeoisie conceived with spider-like, often Hitchcockian cunning – only came into focus with *Les Biches* (1968), initiating a string of highly accomplished works that frequently starred his then-wife Stéphane Audran; among these were *La Femme infidèle* (1968), *Que la bête meure, Le Boucher* (both 1969), *La Rupture* (1970) and *Juste avant la nuit* (1971). His later work was patchier, though a fruitful association with Isabelle Huppert yielded such titles as *Violette Nozière* (1978) and *La Cérémonie* (1995), and even as recently as 2007 he turned out the bracingly bizarre thriller *La Fille coupée en deux*.

Claude Chabrol

Jill Clayburgh

Robert Culp

❧ Other notable French film directors who died in the period under review include **Jacques Baratier**, best known for the Cannes prize-winner *Goha*, who died in November 2009 aged 91, and **Alain Corneau**, who won a César for *Tous les matins du monde* and died in August 2010, aged 67.

JILL CLAYBURGH

Born: *30 April 1944, New York City, New York, USA.*
Died: *5 November 2010, Lakeville, Connecticut, USA.*
Having won success on Broadway, Jill Clayburgh had her start in films with titles like *The Terminal Man* (1973) and *Gable and Lombard* (1976). Despite playing Carole Lombard in the latter, her sophisticated steel only came into true focus with *Silver Streak* (1976) and *Semi-Tough* (1977). She then picked up two Oscar nominations in consecutive years, for Paul Mazursky's *An Unmarried Woman* (1978) and Alan Pakula's *Starting Over* (1979). Yet, after starring in Bernardo Bertolucci's controversial *La Luna* (1979), her 1980s films raised few ripples. She turned instead to TV and further Broadway successes.

ROBERT CULP

Born: *16 August 1930, Oakland, California, USA.*
Died: *24 March 2010, Los Angeles, California, USA.*
Though best known for the TV series *Trackdown* (1957-59) and, pre-eminently, *I Spy* (1965-68), the suavely engaging Robert Culp had early film showcases in three 1963 releases – *PT 109*, *Sunday in New York* and as 'Wild Bill' Hickok in *The Raiders*. He subsequently played Bob in Paul Mazursky's zeitgeist-savvy satire *Bob & Carol & Ted & Alice* (1969), a cultured bounty hunter in *Hannie Caulder* (1971) and directed as well as starred in *Hickey & Boggs* (1972). Later appearances included *Turk 182!* (1984) and a role as the US President in *The Pelican Brief* (1993).

❧ Among other US TV names, **Paul Burke**, star of *Naked City* and best known on film for *Valley of the Dolls* (1967) and *The Thomas Crown Affair* (1968), died in September 2009, aged 83. *Mission: Impossible* star **Peter Graves**, whose films ranged from *Red Planet Mars* (1952) to *Airplane!* (1980), died in March 2010, also at 83. **John Forsythe**, star of *Bachelor Father* and *Dynasty*, had leads in Hitchcock's *The Trouble With Harry* (1955) and *In Cold Blood* (1967) and died in April 2010, aged 92. Finally, **James MacArthur** – indelibly associated with TV's *Hawaii Five-O* but before that the lead in John Frankenheimer's *The Young Stranger* (1956) and a four-time Disney juvenile – died in October 2010, aged 72.

TONY CURTIS

Born: *3 June 1925, New York City, New York, USA.*
Died: *29 September 2010, Henderson, Nevada, USA.*
Marketed as pretty-boy beefcake, Bronx-born Tony Curtis was initially consigned to costume fripperies like *The Prince Who Was a Thief* (1951) and *The Black Shield of Falworth* (1954). But then a co-starring role opposite Burt Lancaster in *Trapeze* (1956) was followed by another, *The Sweet Smell of Success* (1957), in which Curtis really showed his mettle. As the '50s faded, there was an Oscar nomination for *The Defiant Ones*, an iconic role in *Some Like It Hot* and a more nuanced return to the sword and sandal genre in *Spartacus*. Devolving into more functional vehicles in later years, there were still occasional reminders of his halcyon period, as in *The Boston Strangler* (1967), *The Last Tycoon* (1976) and *Insignificance* (1985).

JOHN DANKWORTH

Born: *20 September 1927, Woodford, Essex, England.*
Died: *6 February 2010, London, England.*
As a film composer, jazz giant Johnny Dankworth began by scoring Lindsay Anderson's seminal 1958 documentary *We Are the Lambeth Boys*, then moved

Tony Curtis

Dino De Laurentiis

on to a remarkable run of important British features, among them *The Criminal, Saturday Night and Sunday Morning* (both 1960), *The Servant* (in which he also appeared, 1963), *Darling* (1965), *Modesty Blaise* (1966), *Accident* (1967) and *The Magus* (1968). After such early 1970s titles as *Perfect Friday* and *10 Rillington Place*, he only returned to film scoring with the millennial mobster picture *Gangster No 1*. He was knighted in 2006.

❖ Other composers of note included three nonagenarians. **Vic Mizzy**, who wrote the TV theme for *The Addams Family* as well as film scores for *The Night Walker* and *Don't Make Waves*, died in October 2009, aged 93. **Nathan Scott**, whose many film credits included *Wake of the Red Witch* in 1948, died at 94 the following February, while **Paul Dunlap** – who scored Samuel Fuller's *Shock Corridor* and *The Naked Kiss* amid a slew of exploitation titles – died in March, aged 90.

DINO DE LAURENTIIS
Born: *8 August 1919, Torre Annunziata, Campania, Italy.*
Died: *10 November 2010, Los Angeles, California, USA.*
This colossus among Italian film producers – one of whose characteristic gestures was to counter Cinecittà by building his own studio called Dinocittà – turned out his first film before World War II and in 1948 scored an international neo-realist hit with *Riso amaro* (Bitter Rice). In the 1950s he went into business with Carlo Ponti and sponsored the works of De Sica, Rossellini, Visconti and Fellini. But his more grandiose schemes only bore fruit when he decamped to America. There, he alternated hits like *Serpico* and *Death Wish* with notorious flops like *Hurricane* and *Dune*; he also added a couple of Ingmar Bergman films to his portfolio. Bankrupted in 1988, he pressed on regardless with latterday titles like *The Desperate Hours*, *Body of Evidence* and *Hannibal*.

❖ De Laurentiis' fellow producer **Alfredo Bini** was responsible for, among many others, Pasolini's *Accattone* (1960) and Bresson's *Lancelot du lac* (1974). He was married to Rosanna Schiaffino [qv] and died in October 2010, aged 83.

Bernard-Pierre Donnadieu

BERNARD-PIERRE DONNADIEU
Born: *2 July 1949, Paris, France.*
Died: *27 December 2010, Versailles, France.*
Best known outside France for his chilling performance as the low-key sociopath in George Sluizer's *Spoorloos* (The Vanishing, 1987), the imposing Bernard-Pierre Donnadieu began with small roles for Roman Polanski, Jean-Jacques Annaud, Claude Lelouch and Patrice Chéreau, winning stardom opposite Jean-Paul Belmondo in Georges Lautner's *Le Professionel* (1981). He then played the title role in *Le Retour de Martin Guerre* (1982) and was César-nominated for *Rue Barbare* (1984). Prolific, too, in TV and theatre (and also the

Clive Donner

Blake Edwards

French voice of Harvey Keitel), he was posthumously hailed in *Paris Match* as "un des grands méchants [villains] du cinéma français."

❧ Other notable French actors who died in 2010 include **Pierre Vaneck** (in January, aged 78), **Laurent Terzieff** (July, aged 75), **Bernard Giraudeau** (July, aged 63), **Bruno Cremer** (August, aged 80) and **Julien Guiomar** (November, aged 82).

CLIVE DONNER
Born: *21 January 1926, London, England.*
Died: *6 September 2010, London, England.*
Having edited such films as *Scrooge* (1951) and *Genevieve* (1953), Clive Donner graduated to direction with effective small-scale pictures like *The Secret Place* (1957) and *Heart of a Child* (1958), finally winning box-office success with *Some People* (1962). His two best films, a broodingly atmospheric version of Harold Pinter's *The Caretaker* (1963) and the artfully cynical satire *Nothing But the Best* (1964), were followed by the modishly colourful *What's New Pussycat* (1965)

and *Here We Go Round the Mulberry Bush* (1967). In 1969, however, *Alfred the Great* bombed, and thereafter Donner's sporadic cinema assignments tended to be less impressive than his TV movies.

BLAKE EDWARDS
Born: *26 July 1922, Tulsa, Oklahoma, USA.*
Died: *15 December 2010, Santa Monica, California, USA.*
Blake Edwards' golden period as a director encompassed the early to mid-1960s, when he moved gracefully between the chic romanticism of *Breakfast at Tiffany's*, the psychological shocks of *Experiment in Terror*, the gruelling alcoholic case study *Days of Wine and Roses*, and the classic Inspector Clouseau comedies *The Pink Panther* and *A Shot in the Dark*. After this, a series of damp squibs and outright disasters – *The Great Race*, *Darling Lili*, *The Wild Rovers* – was only redeemed by Edwards' decision, in 1974, to resurrect Clouseau. Revitalised, between 1979 and 1981 he turned out the sex comedy *10*, the bilious film-biz satire *S.O.B.* and the transvestite musical comedy *Victor Victoria* before fading away into more functional projects.

Kathryn Grayson

BEKIM FEHMIU

Born: *1 June 1936, Sarajevo, Bosnia and Herzegovina.*
Died: *15 June 2010, Belgrade, Serbia.*
After five years in the film business, Bekim Fehmiu, already a recipient of two Yugoslavian awards, came to international prominence in Aleksandar Petrovic's *Skupljaci perja* (I Even Met Happy Gypsies, 1967). By 1968 he was starring opposite Candice Bergen in Lewis Gilbert's *The Adventurers*, but the "brooding, earthy sexiness" noted by Gilbert proved insufficient to carry this misconceived Harold Robbins adaptation. Further credits outside Eastern Europe were scarce, among them *The Deserter* (1970), *Permission to Kill* (1975), *Salon Kitty* and *Black Sunday* (both 1976). After many years of self-imposed retirement, in 2010 he suffered an incapacitating stroke and shot himself.

➤ Croatian film star **Vanja Drach** died in September 2009, aged 77. The extraordinarily prolific Catalan character actor **Victor Israel** died the same month, aged 80. The popular Portuguese leading man, **Virgilio Teixeira**, died in December 2010, aged 93.

RUTH FORD

Born: *7 July 1911, Brookhaven, Mississippi, USA.*
Died: *12 August 2009, New York City, New York, USA.*
Having been a member of Orson Welles' Mercury Players, Ruth Ford appeared in the prestige picture *Wilson* (1944) but was otherwise occupied with 'B' films like *Roaring Frontiers* (1941), *Lady Gangster* (1942) and the unusual chiller *Woman Who Came Back* (1945). After much TV and theatre, she returned in *Act One* (1963), *Play It As It Lays* (1972) and *Too Scared to Scream* (1982). By this time she was famous

for the artists' 'salon' she maintained in her Dakota Building apartment; posthumously, she scandalised Manhattan society by leaving her $8.4m estate to her Nepalese butler.

CARMELITA GONZÁLEZ

Born: *11 July 1928, Mexico City, Mexico.*
Died: *30 April 2010, Mexico City, Mexico.*
Carmelita González – occasionally billed as Carmen González – enjoyed a 60-year acting career that ranged from the halcyon days of Mexican cinema to 21st century telenovelas. As well as gracing such post-war south-of-the-border Westerns as *El hijo del bandido* and *Los hijos de María Morales*, she acted for Luis Buñuel in *Subida al cielo* (1952) and the following year made a big impact in the hit 'ranchera' comedy *Dos tipos de cuidado*. She was also involved in the Lucha Libre genre, appearing in *Huracán Ramírez* (1952) and its three 1960s sequels. Much later, she won a Silver Ariel for her performance in Luis Mandoki's 1984 film *Motel*.

➤ Also matched against musical comedy stars Pedro Infante and Jorge Negrete in *Dos tipos de cuidado* was **Yolanda Varela**, who was nominated for a Silver Ariel for the 1956 film *Los Amantes* and died in August 2009, aged 79.

KATHRYN GRAYSON

Born: *9 February 1922, Winston-Salem, North Carolina, USA.*
Died: *17 February 2010, Los Angeles, California, USA.*
Originally intended by M-G-M as a substitute for the errant Deanna Durbin, the beautiful coloratura soprano Kathryn Grayson helped define the post-war Hollywood musical via her roles opposite Gene Kelly

Pamela Green

Corey Haim

June Havoc

and Frank Sinatra in *Anchors Aweigh* (1945), Mario Lanza in *That Midnight Kiss* (1949) and *The Toast of New Orleans* (1950) and, perhaps most memorably, Howard Keel in *Show Boat* (1951), *Lovely to Look At* (1952) and *Kiss Me Kate* (1953). Elsewhere, Warners matched her with Gordon McCrae in *The Desert Song* (1953), then at Paramount she brought her film career to a close with the lavish but underwhelming operetta *The Vagabond King* (1956).

PAMELA GREEN

Born: *28 March 1929, Kingston upon Thames, Surrey, England.*
Died: *7 May 2010, Isle of Wight, England.*
The iconic glamour model Pamela Green occupies a small but perfectly formed niche in cinema history as the first nude included in a mainstream British feature; the film was Michael Powell's 1959 classic *Peeping Tom*. She subsequently starred for her photographer partner Harrison Marks in the quaint but groundbreaking nudie features *Naked – As Nature Intended* (1961) and *The Naked World of Harrison Marks* (1965). Later, she became a stills photographer for the short-lived production company Tyburn, for whom she also played a Parisian prostitute in *Legend of the Werewolf* (1974).

COREY HAIM

Born: *23 December 1971, Toronto, Ontario, Canada.*
Died: *10 March 2010, Burbank, California, USA.*
Corey Haim started out as Teri Garr's son in *Firstborn* (1984) and Sally Field's in *Murphy's Romance* (1985), then got his first lead in the title role of *Lucas* (1986). It was in the modish vampire film *The Lost Boys* (1987) that he broke through to teen idol status, but his impish vitality was squandered in record time by dreary vehicles like *License to Drive* and *Dream a Little Dream* (both 1988); subsequent projects tended to go straight to video. In 2007-8, frequent co-star Corey Feldman joined him in the exhibitionist Reality show *The Two Coreys*.

❧ Exactly one month Haim's senior, German actor **Frank Giering** died in June 2010, aged 38; he was best known for *Funny Games* (1997) and *Baader* (2002).

JUNE HAVOC

Born: *8 November 1912, Vancouver, British Columbia, Canada.*
Died: *28 March 2010, Stamford, Connecticut, USA.*
The tiny vaudeville star Baby June appeared in a few silent films before attaining adult stardom, as June Havoc, in the 1940 Broadway production of *Pal Joey*. Much later, a memoir by her sister, burlesque star Gypsy Rose Lee, became the hit musical *Gypsy*, complete with a Baby June caricature; Havoc countered by writing and directing the autobiographical Broadway drama *Marathon '33*. In the meantime, she had made her film debut proper in *Four Jacks and a Jill* (1942), after which she was seen in, among others, *My Sister Eileen* (1942), *Intrigue*, *Gentleman's Agreement* (both 1947) and *Lady Possessed* (1952).

❧ Other veterans of the silent era included **Virginia Davis**, child star of Walt Disney's 'Alice' comedies, who died in August 2009, aged 90, and **Dorothy Janis**, who starred opposite Ramon Novarro in *The Pagan* (1929) and died aged 98 in March 2010. **Yvonne Howell**, one of Mack Sennett's 'bathing beauties' and subsequently the wife of director George Stevens, was 104 when she died in May 2010.

Dennis Hopper

DENNIS HOPPER

Born: *17 May 1936, Dodge City, Kansas, USA.*
Died: *29 May 2010, Venice, California, USA.*
An iconic actor-director for whom the word 'maverick' might have been coined, Dennis Hopper began as a disciple of James Dean (appearing with him in *Rebel Without a Cause* and *Giant*) and by the turn of the 1960s was starring in beguiling fringe oddities like *Night Tide*. Then in 1969 he delivered the epoch-making counter-cultural hit *Easy Rider*, both directing and starring. But Hopper's follow-up, *The Last Movie*, was deemed a fiasco and ushered in his drug-dependent twilight years. Though *The American Friend*, *Apocalypse Now* and Hopper's third director credit, *Out of the Blue*, date from this 'lost' era, it was only with his hair-raising performance in *Blue Velvet* (1986) that he re-defined himself as Hollywood's favourite senior psychotic, a type showcased most conspicuously in the 1994 hit *Speed*.

❖ Another teen veteran of *Rebel Without a Cause*, **Corey Allen**, died in June 2010, aged 75; moving from acting to directing TV movies, he was also responsible for the odd feature film, notably *Avalanche* (1978).

LENA HORNE

Born: *30 June 1917, New York City, New York, USA.*
Died: *9 May 2010, New York City, New York, USA.*
Singer Lena Horne got her start at the Cotton Club in the 1930s and later became a Tony-winning Broadway star in the 1980s; she was also a campaigner for civil rights. During a brief spell in 1940s Hollywood, her scenes were often compartmentalised in such a way that they could be cut from showings in the South. Even so, she made an impact in *Panama Hattie*, *Broadway Rhythm* and especially *Cabin in the Sky* and *Stormy Weather*; the latter came complete with her same-titled signature tune. Blacklisted during the McCarthy era, she reappeared in *Death of a Gunfighter* (1968) and *The Wiz* (1978).

JOYCE HOWARD

Born: *28 February 1922, London, England.*
Died: *23 November 2010, Santa Monica, California, USA.*
This war-time British star performed at the Old Vic throughout the Blitz and gained her initial film experience in Anthony Asquith's *Freedom Radio* and two John Baxter films, *Love on the Dole* and *The Common Touch* (all 1941). She was one of the seven plucky British girls featured in Leslie Howard's *The Gentle Sex*, appeared in the Arthur Askey vehicle *Back-Room Boy*, and was profitably matched with James Mason in the lurid chiller *The Night Has Eyes* and the taut espionage drama *They Met in the Dark*. She later emigrated to America, becoming a novelist, playwright and TV script editor.

JOHN HUGHES

Born: *18 February 1950, Lansing, Michigan, USA.*
Died: *6 August 2009, New York City, New York, USA.*
Though his last 15 years were spent in self-imposed seclusion, in the 1980s no filmmaker had his finger more astutely on the pulse of American youth than John Hughes. The eight films he directed – including the iconic titles *Sixteen Candles* (1983), *The Breakfast Club* (1984) and *Ferris Bueller's Day Off* (1985) – were made over an industrious eight-year period, with astute changes of pace that accommodated the John Candy comedies *Planes, Trains and Automobiles* (1987) and *Uncle Buck* (1989). As writer and/or producer, he was also responsible for major hits like *Pretty in Pink* (1986), *Home Alone* (1990) and *Beethoven* (1992).

ALAN HUME

Born: *16 October 1924, London, England.*
Died: *13 July 2010, Chalfont St Giles, Buckinghamshire, England.*
After 19 years in the industry, Alan Hume became a cinematographer with the 1961 film *Carry On Regardless*, subsequently notching up a further 15

Lena Horne

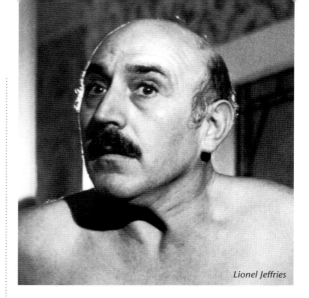

Lionel Jeffries

Alan Hume

Carry Ons as well as several other titles for producer Peter Rogers. He also handled horrors for Hammer (*The Kiss of the Vampire*, 1962) and Amicus (*Dr Terror's House of Horrors*, 1964; *From Beyond the Grave*, 1973), four of Roger Moore's seven James Bond films, and even – to complete his unrivalled breadth of British pop culture phenomena – *Confessions of a Pop Performer* (1975). His last notable credits were the late 1980s hits *A Fish Called Wanda* and *Shirley Valentine*.

TONY IMI

Born: *27 March 1937, London, England.*
Died: *8 March 2010, London, England.*
In his twenties, cinematographer Tony Imi was a stalwart of the BBC's *Wednesday Play* strand, photographing such hand-held, hard-hitting dramas as Ken Loach's *Up the Junction* (1965) and *Cathy Come Home* (1966). Moving into films, he worked frequently with Bryan Forbes (*The Raging Moon*, 1970; *The Slipper and the Rose*, 1975; *International Velvet*, 1978) and shot star-studded action thrillers like *Brass Target* (1978), *North Sea Hijack* (1979) and *The Sea Wolves* (1980). Latterly, amid numerous TV movies, he worked on such disparate titles as *Enemy Mine* (1985), *Buster* (1988), *Shopping* (1994) and *Rancid Aluminium* (1999).

❧ Cinematographers **Richard Moore** and **Rosalío Solano** both died in August 2009, aged 83 and 94 respectively. Moore's credits included *The Wild Angels*, *Myra Breckinridge* and *The Stone Killer*, while Solano

shot nearly 200 Mexican titles across a 60-year period and won three Ariel awards. Cinematographers who died in 2010 ranged from **Derek Vanlint** (February, aged 77), who photographed *Alien* and *Dragonslayer*, to **Gene Polito** (November, aged 92), whose credits included *Prime Cut* and *Westworld*, and **Chris Condon** (December, aged 87), the stereoscopic innovator who photographed *Jaws 3-D*.

LIONEL JEFFRIES

Born: *10 June 1926, London, England.*
Died: *19 February 2010, Poole, Dorset, England.*
This bullet-headed character star had a barely restrained 'could combust at any moment' quality that was equally appropriate for the loathsome Marquis of Queensberry in *The Trials of Oscar Wilde* (1960) and the many apoplectic comedy characters he played in such films as *Blue Murder at St Trinian's* (1957), *Two Way Stretch* (1960) and *The Wrong Arm of the Law* (1962). After iconic roles in the colourful extravaganzas *First Men in the Moon* (1964), *Camelot* (1967) and *Chitty Chitty Bang Bang* (1968), he moved into direction with such perennial favourites as *The Railway Children* (1970) and *The Amazing Mr Blunden* (1972), the gentle tone of which reflected his contempt for the 'permissive society'.

LAMONT JOHNSON

Born: *30 September 1922, Stockton, California, USA.*
Died: *24 October 2010, Monterey, California, USA.*
Lamont Johnson began as an actor, moved into direction via TV series like *Peter Gunn* and *The Twilight Zone*, and made his cinema debut with *A Covenant with Death* (1967). He quickly colonised a wide range of genres – POW drama (*The McKenzie Break*, 1970), Western (*A Gunfight*, 1971), SF thriller (*The Groundstar Conspiracy*, 1971), all-in-the-family horror (*You'll Like My Mother*, 1972) – prior to delivering arguably his best film, *The Last American Hero* (1973). He stumbled, however, with rape-revenge (*Lipstick*, 1976), reserving his best efforts for such classic TV movies as *The Execution of Private Slovik* (1974) and *Lincoln* (1988).

❧ Though chiefly preoccupied with TV, director **Arnold Laven**, who died in September 2009 aged 87, was also responsible for such well-muscled 1950s crime thrillers as *Without Warning* and *Vice Squad*, together with *The Monster that Challenged the World*.

JENNIFER JONES

Born: *2 March 1919, Tulsa, Oklahoma, USA.*
Died: *17 December 2009, Malibu, California, USA.*
Though a major star, Jennifer Jones' career was to some extent impeded by the very man who was determined to build it up – her perfectionist mentor, and latterly husband, David O Selznick. Introduced in the 1943 film *The Song of Bernadette*, for which she won an Oscar, she proceeded to pick up further nominations for *Since You Went Away* (1944), *Love Letters* (1945) and *Duel in the Sun* (1946). Showcased in an unusually earthy role in the latter, she then reached an ethereal (indeed, ghostly) apotheosis in *Portrait of Jennie* (1948). Further credits ranged from *Carrie* (1950), *Ruby Gentry* (1952) and *Beat the Devil* (1953) to *Love is a Many-Splendored Thing* (another Oscar nomination, 1955), *Tender is the Night* (1961) and finally *The Towering Inferno* (1974).

BRENDA JOYCE

Born: *25 February 1912, Excelsior Springs, Missouri, USA.*
Died: *4 July 2009, Santa Monica, California, USA.*
Contracted to Twentieth Century-Fox, Brenda Joyce started strongly as the second female lead in Clarence Brown's *The Rains Came* (1939). After further eye-catching roles in *Public Deb No 1* (1940) and *Marry the Boss's Daughter* (1941), she drifted into second features, including *Pillow of Death* for Universal. She then fetched up at RKO, where she played her most famous – but, for her, most hated – role five times. This was Jane in Sol Lesser's series of Tarzan 'B' pictures, initially opposite Johnny Weissmuller and latterly Lex Barker. She retired in 1948.

Jennifer Jones

Brenda Joyce appeared in the last three of eight Tarzan pictures in which 'Boy' was played by **Johnny Sheffield**. Sheffield, who moved on to his own film series focused on Bomba the Jungle Boy, died in October 2010, aged 79.

ELLIOTT KASTNER

Born: *7 January 1930, New York City, New York, USA.*
Died: *30 June 2010, London, England.*
In the 1960s, in a then-revolutionary move, Elliott Kastner transformed himself from MCA agent and Universal executive into a Pinewood-based independent producer, working in partnership with Jerry Gershwin as Winkast Film Productions. As well as multiple assignments for Marlon Brando

Brenda Joyce

Irvin Kershner

and Richard Burton, Kastner also specialised in adaptations of two very different authors, Raymond Chandler and Alistair Maclean. Among his many credits are *Harper* (1966), *Where Eagles Dare* (1968), *A Severed Head* (1970), *Villain* (1971), *The Long Goodbye* (1973), *The Missouri Breaks* (1975), *Equus* (1977) and *Angel Heart* (1987).

❧ Another filmmaker with a pronounced Alistair Maclean connection was **Geoffrey Reeve**, director of *Puppet on a Chain* and *Caravan to Vaccares*, and producer of several other films; he died in January 2010, aged 77.

TONY KENDALL

Born: *22 August 1936, Rome, Italy.*
Died: *28 November 2009, Rome, Italy.*
Appropriately, given his future in all forms of Euro-exploitation, square-jawed Tony Kendall began as a model for Italian photo-comics. Having made his film debut under his real name, Luciano Stella, in *Femmine tre volta* (1957), he re-emerged as Tony Kendall in Mario Bava's luscious Gothic romance *La frusta e il corpo* (1963). He subsequently achieved fame opposite Brad Harris in a seven-strong sequence of *Kommissar X* thrillers (1965-71), twice played the Western anti-hero

Django, then moved into Spanish horror (*El ataque de los muertos sin ojos*, 1972; *Las garras de Lorelei*, 1973) and Italian gangland rip-offs (*Corleone*, 1978).

IRVIN KERSHNER

Born: *29 April 1923, Philadelphia, Pennsylvania, USA.*
Died: *27 November 2010, Los Angeles, California, USA.*
Though he will remain best remembered for the second *Star Wars* instalment, *The Empire Strikes Back* – which he directed at the request of his former pupil George Lucas – Irvin Kershner made his best films on tighter budgets and much narrower canvases. Having started in the late 1950s with teen melodramas like *Stakeout on Dope Street* and *The Young Captives*, he ranged across several genres in such striking 1960s titles as *The Hoodlum Priest*, *A Face in the Rain*, *The Luck of Ginger Coffey*, *A Fine Madness*, *The Flim-Flam Man* and *Loving*. His later work included two sequels (*The Return of a Man Called Horse* and *RoboCop 2*) and the rogue 007 entry *Never Say Never Again*.

AGNÈS LAURENT

Born: *28 January 1936, Lyon, France.*
Died: *16 February 2010, Grenoble, France.*
Extolled in the July 1958 issue of *Playboy* as the

Agnès Laurent

'Pocket-Size Parisienne', Agnès Laurent was first seen in a couple of André Hunebelle films before graduating to leading roles in *Marchands de filles* (1957) and *Péché de jeunesse* (1958). She was further showcased in Spain (*Un mundo para mí*, 1959) and Italy (*La notte del grande assalto*, 1960), and rounded off her brief star career in Britain, playing the title role in *A French Mistress* (1960) and providing the allure in *Mary Had a Little…* (1961), a contender for the title of Britain's first sex comedy.

◆ Brought over to Hollywood as a Howard Hughes protégée, German actress **Ursula Thiess** appeared in such 1950s titles as *Bengal Rifles* and *The Americano*; she died in June 2010, aged 86.

KARL MALDEN

Born: *22 March 1912, Chicago, Illinois, USA.*
Died: *1 July 2009, Brentwood, California, USA.*
Among Hollywood's greatest post-war character stars, Karl Malden was a graduate of the pre-war Group Theatre. Through director Elia Kazan, he scored a remarkable triptych of 1950s successes with *A Streetcar Named Desire*, *On the Waterfront* and *Baby Doll*, winning an Academy Award for the first. Oscillating between hard-faced villains and empathetic Everyman figures, he also racked up such classic titles as *Ruby Gentry* (1952), *Fear Strikes Out* (1957), *One-Eyed Jacks* (1960), *Birdman of Alcatraz* (1962), *Cheyenne Autumn* (1964), *The Cincinnati Kid* (1965) and *Patton* (1970). In addition, he directed the 1957 film *Time Limit*. And all this before he became a household name via the 1972-77 TV series *The Streets of San Francisco*.

TOM MANKIEWICZ

Born: *1 June 1942, Los Angeles, California, USA.*
Died: *31 July 2010, Los Angeles, California, USA.*
Son of writer-director Joseph L Mankiewicz, Tom Mankiewicz gained his first screenplay credit for *The Sweet Ride* in 1968. Thereafter, starting with *Diamonds Are Forever*, he had a hand in all five of the James Bond films produced during the 1970s. As well as writing the mid-1970s titles *Mother, Jugs and Speed*, *The Cassandra Crossing* and *The Eagle Has Landed*, he was kept busy as a script doctor (notably on the 1978 hit *Superman*) and later turned director with the comedies *Dragnet* (1987) and *Delirious* (1991). He was also a key architect of the hit ABC TV show *Hart to Hart* (1979-84).

ADELE MARA

Born: *28 April 1923, Highland Park, Michigan, USA.*
Died: *7 May 2010, Pacific Palisades, California, USA.*
Spanish-American Adele Mara was signed, aged 18, by Columbia, where she played, among others, Rita Hayworth's sister in *You Were Never Lovelier* (1942). Under contract to Republic from 1944 to 1951, she became a platinum blonde pin-up, played opposite horse-opera heroes Roy Rogers and Gene Autry, contributed an erotic dance routine to *The Vampire's Ghost* (1944) and was matched with John Wayne in

Karl Malden

Adele Mara

Carol Marsh

both *Wake of the Red Witch* (1948) and *Sands of Iwo Jima* (1949). She married TV producer Roy Huggins in 1952 and thereafter appeared in several of his shows.

CAROL MARSH
Born: *10 May 1926, London, England.*
Died: *6 March 2010, London, England.*
Carol Marsh was plucked, aged 20, from the Rank Charm School to play Rose in the Boulting Brothers' classic *Brighton Rock* (1947). Despite the touching luminosity of her performance, and a one-off lead in the 1949 Gainsborough comedy *Helter Skelter*, a fully developed film career never materialised, though she added to *Brighton Rock* supporting roles in two other British classics – *Scrooge* (1951) and *Dracula* (1958). Her strangest assignment was playing the title role in a part-French, part-animated *Alice in Wonderland* in 1948; by coincidence, the film was scheduled at London's National Film Theatre the day after her death.

JOHN McCALLUM
Born: *14 March 1918, Brisbane, Queensland, Australia.*
Died: *3 February 2010, Sydney, New South Wales, Australia.*
Australian-born but of Scots extraction, John McCallum was a handsome leading man in 1940s British cinema, frequently cast alongside his wife Googie Withers. The films that established them, both Ealing releases from 1947, were *The Loves of Joanna Godden* and *It Always Rains on Sunday*, with lesser teamings to follow like *Miranda* (1948) and *Traveller's Joy* (1950). His other leading ladies included

Phyllis Calvert (*Root of All Evil*, 1947), Greta Gynt (*The Calendar*, 1948) and Jean Kent (*The Woman in Question*, 1950). Back in Australia, he directed *Nickel Queen* (1970), starring his wife, and produced several TV series, notably *Skippy* (1967-70).

KEVIN McCARTHY
Born: *15 February 1914, Seattle, Washington, USA.*
Died: *11 September 2010, Hyannis, Massachusetts, USA.*
An actor of irresistible laid-back charm, Kevin McCarthy will be forever remembered for a hair-raising outbreak of the exact opposite, repeatedly shrieking "You're next!" at the climax of Don Siegel's paranoid classic *Invasion of the Body Snatchers* (1955). With 19 Broadway appearances to his credit, he also played Biff in *Death of a Salesman* in the West End and won a Golden Globe (plus an Oscar nomination) when he repeated the role in the 1951 film. Though *Body Snatchers* remained his only lead, his patrician presence distinguished scores of other films, among them *The Misfits* (1960), *The Prize* (1963), *Kansas City Bomber* (1972), *Piranha* (1978) and *Innerspace* (1987). In 2006, he played himself in Anthony Hopkins' bizarre directorial folly, *Slipstream*.

◆ Three other American male leads of the 1950s – **Byron Palmer**, **Fess Parker** and **John Crawford** – died in September 2009 (aged 89), March 2010 (aged 85) and September 2010 (aged 90) respectively. US character actors who died during the period under review include **John Quade** (August 2009, 71), **Henry Gibson**

(September 2009, 73), **John Hart** (September 2009, 91), **Val Avery** (December 2009, 85), **James Gammon** (July 2010, aged 70), **Maury Chaykin** (July 2010, 61) and **Harold Gould** (September 2010, 86). Canadian character stalwart **Lou Jacobi** died in October 2009, aged 95.

DANIEL MELNICK

Born: *21 April 1932, New York City, New York, USA.*
Died: *13 October 2009, Los Angeles, California, USA.*
Beginning in TV, producer Daniel Melnick won two Emmy awards and was the architect of the hit series *Get Smart* (1965-70) and *NYPD* (1967-69). In January 1971, he put his first film project, *Straw Dogs*, into production and the result proved a controversial smash hit; it led to Melnick running both MGM and Columbia at different times during the 1970s. His other production credits were impressively diverse, including *That's Entertainment!* (1974), *All That Jazz* (1979), *Altered States* (1980), *Making Love* (1982), *Footloose* (1984), *Roxanne* (1987), *LA Story* (1991) and *Blue Streak* (1999).

ZAKES MOKAE

Born: *5 August 1934, Johannesburg, South Africa.*
Died: *11 September 2009, Las Vegas, Nevada, USA.*
Zakes Mokae helped bring the injustices of apartheid before an international audience via his decades-long association with actor-playwright Athol Fugard, which finally brought him a Tony award on Broadway in 1982. Mokae's first film, in 1960, was the Anglo-South African *Tremor*; he then appeared in eye-catching but uncredited roles in *Darling* (1965) and *The Rise and Rise of Michael Rimmer* (1969). His greatest visibility on film covered a ten-year period starting in the mid-1980s, including such titles as *Cry Freedom*, *The Serpent and the Rainbow*, *A Dry White Season*, *Dad*, *A Rage in Harlem*, *Dust Devil*, *Outbreak* and *Waterworld*.

MARIO MONICELLI

Born: *16 May 1915, Viareggio, Tuscany, Italy.*
Died: *29 November 2010, Rome, Italy.*
Mario Monicelli started out by directing popular vehicles for Totò before moving on to such stars as Alberto Sordi, Vittorio Gassman and Marcello Mastroianni. Generally writing his own scripts

John McCallum

Kevin McCarthy

Mario Monicelli

in collaboration with Agenore Incrocci and Furio Scarpelli, Monicelli quickly established himself as the architect of a new form of brilliantly observed, frequently bittersweet social comedy, scoring numerous major hits – *I soliti ignoti* (1958), *La grande guerra* (1959), *I compagni* (1963), *Casanova '70* (1965), *L'armata Brancaleone* (1965), *Amici miei* (1975), *Un borghese piccolo piccolo* (1976), *Speriamo che sia femmina*

Brittany Murphy

(1986) and many more. Winner of multiple awards, he directed his final feature, *Le rose del deserto*, aged 91; four years later, having been hospitalised with prostate cancer, he committed suicide.

❥ Italian directors **Luciano Emmer** and **Corso Salani** died, aged 91 and 48 respectively, in September 2009 and June 2010. Other directors of international repute who died in 2009-10 include, from Japan, **Shue Matsubayashi** (August 2009, aged 89); **Ary Fernandes** from Brazil (August 2010, 79); the Spanish **Luis García Berlanga** (November 2010, 89); **Nikos Papatakis** from Greece (December 2010, 92) and, from India, **B S Ranga** (December 2010, 93). In Russia, **Ivan Dykhovichny** died in September 2009, aged 61; **Leonid Nechayev** in January 2010, aged 70; **Pavel Lyubimov** in June 2010 at 71, and **Igor Talankin** in July 2010, aged 82.

BRITTANY MURPHY
Born: *10 November 1977, Atlanta, Georgia, USA.*
Died: *20 December 2009, Los Angeles, California, USA.*
After featuring in the sitcom *Drexell's Class*, Brittany Murphy was just 17 when she played her break-out role in the 1995 teen comedy *Clueless*. The quirky charm that became her stock-in-trade was later subverted by the ensemble intensity of *Girl, Interrupted* (1999) and an edgy performance in the Eminem vehicle *8 Mile* (2002). Her other credits included *Drop Dead Gorgeous* (1999), *Cherry Falls* (2000), *Riding in Cars with Boys* (2001), *Uptown Girls* (2003) and *Sin City* (2005). She also did animation voice work for TV (*King of the Hill*) and film (*Happy Feet*).

PAUL NASCHY

Born: *6 September 1934, Madrid, Spain.*
Died: *30 November 2009, Madrid, Spain.*
As a boy, Paul Naschy fell in love with Lon Chaney Jr's lycanthropic Larry Talbot character, so – after a spell as a champion weightlifter – there was a degree of wish-fulfilment in his taking on the hirsute mantle of macho but melancholy werewolf Waldemar Daninsky. The string of naïve yet spirited Iberian shockers showcasing the character kicked off in 1968 with *La marca del hombre lobo*. Under his real name, Jacinto Molina, Naschy also wrote most of his own vehicles, and in 1976 turned director with *Inquicisión*. Like Chaney Jr, he wasn't always ideally suited to the other famous monsters he played, but he brought a fan's enthusiasm to the task and remains a formidable cult figure.

↪ Another surprising Dracula, US character actor **Michael Pataki**, died in April 2010, aged 72. **Vonetta McGee**, well-remembered for 1970s titles like *Blacula*, *Shaft in Africa* and *The Eiger Sanction*, died in July 2010, aged 65. **Ahna Capri**, whose credits included *Brotherhood of Satan* and *Enter the Dragon*, died the following month, aged 66. And **Margo Johns**, a British stage actress best remembered for the 1961 exploitation absurdity *Konga*, died in September 2009, aged 90.

Paul Naschy

PATRICIA NEAL

Born: *20 January 1926, Packard, Kentucky, USA.*
Died: *8 August 2010, Edgartown, Massachusetts, USA.*
Patricia Neal made her Broadway debut, and won a Tony award, aged only 20. In Hollywood she appeared opposite Gary Cooper in *The Fountainhead* (1949) and Michael Rennie in *The Day the Earth Stood Still* (1951), subsequently wowing critics in Elia Kazan's *A Face in the Crowd* (1957), taking a key supporting role in *Breakfast at Tiffany's* (1961), winning an Oscar for *Hud* (1962) and then a BAFTA for *In Harm's Way* (1964). After being struck down by three debilitating strokes in 1965, she was nursed back to health by her husband Roald Dahl and received another Oscar nomination for *The Subject Was Roses* (1968). Sporadic latterday roles included *Ghost Story* (1981) and *Cookie's Fortune* (1999).

RONALD NEAME

Born: *23 April 1911, London, England.*
Died: *16 June 2010, Los Angeles, California, USA.*
Rounding off more than a decade as a cinematographer, Ronald Neame photographed *Blithe Spirit* in 1944, then turned producer for three further David Lean titles – *Brief Encounter*, *Great Expectations* and *Oliver Twist*. Starting as a director in his own right in 1947, Neame's films included the Gregory Peck vehicle *The Million Pound Note* (1953), several with Alec Guinness, including *The Card* (1952) and *Tunes of Glory* (1960), Judy Garland's last showcase, *I Could Go On*

Patricia Neal

Ronald Neame

Singing (1963), the modish crime caper *Gambit* (1966) and the 1969 evergreen *The Prime of Miss Jean Brodie*. In America, he initiated the 'disaster' cycle with *The Poseidon Adventure* (1972), cannily holding on to five per cent of the considerable profits and making only five further films in its wake.

LESLIE NIELSEN

Born: *11 February 1926, Regina, Saskatchewan, Canada.*
Died: *28 November 2010, Fort Lauderdale, Florida, USA.*
Aptly memorialised in one British newspaper as "the doyen of deadpan," Leslie Nielsen started out as a dependable leading man in 1950s titles like *Forbidden Planet* and *Tammy and the Bachelor*. He then devolved into a dull middle period devoted to somewhat stolid support turns, a highlight among which was his ship's captain in the seminal 1970s disaster film *The Poseidon Adventure*. Then – having given more or less the same straight-faced performance in the ridiculous *Airplane!* – he took on an entirely new 1980s persona as a deadpan droll of the most irresistible kind. His blissfully dense Lt Frank Drebin, in *Naked Gun* and its sequels, has justly entered the pantheon of comic immortals.

DAN O'BANNON

Born: *30 September 1946, St Louis, Missouri, USA.*
Died: *17 December 2009, Los Angeles, California, USA.*
First making a name for himself as co-writer, production designer and co-star of John Carpenter's cult film *Dark Star* (1974), Dan O'Bannon proceeded to notch up an impressive set of writing credits in the horror and SF genres – *Alien* (1979), *Dead & Buried*, *Heavy Metal* (both 1981), *Return of the Living Dead* (1984, which he also directed), *Lifeforce* (1985), *Total Recall* (1990) and *Screamers* (1995), with a detour into action movie thrills for *Blue Thunder* (1983). As well as the smash-hit *Living Dead* film, he also directed the underrated H P Lovecraft adaptation, *The Resurrected* (1991).

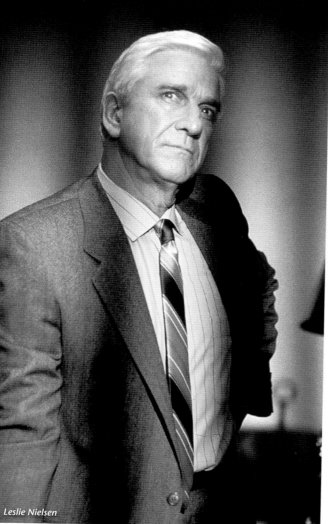
Leslie Nielsen

Per Oscarsson

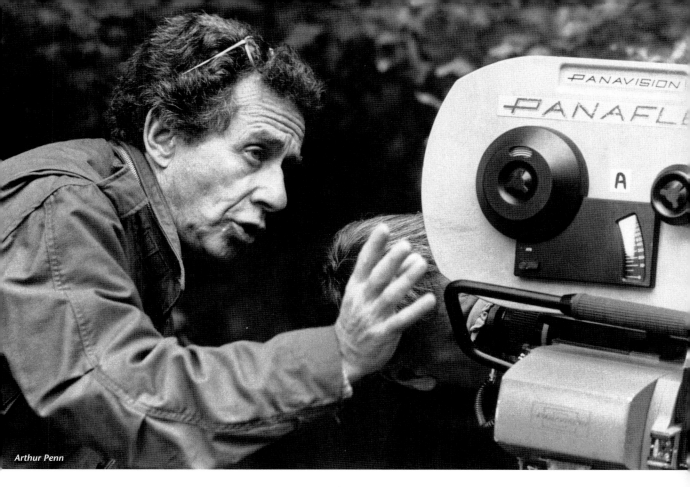

Arthur Penn

PER OSCARSSON

Born: *28 January 1927, Stockholm, Sweden.*
Died: *31 December 2010, Bjärka, Sweden.*

An intense and consistently charismatic screen presence, Per Oscarsson started acting in the mid-1940s and in 1966 made an award-winning breakthrough with the lead role in Henning Carlsen's *Sult* (Hunger). The film triggered a brief flurry of international assignments in the late 1960s and early 1970s, ranging from *A Dandy in Aspic* and *The Night Visitor* (in which he played Max Von Sydow's brother-in-law) to *The Last Valley*, *Endless Night* and *Secrets*. In addition, there were rewarding roles for directors Mai Zetterling, Vilgot Sjöman and Dusan Makavejev, though, strangely, none for Ingmar Bergman. He also played Frankenstein's monster and August Strindberg (twice), and was still working shortly before his tragic death in a New Year's Eve house fire.

❯ Early in his career, Oscarsson was twice directed by **Gösta Werner**, who died in July 2010, aged 101. Oscarsson also appeared in the first of 15 films directed by **Jan Halldoff**, who died – also in July 2010 – at the age of 70.

CLIVE PARSONS

Born: *15 August 1942, Woking, Surrey, England.*
Died: *12 August 2009, London, England.*

Producer Clive Parsons was responsible, with business partner Davina Belling, for an eclectic range of British hits and misses. They started with the controversial *Inserts* (1975), then sandwiched

Alan Clarke's hard-hitting *Scum* (1979) between the sex comedy *Rosie Dixon Night Nurse* (1978) and vulgar teen farce *Party Party* (1982). They also transmuted the TV classic *Rock Follies* into the entirely unrecognisable *Breaking Glass* (1979), then scored heavily with Bill Forsyth's *Gregory's Girl* (1980) and less so with Lindsay Anderson's *Britannia Hospital* (1982). Without Belling, Parsons' credits included two Franco Zeffirelli titles, *Tea With Mussolini* (1998) and *Callas Forever* (2002).

ARTHUR PENN

Born: *27 September 1922, Philadelphia, Pennsylvania, USA.*
Died: *28 September 2010, New York City, New York, USA.*

Having won a golden reputation on Broadway, Arthur Penn directed his first film, *The Left Handed Gun*, in 1957. Four years later he filmed his stage hit *The Miracle Worker* and received his first of three 1960s Oscar nominations. Mid-decade, a teaming with Warren Beatty (*Mickey One*) and an exercise in gruelling violence (*The Chase*) were dazzlingly spliced together in 1966, when Penn shot one of the quintessential American films of the era, *Bonnie and Clyde*. He continued strongly with *Alice's Restaurant* and *Little Big Man*, but began to falter with the mid-'70s duo *Night Moves* and *The Missouri Breaks*. His career concluded with more functional assignments like *Target* (1985) and *Dead of Winter* (1986).

❯ Child actress **Lori Martin** – who appeared in Penn's *The Chase* and, more momentously, J Lee Thompson's *Cape Fear* (1962) – died in April 2010, aged 62.

Ingrid Pitt

INGRID PITT

Born: *21 November 1937, Czestochowa, Poland.*
Died: *23 November 2010, London, England.*
Ingoushka Petrov survived a Nazi concentration camp to become a member of the Berliner Ensemble, subsequently getting a major break in the MGM smash *Where Eagles Dare* (1968). She was then hailed in America's *Cue* magazine as "the world's most lovely vampire" thanks to her fanged appearances in the 1970 films *The Vampire Lovers* (for Hammer) and *The House That Dripped Blood* (for Amicus). After playing the star part in *Countess Dracula* and a truncated role in *The Wicker Man*, Pitt's film opportunities petered out somewhat, but her cult status was assured.

DOROTHY PROVINE

Born: *20 January 1935, Deadwood, South Dakota, USA.*
Died: *25 April 2010, Bremerton, Washington, USA.*
Made famous by the 1960-62 TV series *The Roaring 20's*, Dorothy Provine became a vivacious blonde staple of some of the most high-profile Hollywood comedies of the period. Despite a hard-edged start in the title role of *The Bonnie Parker Story* (1958), she was soon to be seen in *It's a Mad Mad Mad Mad World* (1962), *Good Neighbour Sam* (1964), *The Great Race, That Darn Cat!* (both 1965), *Who's Minding the Mint?* (1967) and, in 1968, *Never a Dull Moment*. The same year, she married director Robert Day and effectively retired.

IRVING RAVETCH

Born: *14 November 1920, Newark, New Jersey, USA.*
Died: *19 September 2010, Los Angeles, California, USA.*
After an apprenticeship in Westerns, Irving Ravetch formed a screenwriting partnership with his wife, Harriet Frank Jr, and turned their joint interest in social issues into eight screenplays for director Martin Ritt. Starting with *The Long, Hot Summer* in 1958, these included the Paul Newman vehicles *Hud* (1962) and *Hombre* (1967), plus *Conrack* (1973), the multi-award-winning *Norma Rae* (1978) and Ritt's last film (theirs too), *Stanley & Iris* (1989). Among the team's other credits were *The Dark at the Top of the Stairs* (1960), *The Cowboys* (1971) and *The Spikes Gang* (1973).

❧ Other US screenwriters who died during 2009-10 included **Larry Gelbart** (September 2009, aged 81), **Rose Kaufman** (December 2009, 70), **Anne Froelich** (January 2010, 96), **Aleen Leslie** (February 2010, 101) and **William W Norton** (October 2010, 85).

LYNN REDGRAVE

Born: *8 March 1943, London, England.*
Died: *2 May 2010, Kent, Connecticut, USA.*
After her 1962 debut in *Tom Jones*, Lynn Redgrave received a BAFTA nomination for *Girl with Green Eyes* and then became a refreshingly alternative exemplar of Swinging London in such mid-'60s movies à la mod as *Georgy Girl* and *Smashing Time*, winning several awards for the former. In the 1970s, she followed *The National Health* with her least likely role, as the titular Xaviera Hollander in *The Happy Hooker*, and then focused on theatre and TV. A latterday return to film brought further awards and such credits as *Getting It Right* (1988), *Shine* (1996), *Gods and Monsters* (1998), *Spider* (2002) and *Peter Pan* (2003).

Dorothy Provine

Lynn Redgrave

Eric Rohmer

Beverly Roberts

➤ Lynn Redgrave was predeceased in April 2010 by her 70-year-old brother **Corin Redgrave**, whose sporadic film credits ranged from *A Man for All Seasons* (1966) to *Glorious 39* (2008).

BEVERLY ROBERTS

Born: *19 May 1914, New York City, New York, USA.*
Died: *13 July 2009, Laguna Niguel, California, USA.*
Initially a cabaret singer, Beverly Roberts was a beautiful, worldly-wise Warner Bros blonde, starring in 21 pictures between 1936 and 1939. Her first film, *The Singing Kid*, matched her with Al Jolson; she later played opposite her good friends Pat O'Brien and Humphrey Bogart in *China Clipper*, starred in the Technicolor Western *God's Country and the Woman*, and vied with Boris Karloff in *West of Shanghai* and Errol Flynn in *The Perfect Specimen*. Feeling overshadowed by Bette Davis and Olivia De Havilland, she opted instead for TV, radio and Broadway.

ERIC ROHMER

Born: *20 March 1920, Tulle, France.*
Died: *11 January 2010, Paris, France.*
Like Claude Chabrol [qv], Eric Rohmer was a graduate of the influential magazine *Cahiers du cinéma*. As writer-director, he came to international attention with *La Collectionneuse* (1966), the Oscar-nominated *Ma Nuit chez Maud* (1968) and *Le Genou de Claire* (1970), three instalments in a self-styled sequence of six 'contes moraux'. He moved on to six 'comédies et

proverbes', including *La Femme de l'aviateur* (1980), *Pauline à la plage* (1982) and *Le Rayon vert* (1986), and then four 'contes' focused on the four seasons. Notwithstanding occasional deviations from these series (including his last film, *Les Amours d'Astrée et de Céladon*, in 2007), all Rohmer's work is marked by a coolly searching view of his loquacious and self-absorbed characters, together with a nuanced insight into human relationships that has drawn comparisons to the 18th century playwright Marivaux.

JEAN ROLLIN

Born: *3 November 1938, Neuilly-sur-Seine, France.*
Died: *15 December 2010, Paris, France.*
Having lost Ingrid Pitt in November 2010, fans of nude 1970s bloodsuckers were further stricken a mere three weeks later by the passing of France's master of shoe-string vampire surrealism, Jean Rollin. Foregrounding plenty of female flesh and displaying an eccentric eye for dreamlike set-pieces, he carved out his unique place in French fantastique with such outré titles as *La Vampire nue* (1969), *Le Frisson des vampires* (1970), *Requiem pour un vampire* (1971), *Les Démoniaques* (1973) and *Lèvres de sang* (1974). His cult status was further consolidated by *Fascination* (1978) and *La Morte vivante* (1981).

➤ **Emilio Vieyra** – director of Argentina's first vampire film, *Sangre de vírgenes* (1967), along with numerous other cult curios – died in January 2010, aged 89. Later the same year, directors **Charles B Pierce** (*The Town That Dreaded Sundown*, 1976) and **David E Durston** (*I Drink Your Blood*, 1970) died in March and May, aged 71 and 88, respectively.

ROSANNA SCHIAFFINO

Born: *25 November 1939, Genoa, Italy.*
Died: *17 October 2009, Milan, Italy.*
Former model Rosanna Schiaffino entered films in the late 1950s, making a major impact in Francesco Rosi's *La sfida* (1958). Her other Italian films included Mauro Bolognini's *La notte brava* (1959), Alberto Lattuada's *La mandragola* (1965) and Roberto Rossellini's segment of

Budd Schulberg

Rosanna Schiaffino

the 1963 portmanteau *Ro.Go.Pa.G*. She also appeared in French films (*Le Miracle des loups*, 1963), British ones (*Drop Dead Darling*, 1966) and Hollywood titles like *Two Weeks in Another Town* (1962) and *The Victors* (1963). She could never quite match the international fame of Claudia Cardinale, however, and retired in the mid-1970s.

◆ Other Italian film actresses who died during the period under review included **Caterina Boratto** (September 2010, aged 95) – who appeared in Federico Fellini's *8½* and *Giulietta degli spiriti* – and **Carla Del Poggio** (October 2010, aged 84). Widow of director Alberto Lattuada, the latter starred in Lattuada and Fellini's *Luci del varietà*.

BUDD SCHULBERG

Born: *27 March 1914, New York City, New York, USA.*
Died: *5 August 2009, West Hampton Beach, Long Island, New York, USA.*
Son of Paramount mogul B P Schulberg, Budd Schulberg was author of the classic anti-Hollywood novel *What Makes Sammy Run?* (1941) and also *The Disenchanted* (1950), which fictionalised his collaboration with the fragmenting F Scott Fitzgerald on the 1939 picture *Winter Carnival*. In between, he collaborated on propaganda films with John Ford and, remarkably, arrested the Nazi director Leni Riefenstahl. Having won an Oscar for his screenplay for *On the Waterfront* (1954), his subsequent films included *The Harder They Fall* (1955), *A Face in the Crowd* (1957) and *Wind Across the Everglades* (1958). In the 21st century, he collaborated with Spike Lee on an as-yet-unmade picture recalling the boxing milieu of *The Harder They Fall*.

ERICH SEGAL

Born: *16 June 1937, New York City, New York, USA.*
Died: *17 January 2010, London, England.*
Even before writing the worldwide bestseller *Love Story*, classics professor Erich Segal had been responsible for the screenplay of the Beatles animation *Yellow Submarine*, together with Michael Winner's *The Games* and Stanley Kramer's *RPM*. In 1970, *Love Story*, both as a book and a film, was a sensation, making Segal's name and fortune. His subsequent screenwriting credits include *Jennifer On My Mind* (1971), the *Love Story* sequel *Oliver's Story* (1978), *A Change of Seasons* (1980) and *Man, Woman and Child* (1983). He was also a sports commentator and author of a provocative 2001 treatise on *The Death of Comedy*.

JEAN SIMMONS

Born: *31 January 1929, London, England.*
Died: *22 January 2010, Santa Monica, California, USA.*
As a teenager in the post-war heyday of British cinema, Jean Simmons gave star-making performances in *The Way to the Stars*, *Great Expectations*, *Black Narcissus*, *Hamlet* (for which she was Oscar-nominated), *The Blue Lagoon* and *So Long at the Fair*. Transplanted to America in 1952, she suffered from Hollywood's inability to 'play' her properly, but nevertheless racked up such distinguished credits as *Angel Face*, *Young Bess*, *Desirée*, *Guys and Dolls* (for which she won a Golden Globe), *The Big Country*, *Home Before Dark* and *Elmer Gantry*, culminating in the 1960 release *Spartacus*. Occupied in latter years by TV and theatre, she nevertheless gained another Oscar nomination (for *The Happy Ending*, 1969) and made one final film, *Shadows in the Sun*, in 2008.

MARIANNE STONE

Born: *23 August 1922, London, England.*
Died: *21 December 2009, London, England.*
Among British character actors, Marianne Stone was without peer for the sheer multiplicity of film appearances she made over a 45-year period; the word 'ubiquitous' scarcely does her justice. She was forever popping up as a nosy neighbour, garrulous charlady, tight-lipped secretary or hard-faced waitress, with a scope that encompassed Hammer horror, Boulting Brothers satire, Norman Wisdom comedy, and no fewer than ten Carry Ons. Her only lead was in the 1956 Merton Park programmer *Person Unknown*; her personal favourite was the role of Gothically enigmatic Vivian Darkbloom in *Lolita* (1962).

JOSEPH STRICK

Born: *6 July 1923, Braddock, Pennsylvania, USA.*
Died: *1 June 2010, Paris, France.*
Coming to prominence with the groundbreaking documentaries *Muscle Beach*, *The Savage Eye* and *Interviews with My Lai Veterans* (winning a BAFTA for the second and an Oscar for the third), writer-director-producer Joseph Strick also mounted controversial feature versions of Genet's supposedly unfilmable play

Marianne Stone

The Balcony (1963) and Joyce's supposedly unfilmable novel *Ulysses* (1967). He moved on to Henry Miller (*Tropic of Cancer*, 1970) and further Joyce (*A Portrait of the Artist as a Young Man*, 1977), interleaving these with the truck-driving curio *Road Movie* (1974). In different vein, he also served as producer on *Ring of Bright Water* (1969) and *Never Cry Wolf* (1983).

GLORIA STUART

Born: *4 July 1910, Santa Monica, California, USA.*
Died: *26 September 2010, Los Angeles, California, USA.*
Gloria Stuart signed with Universal in 1932 and was rapidly featured in a trio of characteristically witty James Whale films – *The Old Dark House* (1932), *The Invisible Man* and *The Kiss Before the Mirror* (both 1933). She also enjoyed eye-catching roles for John Ford (*Air Mail*, 1932; *The Prisoner of Shark Island*, 1936), together with *Roman Scandals* (1933) and *The Three Musketeers* (1939). Other roles, however, were less rewarding. Away from Hollywood for decades, she re-emerged in cameo parts in the 1980s, subsequently gaining an Oscar nomination for her 'Old Rose' in *Titanic* (1997).

PATRICK SWAYZE

Born: *18 August 1952, Houston, Texas, USA.*
Died: *14 September 2009, Los Angeles, California, USA.*
Patrick Swayze fluttered female hearts worldwide in two late 1980s smash hits, as a lithe dance instructor in *Dirty Dancing* (1987) and a still-passionate wraith

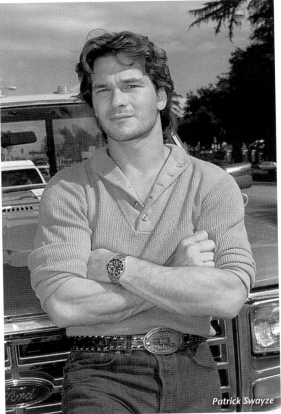

Patrick Swayze

Richard Todd

in the schmaltzy *Ghost* (1990). He first attracted attention in Francis Coppola's *The Outsiders* (1983) and John Milius' *Red Dawn* (1984), and post-*Ghost* starred in *Point Break* (1991) and *City of Joy* (1992); he also took an offbeat role *in To Wong Foo Thanks for Everything, Julie Newmar* (1995). Later roles included *Donnie Darko* (2001), *Waking Up in Reno* (2002) and *Powder Blue* (2007).

⏵ Other actors who made untimely departures in the period under review include **Robert Ginty**, American star of *The Exterminator* (1980) and other action films, who died in September 2009, aged 60; and the Englishmen **James Aubrey** and **Simon MacCorkindale**. The former's first screen work was in Peter Brook's *Lord of the Flies*, aged 15; he died in

April 2010, aged 62. The latter – who appeared in such disparate films as *Death on the Nile* (1978) and *Jaws 3-D* (1983) – died in October 2010, aged 58. The same month, **Lisa Blount**, best known for the early '80s titles *Dead & Buried* and *An Officer and a Gentleman*, died at the age of 53.

RICHARD TODD

Born: *11 June 1919, Dublin, Ireland.*
Died: *3 December 2009, Little Humby, Lincolnshire, England.*
Having taken part in the D-Day Landings, Richard Todd got to repeat the experience on film in both *D-Day the Sixth of June* (1956) and *The Longest Day* (1962). In the interim, he won a Golden Globe (and was Oscar-nominated) for his moving performance in the 1949 film *The Hasty Heart*. He subsequently

worked for Hitchcock in *Stage Fright*, played Robin Hood and Rob Roy for Disney, acted opposite Bette Davis in *The Virgin Queen*, was sincerely touching once again in *A Man Called Peter*, and gained his signature role – as Wing Commander Guy Gibson – in the 1955 evergreen *The Dam Busters*. Among several interesting later films, he was fruitfully cast against true-Brit type in John Guillermin's *Never Let Go* (1960).

HARRY ALAN TOWERS

Born: *19 October 1920, London, England.*
Died: *31 July 2009, Toronto, Ontario, Canada.*
This legendary fly-by-night showman – former child actor, radio producer and pioneering ATV executive – jumped bail when arrested in the US in 1961 and only then began his extraordinary career as a producer (and often writer) of international exploitation films. Among his earliest titles were *Death Drums Along the River* (1963), the first of three attempts at *Ten Little Indians* (1964), and a series of Christopher Lee-Fu Manchu pictures that started out classy but rapidly deteriorated. There was a late-1960s liaison with the equally maverick Spanish director Jesús Franco, a detour into softcore (*Blue Belle*, 1975; *Black Venus*, 1982), and even at the turn of the century he was still peddling ancient properties like *Owd Bob* (1997), *She* (2000) and *Sumuru* (2002).

WENDY TOYE

Born: *1 May 1917, London, England.*
Died: *27 February 2010, Hillingdon, Middlesex, England.*
As a dancer, the remarkable Wendy Toye was something of a child prodigy. As an actress, she made her film debut in *Invitation to the Waltz* (1935). As a choreographer, she worked on films like *South American George* (1941) and *Piccadilly Incident* (1946). Finally, as a director she made the prize-winning short film *The Stranger Left No Card* in 1952, thereafter creating a splendidly creepy vignette in the 1953 portmanteau *Three Cases of Murder*. She then directed the successful comedies *Raising a Riot* (1954), *All for Mary* (1955), *True as a Turtle* (1956) and *We Joined the Navy* (1962). And this is to say nothing of her prolific career as a stage director.

DAVID TREE

Born: *15 July 1915, London, England.*
Died: *4 November 2009, Welwyn Garden City, Hertfordshire, England.*
Scion of a distinguished theatrical family, David Tree was a rising star of British films in the late 1930s. He played opposite Robert Donat in *Knight Without Armour* (1937) and (appropriately for an Old Etonian) *Goodbye, Mr Chips* (1939), as well as becoming part of the combustible Bernard Shaw-Gabriel Pascal set-up in both *Pygmalion* (1938) and *Major Barbara* (1941). Other films included *The Drum* (1938), *French Without Tears* and *Q Planes* (both 1939). He lost a hand during the war, however, and returned to acting only once, at the urging of his director friend Nicolas Roeg, in *Don't Look Now* (1973).

KEITH WATERHOUSE

Born: *6 February 1929, Hunslet, Yorkshire, England.*
Died: *4 September 2009, London, England.*
When fellow Yorkshiremen Keith Waterhouse and Willis Hall translated their successful playwriting partnership to cinema, they began with a remarkable trio of British evergreens – *Whistle Down the Wind* (1961), *A Kind of Loving* (1962) and *Billy Liar* (1963), the latter derived from their play based on Waterhouse's classic novel. In the same period, they also polished off two war films (*The Valiant* and *Man in the Middle*), together with Michael Winner's underrated *West 11*. Later in the decade, they returned with *Pretty Polly* (1967) and *Lock Up Your Daughters!* (1969), after which Waterhouse was fully occupied with a wide range of musicals, TV sitcoms, stage plays and acerbic newspaper columns.

❧ Other British writers who died in 2010 included novelist **Alan Sillitoe** (April 2010, aged 82), originator of the New Wave classics *Saturday Night and Sunday Morning* and *The Loneliness of the Long Distance Runner*. Though chiefly a TV writer, **Troy Kennedy Martin** (September 2009, 77) was also responsible for *Kelly's Heroes* and *The Italian Job*. Similarly, television playwright **Alan Plater** (June 2010, 75) wrote *Keep the Aspidistra Flying* and, much earlier, *The Virgin and the Gypsy*. Yet another TV name, **Mervyn Haisman** (October 2010, 82), wrote, 20 years apart, *Curse of the Crimson Altar* and *Jane and the Lost City*.

PAUL WENDKOS

Born: *20 September 1922, Philadelphia, Pennsylvania, USA.*
Died: *12 November 2009, Malibu, California, USA.*
Director Paul Wendkos started strongly with the

David Tree

Norman Wisdom

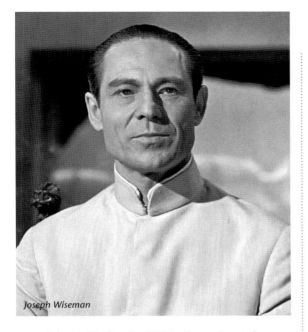

Joseph Wiseman

powerful noir *The Burglar* (1955), the underrated Western *Face of a Fugitive* (1959) and the evangelist exposé *Angel Baby* (1960). He also made the quintessential teen beach movie *Gidget* (1959) and its two sequels, diversifying into war films (*Attack on the Iron Coast*, 1967), occult thrillers (*The Mephisto Waltz*, 1970) and further Westerns (*Guns of the Magnificent Seven*, 1968; *Cannon for Cordoba*, 1970). He then became a pioneer in the nascent art of TV movies – showing a particular flair with classic small-screen chillers like *Fear No Evil* (1969) and *Haunts of the Very Rich* (1972) – and remained in the medium until his retirement in 1999.

NORMAN WISDOM

Born: *4 February 1915, London, England.*
Died: *4 October 2010, Ballasalla, Isle of Man.*
For much of the 1950s and '60s, Norman Wisdom's put-upon 'little man' persona, together with his dextrously physical brand of slapstick comedy, made him one of Britain's biggest stars. His film vehicles – the first batch directed by John Paddy Carstairs, the second by Robert Asher – began with the unexpected smash hit *Trouble in Store* in 1953, continuing with, among others, *Man of the Moment* (1955), *Up in the World* (1956), *The Square Peg* (1958), *The Bulldog Breed* (1960), *On the Beat* (1962), *The Early Bird* (1965) and *Press for Time* (1966). Subsequently, his 1966-67 Broadway success in *Walking Happy* led to his surprise casting in William Friedkin's 1968 film *The Night They Raided Minsky's*.

JOSEPH WISEMAN

Born: *15 May 1918, Montreal, Quebec, Canada.*
Died: *19 October 2009, New York City, New York, USA.*
A major presence on Broadway (appearing in no fewer than 17 productions between 1938 and 2001), Joseph Wiseman gained screen immortality as the unflinching, ice-cold, metal-gauntleted title character in the first James Bond film, *Dr No* (1962). His earliest screen work included edgy, eye-catching performances opposite Kirk Douglas in *Detective Story* (1951) and

Edward Woodward

Marlon Brando in *Viva Zapata!* (1952). Later credits, by no means prolific, included *The Unforgiven* (1960), *The Night They Raided Minsky's* (1968), *The Valachi Papers* (1972), *The Apprenticeship of Duddy Kravitz* (1973), *The Betsy* (1978) and *Seize the Day* (1986).

❖ Another *Dr No* veteran, **Zena Marshall** – who played the duplicitous Miss Taro, as well as appearing in films like *So Long at the Fair* and *Those Magnificent Men in their Flying Machines* – died in July 2009, aged 83.

EDWARD WOODWARD

Born: *1 June 1930, Croydon, Surrey, England.*
Died: *16 November 2009, Truro, Cornwall, England.*
Edward Woodward's signature TV role as grim-faced anti-Bond *Callan* (1967-72) won him a BAFTA prior to yielding a 1973 feature film and 1981 TV movie; an American successor, *The Equalizer* (1985-89), brought him a Golden Globe but no film spin-off. Even so, with powerful star performances in *The Wicker Man* (1972) and *'Breaker' Morant* (1979), he was clearly an actor whose 'cult' credentials were exemplary. In addition, he was a distinguished stage star and put his melodious tenor to good use on a dozen LP releases. Among his final credits was a whiskery cameo in the hit 2006 comedy *Hot Fuzz*.

Afterword

by **Mansel Stimpson**

In the normal course of events this edition of the annual would have covered in full the releases for the first six months of 2011 but, as explained by Michael Darvell in his introduction, our need to start off where the last published edition of the annual ended has made this impossible. We plan to include this material in next year's edition, but this article stands in until then.

With *The King's Speech* released in the first week of 2011, the cinematic year could not have got off to a more auspicious start. This film proved to be a smash hit, drawing back audiences who had not been to the cinema for a very long time (or not since *Mamma Mia!* at any rate). In addition, Colin Firth's performance rightly won awards and, following his outstanding work in *A Single Man*, confirmed his standing as one of our major stars. Further confirmation of an outstanding talent was provided when Carey Mulligan, justly acclaimed for her performance in *An Education*, appeared in *Never Let Me Go*. The film itself may be imperfect but Mulligan herself has never been more luminous.

Great acting was not in short supply during the early months of 2011. The players who shared the screen with Firth in *The King's Speech*

Geoffrey Rush, Colin Firth and Helena Bonham Carter in *The King's Speech*.

were all noteworthy, as were the whole cast of the somewhat overlooked *Barney's Version*, from Paul Giamatti to Dustin Hoffman and with Rosamund Pike giving her best performance ever. Some (but not all) loved the American relationship drama *Blue Valentine*, but everyone agreed that Ryan Gosling and Michelle Williams were remarkable in it. There was acclaim too for rising star Andrea Riseborough for her contribution to the otherwise disappointing new version of *Brighton Rock*, while many felt that Mark Wahlberg scored over the Oscar-awarded Christian Bale in *The Fighter,* if only on points.

That Robert Duvall was largely overlooked for his great turn in *Get Low* (another film with exceptional support provided by all the others in the cast) is a sign of the acting riches of this period. Nor is the talent limited to familiar faces: good as Jeff Bridges was in the Coen Brothers' take on *True Grit,* it was newcomer Hailee Steinfeld who stole the picture. In the field of foreign language films, Javier Bardem turned in an exceptional performance in Alejandro González Iñárritu's *Biutiful,* that tragic but powerful story of a man trying to put things to rights before he dies of cancer.

Left:
Carey Mulligan:
a luminous
performance in
Never Let Me Go.

Below:
Robert Duvall:
overlooked by the
Oscars in *Get Low*.

As has become habitual in recent years, once summer approached what had been a relatively rich range of films gave way, so far as mainstream cinema was concerned, to blockbusters. This meant a diet comprised of three distinct entities, namely kids' movies such as *Kung Fu Panda*, unsubtle youth-orientated comedies led by *The Hangover Part II* and, of course, the special effects movies, ranging from prequels such as *X-Men: First Class* to the final appearance of Harry Potter (that one held back to July).

In this last category it is par for the course to find the world under threat, but the truly major cinematic battle of 2011 lay in the attempt to persuade audiences that what they wanted was films in 3D. It was clear enough that Hollywood wanted it; much money had been spent on its promotion and it was accepted that the price of seats for a 3D presentation would be higher. Initially it may have seemed that in this country the critic Mark Kermode was a sole voice questioning the whole thing and preferring the 2D version of titles that arrived in both formats. But gradually other critical voices were raised, there was talk of how much darker the images often seem in 3D, and before long reports were coming in of American audiences selecting 2D screenings in preference when given the choice.

However, with big money involved it may be some time before the issue of 3D vs 2D is resolved, and in the meantime some distinguished film-makers are stepping in to embrace 3D. In the period covered here Werner Herzog did it with *Cave of Forgotten Dreams* and Wim Wenders with *Pina*, both documentaries. That's a category that continued to do well in 2011. As even its title indicated, the impressive

Jeff Bridges, good in *True Grit*, but Hailee Steinfeld stole the film.

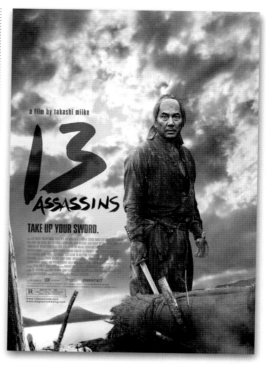

Above:
Javier Bardem
gave an
exceptional
performance
playing in *Biutiful.*

Above right:
Miike Takashi's *13
Assassins* featured
stunningly good
action sequences.

TT 3D Closer to the Edge invested in 3D, but the other outstanding documentaries from the UK and America did not. They include such memorable works as *A Small Act*, *Client 9*, the Oscar-winning *Inside Job* and, arguably the finest of them all, Asif Kapadia's *Senna*. A portrait of the Formula 1 driver who died tragically aged only 34, it proved to be an engrossing work of far wider appeal than might have been anticipated. You didn't have to be interested in motor racing to like it, only in people.

Another genre which remains a staple is the animated feature. In this period the most interesting and indeed the most individual was *My Dog Tulip*, derived from J R Ackerley's celebrated memoir, with magnificent work from Christopher Plummer as the voice of Ackerley himself. But if the continuing tendency to release as many as ten films a week theoretically promises a great choice of movies, the fact is that among the dross many really good movies get lost and fail to attain as wide a release as they deserve. In this category I would include two titles already mentioned – *Barney's Version* and *Get Low* – but to some extent it applies also to another appealing film starring Paul Giamatti, *Win Win*, and to the Allen Ginsberg biopic *Howl*, which centres on the eponymous poem and features a superb performance by James Franco.

Among those movies not seen as widely as they should have been, two other undervalued films also stand out: *West Is West* (which I found much superior to *East Is East* despite the popularity of that earlier work, to which this is a sequel) and *How Do You Know* which, as an example of mainstream rom-com, should have done well. This latter piece has a talented cast led by Reese Witherspoon, Owen Wilson, Paul Rudd and Jack Nicholson; if hardly original, it is as professional and assured as one would expect of writer/director James L Brooks. However, it was dismissed by most critics (the reviewer in *Sight & Sound* an honourable exception) and made no mark.

When it comes to foreign language pictures, *Biutiful*, mentioned earlier for Javier Bardem's acting, was awaited with expectations that were rewarded, but some of the best work took one by surprise. The films of Mahamat-Saleh Haroun set in Chad have hitherto been heartfelt but less than wholly satisfying, but with *A Screaming Man* he has given us a superb work of great human feeling with a father/son relationship at its centre. Even more unexpected is the success of the French Canadian movie *Incendies*. A powerful drama set initially in Canada but then in the Middle East, it uses a double time scale to show two adult children crossing the ocean to discover key events in the life of their now deceased mother. Cutting back and forth between the present and the past (the 1970s and '80s), the film puts us in the centre of a drama which proves stunning whether viewed as a family tale or as a comment on the tragedy and foolishness of military conflicts. The writer/director Denis Villeneuve made *August 32nd On Earth* back in

1998, which I found pretentious and tiresome, so I didn't expect to be knocked for six by *Incendies* – but I was.

Outstanding too is *13 Assassins* from Japan's Miike Takashi. Whereas Kitano Takeshi's *Zatoichi* from 2003 betrayed the spirit of the traditional samurai films by bringing the genre gorily up to date and relishing it, *13 Assassins*, in reworking a 1960s movie, respects the outlook of such films as *Seven Samurai*. Simultaneously it creates stunning choreography for its fierce action scenes, which include a climactic set-piece that lasts at least 45 minutes! Some people have raved about the highly poetic Italian film *Le quattro volte* by Michelangelo Frammartino, set in rural Calabria. Uniquely it brings a touch of Jacques Tati humour to its wordless view of life in a small town. Although the film is close to documentary, it is at heart a metaphysical work. I am not certain that on that level the ideas are fully communicated, but it's one for the adventurous viewer. Even more so in my estimation is the latest documentary from Nicolas Philibert, who gave us *Être et Avoir*. This is *Nénette*, a study of an orang-utan in the Jardin des Plantes in Paris. No less unique than Frammartino's film, it relies for its effect on what the viewer brings to it, since we are invited to meditate on what is suggested to us by what we see and learn of this animal. *Nénette* came and went in a twinkling in London, but I regard it as exceptional.

Releases such as the last two are likely to divide audiences, and in terms of popular taste the most appealing foreign item could well be François Ozon's *Potiche*, a title which has been translated as 'trophy wife'. In France *Little White Lies*, also seen here in 2011, was a box-office phenomenon but, writing just ahead of its release, I would expect British audiences to prefer *Potiche*. Based on a stage play but not grounded by that, this is a comedy about a wife who asserts herself when given the opportunity to take over her husband's factory when he falls ill. The stars are Catherine Deneuve and Gérard Depardieu, both on such great form that their fans will be delighted.

While controversy can be expected over the more unusual ventures in art-house cinema, it is rarer but not unknown within the mainstream. However, a striking example of it came up early in 2011 with Darren Aronofsky's *Black Swan*, which won Natalie Portman the Oscar for Best Actress. What was promoted in some quarters as a film in the spirit of Powell and Pressburger's classic *The Red Shoes* proved to be a cross between a conventional drama of the ballet and a Grand Guignol tale with lesbian trimmings. Given that bizarre mix it was not surprising that some dismissed it as tosh, however well made, while others proclaimed it to be brilliant. What was unexpected was that some reviewers brought the two extremes together by declaring that *Black Swan* was to be relished as trash that was

Catherine Deneuve, on great form in François Ozon's *Potiche*.

positively brilliant! This reminds us of how diverse reactions can be.

As we wait to see what is on offer in mainstream cinema following the summer's blockbusters (there's talk of an exciting new *Jane Eyre* and we wait to see if Colin Firth can pull off a hat-trick with his appearance in the film of John Le Carré's *Tinker, Tailor, Soldier, Spy*), the reports from the 2011 Cannes Film Festival point to many titles which we can look out for eagerly. Let us hope, therefore, that the promise is realised and that next year's *Film Review* annual will have plenty of films to recommend.

Natalie Portman in *Black Swan*: brilliant, bunkum or both?

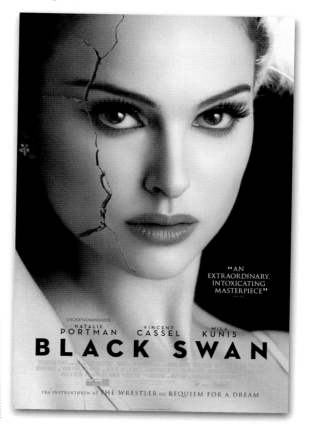

Carey Mulligan and Peter Sarsgaard
in Lone Scherfig's *An Education*.

Title Index